Frommer's®

W9-BBZ-606

Toronto 2011

by Pamela Cuthbert

WILEY

John Wiley & Sons Canada, Ltd.

Published by:

JOHN WILEY & SONS CANADA, LTD.

6045 Freemont Blvd.

Mississauga, ON L5R 4J3

ISBN 978-0-470-96372-2

e-pdf: 978-0-470-96490-3; Mobi: 978-0-470-96491-0; ePub: 978-0-470-96492-7

Editor: Gene Shannon
Developmental Editor: Melissa Klurman
Production Editor: Pamela Vokey
Project Coordinator: Lynsey Stanford
Editorial Assistant: Katie Wolsley
Cartographer: Lohnes Wright
Photo Editor: Richard Fox
Vice President, Publishing Services: Karen Bryan
Production by Wiley Indianapolis Composition Services
Front cover photo: Toronto downtown panorama view from Centre Island,
restaurant in foreground ©Andrew Rubtsov / Alamy Images
Back cover photo: Geodesic dome containing an Imax theatre in the Ontario Place
amusement park in Toronto, Ontario, Canada ©Bill Brooks / Alamy Images

For reseller information, including discounts and premium sales, please call our sales department: Tel. 416/646-7992. For press review copies, author interviews, or other publicity information, please contact our marketing department: Tel. 416/646-4584; Fax: 416/236-4448.

Manufactured in the United States of America

1 2 3 4 5   RRD   15 14 13 12 11

CONTENTS

LIST OF MAPS

ABOUT THE AUTHOR

Pamela Cuthbert is an award-winning food writer and editor published in *Macleans, Saveur, The Walrus, The Toronto Star, The Economist, Common Dreams,* and elsewhere. A past editor with *Time Out Toronto,* she has also contributed to other books, including The *Edible City* and the *Slow Food Almanac.* A native Torontonian, she lives in her hometown with her husband and young son.

ACKNOWLEDGMENTS

Many thanks to my terrific editor Gene Shannon and to the Frommer's team who together made this assignment a pleasure. A heartfelt thanks to my husband, Paul French, whose keen observations of Toronto's many idiosyncrasies fuelled new discoveries. And a special thanks to my son Dylan who shows me around his town: a place that is bright and fascinating in its own right.

HOW TO CONTACT US

In researching this book, we discovered many wonderful places—hotels, restaurants, shops, and more. We're sure you'll find others. Please tell us about them, so we can share the information with your fellow travelers in upcoming editions. If you were disappointed with a recommendation, we'd love to know that, too. Please write to:

Frommer's Toronto 2011
John Wiley & Sons Canada, Ltd. • 6045 Freemont Blvd. • Mississauga, ON L5R 4J3

AN ADDITIONAL NOTE

Please be advised that travel information is subject to change at any time—and this is especially true of prices. We therefore suggest that you write or call ahead for confirmation when making your travel plans. The authors, editors, and publisher cannot be held responsible for the experiences of readers while traveling. Your safety is important to us, however, so we encourage you to stay alert and be aware of your surroundings. Keep a close eye on cameras, purses, and wallets, which are all favorite targets of thieves and pickpockets.

FROMMER'S STAR RATINGS, ICONS & ABBREVIATIONS

Every hotel, restaurant, and attraction listing in this guide has been ranked for quality, value, service, amenities, and special features using a star-rating system. In country, state, and regional guides, we also rate towns and regions to help you narrow down your choices and budget your time accordingly. Hotels and restaurants are rated on a scale of zero (recommended) to three stars (exceptional). Attractions, shopping, nightlife, towns, and regions are rated according to the following scale: zero stars (recommended), one star (highly recommended), two stars (very highly recommended), and three stars (must-see).

In addition to the star-rating system, we also use seven feature icons that point you to the great deals, in-the-know advice, and unique experiences that separate travelers from tourists. Throughout the book, look for:

special finds—those places only insiders know about

fun facts—details that make travelers more informed and their trips more fun

kids—best bets for kids and advice for the whole family

special moments—those experiences that memories are made of

overrated—places or experiences not worth your time or money

insider tips—great ways to save time and money

great values—where to get the best deals

The following abbreviations are used for credit cards:

AE	American Express	DISC	Discover	V	Visa
DC	Diners Club	MC	MasterCard		

TRAVEL RESOURCES AT FROMMERS.COM

Frommer's travel resources don't end with this guide. Frommer's website, www.frommers. com, has travel information on more than 4,000 destinations. We update features regularly, giving you access to the most current trip-planning information and the best airfare, lodging, and car-rental bargains. You can also listen to podcasts, connect with other Frommers. com members through our active-reader forums, share your travel photos, read blogs from guidebook editors and fellow travelers, and much more.

THE BEST OF TORONTO

I grew up in downtown Toronto, and it's where I still choose to live with my family. It's an ever-evolving version of the multicultural city I remember from childhood: an interlocking collection of neighborhoods that change every year with new arrivals. Toronto is friendly in a somewhat reserved way, a generally safe place to explore, and it has plenty to discover, from restaurants to museums, festivals to towers, arts to shopping, with loads of green spaces throughout. Sure, times have changed since I was kid, and crime has risen along with traffic, but it's still relatively safe for a metropolis with a 5 million-plus population. It also, happily, ranks as one of the world's most diverse cities.

Toronto has a sprawling layout and miles of suburbs, but if you stay focused on its core, the density of attractions and vibrant communities makes it an incredibly approachable place to explore. For example, just stepping out my front door leads me to great cafes for people watching; lip-smacking charcuterie; the Art Gallery of Ontario, MOCCA, the Cinematheque, and assorted galleries for inspiration; funky pubs with great live music; and a handful of parks.

Exploring Toronto is easy. Hop on a red-rocket streetcar and ride with the locals. Get your bearings from the top of the CN Tower or from a rooftop lounge. Take a ferry ride if the weather is good or opt for a bracing walk along the waterfront. Look up to see the city's great architecture. Look down to navigate the city's mazelike underground. Be prepared to shop until you drop. Eat till you're stuffed. Dance till dawn. Walk, and then walk some more. The

Metropolitan Toronto

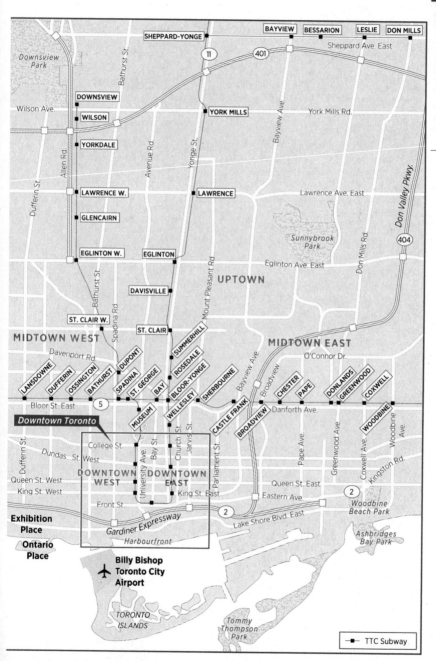

reward: In just a few days, you can tour the town and leave with the feeling that you've got the hang of the place. A great, and lasting, souvenir.

THE most MEMORABLE TRAVEL EXPERIENCES

o **Taking in the Thomson Collection at the Art Gallery of Ontario:** Locals are thrilled with local boy Frank Gehry's renovation of the AGO. His design has brilliantly revised (and expanded) the space, but the very best thing about the newly reopened AGO is the 2,000 works of art (great paintings, miniature sculptures, model ships) donated by local media magnate Ken Thomson. See p. 119.

o **Checking Out Local Theater and Music:** Sure, Toronto mounts its fair share of blockbusters. But the fine, and often more rewarding, offerings from Soulpepper, Opera Atelier, the Canadian Stage Company, Tafelmusik, and the Lorraine Kimsa Theatre for Young People are innovative and generally excellent. And seeing the Canadian Opera Company onstage at the Four Seasons Centre for the Performing Arts is breathtaking. See "The Performing Arts," in chapter 10.

o **Exploring the Distillery District:** Not only is this carefully restored area a remarkably intact example of 19th-century industrial architecture, largely thanks to its recent past as a stage set for movies and other productions, it's also a hive of activity. In addition to art galleries, shops, restaurants, and the city's finest chocolate emporium, Soma, you can hear live music or visit the farmers' market. See p. 123.

o **Bar Hopping along Ossington Avenue:** This once downtrodden strip is so hot that the city recently passed a bill to prevent more establishments from opening in what is largely a residential neighborhood. You can dine at the excellent restaurants or grab a great pizza, sip a cocktail at an intimate club or a tiny bar, take in some live music and then stroll the streets that frame the area and get a look at how the locals live—in Victorian-era homes side-by-side with family-owned shops. Utterly charming. See chapter 10.

o **Visiting the Toronto Islands:** Toronto is blessed with a chain of leafy islands just a brief ferry ride away that are mostly residential and offer a pretty, quiet, car-free spot for a stroll or a bike ride. The main attraction, Centre Island, is wide open parkland with an old-fashioned theme park, complete with pony rides and cotton candy (needless to say, it's great for kids). From the islands, you'll have a perfect view of Toronto's ever-evolving skyline. Pack a picnic, paddle a canoe, go bare if you dare at the sandy nudist beach, or take in the amusement park for a vacation within your vacation.

THE best SPLURGE HOTELS

o **Park Hyatt Toronto** (4 Avenue Rd.; (C) **800/233-1234**): The Park Hyatt is a perennial favorite, with top-notch service and one of the best views in the city from the rooftop terrace lounge. This is a place to relax and let yourself be pampered, especially in the on-site Stillwater spa. See p. 84.

o **The Gladstone Hotel** (1214 Queen St. W.; ✆ **416/531-4635**): This groovy hotel is moderately priced overall, but the double-decker "Rock Star Suite," located in the hotel's Gothic tower, is a unique splurge—and its view makes the downtown Toronto core look like a faraway metropolis. See p. 77.

o **Thompson Toronto** (550 Wellington St. W.; ✆ **866/345-9501**): The hip, luxury brand that started in New York City has landed in Toronto. Smartly situated in the King West district, this super-hot new hotel opened in summer 2010. Sixteen floors of fine modern design are complemented by floor-to-ceiling windows, a rooftop pool, private screening room, sushi bar, all-night diner, an outpost of New York City's Scarpetta restaurant, and excellent service. See p. 74.

THE best MODERATELY PRICED HOTELS

o **Delta Chelsea** (33 Gerrard St. W.; ✆ **800/243-5732**): This is a longtime favorite with budget-minded families. Perks include a playroom with live bunnies and fish, a video arcade, and a waterslide. It also offers children's programs, a day-care center, and kid-friendly restaurants. Many rooms have fridges or kitchenettes. See p. 77.

o **Hotel Victoria** (56 Yonge St.; ✆ **800/363-8228**): This property offers the best value in town. Double rooms start at C$120 per night and, for this, you get excellent service; a smallish but well-appointed room; and proximity to the Eaton Centre, St. Lawrence market, top theaters, and the Financial District. See p. 79.

o **Fairmont Royal York** (100 Front St.; ✆ **800/441-1414**): This historic grande dame is at the higher end of the moderate price range, but it's also a place where great deals are often available (it's possible to score a room for as low as C$119, if you keep an eye on the special deals on its website). It's a piece of historic Toronto, plus it has some fine dining, too. See p. 76.

THE most MEMORABLE DINING EXPERIENCES

o **The Black Hoof & Hoof Café** (928 & 923 Dundas St. W.; ✆ **416/551-8854** or 416/762-7511): Nose-to-tail eating is taken to extremes—and to truly tasty heights—at this brilliant resto-bar and its sister brunch spot right across the street. Co-owner/chef Grant van Gameren's hand-crafted charcuterie is the main draw (the tongue sandwich draws raves), but the pastas and mains are equally inspired. At the Café, try the delicious bone-marrow donuts and suckling-pig eggs benedict for brunch. See p. 99.

o **Canoe** (TD Tower, 66 Wellington St. W.; ✆ **416/364-0054**): The panorama from the 54th floor of this iconic bank tower in the heart of the Financial District is stunning, but as the many regulars can attest, the food is so good you might forget all about the view. It's Canadian cuisine with rarities such as Nunavut caribou and Québec foie gras, all handled with delicacy and brilliant technique.

The menus, wine list, and service are as dazzling as the locale. The daytime vibe is corporate; evening is more romantic. See p. 93.

o **Gilead Bistro** (4 Gilead Place; © **647/288-0680**): Local top chef Jamie Kennedy is behind the stove at this small, beautiful *boîte*. In other words, the food is sublime. Come for a light breakfast, a simple yet lovely lunch, or a real treat: a memorable dinner where local, seasonal ingredients are the stars. Great value, too. Finding your way can be tricky: It's situated in a tiny alley in Corktown. See p. 105.

o **The Local Kitchen** (1710 Queen St. W.; © **416/534-6700**): Parkdale's latest hot spot is part authentic Italian trattoria, part contemporary Toronto. The crowded, convivial room is idiosyncratic, the service pro yet friendly, and the food absolutely fantastic. Chef Fabio Bondi arrives pre-dawn each morning to make stunning fresh pasta such as smoked gnocchi with creamy *taleggio*. The wine list is simple yet superb. See p. 100.

o **Scaramouche** (1 Benvenuto Place; © **416/961-8011**): Chef Keith Froggett and maitre d' Carl Corte have been quietly perfecting one of the city's finest restaurants for over 25 years. The formal dining room, which is best for special occasions, is complemented by the adjoining casual pasta bar and grill. Located in a tony apartment building in midtown, there are beautiful views over the city. See p. 115.

THE best THINGS TO DO FOR FREE (OR ALMOST)

o **Seeing Great Museums When They're Discounted—or Free:** Admissions to the Royal Ontario Museum and the Art Gallery of Ontario have jumped since their massive renovations. However, you can pay less—or nothing—if you know when to go. See "Saving on Admission Costs," on p. 128.

o **Listening to a Concert at the Toronto Music Garden:** Cellist Yo-Yo Ma co-designed this serene space that's intended to evoke Bach's First Suite for Unaccompanied Cello. It's easy on the eyes, but the best time to come here is for a summertime concert. Pure bliss. See p. 143.

o **Wandering through Riverdale Farm:** In case you need more proof that Toronto is a very green city, it has a working farm in its midst. Cows, sheep, pigs, goats, and other critters call it home. See p. 147.

o **Strolling the Lakeside Boardwalk:** You can choose from a number of starting points, but don't miss the quirky parks, open-air concert venues, and wintertime skating rink near Habourfront. Or venture east to the long boardwalk in the neighborhood called the Beach, where you'll share the lake views with locals and their many dogs and youngsters. See p. 61.

o **Visiting Harbourfront Centre and the Power Plant Gallery:** The collection of studios, stages, open-air exhibits (especially in summer), and the Power Plant Gallery itself together offer an always-interesting, ever-changing attraction. You might call it a living museum. Watch for the many free special events. See p. 123.

THE best MUSEUMS

- **Royal Ontario Museum** (100 Queen's Park; ☎ **416/586-8000**): Good for the whole family, especially with the massive dinosaur collection and creepy bat cave, the impressive exhibits also include Chinese temple art, Roman statues, and Middle Eastern mosaics. See p. 127.

- **Ontario Science Centre** (770 Don Mills Rd.; ☎ **416/696-3127**): You don't have to be a tyke to appreciate the impressive interactive displays here that take in the realm of science disciplines, from biology to technology, and make them fun and interactive. See p. 126.

- **University of Toronto Art Centre** (15 King's College Circle; (☎ **416/978-1838**): This intimate gallery is one of the city's secret treasures. Visit it for the special exhibits or for the stunning permanent collection of Byzantine art. See p. 132.

- **Casa Loma** (1 Austin Terrace; ☎ **416/923-1171**): Toronto has its own castle, and it's a smashing example of architecture. Perhaps the man who built it was a little obsessive, but how can you not admire the fact that it has both a Scottish *and* a Norman tower? See p. 136.

THE best PLACES TO HANG WITH THE LOCALS

- **The Drake Hotel** (1150 Queen St. W.; ☎ **416/531-5042**): Set in the middle of the Art & Design District, this hotel fosters a sense of community by hosting music events, literary readings, and other festivities. If you hate feeling like a tourist, this place is for you. See p. 74.

- **The Rogers Centre or the Air Canada Centre:** The Rogers Centre is home base for the Toronto Blue Jays baseball team. The Air Canada Centre is where the Maple Leafs (hockey) and the Raptors (basketball) play. Torontonians come out to support them in droves. See p. 140.

- **Comedy Clubs:** Maybe it's something in the water: Toronto has produced more than its share of top-notch comedians, including the shagadelic Mike Myers, Jim Carrey, Dan Aykroyd, and the late John Candy. Checking out local talent or international stand-up stars at one of the many comedy clubs is a favorite pastime for Torontonians. See p. 215.

- **Treasure Hunting for Vintage Clothing in Kensington Market:** How can one small area have a dozen vintage-clothing vendors? And how do they keep prices low and the quality high? Haphazard Kensington Market is a big draw for local bargain hunters. See "Walking Tour 1: Chinatown & Kensington Market," in chapter 8, and "Hunting for Vintage," in chapter 9.

TORONTO IN DEPTH

2

Toronto is Canada's biggest city and the country's economic epicenter. With a population of 5.6 million in the greater metropolitan area and growing each year with new arrivals, most of them coming not from maternity wards but from around the globe, Toronto is a modest metropolis with an international feel. It's known as a clean, safe, and affordable destination. Fortunately, especially for its residents, the truth is a lot more interesting and sometimes downright enthralling.

Worldwide, Toronto is known for its multicultural makeup, which, in fact, provides the best reason to visit the city. Tourist attractions rate, too, if that's your thing, but the city's sheer cultural diversity, which has been compared with London's, is what ultimately gives pulse to the place, from great dining spots to music and other cultural festivals.

Visitors who knew the former Toronto of even a few decades ago won't recognize the place. It has shed its stodgy, provincial past and is embracing a collective enthusiasm as one of the most desirable cities in which to live. It's a young city (turning 177 in 2011) and draws on its vast international pedigree to give it shape and definition: The polyglot Toronto *is* the Toronto story.

Toronto is a patchwork of neighborhoods remarkable for its vibrant downtown core. Where most North American urbanites know the heart of their metropolis as a workplace and occasional shopping destination, Torontonians eat, play, sleep, and work within the city-center limits. If you're coming in from Pearson International Airport, the city might seem sprawling—and the Greater Toronto Area, including its former boroughs, is big—but once you're grounded downtown, everything is here: shoulder-to-shoulder condo towers, office buildings, theaters, parks, schools, restaurants and cafes, bars and nightclubs, taverns, and places of worship.

Stroll Kensington Market, an inner-city enclave—part Third World bazaar, part breeding ground for artistic movements—to get a feel for its lifeblood.

Or venture along its sylvan streets and ravines, and consider them as tentacles reaching into the vast expanse of wilderness that lies somewhere in the Canadian imagination and starts Up North and stretches for thousands of miles. For the most part a livable and low-crime place, Toronto has its fair share of trouble, especially with more guns crossing the border from the U.S. and the ensuing incidents. However, most visitors would have little reason to see Toronto as anything but a peaceable destination plagued with the usual urban problems, especially in North America, of homelessness and petty crime.

In a rush to grow up, the city has shamefully demolished much of its past in the name of progress. Visitors and locals alike, however, get to witness a Toronto reinventing itself today with bold new initiatives to reclaim the waterfront from industrial decay, remake failed social housing experiments from the post-war era, and try to accommodate all who want to make Toronto their home.

TORONTO TODAY

Toronto's downtown core is bustling. It was never abandoned like the city centers of so many American cities that empty after 5pm. The city was a pioneer in converting office towers into condos and has benefited hugely from maintaining a downtown as an attractive alternative to the suburban commute. Even still, one of the biggest challenges in the Greater Toronto Area (GTA) is coming to grips with invasive sprawl.

Move over Los Angeles. Commuter drive times in the GTA ranked among the top of 20 Western cities in a 2010 study. Clogged arteries of snarled traffic are now a daily occurrence and one that threatens the economic viability of a city that seems unable to manage its rapidly growing population with infrastructure upgrades. The local government has neither the funds nor the political will to address the matter through road tolls, better transit service, or even upgrading bike lanes. As more people move into the GTA—1 million more are expected over the next 20 years, bringing the total population of the GTA to 7.5 million—getting around may soon grind to a halt.

Meanwhile, the city by the lake is taking strides to reclaim its final frontier along the waterfront. After years of political dithering while developers erected a concrete curtain of condos that deprived downtown of lake views and cooling on-shore breezes, some visible progress is taking shape to replace the city's derelict shipping and industrial past at the water's edge. The impetus that finally spurred development was the city's winning the right to host the Pan Am Games in 2015. This Olympics-lite requires scads of housing for athletes, which is rising around the mouth of the Don River just to the east of downtown.

Parks are quicker to throw together than housing, so new parks have appeared first: **Sugar Beach,** at the foot of Jarvis Street, refers to one of the last remaining industrial uses on the waterfront. A stretch of powdery white sand beckons across the quay from the Redpath sugar refinery. The 3.2-hectare (8-acre) **Sherbourne Park** extends back from the water's edge surrounded by birch trees and some water channels. And **Don River Park,** when completed in fall 2011, will invite people to the previously uninviting Don River in a re-naturalized 7.3-hectare (18-acre) site with views of the city from a pavilion and playground on top of a newly-built hill.

Toronto is basking in the afterglow of a cultural renaissance that saw major additions to its key arts institutions over the past few years with works by leading architects.

The transformation elevated discussion of the public realm by adding controversy to the mix with some less-than-universally-accepted remakes of the city's beloved attractions.

Prime among them is David Libeskind's crystal add-on to the **Royal Ontario Museum** on Bloor Street. Love it or loathe it, it got people talking. Local boy Frank Gehry finally added his imprimatur to the cityscape with a favorable remake of the **Art Gallery of Ontario.** There is no Bilbao-effect here: just a tasteful rendering of the space to accommodate the AGO's wonderful art collection. Another local, Jack Diamond, designed Canada's first purpose-built opera house, the **Four Seasons Centre for the Performing Arts,** whose exterior lights up University Avenue with its glass façade and whose interior provides wonderful sightlines and acoustics for the opera and ballet crowd. And the newest addition, the **Bell Lightbox,** provides even more wattage to the Toronto International Film Festival with a gallery and year-round screening rooms on King Street West.

But it's not just the shiny and new buildings that are getting all the attention. As the city grows, heritage-minded preservationists are stepping up to do their part. Three recent additions bridge past and present. **Artscape Wychwood Barns** is an artist's colony and local food resource center fashioned from streetcar repair barns from the 1920s. **The Toronto Railway Heritage Centre,** just a fly-ball away from the Rogers Centre, is set in an old railroad roundhouse. And **Evergreen Brick Works** has transformed a quarry into a center for sustainable living.

Even City Hall, the Modernist marvel with a space ship–looking pod embraced by two curving towers, is being refashioned for the times. The building remains untouched: what's new is the wonderful garden on the elevated podium above the entrance.

Toronto continues to be very much a work in progress. As the skyline continues to grow at a clip, there's a noticeable increase in street life and energy as all those rising condos fill up. This dynamic metropolis beckons with an embrace of diverse and cosmopolitan cultures that gives shape to an ever-changing city.

LOOKING BACK AT TORONTO
Early Settlement in "Muddy York"

Native Canadians had long stopped here—at the entrance to the Toronto Trail, a short route between the lower and upper Great Lakes. In 1615, French fur trader Étienne Brûlé was the first European to travel the trail. It wasn't until 1720 that the French established the first trading post, known as Fort Toronto (the Huron word *Toronton* meant "place of meetings"), to intercept the furs that were being taken across Lake Ontario to New York State by English rivals. Fort Rouillé, built on the site of today's Canadian National Exhibition (CNE) grounds, replaced the trading post in 1751. When the 1763 Treaty of Paris ended the Anglo-French War after the fall of Québec, French rule in North America effectively ended, and the city's French antecedents were all but forgotten.

In the wake of the American Revolution, the Loyalists fled north, and the British decided it was time to carve a capital city out of the northern wilderness. In 1791, the British established Upper Canada (modern-day Ontario) as a province. Its first lieutenant governor, John Graves Simcoe, made Toronto its capital. His wife, Elizabeth, and the Queen's Rangers arrived in Toronto in 1793, which Simcoe immediately renamed "York" in honor of Frederick, Duke of York (one of George III's sons). Simcoe ordered a garrison built and laid it out in a 10-block rectangle around King, Front, George, and Berkeley streets. Beyond stretched a series of 40-hectare (100-acre) lots from Queen to Bloor, which were granted to mollify government officials who resented having to move to the mosquito-plagued, marshy outpost. York was notorious for its always-muddy streets, earning it the nickname "Muddy York."

By 1796, the hamlet had grown, and the first parliament buildings were erected. Simcoe also surveyed Yonge Street, which would eventually become the longest street in the world (in Simcoe's time, it facilitated trade by fur-trappers and farmers, and offered an escape route in case of an American attack). The first Parliament meeting confirmed York as the capital of Upper Canada.

The War of 1812 & Its Aftermath

When America declared war on Britain in the War of 1812 (actually 1812–1815), President Madison assumed it would be simple to invade and hold Canada. The opposite proved to be true. In April 1813, 14 ships carrying 1,700 American troops invaded York (population 625), looting and destroying the Parliament buildings, the Fort York garrison, and much of the settlement. It was a Pyrrhic victory because the Americans suffered heavy losses and failed to take any more Canadian territory. In retaliation, British and Canadian troops marched on Washington, D.C., in 1814 and burned all government buildings, including the American president's residence. (The Americans later whitewashed it to hide the charred wood—hence, the White House.)

Perhaps unsurprisingly given the events of the war, York's ruling oligarchy shared a conservative pro-British outlook. Called the Family Compact, the group consisted of William Jarvis, a New England Loyalist who became provincial secretary; John Beverley Robinson, son of a Virginia Loyalist, who became attorney general at age 22 and, later, chief justice of Upper Canada; and Scottish-educated Dr. John Strachan, a schoolmaster who became an Anglican rector and, eventually, the most powerful figure in York. Anglo-Irish Dr. William Warren Baldwin, doctor, lawyer, architect, judge, and parliamentarian, laid out Spadina Avenue as a thoroughfare leading to his country house; the Boultons were prominent lawyers, judges, and politicians—Judge D'Arcy Boulton built a mansion, the Grange, which later became the core of the art museum and still stands today.

The Early 1800s Rebellion & Immigration

In 1834, the city was incorporated, and York became Toronto, a city bounded by Parliament Street to the east, Bathurst Street to the west, the lakefront to the south, and 366m (1,201 ft.) north of the current Queen Street (then called Lot) on the northern edge. Outside this area—west to Dufferin Street, east to the Don River,

Muddy York

Just how muddy was the early settlement of Muddy York? It was a subject of continuous complaint by early settlers. One apocryphal story tells of a man who saw a hat lying in the middle of a street and went to pick it up. When he did, he found the head of a live man submerged in the muck below it.

and north to Bloor Street—laid the "liberties," out of which the city would later carve new wards. North of Bloor, local brewer Joseph Bloor and Sheriff William Jarvis were already drawing up plans for the village of Yorkville. In 1843, the University of Toronto opened; this was an intellectual achievement but also an aesthetic one, as the university added new and beautiful architecture to the city.

As increasing numbers of immigrants arrived, demands arose for democracy and reform. Among the reformers were such leaders as Francis Collins, who launched the radical paper *Canadian Freeman* in 1825; lawyer William Draper; and, most famous of all, fiery William Lyon Mackenzie, who was elected Toronto's first mayor in 1834.

Immigration was changing Toronto more than anything else. During the 1820s, 1830s, and 1840s, immigrants—Irish Protestants and Catholics, Scots, Presbyterians, Methodists, and other nonconformists—arrived in droves. In 1822, York got its first Catholic church, St. Paul's, built on the eastern outskirts of town. Slavery was outlawed throughout the British Empire in 1834; by the 1850s, roughly 3% of Toronto's population was black. But the biggest change was the arrival of the Irish. In early 1847, Toronto's population stood at 20,000. That summer 38,000 Irish immigrants fleeing the Great Famine landed in Toronto, forever changing the city. Many were sick with typhus, and more than 1,000 perished after arriving in Toronto. While some of the Irish settlers were Ulster Protestants, many more were Catholics, and the old-country Orange and Green conflicts flared into mob violence every year on July 12th.

Canadian Confederation & the Late Victorian Era

During the 1850s, the building of the railroads accelerated Toronto's booming economy. By 1860, it was the trading hub for lumber and grain imports and exports. Merchant empires were founded, railroad magnates emerged, and institutions such as the Bank of Toronto were established. The foundations of an industrial city were laid: Toronto gained a waterworks, gas, and public transportation. Many municipal facilities were built, including a city hall, the Royal Lyceum Theatre (1848), St. Lawrence Hall (1851), and the Toronto Stock Exchange (1852).

The Toronto Rebellion

William Lyon Mackenzie, Toronto's first mayor, founded the *Colonial Advocate* to crusade against the narrow-minded Family Compact, calling for reform and challenging their power to such an extent that some of them broke into his office and dumped his presses into the lake. By 1837, Mackenzie, undaunted, was calling for open rebellion. The city's financial turmoil in the wake of some bank failures made his wish come true. On December 5, 1837, 700 rebels gathered at Montgomery's Tavern outside the city (near modern-day Eglinton Ave.). Led by Mackenzie on a white mare, they marched on the city. But Sheriff Jarvis was waiting for them, and his militia crushed the rebellion. Mackenzie fled to the United States, but two other rebellion leaders were hanged (their graves are in the Toronto Necropolis). Mackenzie was later pardoned, returned to Toronto in 1849, and was elected to the Upper Canada legislature.

Revolutionary Shopping

Toronto's burgeoning urban market helped spawn two great Toronto merchants—Timothy Eaton and Robert Simpson—who moved to Toronto from Ontario towns to open stores at Queen and Yonge streets in 1869 and 1872, respectively. Eaton developed his reputation on fixed prices, cash sales only, and promises of refunds if the customer wasn't satisfied—all unique gambits at the time. Simpson copied Eaton and competed by providing better service, such as two telephones to take orders instead of one. Both enterprises developed into full-fledged department stores, and both entered the mail-order business, conquering the country with their catalogs.

Despite its wealth, Toronto lagged behind Montréal, which had twice Toronto's population in 1861. But Toronto increasingly took advantage of its superior links to the south, and that edge eventually helped it overtake its rival. Under the Confederation of 1867, the city was guaranteed another advantage: As the capital of the newly created Ontario province, Toronto, in effect, controlled the minerals and timber of the north.

By 1891, Toronto's population was 181,000. The business of the city was business, and amassing wealth was the pastime of such figures as Henry Pellatt, stockbroker, president of the Electrical Development Company, and builder of Casa Loma; E. B. Osler; George Albertus Cox; and A. R. Ames. Although these men were self-made entrepreneurs, not Family Compact officials, they formed a traditional, socially conservative elite linked by money, tastes, investments, and religious affiliation. And they were staunchly British. They, and the rest of the citizens, celebrated the Queen's Jubilee in 1897 with gusto and gave Toronto boys a rousing send-off to fight in the Boer War in 1899. The prominent businessmen also had a fondness for clubs—the Albany Club for the Conservatives and the National Club for the Liberals. As in England, their sports clubs (notably the Royal Canadian Yacht Club, the Toronto Cricket Club, the Toronto Golf Club, and the Lawn Tennis Club) carried a certain cachet.

The boom spurred new commercial and residential construction. Projects included the first steel-frame building—the Board of Trade Building (1889) at Yonge and Front Streets—George Gooderham's Romanesque-style mansion (1890) at St. George and Bloor (now the York Club), the provincial parliament buildings in Queen's Park (1886–92), and the city hall (1899) at Queen and Bay. Public transit improved, and by 1891, the city had 109km (68 miles) of tracks for horse-drawn cars. Electric lights, telephones, and electric streetcars appeared in the 1890s.

From Boomtown to the Great Depression

Toronto's Great Fire of 1904 demolished 5.6 hectares (14 acres) of downtown, and the damage was an estimated C\$10 million (in 1904 dollars). Miraculously, no one died in the fire, the cause of which was never discovered. Less impressively, insurance companies raised all premiums for businesses in the torched area by 75%, retroactive to the night of the fire, April 19th.

Between 1901 and 1921, Toronto's population more than doubled, climbing from 208,000 to 521,893. The economy continued to expand, fueled by the lumber, mining, wholesale, and agricultural machinery industries, and after 1911, by hydro-electric power. Much of the new wealth went into construction, and three marvelous buildings from this era can still be seen today: the Horticultural Building at the Exhibition Grounds (1907), the King Edward Hotel (1903), and Union Station (1914–1919).

The booming economy and its factories attracted a wave of new immigrants—mostly Italians and Jews from Russia and Eastern Europe—who settled in the city's emerging ethnic enclaves. By 1912, Kensington Market was well established, and the garment center and Jewish community were firmly ensconced around King Street and Spadina Avenue. Little Italy clustered around College and Grace. By 1911, more than 30,000 Torontonians were foreign-born, and the slow march to change the English character of the city had begun.

Increased industrialization brought social problems, largely concentrated in Cabbagetown and the Ward, a large area that stretched west of Yonge Street and north of Queen Street. Here, poor people lived in crowded, wretched conditions: Housing was inadequate; health conditions were poor; and rag picking, or sweatshop labor, was the only employment.

As industry grew, unionism also increased, but the movement, as in the United States, failed to organize politically. Two major strikes—at Bell, in 1907, and in the garment industry, in 1912—were easily broken.

As it became larger and wealthier, Toronto also became an intellectual and cultural magnet. Artists such as Charles Jefferys, J. H. MacDonald, Arthur Lismer, Tom Thomson, Lawren Harris, Frederick Varley, and A. Y. Jackson, most associated with the Group of Seven, set up studios in Toronto. Their first group show opened in 1920. Toronto also became the English-language publishing center of the nation, and such national magazines as *Maclean's* (1896) and *Saturday Night* (1887) were launched. The Art Gallery of Ontario, the Royal Ontario Museum, the Toronto Symphony Orchestra, and the Royal Alexandra Theatre all opened before 1914.

Women advanced, too, at the turn of the 20th century. In 1880, Emily Jennings Stowe became the first Canadian woman authorized to practice medicine. In 1886, the University of Toronto began to accept women. Clara Brett Martin was the first woman admitted to the law courts. The women's suffrage movement gained

"Toronto the Good"

Toronto's reputation for conservatism was well deserved. While the city was blessed with many beautiful churches, its nickname, "Toronto the Good," had less to do with religion and more to do with legislation against fun. This was, after all, the city that, in 1912, banned tobogganing on Sunday. As late as 1936, 30 men were arrested at the lakeshore resort of Sunnyside because they exposed their chests—even though the temperature was 105°F (41°C)! In 1947, cocktail lounges were approved, but it wasn't until 1950 that playing sports on Sunday became legal. Leopold Infeld, a University of Toronto physicist who worked with Einstein, famously said: "I dreaded the Sundays and prayed to God that if he chose for me to die in Toronto he would let it be on a Saturday afternoon to save me from one more Toronto Sunday."

strength, led by Dr. Stowe, Flora McDonald Denison, and the Women's Christian Temperance Union.

When Britain entered World War I, Canada was immediately pulled into it, as well. During the war, Toronto sent 70,000 men to the trenches; about 13,000 were killed. At home, the war had a great impact economically and socially: Toronto became Canada's chief aviation center; factories, shipyards, and power facilities expanded to meet the needs of war; and women entered the workforce in great numbers.

> ### Impressions
>
> *In the eyes of the rest of the country, Toronto is a kind of combination Sodom and Mecca.*
> —Pierre Berton, 1961

After the war, the city took on much more of the aspect and tone that characterize it today. Automobiles appeared on the streets, and one or two skyscrapers appeared. Although 80% of the population was of British origin, ethnic enclaves were clearly defined.

The 1920s roared along, fueled by a mining boom that saw Bay Street turned into a veritable gold-rush alley, where everyone was pushing something hot. The Great Depression followed, inflicting 30% unemployment in 1933. The only distraction from its bleakness was the opening of Maple Leaf Gardens in 1931. Besides being an ice-hockey center, it was host to large protest rallies during the Depression and later to such diverse entities as the Jehovah's Witnesses, Billy Graham, the Ringling Bros. Circus, and the Metropolitan Opera.

As in the United States, hostility toward new immigrants was rife during the '20s. It reached a peak in 1923, when the Chinese Exclusion Act was passed, banning Chinese immigration. In the 1930s, antagonism toward Jews intensified. Signs such as NO JEWS, NIGGERS, OR DOGS were posted occasionally at Balmy and Kew beaches. In August 1933, the display of a swastika at Christie Pits Park caused a battle between Nazis and Jews. As if things weren't bad enough, a polio epidemic broke out in 1936.

World War II & Aftermath

Unlike World War I, Canada wasn't automatically bound to enter World War II by Britain's declaration of war. However, the Canadian Parliament voted to declare war on Germany on September 10, 1939, a move that was widely supported by Canadians.

The Second World War brought new life to Toronto—literally. Toronto men rushed to volunteer to serve while women took their place in the factories. At the same time, 8,000 British children were sent to Toronto by their parents, to keep them safe from the war. Toronto became a major aviation center, manufacturing roughly 3,000 planes, as well as weapons, including machine guns. Torontonians endured rationing—one bottle of liquor a month, and limited supplies of sugar, tea, and other staples—while they listened to the war-front news delivered by future *Bonanza* star Lorne Greene.

After World War II, prosperous Toronto continued to expand. The suburbs alone added more than 200,000 to the population between 1940 and 1953. By the 1950s, the urban area had grown so large, disputes between city and suburbs were so frequent, and the need for social and other services was so great that an effective administrative solution was needed. In 1953, the Metro Council, composed of equal numbers of representatives from the city and the suburbs, was established.

Mid- & Late 20th Century

Toronto became a major city in the 1950s, with the Metro Council providing a structure for planning and growth. The Yonge subway opened, and a network of highways was constructed. It linked the city to the affluent suburbs. Don Mills, the first post-war planned community town, was built between 1952 and 1962; Yorkdale Centre, a mammoth shopping center, followed in 1964. American companies began locating branch plants in the area, fueling much of the growth.

The city also began to loosen up. While the old social elite continued to dominate the boardrooms, politics, at least, had become more accessible and fluid. In 1954, Nathan Phillips became the first Jewish mayor, signifying how greatly the population had changed. In 1947, the Chinese Exclusion Act of 1923 was repealed, opening the door to relatives of Toronto's then-small Chinese community. After 1950, the door swung open farther. Germans and Italians were allowed to enter, adding to the communities that were already established; then, under pressure from the United Nations, Poles, Ukrainians, Central European and Russian Jews, Yugoslavs, Estonians, Latvians, and other East Europeans poured in. Most arrived at Union Station, having journeyed from the ports of Halifax, Québec City, and Montréal. At the beginning of the 1950s, the foreign-born were 31% of the population; by 1961, they were 42%, and the number of people claiming British descent had fallen from 73% to 59%. The 1960s brought an even richer mix of people—Portuguese, Greeks, West Indians, South Asians, Chinese, Vietnamese, and Chilean refugees—changing the city's character forever.

In the 1960s, the focus shifted from the suburbs to the city. People moved back downtown, renovating the handsome brick Victorians so characteristic of today's downtown. Yorkville emerged briefly as the hippie capital—the Haight-Ashbury of Canada. Gordon Lightfoot and Joni Mitchell sang in the coffeehouses, and a group called the Toronto Anti-Draft Programme helped many Americans fleeing the Vietnam draft settle in Toronto.

During the 1970s, the provincial government also helped develop attractions that would polish Toronto's patina and lure visitors: Ontario Place in 1971, Harbourfront in 1972, and the Metro Zoo and the Ontario Science Centre in 1974. The CN Tower is another development from that era, and for more than 3 decades it was the tallest free-standing structure in the world (now surpassed by the Burj Dubai tower).

Montréal's Loss, Toronto's Gain
In the 1970s, Toronto became the fastest-growing city in North America. For years, it had competed with Montréal for first-city status, but it was the election of the separatist Parti Québécois, in 1976, that boosted Toronto over the top. Montréal's loss was Toronto's gain, as English-speaking families and large companies chose Toronto over French-speaking Québec. The city overtook Montréal as a financial center, boasting more corporate headquarters. Its stock market was more important, and it remained the country's prime publishing center.

Unfortunately, in spite of strong efforts by preservationists, Toronto lost many historic buildings in the 1960s and '70s (a few, such as the Royal Alexandra Theatre, were recognized for their historic importance in this period).

The 1980s were an interesting time in Toronto. On the one hand, the city fell into the habit of conspicuous consumption that seemed to define the era. Yorkville was transformed from hippie coffeehouse central into a hive of chic boutiques. But, on a more positive note, previously neglected neighborhoods such as the Annex and Cabbagetown were revitalized, the grand mansions brought back to life by a new wave of residents. In fairness to the oft-mocked 1980s, this was a time when people began to appreciate Toronto's historic architecture, working to restore it rather than tear it down as they had in the 1970s. The Elgin and Winter Garden theaters were fully renovated and reopened, as was the Pantages Theatre (now called the Canon). In 1986, Toronto's Mirvish family (of "Honest Ed's" fame) created Mirvish Productions, which (along with the now-defunct Livent group) ushered in a renaissance on the Toronto theater scene. There was also important new construction in the city: Roy Thomson Hall opened in 1982, and SkyDome (now called the Rogers Centre) debuted in 1989.

In the 1990s, the GTA really began to boom, fueled in part by rising immigration to the city. In 1998, the megacity merger forced the former city of Toronto into a union with five previously independent boroughs, causing cuts in public services as the provincial government off-loaded transit and welfare costs to the city.

The 21st Century

The new century began with a renewal of the city's cultural inventory. At long last, the city got a purpose-built opera house, the **Four Seasons Centre for the Performing Arts,** which opened in 2006 (see p. 208). Also, the **Royal Ontario Museum** (see p. 127), **the Art Gallery of Ontario** (see p. 119), **the Ontario Science Centre** (see p. 126), the **Royal Conservatory of Music** (see p. 214), the **National Ballet School,** and the **Gardiner Museum of Ceramic Art** (see p. 131) have all undergone extensive renovations.

By 2008, Toronto had become North America's largest condo market, with towers going up all over the city. The trend continues unabated, and Toronto's future seems destined to become a city of high-rise living.

TORONTO'S ARCHITECTURE

Toronto contains a wealth of architectural styles, from Gothic Revival churches to Romanesque civic buildings to the Modernist bank towers in the Financial District. While it lacks any unique and defining Toronto style, the city's push for sustainable architecture that is environmentally aware will characterize the future of its buildings.

The Settling of York (1793–1837)

Early architecture in what was York and, after 1834, Toronto took its stylistic cues from England. The most notable style of the era was:

GEORGIAN These buildings are characterized by their formal, symmetrical design and by their classically inspired details, such as columns and pediments. There are few examples in Toronto, but an outstanding one is **Campbell House**

at 160 Queen St. W. (p. 139). Built for Sir William Campbell in 1822 (he was a Loyalist and a chief justice of Upper Canada), it was moved 1.5km (1 mile) from its original location in 1972 to save it from being demolished in favor of a parking lot. Campbell House is currently a museum. Another example of Georgian architecture is the **Grange** (p. 119), which is part of the Art Gallery of Ontario and sits behind the AGO's Dundas Street West main building. Built in 1817, the Grange is now the members' lounge at the AGO.

Early Victorian (1837–1860)

The Victorian era in Toronto was a creative time in which a variety of different architectural styles were employed. There was a strong tendency to look at the styles of the past and reinterpret them for the present. The chief ones were:

GOTHIC REVIVAL   This fanciful style was part of a literary and aesthetic movement in England in the 1830s and 1840s, and became incredibly popular in Toronto. Gothic Revival design was asymmetrical, with pointed arches and windows, extensive ornamentation, and steeply pitched roofs; towers were often incorporated into the design. While the inspiration for Gothic Revival buildings was the great churches of the past, the style was applied to many types of buildings in Toronto. **St. James' Cathedral** (p. 138), built between 1850 and 1874, is a perfect example of the style with its 30m-tall (100-ft.) bell tower and its Romantic-inspired stained glass windows. **St. Michael's Cathedral** (p. 138) and the **Church of St.-Stephen-in-the-Fields** (p. 160) are also prime examples of Gothic Revival religious architecture. The **Toronto Necropolis** (p. 144), a cemetery that was established in 1850, is another fine example. **Hart House** (p. 131), at the University of Toronto, is another, though it was built much later than the others and completed during the First World War.

> ### Impressions
>
> *You build your stations like we build our cathedrals.*
> —The Prince of Wales, speaking at the official opening of Toronto's Union Station in 1927

GREEK REVIVAL   Influenced by Greece's fight for independence in the 1820s (in which the Romantic poet Lord Byron famously perished), there was a revival in interest in the country's history, arts, and architecture. Picture the classical columns, friezes, and low-pitch pediment of a Greek temple, and you have a general outline of the style. Few Greek Revival buildings have survived in Toronto. One example stands at **15 Wellington St. W.,** an 1845 bank building now stripped of its signage. A smaller example is **Mackenzie House** (p. 140), where the would-be revolutionary William Lyon Mackenzie lived after returning from his exile in America. The house, built in the 1850s, includes a decorative frieze.

RENAISSANCE REVIVAL   Just as ancient Greece fascinated the Victorian mind, so did the ideals of the Italian Renaissance. Buildings designed in this style tended to be large, impressive, and formal, with a symmetrical arrangement of the facade, quoins (cornerstones that give an impression of strength and solidity), columns separating windows, and large blocks of masonry on the lowest floor. Toronto's **St. Lawrence Hall** (next to the St. Lawrence Market, p. 201), built in 1850, is a textbook example of Renaissance Revival. Improving the sightlines of this building

BE AN archi-tourist

From blogs to talks to walks, there are many ways to stay on top of the city's ever-changing skyline:

- The **Toronto Society of Architects** offers walking tours on architectural themes from June through September. Tours have included "Toronto's Cultural Renaissance: Buildings of the 21st Century" and "Skyscrapers of the Financial District." For details and schedules, visit torontosocietyofarchitects.ca.

- **Doors Open Toronto** is a popular, free celebration of buildings in and around the city. Each year, during the last weekend in May, more than 150 architecturally significant buildings—many of them otherwise not accessible to the public—open their doors to the public. For details, visit www.toronto.ca/doorsopen.

- **Jane's Walk** is named for the late Toronto-based writer and urban activist Jane Jacobs and allows impassioned residents to lead tours of their neighborhoods

each May. What began in 2007 as a local commemoration is now an international phenomenon with Jane's Walks in 68 cities around the world. For more, see www.janeswalk.net.

- The **Design Exchange** (see p. 130) has year-round programming on architecture themes with exhibits, talks, and film screenings, and its blog gives great insight into local trends. See www.dx.org.

- The **Pug Awards** were launched in 2004 as a way to raise awareness of architectural and design issues in Toronto. The public votes via the Web for the best and worst new buildings of the year. The exposure has shamed developers and lauded unsung works. The Pugs are raising the bar, and hopes, for a better-built tomorrow. There's also a lecture series, "Pug Talks," held throughout the year. For more, see www.pugawards.com.

is a key element in the new design for the north building at St. Lawrence Market, which will open in 2013.

VICTORIAN CLASSICAL   Some buildings in Toronto were constructed in the spirit of several different revivals (an eclectic approach to architecture that is still relevant today). They don't fit well into any particular style, and so are grouped together as Victorian Classical. **Osgoode Hall** (p. 177), which was built, rebuilt, and expanded multiple times between 1829 and 1858, is referred to this way for its unique design.

Late Victorian (1860–1901)

Later in the Victorian period, Toronto was still being influenced by Britain, but the city was also becoming more original in its design:

RICHARDSONIAN ROMANESQUE   Arguably old Toronto's most beloved architectural style. In England, there was a Romanesque Revival, though the style was usually called Norman, calling on elements of 11th- and 12th-century castle and church design. Toronto's Richardson Romanesque buildings were influenced by the

American architect Henry Hobson Richardson. The style is immediately identifiable by its massive scale, rounded archways, belt courses (continuous rows of bricks in a wall), decorative arcading, and large towers. The **Ontario Legislature** at Queen's Park (p. 137), built in 1893, is a Richardsonian Romanesque masterpiece in rose-tinted sandstone and granite. So is **Old Toronto City Hall** (p. 136), though its design is less orthodox with its two-tone sandstone exterior and prominent gargoyles.

BAY-AND-GABLE   Closely related to Gothic Revival architecture, this is a style that is considered unique to Toronto. It applies some of the most visually spectacu-lar elements of Gothic Revival to single-family homes. Lots in 19th-century Toronto were oddly long and narrow (6.1×4m/20×13 ft.), and the Bay-and-Gable style, with its sharply peaked roofs, large bay windows (often filled with stained glass), and extensive decorative gabling managed to fit into these lots perfectly (most stand three stories tall). There are excellent examples of Bay-and-Gable in **Cabbagetown** (see Walking Tour 4 on p. 167), as well as in the **Annex** and in **Little Italy.**

Early & Mid–20th Century (1901–1970)

Toronto erected its first skyscraper in 1894—the Beard Building—but unfortunately, it has been demolished. In the first decades of the 20th century, the city became less interested in looking back at the past and more intrigued by the future. When the decision was made to create a new city hall in the 1950s, Torontonians voted down a classically designed city hall, eventually favoring a modern building based on Inter-national Style (see below).

EARLY SKYSCRAPER   The **Royal Bank Building** at the corner of King and Yonge streets was the tallest building in the British Commonwealth when it was completed in 1914. The **Royal York Hotel** (now called the Fairmont Royal York, p. 76) was even taller, but by the time it opened, there was more competition (it was the tallest building in Toronto from the year it opened, 1929, until 1931).

BEAUX ARTS   Taking its name from the Ecole des Beaux-Arts in Paris, this style was an idealization of classical Greek and Roman architecture. These grand build-ings featured sweeping staircases and archways, classical columns, and frequently classical decoration (including statues and friezes). Toronto's most beloved example of Beaux Arts style is **Union Station** (p. 66), which was built between 1914 and 1921, but not used as a rail station until 1927 because of a legal dispute.

INTERNATIONAL STYLE   In the 1930s, this was modern architecture. These stark, rectangular buildings, which frequently were surfaced with glass, were influ-enced by Germany's Bauhaus School. They were simple in design (as least, to the naked eye), unornamented, and seriously functional. The **Toronto-Dominion Bank Tower,** at 66 Wellington St. W., was designed by Mies van der Rohe, perhaps the most famous of the Modernist architects. Built in 1967, it is distinctive for its black steel structure and black-glazed glass.

Late 20th Century & Beyond (1970–Present)

Toronto architecture in the past 4 decades has veered from the Postmodern to the wildly eclectic. It's hard to group works together in a cohesive style, though they do share elements of whimsy and improbability. In the 1970s, a postmodern approach, in which classical or historical references were incorporated into the design of a building, became popular. There was a great deal of leeway in terms of the overall shape of a building, rather than using a simple rectangle. The **Toronto Reference Library** (p. 139) and the **Bata Shoe Museum** (p. 128), both designed by Toronto architect Raymond Moriyama, are two visually stunning counterpoints within walking distance of each other. The **Royal Ontario Museum** (p. 127) and the **Art Gallery of Ontario** (p. 119) have engaged high-profile architects to reinvent their traditional spaces, with eye-popping results. The **Sharp Centre for Design** (p. 136), which opened in 2004, still shocks many visitors. Best described as a checkerboard on colorful stilts, it was designed by the English architect Will Alsop for the Ontario College of Art and Design and captures a sense of possibility and playfulness in contemporary architecture. (Alsop is also creating a subway station in the suburbs for an extension of the University Avenue line.)

Currently, one of the most cherished buildings in the city is getting a makeover rather than the wrecking ball: **Maple Leaf Gardens.** This hockey shrine on Carlton Street has sat empty for a decade since the Leafs decamped to the Air Canada Centre. Its future was in doubt but was secured when a grocery chain and Ryerson University teamed up to preserve it. Scheduled to re-open in mid-2011, the mixed-use facility will become Ryerson's hockey rink and will also offer groceries at street level. The designers say they will retain as much character of the legendary arena as possible.

The biggest trend in architecture in the city right now is one not always visible to the naked eye: Sustainable design. LEED (Leadership in Energy and Environmental Design) buildings incorporate energy-saving systems such as green roofs, lake water to cool buildings instead of conventional air conditioning, and new window glazing and shading techniques to prevent heat build-up. Some buildings on the vanguard of these principals include the **Evergreen Brick Works, One Cole** condominium in the renewed Regent Park, and new campus buildings at **University of Toronto.**

Cabbagetown

"A few houses on almost every street were as verminous and tumbledown as any in the city, but next door or across the street was the same type of house, clean and in good repair, reflecting the decency or pride of the occupants, or reflecting the fact that the tenant was buying it. In 1929, most Cabbagetown-ers rented their homes, from the ingrained habit of generations or because they refused to tie themselves down to the district. This was a neighborhood almost without tenements, and the streets were lined with single-family houses, many of whose upper stories accommodated a second family.

The citizens of Cabbagetown believed in God, the Royal Family, the Conservative Party, and private enterprise. They were suspicious and a little condescending towards all heathen religions, higher education, 'foreigners,' and social reformers. They were generally unskilled working people, among whom were scattered, like raisins in a ten-cent cake, representatives of the State—such as postmen, civic employees, streetcar conductors, and even a policeman or two."

—From *Cabbagetown,*
by Hugh Garner, 1950

"I DIDN'T KNOW SUPERMAN WAS FROM TORONTO. . ."

Torontonians show up in films, television, music, and literature that's famous the world over, and their scientific, architectural, and political accomplishments have had a global impact. How many people on this list did you know were from Toronto?

- **Margaret Atwood** (b. 1939): Canada's most famous literary luminary—her books have been translated into more than 20 languages, and there's a university in Sweden that teaches a course just in the use of comedy in her novels—Atwood is best known for her futuristic novel *The Handmaid's Tale*, which was made into a Hollywood film. Her body of work includes *The Edible Woman, The Robber Bride, Alias Grace,* and *Oryx and Crake* (all published by Emblem Editions).
- **Sir Frederick Banting** (1891–1941): Banting was the co-discoverer of insulin at the University of Toronto; in 1923, he was awarded the Nobel Prize for his life-saving research. He also distinguished himself as a captain in the Army Medical Corps in World War I and, later in life, as an artist.
- **John Candy** (1950–1994): The well-loved funnyman and Toronto native got his start in comedy with the local Second City troupe, playing a succession of crazy characters on "SCTV." In Hollywood, he made a succession of popular films that included *Only the Lonely, Uncle Buck,* and *Planes, Trains and Automobiles*. He was also a co-owner of the Toronto Argonauts football team.
- **Jim Carrey** (b. 1962): Before striking it rich in Hollywood with

movies such as *The Mask, Ace Ventura: Pet Detective, Dumb and Dumber, The Truman Show,* and *Eternal Sunshine of the Spotless Mind,* Carrey lit up the stage at Toronto comedy clubs.
- **Atom Egoyan** (b. 1960): His films—including *Exotica, The Sweet Hereafter,* and *Felicia's Journey*—have been critical successes. Born in Cairo and raised in western Canada, Egoyan studied at the University of Toronto. His latest film, *Chloe,* unabashedly uses Toronto, especially its ravines, to portray a tale of infidelity and revenge.
- **Frank Gehry** (b. 1929): Arguably the world's most famous living architect, Gehry put Bilbao, Spain, on the map with the swooping titanium shape of its Guggenheim Museum. In a more subdued way, Gehry refashioned the Art Gallery of Ontario to fit within the context of its residential neighborhood, where he grew up.
- **Norman Jewison** (b. 1926): This multiple award-winning director found fame south of the border making films that include *Fiddler on the Roof, The Cincinnati Kid, Jesus Christ Superstar, Agnes of God,* and *Moonstruck.* In 1986, the Toronto native established the Canadian Centre for Film Studies in his hometown.
- **k-os** (b. 1972): His real name is Kevin Brereton, but he's better known as k-os in his work as a rapper, singer, songwriter, and producer. He frequently references places and events in Toronto in his songs.

- **K'naan** (b. 1978; aka Keinan Abdi Warsame): This Somalia-born poet, rapper, and singer gained global exposure for writing *Wavin' Flag*, Coca Cola's anthem for the 2010 FIFA World Cup of Soccer, and continues to win over fans with songs about the immigrant experience in Canada.
- **Marshall McLuhan** (1911–1980): The man who is best known for coining the phrases "the medium is the message" and "the global village" was a professor of English and the director of the Centre for Culture and Technology at the University of Toronto. His seminal works include *The Gutenberg Galaxy* (University of Toronto Press), *Understanding Media* (MIT Press), and *War and Peace in the Global Village* (Ginkgo Press).
- **Lorne Michaels** (b. 1944): Ever wonder why *Saturday Night Live* has featured so many Canadian performers? That may have had something to do with the fact that the show's creator was born and raised in Toronto. Michaels has also produced SNL alumni movies such as *Wayne's World* and *Baby Mama*, and TV shows including *30 Rock*.
- **Mike Myers** (b. 1963): Myers became a celebrity when he starred on "Saturday Night Live" from 1989 to 1994 playing a series of characters that included metal-head rocker Wayne Campbell and German aesthete Dieter. On the big screen, Myers has struck gold writing and starring in such films as *Wayne's World* and *Austin Powers* (and their respective sequels).
- **Michael Ondaatje** (b. 1943): Ondaatje is perhaps best known for his novel *The English Patient* (Knopf Canada), which was adapted into an Oscar-winning film. Born in Sri Lanka, he earned his BA from the University of Toronto and taught English literature at Toronto's York University from 1971 to 1988. His acclaimed body of work includes *Running in the Family, In the Skin of a Lion,* and *Anil's Ghost* (all published by Knopf Canada).
- **Joe Shuster** (1914–1992): Poor Joe Shuster—if only he and his Superman co-creator Jerome Siegel had known what a success their cartoon character would be one day, they wouldn't have sold the rights to D.C. Comics for a pittance in 1940. Shuster had been a newspaper boy for the *Toronto Star,* and in the early Superman strips, Clark Kent worked for the *Daily Star* (later rechristened the *Daily Planet*). Toronto purportedly served as the model for the city of Metropolis.
- **Michael Cera** (b. 1988): This fast-rising Hollywood actor was born and raised in the suburb of Brampton, Ontario. His films include *Superbad, Juno,* and *Scott Pilgrim vs. the World,* and he appeared in the cult-hit television series *Arrested Development.*
- **Neil Young** (b. 1945): Maybe Neil shouldn't be on this list—the genius singer/songwriter is likely the only famous person Toronto has produced that people actually realize is *from* Toronto.

TORONTO IN POPULAR CULTURE

Toronto has had a reputation of always being the bridesmaid and never the bride when it comes to its portrayal in the movies. As a stand-in for large American cities, it has fueled a busy film-production industry but done little to attract the curious since its streets and skyline always depict some other place.

As a city on the page, however, Toronto can claim a rich legacy of settings and inspirations brought to life in many a page-turner. Being the home of many of the country's most prolific and acclaimed writers hasn't hurt its literary leanings, either.

Margaret Atwood's *The Robber Bride* (Emblem Editions) pays homage to Toronto with a story that covers three decades of life in the city. Some of her other novels— *The Edible Woman, Cat's Eye,* and *The Blind Assassin* (all published by Emblem Editions)—also use Toronto as a backdrop. *In the Skin of a Lion,* by Michael Ondaatje, the celebrated author of *The English Patient* (both published by Knopf Canada), is a moving love story that brings the city's landmarks to life. Carol Shields, who died in 2003, set her final novel, *Unless* (Harper Perennial), in Toronto's streets. Michael Redhill's *Consolation* (Doubleday, Canada) bounces back and forth between contemporary Toronto and the city in the 19th-century.

Another notable novel is *Cabbagetown,* by Hugh Garner, the story of the fight to survive in a Toronto slum in the 1930s. (Cabbagetown was famous as the largest Anglo-Saxon slum in North America.)

For those more interested in possible futures than the past, there's an Afro-futurist/sci-fi novel called *Brown Girl in the Ring,* by Nalo Hopkinson (Warner Books). Some other books to consider: *Noise* (Porcupine's Quill) and *How Insensitive* (Doubleday Canada), by Russell Smith; *Headhunter,* by Timothy Findley (Harper-Collins Canada); *Then Again,* by Elyse Friedman (Random House Canada); *Lost Girls,* by Andrew Pyper (Harper Collins Canada); and *The Origin of Waves,* by Austin Clarke (McClelland & Stewart). Clarke has also written three novels that are collectively known as the Toronto Trilogy: *The Meeting Point, Storm of Fortune,* and *The Bigger Light* (all published by Knopf Canada). The literary legend Robertson Davies was working on the third novel in his own Toronto Trilogy when he died in 1995. The first two books, *Murther and Walking Spirits* and *The Cunning Man* (both published by Penguin Books), were published in 1991 and 1994, respectively.

If you like the look of Old City Hall, pick up the eponymous novel, *Old City Hall,* by Robert Rotenberg. Published in 2009, the story—written by a veteran criminal lawyer—explores Toronto's noir side.

Insightful books on architecture include *Emerald City: Toronto Revisited,* by John Bentley Mays (Viking), and as handy reference to recent buildings, *A Guidebook to Contemporary Architecture in Toronto,* by Margaret and Phil Goodfellow (Douglas & McIntyre), covers the bases.

EATING & DRINKING IN TORONTO

Dining out is nothing short of a passion in Toronto. It's not that residents are too lazy to cook, but we are spoiled by the embarrassment of edible riches in all parts of the city. The city is a restaurant-goer's nirvana for a wealth of reasons. For starters, there

ICE WINE & OTHER ontario whites

Ontario vintners' greatest successes so far have been mostly with white wines (although cool-climate red varietals like pinot noir are on the rise). Delicious, crisp, and complex, they're often impossible to resist, and include fine Rieslings, Gewürztraminers, chardonnays, and special, late-harvest vintages. These wines are taking home gold medals at international competitions and winning accolades from wine writers the world over.

At dessert time, a highlight is Ontario ice wine, a very sweet and sometimes heavenly creation. To create this special varietal, grapes are left on the vine through December and most or all of January. When the first frost descends, everyone is out in the fields harvesting, regardless of whether it's day or night—timing is everything when the fruit has been kissed by frost (which sends grapes' sweetness through the roof). It's not an easy process, but the hard work can pay off in huge rewards, as it did for Inniskillin in 1991, when the Ontario winery won the Grand Prix d'Honneur for its 1989 Vidal ice wine. Since then, dozens of other vintners, from artisan wineries to large-scale producers, have produced award-winning ice wines. To learn more about Ontario wine before your visit, check out the Ontario Wine Council at **www.winesofontario.org**. And be sure to buy VQA (the acronym for the Vintners' Quality Alliance), which guarantees wines made from 100% Ontario-grown grapes.

are more than 7,000 places to choose from. They represent cooking styles from any country or nationality you can name, making Toronto's culinary scene both eclectic and palate-teasing. Eating out is also remarkably affordable: While the most expensive restaurants have broken the C$50-an-entree mark, there are many, many reasonably priced options that offer inventive cooking and attentive service.

Toronto is a place where chefs can become stars. Some of the best-known talent in the Toronto firmament includes Jamie Kennedy of **Gilead Café** (p. 96), Mark McEwan of **North 44** (p. 115), Marc Thuet of **Conviction** (p. 97), Edward Levesque of **Edward Levesque's Restaurant** (p. 105), and Chris McDonald of **Cava** (p. 116). If you're a foodie who has only a long weekend in the city, it will be a tough challenge to figure out where to dine.

Generally, Mediterranean and Asian cuisines dominate the scene—and often appear on the same plate. Fusion cooking caught on big here and has not yet lost its steam. Many restaurants that started out as, say, Italian have incorporated ingredients and cooking styles from Southeast Asia and North Africa, among other regions. Each wave of immigration has carried new ideas and flavors to the city. Some of the newer restaurants, such as **The Black Hoof** (p. 99) and **C5** (p. 106) are mixing powerful flavors in unexpected ways.

While restaurants of all descriptions are found across the city, certain neighborhoods are renowned for their specialties: Little Italy for its *trattorias,* Chinatown for its Chinese and Vietnamese eateries, and the Danforth for its Greek tavernas. King Street West, in the past several years, has unexpectedly become a magnet for gourmet restaurants, offering a bevy of bistros and *boîtes.* One thing that's particularly wonderful about Toronto's dining scene is that it's entirely possible to have a great meal at a bargain price. Restaurants such as **Torito Tapas Bar** (p. 104), **Supermarket** (p. 218), and **Gilead Café** (p. 105) let you dine well without breaking the bank.

Here's one more indulgence, if you have the time for a day trip. Just south and west of Toronto is the Niagara region, which is the best wine country in Canada. Follow its Wine Route to discover for yourself the reason local vintners, such as Inniskillin, Henry of Pelham, and Pillitteri, are winning international competitions. Niagara's wineries use imported European vines, and because the region lies on the same latitude as France's Burgundy region, this meeting of Old and New World results in bottles of Riesling, Sauvignon Blanc, Chardonnay, Pinot Noir, and Cabernet Sauvignon that are consistently excellent.

On second thought, even if you don't have the time for a day trip, you can try many of these wines at the local restaurants. Even those who don't normally save room for dessert won't be able to resist a small glass of Niagara ice wine to polish off a perfect meal. *Bon appétit!*

PLANNING YOUR TRIP TO TORONTO

Toronto is an easy place to go for a spur-of-the-moment visit. Still, whether you're traveling on a whim or charting your course months in advance, some planning will help you make the most of your trip. This chapter will help you prepare.

For additional assistance and on-the-ground resources in Toronto, please turn to "Fast Facts," on p. 258.

WHEN TO GO

Toronto is a city with four distinctive seasons. Autumn is a particularly good time to visit: The climate is brisk but temperate, the skies are sunny, the trees are a riot of color, and the cultural scene is in full swing. Another great time to see the city—if you don't mind a dusting of snow—is early winter in December, with holiday festivities for everyone. Spring is pretty, although rainy and cool days can make for a moody stay. Midsummer can be oppressive with heat, but there are plenty of parks and other places to cool down, like Ontario Place's busy water park and the Toronto Islands. Really, the only time the city can seem unwelcoming is on a windy February day when the temperature hits −22°F (−30°C). In fact, bone-chilling days are less frequent as the planet warms: you could call it a boost for Torontonians and the city's visitors, at least, for now.

Never mind what the calendar says; these are Toronto's true seasons: **Spring** runs from late March to late May (though occasionally there's snow in April); **summer,** June to early September; **fall,** mid-September to mid-November; and **winter,** late November to sometime in March. The highest recorded temperature is 105°F (41°C); the lowest, −27°F (−33°C). The average date of first frost is October 29; the average date of last frost is April 20. The windblasts from Lake Ontario can be fierce, even in June. Even in summer, bring a light jacket.

Toronto's Average Temperatures °F (°C)

	JAN	FEB	MAR	APR	MAY	JUNE	JULY	AUG	SEPT	OCT	NOV	DEC
HIGH	28 (-2)	29 (-2)	39 (4)	52 (11)	65 (18)	73 (23)	79 (26)	77 (25)	68 (20)	56 (13)	44 (7)	33 (1)
LOW	15 (-9)	15 (-9)	24 (-4)	35 (2)	45 (7)	54 (12)	60 (16)	58 (14)	50 (10)	39 (4)	31 (-1)	20 (-7)

Holidays

Toronto celebrates the following holidays: New Year's Day (Jan 1), Family Day (third Mon of Feb), Good Friday and Easter Monday (Mar or Apr), Victoria Day (Mon following the third weekend in May), Canada Day (July 1), Simcoe Day (first Mon in Aug), Labour Day (first Mon in Sept), Thanksgiving (second Mon in Oct), Remembrance Day (Nov 11), Christmas Day (Dec 25), and Boxing Day (Dec 26).

On Good Friday and Easter Monday, schools and government offices close; most corporations close on one or the other, and a few close on both. Only banks and government offices close on Remembrance Day (Nov 11).

Calendar of Events

January, February, March, and April are dominated by trade shows, such as the International Boat and Automobile shows, Metro Home Show, Outdoor Adventure Sport Show, and more. For information, call **Tourism Toronto** (✆ **800/499-2514** or 416/203-2600; www.torontotourism.com).

For an exhaustive list of events beyond those listed here, check http://events.frommers.com, where you'll find a searchable, up-to-the-minute roster of what's happening in cities all over the world.

JANUARY

Toronto WinterCity Festival, citywide. Formerly known as WinterFest, this 2-week celebration blankets the city with fun, mostly outdoor, events. It features ice-skating shows, snow play, performances, art shows, and more. For information, visit **www.toronto.ca/special_events.** Late January through early February.

Winterlicious, citywide. Baby, it's cold outside, but Toronto's restaurants really know how to heat things up. Roughly 150 of the city's finest eateries offer prix-fixe lunch (C$15–C$30) and dinner (C$25–C$45) menus. See **www.toronto.ca/special_events** for a complete listing. Late January through early February.

FEBRUARY

Chinese New Year Celebrations, various sites in the city. In 2011, the Year of the Rabbit is celebrated. Festivities include traditional and contemporary performances of Chinese opera, dancing, music, and more. For **Harbourfront** celebration information, call ✆ **416/973-4000** or visit **www.harbourfrontcentre.com;** for the **Rogers Centre,** call ✆ **877/666-3838** or check **www.rogerscentre.com.** The 2011 new year starts on February 3.

Don't Forget the Sunscreen

Because of Canada's image of a land of harsh winters, many travelers don't realize that summer can be scorching. "The UV index goes quite high, between 7 and 10, in Toronto," says Dr. Patricia Agin of the Coppertone Solar Research Center in Memphis. A UV index reading of 7 can mean sunburn, so don't forget to pack your sunscreen and a hat, especially if you're planning to enjoy Toronto's many parks and outdoor attractions.

International Readings at Harbourfront, Harbourfront. This weekly series invites authors from around the globe to read from their most recent works. Participants have included David Sedaris, Pico Iyer, and Jhumpa Lahiri. For information, call Harbourfront at ✆ **416/973-4000** or go to **www.readings.org.** February through June.

MARCH

Canada Blooms, Metro Toronto Convention Centre. At this time of year, any glimpse of greenery is welcome. Canada Blooms treats visitors to 2.5 hectares (6¼ acres) of indoor garden and flower displays, seminars with green-thumb experts, and competitions. For information, call ✆ **416/593-0223** or visit **www.canadablooms.com.** Second or third week of March.

St. Patrick's Day Parade, downtown. Toronto's own version of the classic Irish celebration. For information, call ✆ **416/487-1566** or visit **www.topatrick.com.** March 17.

Toronto Festival of Storytelling, Harbourfront. Now in its 32nd year, this event celebrates international folklore, with storytellers imparting legends and fables from around the world. For information, call ✆ **416/973-4000** or check **www.torontofestivalofstorytelling.ca.** March 25 to April 3, 2011.

One-of-a-Kind Craft Show & Sale, Exhibition Place. More than 400 crafts artists from across Canada display their unique wares at this show. For information, visit **www.oneofakindshow.com.** March 31 to April 4, 2010.

APRIL

Blue Jays Season Opener, Rogers Centre. Turn out to root for your home-away-from-home team. For tickets, call ✆ **888/OK-GO-JAY** (888/654-6529) or 416/341-1234, or visit **http://toronto.bluejays.mlb.com.** Mid-April.

The Shaw Festival, Niagara-on-the-Lake, Ontario. This festival presents the plays of George Bernard Shaw and his contemporaries, as well as modern Canadian works.

Call ✆ **800/511-7429** or 905/468-2172, or visit **www.shawfest.com.** Mid-April through first weekend of November.

Hot Docs Film Festival, citywide. North America's largest documentary festival has grown from a modest celebration to an 11-day extravaganza with over 170 films from more than 40 countries. Call ✆ **416/203-2155** or visit **www.hotdocs.ca.** Late April to early May.

Total Health Show, Metro Convention Centre. Founded in 1975, this 3-day event organizes panels and events with medical professionals, authors, alternative practitioners, organic farmers, and local chefs to talk about public and personal health issues. For information, call ✆ **416/924-9800** or visit **www.totalhealthshow.com.** Mid-April.

MAY

CONTACT Photography Festival, citywide. This annual month-long event shows the work of more than 500 Canadian and international photographers. For information, call ✆ **416/539-9595** or visit **www.contactphoto.com.** May 1 to 31.

Salut Toronto Food + Wine Festival, Yorkville. Formerly known as Santé, this week-long event celebrates international wines, as well as Ontario vintages, great cocktails, and the best in food. For information, visit **www.salutwinefestival.com.** Early May.

The Stratford Festival, Stratford, Ontario. Featuring a wide range of contemporary and classic plays, this festival always includes several works by Shakespeare. Call ✆ **800/567-1600** or check out **www.stratfordfestival.ca.** Early May through mid-November.

ALOUD: A Celebration for Young Readers, Harbourfront. A 3-day literary fun fest for kids. For information, call Harbourfront at ✆ **416/973-4000** or go to **www.readings.org.** Mid-May.

Inside Out Lesbian and Gay Film Festival, citywide. Toronto has no shortage of film festivals, but Inside Out, now in its 21st year, is unique. This 11-day event has nurtured plenty of new talent and supported many established artists. Call ✆ **416/977-6847** or check out **www.insideout.on.ca.** Mid-May.

Doors Open Toronto, citywide. Hugely popular, this weekend event invites city residents and visitors alike to tour some of Toronto's architectural marvels. Some of the more than 150 participating buildings aren't normally open to the public, and all are free of charge. Visit **www.toronto.ca/doorsopen.** Late May.

JUNE

Luminato, citywide. First launched in 2007, this 9-day festival of "arts + creativity" has quickly become a highlight of the city's calendar. Featuring music, dance, theater, art, and educational programs, it really does offer something for the whole family. For information, visit **www.luminato.com.** Early to mid-June.

North by Northeast Festival, citywide. Known in the music biz as NXNE, this hot 3-day event features rock and indie bands at multiple venues around town. For information, visit **www.nxne.com.** Mid-June.

Waterfront Blues, Woodbine Park in the Beaches. This used to be the Distillery District's blues fest. Toronto shows that it's got soul in this 3-day festival of Canada's best blues musicians. The event is free; no tickets are required. For information, visit **www.waterfrontblues.ca.** First or second weekend in June.

Telus Toronto International Dragon Boat Festival, Centre Island. More than 160 teams of dragon-boaters compete in the 2-day event, which commemorates the death of the Chinese philosopher and poet Qu Yuan. For information, visit **www.dragonboats.com.** Third weekend in June.

Pride Week & Pride Parade, citywide. Celebrating Toronto's gay and lesbian community, Pride Week features events, performances, symposiums, and parties. It culminates in an extravagant Sunday parade, one of the biggest in North America. For information, call ✆ **416/92-PRIDE** (416/927-7433) or 416/927-7433, or visit **www.pridetoronto.com.** Late June.

TD Canada Trust Toronto Jazz Festival, citywide. This 10-day festival showcases international artists playing every jazz style—blues, gospel, Latin, African, traditional—at venues around town. For information, call ✆ **416/928-2033** or check out **www.tojazz.com.** Late June.

The Fringe: Toronto's Theatre Festival, citywide. More than 90 troupes participate in this 12-day festival of contemporary and experimental theater. Shows last no more than an hour. For information, call ✆ **416/966-1062** or visit **www.fringetoronto.com.** Late June to early July.

JULY

Canada Day Celebrations, citywide. July 1, 2011, marks the nation's 144th birthday. Street parties, fireworks, and other special events commemorate the day. For information, contact **Tourism Toronto** (✆ **800/363-1990** or 416/203-2600; www.seetorontonow.com). July 1.

Canada Dry Festival of Fire, Ontario Place. Formerly known as the Symphony of Fire, this fireworks extravaganza lights up Toronto's waterfront, with the pyrotechnics synchronized to music. For information, call ✆ **416/314-9900** or visit **www.ontarioplace.com.** Early July.

Summerlicious, citywide. It's just like January's Winterlicious event, except that you can dine alfresco. The prix-fixe menus (C$15–C$30 lunch, C$25–C$45 dinner) are some of the best deals around. See **www.toronto.ca/special_events** for a complete list. First 2 weeks of July.

Honda Indy, the Exhibition Place Street circuit. Formerly known as the Molson Indy, this is one of Canada's major races on the IndyCar circuit. Away from the track, you'll find live music and beer gardens. For information, call ✆ **416/922-7477** or visit **www.hondaindytoronto.com.** Second weekend in July.

Just For Laughs, citywide. This offshoot of the successful Montreal-based comedy festival brings to town the world's top comics, alongside emerging talent. Visit **www.hahaha.com/toronto** for more information. Early to mid-July.

RBC Canadian Open, Glen Abbey Golf Club, Oakville. Formerly called the PGA Tour Canadian Open, Canada's national golf tournament has featured the likes of Greg Norman and Tiger Woods. Visit **www.rbccanadianopen.com** for more information. Mid- to late July.

Beaches International Jazz Festival, Queen Street East, between Woodbine and Beech avenues. Both local and international jazz artists turn out for this annual festival, which plays out over 9 days. All of the performances are free. For information, visit **www.beachesjazz.com.** Late July.

Caribana, citywide. Toronto's version of Carnival transforms the city. It's complete with traditional foods from the Caribbean and Latin America, ferry cruises, picnics, children's events, concerts, and arts-and-crafts exhibits. Visit **www.caribana.com.** Late July through early August.

AUGUST

Beerlicious, Fort York. More than 70 major Ontario breweries and microbreweries turn out for this celebration of suds. There's also a wide selection of food from local restaurants, as well as live blues, swing, and jazz music. *Note:* Fort York is normally a great spot for kids, but no one under 19 is allowed at this event. For info, call © **416/698-7206** or visit **www.beerfestival.ca.** First weekend in August.

Canadian National Exhibition, Exhibition Place. It's an old-style touring amusement fair. One of the world's largest exhibitions, this 18-day extravaganza features midway rides, display buildings, free shows, and grandstand performers. The 3-day Canadian International Air Show (first staged in 1878) is a bonus. Call © **416/393-6300** or visit **www.theex.com** for information. Mid-August through Labour Day.

Rogers Cup, Rexall Centre at York University. This international tennis championship is an important stop on the pro tennis tour. In 2011, the women play in Toronto and the men in Montreal. In 2012, they'll swap. For information, call © **877/283-6647** or visit **www.lovemeansnothing.ca.** Mid- August.

SEPTEMBER

Toronto International Film Festival, citywide. The stars come out for the second-largest film festival in the world. More than 250 films from 70 countries are shown over 10 days. For information, call © **416/968-FILM** (416/968-3456) or surf over to **www.tiff.net.** Mid-September.

Word on the Street, Queen's Park. This open-air event celebrates the written word with readings, discounted books and magazines, and children's events. Other major Canadian cities hold similar events on the same weekend. For information, call © **416/504-7241** or visit **www.thewordonthestreet.ca.** Last weekend in September.

The Clothing Show, Exhibition Place. More than 300 booths, featuring everything from indie design to vintage couture, all under one roof. For information, call © **416/516-9859** or visit **www.theclothingshow.com.** Last weekend of September.

OCTOBER

Oktoberfest, Kitchener–Waterloo, about 1 hour from Toronto. This famed 9-day drink-fest features cultural events, plus a pageant and parade. For information, call © **888/294-4267** or 519/570-4267, or visit **www.oktoberfest.ca.** Mid-October.

International Festival of Authors, Harbourfront. Founded in 1980, this renowned 10-day literary festival is arguably the most prestigious in Canada. It draws the absolute top writers from around the world and at home, and has also proven to be an important stage for discovering new talent. Among the literary luminaries who have appeared are Salman Rushdie, Margaret Drabble, Thomas Kenneally, Joyce Carol Oates, A. S. Byatt, and Margaret Atwood. For information, call Harbourfront at

© 416/973-4000 or visit **www.readings. org.** Last 10 days of October.

Toronto Maple Leafs Opening Night, Air Canada Centre. Torontonians love their hockey team, and opening night is always a big event. For tickets, call © **416/872-5000** or visit **http://mapleleafs.nhl.com.** October.

NOVEMBER

Royal Agricultural Winter Fair and Royal Horse Show, Exhibition Place. The 12-day show is the largest indoor agricultural and equestrian competition in the world. Displays include giant vegetables and fruits, homey crafts, farm machinery, livestock, and more. A member of the British royal family traditionally attends the horse show; in 2010, Prince Charles and Camilla cut the ribbon. Call © **416/263-3400** or check **www.royalfair.org** for information. Mid-November.

Santa Claus Parade, downtown. A favorite with kids since 1905, it features marching bands, floats, clowns, and jolly St. Nick. American visitors are usually surprised that the parade's in November, but it's better than watching Santa try to slide through slush. For information, contact **Tourism Toronto** (© **800/363-1990** or

416/203-2600; **www.thesantaclausparade. com**). Third Sunday of November.

Cavalcade of Lights, Nathan Phillips Square. This holiday celebration brings to life the skating rink at City Hall with a fantastic light show, performances, parties, and fireworks. Visit **www.toronto.ca** for more information. Late November through late December.

Canadian Aboriginal Festival, Hamilton. More than 1,500 Native American dancers, drummers, and singers attend this weekend celebration. There are literary readings, an arts-and-crafts market, lacrosse-playing, and traditional foods. Call © **519/751-0040** or visit **www.canab.com.** Last weekend in November.

DECEMBER

First Night Toronto and New Year's Eve at City Hall. First Night is an alcohol-free family New Year's Eve celebration. There is a variety of musical, theatrical, and dance performances at downtown venues. In Nathan Phillips Square and in Mel Lastman Square in North York, concerts begin at around 10pm to usher in the countdown to the New Year. Visit **www.toronto.ca** for more information. December 31.

ENTRY REQUIREMENTS
Passports & Visas

A change in U.S. regulations that kicked in on June 1, 2009, requires Americans who visit Canada to hold a U.S. passport to return home. Previously, a passport was not required at land crossings, but this is the new norm.

Lawful permanent residents of the U.S. must have their **permanent resident cards (green cards)** with them to enter Canada and reenter the U.S. More details are available from U.S. Customs and Border Protection (**www.cbp.gov**).

For citizens of many countries, only a passport is required to visit Canada for up to 90 days; no visas or proof of vaccinations are necessary. This is true for citizens of Andorra, Antigua and Barbuda, Australia, Austria, Bahamas, Belgium, Botswana, Brunei, Denmark, Estonia, Finland, France, Germany, Iceland, Ireland, Israel, Italy, Japan, Korea, Lithuania, Liechtenstein, Luxembourg, Malta, Monaco, Namibia, the Netherlands, New Zealand, Norway, Papua New Guinea, Poland, Portugal, St. Kitts and Nevis, St. Lucia, St. Vincent, San Marino, Singapore, Slovakia, Slovenia, Solomon Islands, Spain, Swaziland, Sweden, Switzerland, the United Kingdom, and the

jump UP!

One of the undisputed highlights of summer in Toronto is the annual Caribana festival. Created in 1967 as a community heritage celebration to tie in with Canada's centennial, Caribana has become North America's largest street festival, drawing more than a million visitors from North America, Britain, and the Caribbean each year. Originally based on Trinidad's Carnival, the festival now draws on numerous cultures—Jamaican, Guyanese, Brazilian, and Bahamian, to name a few—for its music, food, and events.

During the 2 weeks that it runs, you will see the influence of Caribana around town. It starts with a bang—think steel drums—at Nathan Phillips Square with a free concert featuring calypso, salsa, and soca music. In the days that follow, there are boat cruises, dances, and concerts; the King and Queen Extravaganza, which showcases some of the most amazing costumes you'll ever hope to see; and an arts festival. The highlight is the Caribana Parade, which brings together masquerade and steel-drum bands, dancers, and floats in a memorable feast for all the senses. This is one party you just can't miss.

United States. For the most up-to-date list of visitor visa exemptions, visit **Citizenship and Immigration Canada** at www.cic.gc.ca.

If you are driving into Canada, be sure to have your **car registration** with you. U.S. citizens do not need an international driver's license—a state-issued **driver's license** is fine. It's also a good idea to have a **copy of your car insurance**.

Frequent travelers from the U.S. may want to consider a **NEXUS membership,** which gets you preapproved by U.S. Customs and Border Protection and can speed the trip across the border (there is a special car lane at the border for NEXUS members). For details, call © **866-NEXUS26** (639-8726) or visit www.cbp.gov.

Note for young travelers: Anyone 18 and younger and traveling without a parent must have **proof of citizenship and a letter from both parents (or guardians)** detailing the length of stay, providing the parents' telephone numbers, and authorizing the person waiting for them to take care of them while they are in Canada. While the U.S. defines a minor as 16 years or younger, Canada defines a minor as 18 years or younger.

Note for parents traveling with children: Because of international concerns about child abduction, if you are divorced, separated, or traveling without your spouse and are bringing your children to Canada, you will need **proof of custody or a notarized letter from the other parent** giving permission for foreign travel. The letter should include addresses and phone numbers where the parents or guardians can be reached and identify a person who can confirm that the children are not being abducted or taken against their will. Passport requirements apply to children of all ages.

Note on DWIs: If you have ever been convicted for driving while intoxicated, you may be denied entrance into Canada. An **approval of rehabilitation** (also referred to as waiver of exclusion) may be obtained for a fee from a Canadian consulate in the U.S.

Note about passport expiration: The U.S. Department of State recommends renewing passports approximately 9 months before they expire because many countries require that a passport have at least 6 months left before its expiration. In Canada, your passport must be valid for at least one day beyond your stay.

For information on how to obtain a passport, go to "Passports" in the "Fast Facts" chapter (p. 261).

Customs

WHAT YOU CAN BRING INTO CANADA

Generally speaking, Canadian Customs regulations are generous, but they get complicated when it comes to firearms, plants, meat, and pets. Visitors can bring rifles into Canada during hunting season; handguns and automatic rifles are not permitted. Fishing tackle poses no problem (provided the lures are not made of restricted materials—specific feathers, for example), but the bearer must possess a nonresident license for the province or territory where he or she plans to use it. You can bring in, free of duty, up to 50 cigars, 200 cigarettes, and 200g (7 oz.) of tobacco, provided you're at least 18 years of age. You are also allowed 1.2L (40 oz.) of liquor or 1.5L (51 oz.) of wine as long as you're of age in the province you're visiting (19 in Ontario). There are no restrictions on what you can take out (but if you're thinking of bringing Cuban cigars back to the United States, beware—they can be confiscated, and you could face a fine). In terms of pets, visitors from the U.S., the U.K., Ireland, Australia, and New Zealand can bring a cat or dog without quarantine. For more information (and for updates on these policies), check with the **Canada Border Services Agency** (*©* **204/983-3500** or 506/636-5064; www.cbsa.gc.ca).

passport cards: THE NEW WAY TO ENTER CANADA FOR U.S. CITIZENS

If you are traveling to and from Canada by land or sea in 2011, you can do so with the new **passport card** issued by the U.S. Department of State. The department adopted this idea in 2008 after vociferous complaints by border communities that requiring expensive passports for all visitors would harm local businesses dependent on easy cross-border access. Less expensive and more portable than the traditional passport book, the wallet-size passport card has the same validity period as a passport book: 10 years for adults, 5 years for children 15 and younger. Adults who already have a passport book may apply for the card as a passport renewal and pay only $20. First-time applicants are charged $45 for adult cards and $35 for children.

The passport card contains a vicinity-read radio frequency identification (RFID) chip that links the card to a stored record in government databases. No personal information is written to the RFID chip itself. Note that **the passport card is valid for entry by land or sea only;** air travelers must have a valid U.S. passport. If you already have a passport, you may, of course, use that to enter Canada by land or sea. The passport card cannot be used for other international travel. First-time applicants can apply at any one of the 9,300 Passport Acceptance Facilities across the U.S. For more information on passport cards and to locate the application office nearest you, visit http://travel.state.gov.

WHAT YOU CAN TAKE HOME FROM CANADA

For information on what you're allowed to bring home, contact one of the following agencies:

U.S. Citizens: U.S. Customs & Border Protection (CBP), 1300 Pennsylvania Ave., NW, Washington, DC 20229 (② **877/287-8667;** www.cbp.gov).

U.K. Citizens: HM Customs & Excise at ② **0845/010-9000** (from outside the U.K., 020/8929-0152), or consult their website at **www.hmce.gov.uk.**

Australian Citizens: Australian Customs Service at ② **1300/363-263** or **www. customs.gov.au.**

New Zealand Citizens: New Zealand Customs, the Customhouse, 17–21 Whitmore St., Box 2218, Wellington (② **04/473-6099** or 0800/428-786; www. customs.govt.nz).

Medical Requirements

Unless you're arriving from an area known to be suffering from an epidemic (particularly cholera or yellow fever), inoculations or vaccinations are not required for entry into Canada.

GETTING THERE & GETTING AROUND

Getting to Toronto

BY PLANE

Pearson International Airport (YYZ) is the busiest airport in Canada, and its terminals are massive (particularly Terminal 1). Almost all flights into Toronto arrive here. Expect a long walk to the Immigration and Customs area, which you will have to clear in Toronto, even if you're flying on to another Canadian destination. (There are maps of both terminals online at www.gtaa.com.) There are tourism information booths at both terminals.

Canada's only national airline, **Air Canada** (② **888/247-2262;** www.aircanada. ca), operates direct flights to Toronto from most major American cities and many smaller ones. It also flies from major cities around the world and operates connecting flights from other U.S. cities. It is based in Pearson's Terminal 1. **WestJet** (② **888/937-8538;** www.westjet.com), based in Calgary, has become an increasingly popular choice for anyone coming to Toronto from the United States, as well as some locations in the Caribbean and Mexico.

Upstart **Porter Airlines** (② **888/619-8622** or 416/619-8622; www.flyporter. com) has gained a great reputation for service and flies to **Toronto City Centre Airport** from four U.S. locations—Newark, Chicago, Boston, and Myrtle Beach—as well as a rapidly increasing number of Canadian cities, including Halifax, Montréal, Québec City, St. John's, and Ottawa. Porter, along with a handful of commuter flight services, is the only airline that flies to the Toronto City Centre Airport, which is located on the western side of the Toronto Islands.

To find out which airlines travel to Toronto, see "Airline Websites," p. 263.

Getting into Town from the Airport

To get from the airport to downtown, take Highway 427 south to the Gardiner Expressway East. A **taxi** costs about C$50 if you're going downtown (it's higher if you're heading to north or east Toronto).

The convenient **Airport Express bus** (✆ **905/564-6333;** www.torontoairport express.com) travels between the airport, the bus terminal, and major downtown hotels—the Westin Harbour Castle, Fairmont Royal York, Sheraton Centre Toronto, and Delta Chelsea—every 20 to 30 minutes, from 4:55am to 12:55am. The fare is C$20 one-way, C$33 round-trip.

The cheapest way to go is by **bus and subway,** which takes about an hour. During the day, you have three options: the no. 192 "Airport Rocket" bus to Kipling station, the no. 58A bus to Lawrence West station, or the no. 307 bus to Eglinton West station. In the middle of the night, you can take the no. 300A bus to Yonge and Bloor Streets. The fare of C$3 includes free transfer to the subway (which is available till 1:30am). All buses make stops at both airport terminals 1 and 3. It doesn't matter which bus you use; they all take roughly the same amount of time. (The Airport Rocket reaches the subway fastest, but the subway ride to downtown is twice as long as from the other stations.) For more information, call the **Toronto Transit Commission,** or TTC (✆ **416/393-4636;** www3.ttc.ca).

Don't Stow It—Ship It

Though pricey, it's sometimes worth-while to travel luggage-free, particularly if you're toting sports equipment, meetings materials, or baby equipment. Specialists in door-to-door luggage delivery include **SkyCap International** (www. skycapinternational.com) and **Sports Express** (www.sportsexpress.com).

BY CAR
Crossing the border between Canada and the U.S. by car gives you a lot of options—the U.S. highway system leads directly into Canada at 13 points. If you're driving from Michigan, you'll enter at Detroit-Windsor (I-75 and the Ambassador Bridge) or Port Huron–Sarnia (I-94 and the Bluewater Bridge). If you're coming from New York, you have more options. On I-190, you can enter at Buffalo–Fort Erie; Niagara Falls, New York–Niagara Falls, Ontario; or Niagara Falls, New York–Lewiston. On I-81, you'll cross the Canadian border at Hill Island; on Route 37, you'll enter at either Ogdensburg-Johnstown or Rooseveltown-Cornwall.

From the United States, you are most likely to enter Toronto from the west on Highway 401 or Highway 2 and the Queen Elizabeth Way. If you come from the east, via Montréal, you'll also use highways 401 and 2.

Here are approximate driving distances to Toronto: from Boston, 911km (566 miles); Buffalo, 155km (96 miles); Chicago, 859km (534 miles); Cincinnati, 806km (501 miles); Detroit, 379km (235 miles); Minneapolis, 1,564km (972 miles); Montréal, 545km (339 miles); New York, 797km (495 miles); Ottawa, 453km (281 miles); and Québec City, 790km (491 miles).

Be sure you have your driver's license and car registration if you plan to drive your own vehicle into Canada. It isn't a bad idea to carry proof of automobile liability insurance, too.

If you are a member of the American Automobile Association (AAA), the **Canadian Automobile Association (CAA),** Central Ontario Branch, in Toronto (✆ **416/221-4300;** www.caa.ca), provides emergency road service.

I don't recommend driving in Toronto, but if you're planning to make side trips outside of the city, you may wish to rent a car in Toronto or at Pearson International

COPING WITH jet lag

Jetlag is a pitfall of traveling across time zones. If you're flying north–south and you feel sluggish when you touch down, your symptoms will be the result of dehydration and the general stress of air travel. When you travel east–west or vice-versa, your body becomes confused about what time it is, and everything from your digestive system to your brain is knocked for a loop. Traveling east is more difficult on your internal clock than traveling west because most peoples' bodies are more inclined to stay up late than to fall asleep early.

Here are some tips for combating jet lag:

- **Reset your watch** to your destination time before you board the plane.
- **Drink lots of water** before, during, and after your flight. Avoid alcohol.
- **Exercise and sleep well** for a few days before your trip.
- If you have trouble sleeping on planes, **fly eastward on morning flights.**
- **Daylight** is the key to resetting your body clock. At the website for **Outside In** (www.bodyclock. com), you can get a customized plan of when to seek and avoid light.

Airport. If you pay with credit card, you might get automatic coverage (check with your credit card issuer before you go). Be sure to read the fine print of the rental agreement—some companies add conditions that will boost your bill if you don't fulfill certain obligations, such as filling the gas tank before returning the car.

BY TRAIN

Amtrak's (©**800/USA-RAIL** or 800/872-7245; www.amtrak.com) "Maple Leaf" service links New York City and Toronto via Albany, Buffalo, and Niagara Falls. It departs daily from Penn Station. The journey takes 12½ hours. Note that the lengthy schedule allows for extended stops at Customs and Immigration checkpoints at the border. VIA Rail Canada (©**888/VIA-RAIL** or ©888/842-7245; www.viarail.ca) is the nation's top rail line and offers many routes and generally pleasant service. Trains arrive in Toronto at Union Station on Front Street, 1 block west of Yonge Street, opposite the Fairmont Royal York Hotel (see p. 76). The station has direct access to the subway.

BY BUS

Greyhound (© 800/231-2222; www.greyhound.com) is the best-known bus company that crosses the U.S. border. You can travel from almost anywhere in the United States and Canada. You'll arrive at the Metro Coach Terminal downtown at 610 Bay St., near the corner of Dundas Street. Another option is **Coach Canada** (www.coachcanada.com), which travels from many places in the United States, as well as from Québec, to Ontario.

The bus may be faster and cheaper than the train, and its routes may be more flexible if you want to stop along the way. Bear in mind that it's more cramped, toilet facilities are meager, and meals are taken at fast-food rest stops.

Depending on where you are coming from, check into Greyhound's special unlimited-travel passes and discount fares. It's hard to provide sample fares because

3

PLANNING YOUR TRIP TO TORONTO | Getting There & Getting Around bus companies, like airlines, are adopting yield-management strategies, causing prices to change from day to day.

Getting Around

BY PUBLIC TRANSPORTATION

The **Toronto Transit Commission,** or TTC (✆ **416/393-4636** for 24-hr. information; recordings available in 18 languages; www3.ttc.ca), operates the subway, bus, streetcar, and light rapid transit (LRT) systems.

Fares, including transfers to buses or streetcars, are C$3 or 5 tokens for C$13 for adults. Seniors and students ages 13 to 19 with valid ID pay C$2, or 10 tickets for C$17; children 12 and under pay C$0.75, or 10 tickets for C$5.50. You can buy a special day pass for C$10 that's good for unlimited travel for one adult on weekdays and for up to two adults and four children on weekends.

For surface transportation, you need a token, a ticket (for seniors or kids), or exact change. You can buy tokens and tickets at subway entrances and at authorized stores that display the sign TTC TICKETS MAY BE PURCHASED HERE. Bus drivers do not sell tickets, nor will they make change. Always obtain a free transfer where you board the train or bus, in case you need it. In the subways, use the push-button machine just inside the entrance. On streetcars and buses, ask the driver for a transfer.

THE SUBWAY   The TTC faced some serious public-relations issues in 2010, including a drunken bus driver, but it nonetheless remains fast (especially compared with snarled surface traffic), clean, and very simple to use. There are two major lines—Bloor-Danforth and Yonge-University-Spadina—and one smaller line, Sheppard, in the northern part of the city. The Bloor Street east-west line runs from Kipling Avenue in the west to Kennedy Road in the east (where it connects with Scarborough Rapid Transit to Scarborough Centre and McCowan Rd.). The Yonge Street north-south line runs from Finch Avenue in the north to Union Station (Front St.) in the south. From there, it loops north along University Avenue and connects with the Bloor line at the St. George station. A Spadina extension runs north from St. George to Downsview station at Sheppard Avenue. The Sheppard line connects only with the Yonge line at Sheppard Station and runs east through north Toronto for just 6km (3¾ miles).

The LRT system connects downtown to Harbourfront. The fare is one ticket or token. It runs from Union Station along Queens Quay to Spadina Avenue, with stops at Queens Quay ferry docks, York Street, Simcoe Street, and Rees Street; then it continues up Spadina to the Spadina subway station. The transfer from the subway to the LRT (and vice versa) at Union Station is free.

The subway operates Monday to Saturday from 6am to 1:30am and Sunday from 9am to 1:30am. From 1am to 5:30am, the Blue Night Network operates on basic surface routes. It runs about every 30 minutes. For route information, pick up a *Ride Guide* at subway entrances or call ✆ **416/393-4636.** Multilingual information is available.

BUSES & STREETCARS   Where the subway leaves off, buses and streetcars take over. They run east-west and north-south along the city's arteries. When you pay your fare (on bus, streetcar, or subway), always pick up a transfer so that you won't have to pay again if you want to transfer to another mode of transportation.

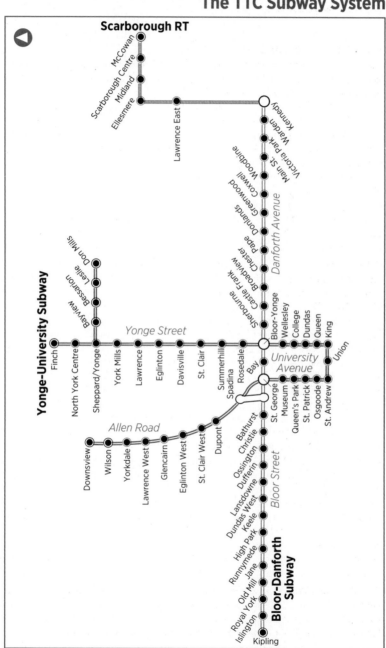

The TTC Subway System

Scarborough RT

McCowan
Scarborough Centre
Midland
Ellesmere
Lawrence East
Kennedy
Warden
Victoria Park
Main St.
Woodbine
Coxwell
Greenwood
Donlands
Pape
Chester
Broadview
Castle Frank
Sherbourne

Danforth Avenue

Yonge-University Subway

Don Mills
Leslie
Bessarion
Bayview

Yonge Street

Finch
North York Centre
Sheppard/Yonge
York Mills
Lawrence
Eglinton
Davisville
St. Clair
Summerhill
Spadina
Rosedale
Bay
Bloor-Yonge
Wellesley
College
Dundas
Queen
King
Union

University Avenue

St. George
Museum
Queen's Park
St. Patrick
Osgoode
St. Andrew

Allen Road

Downsview
Wilson
Yorkdale
Lawrence West
Glencairn
Eglinton West
St. Clair West
Dupont
Bathurst
Christie
Ossington
Dufferin
Lansdowne
Dundas West
Keele
High Park
Runnymede
Jane
Old Mill
Royal York
Islington
Kipling

Bloor Street

Bloor-Danforth Subway

TAXIS In many cities, taxis are an expensive mode of transportation, but this is especially true of Toronto. In 2008, rates were raised (again) because of the high cost of fuel. It's C$4 the minute you step in and C$0.25 for each additional 155m (509 ft.). Fares can quickly mount up. You can hail a cab on the street, find one in line in front of a big hotel, or call one of the major companies—**Diamond** (𝄞 **416/366-6868**), **Royal** (𝄞 **416/777-9222**), or **Metro** (𝄞 **416/504-8294**). If you experience problems with cab service, call the **Metro Licensing Commission** (𝄞 **416/392-3082**).

FERRY SERVICE Toronto Parks and Recreation operates ferries that travel to the Toronto Islands. Call 𝄞 **416/392-8193** for schedules and information. Round-trip fares are C$6.50 adults, C$4 seniors and children 15 to 19, C$3 children under 15.

BY CAR

Toronto is a rambling city, but that doesn't mean the best way to get around is by car. There are long traffic jams, especially during morning and afternoon rush hours. A reputation for "two seasons: winter and construction" means the warmer months are especially busy with road work. And to make matters worse, there is an escalating turf war between the numerous cyclists and motorists sharing the road.

Parking can be very expensive, too, and the city's meter maids are notoriously aggressive in issuing pricey parking tickets at any opportunity.

RENTAL CARS If you decide to rent a car, try to make arrangements in advance. Companies with outlets at Pearson International Airport include **Thrifty, Budget, Avis, Hertz, National,** and **Enterprise** (see "Fast Facts" p. 258, for toll-free phone numbers). The rental fee depends on the type of vehicle, but do keep in mind that the quoted price does not include an added sales tax. It also does not include insurance; if you pay with a particular credit card, you might get automatic coverage (check with your credit card issuer before you go). *Note:* If you're under 25, check with the company—many will rent on a cash-only basis, some only with a credit card, and others will not rent to you at all. Also, keep in mind that you must be 21 or older to rent a car.

Car-rental insurance probably does not cover liability if you cause an accident. Check your own auto insurance policy, the rental company policy, and your credit card coverage for the extent of coverage: Is your destination covered? Are other drivers covered? How much liability is covered if a passenger is injured? (If you rely on your credit card for coverage, you may want to bring a second credit card with you, as damages may be charged to your card and you may find yourself stranded with no money.)

PARKING It can be a hassle to find parking in downtown Toronto, and parking lots have a wide range of fees. Generally speaking, the city-owned lots, marked with a big green "P," are the most affordable. They charge about C$2 per half-hour. After 6pm and on Sunday, there is usually a maximum rate of C$12. Observe the parking restrictions—otherwise, the city will tow your car away, and it'll cost more than C$100 to get it back.

DRIVING RULES A right turn at a red light is legal after coming to a full stop, unless posted otherwise. Passengers must wear seat belts; if you're caught not wearing one, the fine is substantial. The speed limit in the city is 50kmph (31 mph). You must stop at pedestrian crosswalks. If you are following a streetcar and it stops, you must stop well back from the rear doors so passengers can exit easily and safely. (Where there are concrete safety islands in the middle of the street for streetcar stops, this rule does not apply, but exercise care, nonetheless.) Radar detectors are illegal.

MONEY & COSTS

THE VALUE OF THE CANADIAN DOLLAR VS. OTHER POPULAR CURRENCIES

Can$	US$	UK£	Euro (€)	Aus$	NZ$
1.00	1.00	0.65	0.74	1.06	1.35

Frommer's lists exact prices in the local currency. The currency conversions quoted above were correct at press time. However, rates fluctuate, so before departing, consult a currency exchange website, such as **www.oanda.com/currency/converter,** to check up-to-the-minute rates.

Toronto is one of Canada's most expensive cities (along with Vancouver), but compared with other major world cities such as New York, London, and Tokyo, it's very affordable. There are some exceptions, like the above-mentioned high taxi fares, pricey museum admissions (especially compared with the recent, progressive programs in places like London that draw crowds with discounted or free admissions), high sales taxes, and, thanks to the government monopoly on alcohol, inflated prices for wine, beer, and cocktails.

Currency

Canadians use **dollars** and **cents:** Paper currency comes in C$5, C$10, C$20, C$50, and C$100 denominations. Coins come in 1-, 5-, 10-, and 25-cent, and 1- and 2-dollar denominations. The gold-colored C$1 coin is a "loonie"—it sports a loon on its "tails" side—and the large gold-and-silver-colored C$2 coin is a "toonie." If you find these names somewhat . . . ah, colorful, just remember that there's no swifter way to reveal that you're a tourist than to say "one-dollar coin."

Ideally, you should exchange enough petty cash to cover airport incidentals, tipping, and transportation to your hotel before you leave home; however, it's very easy to withdraw money upon arrival at an ATM at Pearson airport. Check with your local American Express or Thomas Cook office, or with your bank. American Express cardholders can order foreign currency over the phone at © **800/807-6233.**

It's best to exchange currency or traveler's checks at a bank, not a currency exchange, hotel, or shop. Get up-to-the-minute exchange rates online before you go at **www.oanda.com/currency/converter** or **www.xe.com/ucc.**

WHAT THINGS COST IN TORONTO	C$
Taxi from the airport to downtown	50.00
Subway ride	3.00
Round-trip ticket for the Toronto Island Ferry	6.50
Local telephone call	0.50
Double at the Delta Chelsea Hotel (moderate)	189.00

Gilead Café (moderate)*	$23.00
Three-course dinner for one at Grano (moderate)*	$50.00
Pint of beer at Mill Street Brew Pub	$7.00
Coca-Cola (355mL/12-oz. can)	$1.50
Cup of coffee (black, not latte)	$2.00
Admission to the Art Gallery of Ontario	$18.00
Movie ticket	$12.99
Ticket for the Canadian Opera Company	$20.00–317.53
Show at the Second City comedy club	$30.00
375mL (12.7-oz.) bottle of Inniskillin Vidal ice wine (LCBO)	$79.00

*Includes tax and tip, but not wine.

ATMs

The easiest and best way to get cash away from home is from an ATM (automated teller machine), sometimes referred to as a "cash machine," or a "cashpoint." The **Cirrus** (© 800/424-7787; www.mastercard.com) and **PLUS** (© 800/843-7587; www.visa.com) networks span the globe. Go to your bank card's website to find ATM locations at your destination. Be sure you know your daily withdrawal limit before you depart. *Note:* Many banks impose a fee every time you use a card at another bank's ATM, and that fee can be higher for international transactions than for domestic ones. In addition, the bank from which you withdraw cash may charge its own fee. For international withdrawal fees, ask your bank.

Note: Banks that are members of the **Global ATM Alliance** charge no transaction fees for cash withdrawals at other Alliance member ATMs; these include Bank of America, Scotiabank (Canada, Caribbean, and Mexico), Barclays (U.K. and parts of Africa), Deutsche Bank (Germany, Poland, Spain, and Italy), and BNP Paribas (France).

Credit Cards

MasterCard and Visa are almost universally accepted in Toronto; American Express has become more common, but many independent boutiques and small restaurants still don't accept it. Overall, credit cards are a smart way to "carry" money. They also provide a convenient record of all your expenses, and they generally offer relatively good exchange rates. You can withdraw cash advances from your credit cards at banks or ATMs, but high fees make credit card cash advances a pricey way to get cash. Keep in mind that you'll pay interest from the moment of your withdrawal, even if you pay your monthly bills on time. Also, note that many banks now assess a 1% to 3% "transaction fee" on *all* charges you incur abroad (whether you're using the local currency or your native currency).

Traveler's Checks

Traveler's checks are something of an anachronism in Toronto, since ATMs have made getting cash accessible at any time. However, traveler's checks are still widely accepted—and unlike cash, can be replaced if lost or stolen.

You can buy traveler's checks at most banks. They are offered in denominations of $20, $50, $100, $500, and sometimes $1,000. Generally, you'll pay a service charge ranging from 1% to 4%.

The most popular traveler's checks are offered by **American Express** (📞 **800/807-6233,** or 📞 800/221-7282 for card holders—this number accepts collect calls, offers service in several foreign languages, and exempts Amex gold and platinum cardholders from the 1% fee); **Visa** (📞 **800/732-1322**); and **Master-Card** (📞 **800/223-9920**).

Be sure to keep a record of the traveler's checks serial numbers separate from your checks, in the event that they are stolen or lost. You'll get a refund faster if you know the numbers.

Another option is the new prepaid traveler's check cards, reloadable cards that work much like debit cards but aren't linked to your checking account. The **American Express Travelers Cheque Card,** for example, requires a minimum deposit, sets a maximum balance, and has a one-time issuance fee of $15. You can withdraw money from an ATM (for a fee of $2.50 per transaction, not including bank fees), and the funds can be purchased in dollars, euros, or pounds. If you lose the card, your available funds will be refunded within 24 hours.

HEALTH

Staying Healthy

While Toronto has excellent doctors and fine hospitals, it is common sense to prepare for the trip as you would for any other. The SARS outbreak here in 2003 was huge news at the time, but there has not been a subsequent outbreak.

GENERAL AVAILABILITY OF HEALTH CARE

Toronto has excellent hospitals and doctors—though hopefully you won't have any occasion to need these services. Bring any prescriptions you might require with you. Decongestants, cough and cold remedies, and allergy medications are available without prescription in pharmacies. Two major chains dominate. **Pharma Plus** has many locations around town, including one at 63 Wellesley St., at Church Street

---

Avoiding "Economy-Class Syndrome"

Deep-vein thrombosis, or as it's known in the world of flying, "economy-class syndrome," is a blood clot that develops in a deep vein. It's a potentially deadly condition that can be caused by sitting in cramped conditions—such as an airplane cabin—for too long. During a flight (especially a long-haul flight), get up, walk around, and stretch your legs every 60 to 90 minutes to keep your blood flowing. Other preventative measures include frequent flexing of the legs while sitting, drinking lots of water, and avoiding alcohol and sleeping pills. If you have a history of deep-vein thrombosis, heart disease, or another condition that puts you at high risk, some experts recommend wearing compression stockings or taking anticoagulants when you fly; always ask your physician about the best course for you. Symptoms of deep-vein thrombosis include leg pain or swelling, or even shortness of breath.

(📞 416/924-7760) that's open daily from 8am to midnight. Other Pharma Plus branches are in College Park, Manulife Centre, Commerce Court, and First Canadian Place. **Shopper's Drug Mart** is also everywhere. The only 24-hour drugstore near downtown is the **Shopper's Drug Mart** at 700 Bay St., at Gerrard Street West (📞 416/979-2424).

What to Do If You Get Sick Away from Home

In downtown Toronto, the **University Health Network** manages three hospitals: **Toronto General** at 200 Elizabeth St., **Princess Margaret** at 610 University Ave., and **Toronto Western** at 399 Bathurst St. The UHN has a central switchboard for all three (📞 416/340-3111).

The staff or concierge at your hotel should be able to help you locate a doctor. You can also call the **College of Physicians and Surgeons of Ontario** (80 College St.; 📞 416/967-2626) for a referral from 8am to 5pm Monday through Friday.

For emergency dental services from 8am till midnight, call the **Dental Emergency Service** (📞 416/485-7121). After midnight, your best bet is the **University Health Network.** Otherwise, ask the front-desk staff or concierge at your hotel.

We list additional **emergency numbers** in the "Fast Facts" chapter, p. 258.

SAFETY

Toronto enjoys an unusually safe reputation as far as big cities go, although a steady supply of guns coming across the border from the U.S. is damaging the now worn-out reputation of "Toronto the Good." But keep in mind that it is a big city, with all of the difficulties that implies. While lovely parks such as Allan Gardens and Trinity Bellwoods have been cleaned up in recent years, it's best to avoid all big parks after dark unless you're attending a special event such as a theater performance. During the day, keep your valuables close and your eyes peeled for pickpockets. This is important to keep in mind when you're at a major tourist attraction, on a crowded shopping strip such as Yonge Dundas Square, and on the subway or streetcar.

More about safety on Toronto's public transit system: If it's late and you're alone on an almost-empty platform, wait for the train by the big "DWA" sign (it stands for **"Designated Waiting Area,"** and it has an intercom and a closed-circuit TV camera trained on it). There is a DWA area at every TTC station. If there is an incident on a subway car, press the alarm—the yellow strip is very visible—and note that it is silent. If you are traveling by bus, there is a **"Request Stop"** program in effect between 9pm and 5am, in which female passengers traveling alone can disembark at streets in between regular TTC bus stops. For information about these safety features, visit **http://www3.ttc.ca/Riding_the_TTC/Safety_and_Security/index.jsp.**

SPECIALIZED TRAVEL RESOURCES

Gay & Lesbian Travelers

Toronto is a member of the Big Four, the term for the North American cities with the largest gay communities (the others are San Francisco, New York, and Chicago). For the city's large gay population, estimated at more than 250,000 and growing, community life is no longer restricted to a "gay ghetto," although the former hub of gay community life still hums at the intersection of Church and Wellesley streets. Gay-friendly establishments are located throughout the entire city. Gay marriage, after all, was legalized here in 2003. One of Toronto's most celebrated events is Pride Week in June (see "Calendar of Events," p. 28). Also, Toronto has become a popular spot for gay and lesbian couples to marry; see "Wedded Bliss for Gay & Lesbian Couples," below, for details.

Gay and lesbian travelers can pick up a copy of the free biweekly *Xtra!* at many bookstores, including the **Glad Day Bookshop** (598A Yonge St., second floor; © 416/961-4161). To read *Xtra!* before you get to town, log in to **www.xtra.ca.** You can also sign up for its Toronto e-mail list, with information about local events and breaking news.

Another resource is **Gay Toronto** (www.gaytoronto.com), which lists gay-friendly restaurants, bars, nightclubs, guesthouses, travel agencies, and other businesses and organizations. The daily news website **www.365gay.com** features Toronto travel information.

The International Gay and Lesbian Travel Association (IGLTA; © 800/448-8550 or 954/776-2626; www.iglta.org) is the trade association for the gay and lesbian travel industry and offers an online directory of gay- and lesbian-friendly travel businesses and tour operators.

Gay.com Travel (© 800/929-2268 or 415/644-8044; www.outandabout.com) is an excellent online successor to the popular *Out & About* print magazine. It provides regularly updated information about gay-owned, gay-oriented, and gay-friendly

---

WEDDED BLISS FOR gay & lesbian COUPLES

Niagara Falls used to be one of the most popular places to honeymoon, but Toronto today is one of the most in-demand wedding destinations. After same-sex marriage became legal in Ontario in 2003, gay and lesbian couples flocked to the city to marry. (In July 2006, the Civil Marriage Act legalized same-sex marriage across Canada. The new law will apply to civil ceremonies—religious institutions will not be bound by it.)

If you want to get married in Toronto, it's pretty simple: Go with your partner to the Registrar General's office at 900 Bay St. (at Wellesley), bring ID (including your passport and birth certificate), pay a small fee, and the marriage license will be yours; there's no residency requirement. See **www.toronto.ca** for details and an application form that you can download. For help organizing

a wedding beyond the confines of city hall, check out the wedding-planner pages at **www.toronto.com.** One company that specializes in planning same-sex weddings is **I Do in Toronto** (© **888/418-1188;** www.idointoronto. com). While many wedding ceremonies are being conducted at the **Toronto Civic Wedding Chambers** (100 Queen St. W.; © **416/363-0316**), couples are increasingly choosing to wed elsewhere. One popular place is the **Metropolitan Community Church of Toronto** (© **416/406-6228;** www.mcctoronto. com), which has been very active in the battle for same-sex marriage rights.

Keep in mind that while some U.S. states, such as New York, will recognize a same-sex marriage that took place in Canada, many other states will not. Legislation on the issue varies from state to state.

lodging, dining, sightseeing, nightlife, and shopping establishments in every important destination worldwide. British travelers should go to **www.gaytravel.co.uk** for advice and gay-friendly trip ideas.

The Canadian website **GayTraveler** (www.gaytraveler.ca) offers ideas and advice for gay travel all over the world.

For more gay and lesbian travel resources, visit Frommers.com.

Travelers with Disabilities

Most disabilities shouldn't stop anyone from traveling. There are more options and resources out there than ever before.

Toronto is a very accessible city. Curb cuts are well made and common throughout the downtown area; special parking privileges are extended to people with disabilities who have special plates or a pass that allows parking in no-parking zones. The subway and trolleys are not accessible, but the city operates **Wheel-Trans,** a special service for those with disabilities. Visitors can register for this service. For information, call ✆ **416/393-4111** or visit **http://www3.ttc.ca/TTC_Accessibility/index.jsp.**

Community Information Toronto (425 Adelaide St. W., at Spadina Ave.; ✆ **416/397-4636**), may be able to provide limited information and assistance about social-service organizations in the city. It does not have specific accessibility information on tourism or hotels, though. It's open daily from 8am to 10pm.

Organizations that offer a vast range of resources and assistance to travelers with disabilities include **MossRehab** (✆ **800/CALL-MOSS** [800/225-5667]; www.mossresourcenet.org); the Canadian National Institute for the Blind (CNIB; ✆ **416/486-2500;** www.cnib.ca) or the **American Foundation for the Blind** (**AFB;** ✆ **800/232-5463;** www.afb.org); and **SATH** (Society for Accessible Travel & Hospitality; ✆ **212/447-7284;** www.sath.org). **AirAmbulanceCard.com** is now partnered with SATH and allows you to preselect top-notch hospitals in case of an emergency. **Flying with Disability** (www.flying-with-disability.org) is a comprehensive information source on airplane travel.

For more on organizations that offer resources to travelers, go to Frommers.com.

Family Travel

Toronto is a kid-friendly town. There are plenty of great attractions, such as the water park at Ontario Place; the idiosyncratic Ontario Science Centre; Paramount Canada's Wonderland, a conventional theme park on the outskirts of town noted for its super roller coasters; the artsy Harbourfront centre; and the Toronto Zoo, which rivals the great zoos of the world.

A new attraction in nearby Niagara Falls is the indoor water park and family resort Great Wolf Lodge, a popular chain across the U.S. and Canada.

For more suggestions on family and kid-oriented entertainment in Toronto, see "Especially for Kids," in chapter 7. If you're already in town, pick up a copy of *Toronto Families,* a free magazine produced by the publishers of *Today's Parent Toronto* (an award-winning national magazine). You can also check it out online at **www.torontofamilies.ca.**

Helpful features in this guide include "Family-Friendly Hotels" (p. 80). To locate those accommodations, restaurants, and attractions that are particularly kid friendly, refer to the "Kids" icon throughout this guide.

Recommended family travel websites include **Help! We've Got Kids** (www.helpwevegotkids.com); **Family Travel Forum** (www.familytravelforum.com), a comprehensive site that offers customized trip planning; **Family Travel Network** (www.familytravelnetwork.com), an online magazine providing travel tips; and **TravelWithYourKids.com,** a comprehensive site written by parents for parents offering sound advice for long-distance and international travel with children.

For a list of more family-friendly travel resources, turn to the experts at Frommers.com.

Women Travelers

Toronto is an easy place to be for solo travelers, male or female. At night, take note of the TTC's "Request Stop" program for women traveling on buses (see "Safety," above). Check out the award-winning website **Journeywoman** (www.journeywoman.com), a "real-life" women's travel-information network, where you can sign up for a free e-mail newsletter and get advice on everything from etiquette and dress to safety. The travel guide *Safety and Security for Women Who Travel, 2nd edition,* by Sheila Swan and Peter Laufer (Travelers' Tales), offers common-sense tips on safe travel. For general travel resources for women, go to Frommers.com.

Senior Travel

The term "seniors" is proving to be more elastic than most face-lifts. Boomers in the above-50 group should check out the local magazine *Zoomer,* which is connected to **CARP** (Canadian Association for Retired Persons; ✆ **416/363-8748;** www.carp.ca). Members of **CARP** or **AARP** (the American analog; ✆ **888/687-2277;** www.aarp.org), can get discounts on hotels, airfares, and car rentals. Otherwise, seniors can expect to receive discounts on the TTC (subway and bus), and on many (but not all) admissions to attractions. Keep in mind that it is usually necessary to show photo identification when purchasing discounted tickets or admissions.

Frommers.com offers more information and resources on travel for seniors.

Vegetarian Travelers

To get an idea of how mainstream vegetarianism is in Toronto, consider Meatless Mondays, a program launched in 2010 that encourages citizens to go meat-free at least one day a week. For up-to-date information, check out the **Toronto Vegetarian Association** (www.veg.ca). Its long list of resources includes a vegetarian directory to the city. **Happy Cow's Vegetarian Guide to Restaurants & Health Food Stores** (www.happycow.net) has an international restaurant guide with more than 6,000 recommendations and 70 or so located in Toronto. **VegDining.com** also lists vegetarian restaurants (with profiles) around the world **Vegetarian Vacations** (www.vegetarian-vacations.com) offers vegetarian tours and itineraries.

There are many vegetarian restaurants (or restaurants with impressive vegetarian options) listed in chapter 6.

SUSTAINABLE TOURISM/ ECOTOURISM

By North American standards, Toronto is an exceptionally green city. It boasts good eco-initiatives such as composting and recycling programs, a powerful local-foods movement, and more. The city's wealth of parkland, even in the downtown core, is

IT'S easy BEING GREEN

We can all help conserve fuel and energy when we travel. Here are a few simple ways you can help preserve your favorite destinations:

○ Each time you take a flight or drive a car greenhouse gases release into the atmosphere. You can help neutralize this danger to the planet through "carbon offsetting"—paying someone to invest your money in programs that reduce greenhouse gas emissions by the same amount you've added. Before buying carbon offset credits, just make sure that you're using a reputable company such as **Carbonfund** (www.carbonfund.org), **TerraPass** (www.terrapass.org), or **Carbon Neutral** (www.carbonneutral.org). **Air Canada** partnered with **Zerofootprint,** a not-for-profit organization, to offset flight emissions when you book on **www.air canada.com.** In February 2010, they tallied the program's savings: Since 2007, the offsets were 15,108 tons of carbon dioxide or the equivalent of removing 3,740 cars from the road.

○ Whenever possible, choose non-stop flights; they generally require less fuel than indirect flights that stop and take off again. Try to fly during the day—some scientists estimate that nighttime flights are twice as harmful to the environment. And pack light—each 6.8kg (15 lb.) of luggage on a 8,047km (5,000-mile) flight adds up to 23kg (50 lb.) of carbon dioxide emitted.

○ Call the **Green Tourism Association of Toronto** for inspiration and advice about eco-friendly travel (☎ **416/392-1288**).

○ Rely on public transportation to get around Toronto: The **TTC** is safe and clean, and it makes it easy to get to downtown, mid-town, and uptown sights. Or rent a bike: Check out **Bikeshare** (☎ **416/504-2918**; http://communitybicyclenetwork.org/bike_rentals).

○ If renting a car is necessary for a side trip (such as to Niagara-on-the-Lake), ask for a hybrid or rent the most fuel-efficient car

a standout. And, although there is nothing on the scale of say Central Park, there are green spaces scattered throughout, from tiny plots in the Financial District to neighborhood gems like Riverdale, Allan Gardens, Trinity Bellwoods, Dufferin Grove, and High Park. (The green spaces are well maintained, but you may notice a fair number of weeds because cosmetic use of pesticides is banned in the city.)

Cycling is a popular mode of transit, and the city has ambitious plans to expand the number of dedicated bicycle lanes as part of a proposed 1,000km-plus (621-mile) Bikeway Network. There are biking trails through most of the city's parks and more than 29km (18 miles) of street bike routes. Favorite pathways include the **Martin Goodman Trail** (from the Beaches neighborhood to the Humber River along the waterfront); the **Lower Don Valley** bike trail (from the east end of the city north to Riverdale Park); **High Park** (with winding trails over 160 hectares/395 acres); and the best of them all for bi-pedal fans: the **Toronto Islands,** where bikes available. You'll use less gas and save money.

o Take a look at **"The City of Toronto Green Guide"** online at www.toronto.ca/greenguide. And pick up a copy of *Green Living Magazine* for good resources, also online at **www.greenliving online.com.**

o Where you stay during your travels can have a major environmental impact. To determine the green credentials of a property, ask about trash disposal and recycling, water conservation, and energy use; also whether sustainable materials were used in the construction of the property. The website **www. greenhotels.com** recommends green-rated member hotels around the world that fulfill the company's stringent environmental requirements. Also consult **www.environmentallyfriendly hotels.com** for more green accommodation ratings.

o At hotels, request that your sheets and towels not be changed daily. (Many hotels already do this.) Turn off the lights and air-conditioner when you leave your room.

o Last, but definitely not least, eat at locally owned and operated restaurants that use local, seasonal, and, wherever possible, organic produce. Ditto for meats: Look for pasture-raised and non-industrial suppliers. Not only do these choices contribute to the local economy, they cut down on greenhouse gas emissions. Check out the city's farmers markets and, when shopping at supermarkets, look for the Local Food Plus (www.localfoodplus.ca) label, which identifies local producers that aim for sustainable practices. Toronto has too many restaurants that support the local foods movement to list here, but some suggestions include Gilead Café and Bistro (see p. 105), Zucca (see p. 116), Trattoria Giancarlo (see p. 98), Cowbell (see p. 96), The Local Kitchen (see p. 100), and Scaramouche (see p. 115).

rule and cars are forbidden. Bike lanes, which are clearly marked, include routes along College/Carlton streets, the Bloor Street Viaduct leading to Danforth Avenue, Beverly/St. George streets, Jarvis Street, and Davenport Road. For cycling maps, rentals, and more information, visit www.toronto.ca/cycling.

SPECIAL-INTEREST TRIPS & ESCORTED GENERAL-INTEREST TOURS

Architectural & Cultural Tours

Toronto is a city for walking, and there's no shortage of options for those willing to pound the pavement. The **Royal Ontario Museum** has a **ROMwalks** program

(© 416/586-5513) throughout the summer that offers guided tours of architectural highlights and neighborhoods from the Entertainment District to the Danforth. During the summer, **Heritage Toronto** (© 416/338-0684; www.heritagetoronto. org) offers walking tours of several neighborhoods, including Cabbagetown and Rosedale. If you're in town on the first weekend of May, check out Jane Walks (www. janeswalk.net), in honor of the late Jane Jacobs, the city's beloved author, thinker, and believer in "cities planned for and by people."

Bike Tours

Year-round, **A Taste of the World Neighbourhood Bicycle Tours and Walks** ★ (© 416/923-6813; www.torontowalksbikes.com) leads visitors through the nooks and crannies of such places as Chinatown, Yorkville, and Rosedale. It's particularly well known for its "haunted" tours, including one about the ghosts of Yorkville (remember, that chic neighborhood stands atop a former cemetery).

Another option is the **Toronto Bicycling Network** (© 416/766-1985; www. tbn.ca). The association organizes tours and provides information about routes you can explore in and around the city.

Chefs & Gourmets

Bonnie Stern is a local legend, and the **Bonnie Stern Cooking School** is a wonderful place to pick up some of her culinary secrets (she teaches many of the classes herself). The school is located at 6 Erskine Ave. (3 blocks north of the Eglinton subway station); call © 416/484-4810 or visit **www.bonniestern.com** for information. The school offers classes in everything from challah baking to Moroccan cooking.

The Fairmont Royal York runs a popular Shop with a Chef package that includes a tour of St. Lawrence market and a delicious meal led by the eco-minded executive chef David Garcelon. Winery tours in the Niagara Region are popular and plenty. For more information, go to **www.tourismniagara.com/wine_country.html.**

Ecology & Wildlife

If you're interested in exploring the Toronto region's natural wonders, contact **Toronto and Region Conservation** at ✆ **416/661-6600** or visit **www.trcaparks.ca.** The organization offers tours that include bird-watching and wildlife viewing.

Harbor Tours

Mariposa Cruise Line (✆ **800/976-2442** or 416/203-0178; www.mariposa cruises.com) operates 1-hour narrated tours of the waterfront and the Toronto Islands from mid-May to September. Tours leave from the Queen's Quay Terminal at 207 Queens Quay W.

The *Kajama,* a three-masted, 50m (164-ft.) schooner, offers 90-minute cruises. The schedule varies, but in July and August, three tours a day take place on weekdays and weekends. For more information, call the **Great Lakes Schooner Company** (249 Queens Quay W., Ste. 111; ✆ **800/267-3866** or 416/260-6355; www. greatlakesschooner.com).

Escorted General-Interest Tours

Do you really need a package tour to visit Toronto? Generally speaking, no—it's easy to arrange accommodations and show tickets yourself. However, if you're determined to see a particular show (or the Canadian Opera Company, whose performances often sell out), a package is a good idea. Package tours are simply a way to buy the airfare, accommodations, and other elements of your trip (such as car rentals, airport transfers, and sometimes even activities) at the same time and often at discounted prices.

One good source of package deals is **Tourism Toronto** itself, which lists deals on its website (www.seetorontonow.com). Several of Toronto's hotels (including the **Park Hyatt, the Fairmont Royal York,** and the **Delta Chelsea**) offer special

 ASK before YOU GO

Before you invest in a package deal or an escorted tour:

- Always ask about the **cancellation policy.** Can you get your money back? Is there a deposit required?
- Ask about the **accommodations choices and prices** for each. Then, look up the hotels' reviews in a Frommer's guide and check their rates online for your specific dates of travel. Also, find out what types of rooms are offered.

- Request a complete **schedule** (escorted tours only).
- Ask about the **size** and demographics of the group (escorted tours only).
- Discuss what is included in the **price**—transportation, meals, tips, airport transfers, and so on (escorted tours only).
- Finally, look for **hidden expenses.** Ask whether airport departure fees and taxes, for example, are included in the total cost—they rarely are.

Hey, Google, Did You Get My Text Message?

It's bound to happen: The day you leave this guidebook back at the hotel for an unencumbered stroll through Leslieville, you'll forget the address of the lunch spot you had earmarked. If you're traveling with a mobile device, send a text message to © GOOGL (46645) for a lightning-fast response. For instance, type "edward levesques kitchen toronto" and within 10 seconds, you'll receive a text message with the address and phone number. This nifty trick works in a range of search categories: Look up weather ("weather toronto"), language translations ("translate goodbye in chinese"), currency conversions ("10 pounds in csd"), movie dates and times ("harry potter 60610"), and more. If your search results are off, be more specific ("sailor gay bar church street"). For more tips and search options, see www.google. com/sms. Regular text-message charges apply.

packages; see chapter 5. Several big **online travel agencies**—Expedia.com, Travelocity, Orbitz, and Lastminute.com—also do a brisk business in packages.

Maxxim Vacations (© **800/567-6666;** www.maxximvacations.com) is a Canadian company that has a long track record with Toronto package tours. One advantage with their packages is that you can guarantee you get to see the show (or shows) you have your heart set on while in town.

Travel packages are also listed in the travel section of your local weekend newspaper and sometimes in midweek editions. Or check ads in national travel magazines such as *Arthur Frommer's Budget Travel Magazine, Travel + Leisure, National Geographic Traveler,* and *Condé Nast Traveler.*

Escorted tours are structured group tours, with a group leader. The price usually includes everything from airfare to hotels, meals, tours, admission costs, and local transportation.

There are some great special-interest tours you can take part in while you're in town (see above), and the city is easy to navigate and explore without a group. However, if you do want an escorted tour, there are several options, including **Great Adventure Tours** (© **800/638-3945;** www.greatadventuretours.com), which explores Toronto and Niagara, and **SWT Tours** (© **212/988-1359;** www.posh nosh.com), which specializes in theater tours.

For more information on escorted general-interest tours, including questions to ask before booking your trip, see Frommers.com.

STAYING CONNECTED

Telephones

To call Toronto from the U.S.: Canada and the U.S. use the same area-code system. Simply dial 1, the Toronto area code (416 or 647), and the number.

To call Toronto from other countries:

1. Dial the international access code: 00 from the U.K., Ireland, or New Zealand; or 0011 from Australia.
2. Dial the country code 1.

3. Dial the city code 416 or 647, and then the number.

To make international calls: To make international calls from Toronto, first dial 00 and then the country code (U.K. 44, Ireland 353, Australia 61, New Zealand 64). Next, dial the area code and number. However, if you are calling the U.S. from Toronto, you need only to dial 1 and then the area code and phone number.

For directory assistance: Dial ✆ **411** if you're looking for a phone number; online, visit **www.canada411.com.**

For operator assistance: If you need operator assistance in making a call, dial ✆ **0** (zero).

Toll-free numbers: Numbers beginning with 800 or 866 are toll-free within Canada and the U.S. However, calling an 800 number from other countries is not toll-free. In fact, it costs the same as an overseas call.

Cellphones

The three letters that define much of the world's wireless capabilities are **GSM** (Global System for Mobile Communications), a big, seamless network that makes for easy cross-border cellphone use throughout Europe and dozens of other countries worldwide. In the U.S., T-Mobile and AT&T Wireless use this quasi-universal system; in Canada, Rogers customers are GSM, and all Europeans and most Australians use GSM. GSM phones function with a removable plastic SIM card, encoded with your phone number and account information. If your cellphone is on a GSM system and you have a world-capable multiband phone—such as many Sony Ericsson, Motorola, or Samsung models—you can make and receive calls across civilized areas around much of the globe. Just call your wireless provider and ask for "international roaming" to be activated on your account.

For many, **renting** a phone is a good idea. While you can rent a phone from any number of sites, including kiosks at airports and at car-rental agencies, we suggest renting the phone before you leave home. Americans can rent one before leaving home from **InTouch USA** (✆ **800/872-7626;** www.intouchglobal.com) or **Road-Post** (✆ **888/290-1606** or 905/272-5665; www.roadpost.com).

Most U.S. cellphone carriers have roaming agreements with Canadian cellphone carriers. Before leaving home, check with your carrier for rates and availability. You can rent a cellphone in Toronto from **Hello Anywhere** (✆ **888/729-4355** or 416/367-4355; www.helloanywhere.com). Also, cellphone rentals are available

---

House-Swapping

House-swapping is becoming a more popular and viable means of travel; you stay in their place, they stay in yours, and you both get an authentic and personal view of the area. Try **HomeLink International** (www.homelink.org), the largest and oldest home-swapping organization, founded in 1952, with over 11,000 listings worldwide. Smaller but also-reliable associations include **HomeExchange.com** and **InterVac.com**. Many travelers find great housing swaps on **Craigslist** (www.craigslist.org), too, though the offerings cannot be vetted or vouched for. Swap at your own risk.

ONLINE toolbox

Veteran travelers usually carry some essential items to make their trips easier. Following is a selection of handy online tools to bookmark and use:

o **Airplane Food** (www.airline meals.net)

o **Airplane Seating** (www.seatguru. com and www.airlinequality.com)

o **City of Toronto** (www.toronto.ca) is the official municipal guide to Toronto, a straightforward source of practical information peppered with profiles of fun places to visit and announcements of festivals, free concerts, kids' events, and more.

o *Globe and Mail* (www.globeand mail.com) has a weekend edition with restaurant reviews and other useful services.

o **Help! We've Got Kids** (www. helpwevegotkids.com) is just what parents of young children need: comprehensive listings of special events, attractions, and services that work for the small fry.

o **Maps** (www.mapquest.com)

o **Ticketmaster** (www.ticket master.ca)

o **Time and Date** (www.timeand date.com)

o **Toronto.com** (www.toronto.com) boasts articles on arts and culture, as well as a hotel directory, restaurant reviews, community news, and events listings. One of its best features is its extensive use of photographs.

o **Toronto Arts & Culture** (www. livewithculture.ca) is a new initiative from local government to have all of the cultural events, festivals, and concerts that happen in Toronto listed in one place.

o *Toronto Life* (www.torontolife. com) has extensive restaurant listings, as well as links for events, activities, and nightlife.

o *Toronto Star* (www.thestar.com) includes everything from theater, restaurant, and concert reviews to local news and weather conditions.

o **Toronto Transit Commission** (www3.ttc.ca)

o **Toronto Vegetarian Association** (www.veg.ca)

o **Travel Warnings** (http://travel. state.gov, www.fco.gov.uk/travel, www.voyage.gc.ca, or www.dfat. gov.au/consular/advice)

o **Universal Currency Converter** (www.xe.com/ucc)

o **Visa ATM Locator** (www.visa. com); **MasterCard ATM Locator** (www.mastercard.com)

o **Weather** (www.intellicast.com and www.weather.com)

through many of Toronto's more upscale hotels, including the **Park Hyatt Toronto,** the **Metropolitan Hotel,** and the **Sutton Place Hotel.**

Voice over Internet Protocol (VoIP)

If you have Web access while traveling, you might consider a broadband-based telephone service (in technical terms, **Voice over Internet Protocol,** or **VoIP**) such as Skype (www.skype.com) or Vonage (www.vonage.com), which allows you to make free international calls if you use their services from your laptop or in a cyber-cafe. The people you're calling must also use the service for it to work; check the sites for details.

TIPS ON ACCOMMODATIONS

Whether you're seeking an historic hotel with old-world elegance or looking for all the conveniences of the office in your "home" away from home, you'll find a perfect place to stay in Toronto. The city's accommodations run the gamut from intimate boutique hotels to large, comfortable convention destinations. Proximity to major attractions (such as the CN Tower, Harbourfront, the Rogers Centre, and the Eaton Centre) can cost a bundle. Even budget hotels charge more than C$100 a night in the high season, which runs from April to October. And remember to factor in the 5% accommodations tax and the new 13% HST or "harmonized" sales tax—a combination of the federal Goods & Services Tax (GST) and the provincial sales tax. Before you make a reservation, it's important to have some sense of what you'd like to see and do in town. Toronto is a sprawling metropolis, with attractions, dining districts, and ethnic communities scattered throughout. Keep in mind that you want to be as close as possible to the sights that interest you most.

For tips on finding hotel deals online, visit Frommers.com.

SUGGESTED TORONTO ITINERARIES

4

Toronto is a patchwork of neighborhoods with a remarkably vibrant downtown core. (Once you're in the heart of the city, you can head in just about any direction and end up somewhere with plenty to see, eat, and do.) Where most North American urbanites know the heart of their metropolis as a workplace, a practical day-time shopping network, and occasional night-time destination, nearly 200,000 Torontonians eat, play, and sleep in addition to working in the downtown core. If you're coming in from Pearson International Airport, the city might seem sprawling, but once you're grounded downtown, every-thing is here: shoulder-to-shoulder condo towers, office buildings, theaters, parks, schools, restaurants and cafes, bars and nightclubs, and places of worship.

Where most of the world is still proceeding with post-recessionary caution, the building here keeps booming, from new five-star hotel/residence developments to exciting architectural destinations. The city's diverse cultural life, historic and ever-evolving, thrives everywhere, from residential laneways still lined with garages where wine and tomato sauces are made in late summer to dazzling architecture projects as well as restaurants, galleries, and shops, to keep the citizens engaged.

Start anywhere in the downtown core, walk in any direction for no more than 15 minutes, and you'll see eclectic modern buildings side by side with neo-Gothic and Art

Deco architecture, or catch a fair glimpse of the city's ethnic spectrum. Sometimes, you'll walk right into a pleasing patch of greenery.

This is a happy coincidence because the layout and organization of the city mean you *will* almost certainly get lost at least once during your stay. Streets have names, not numbers, and they have a crazy-making habit of changing their monikers as they go along. In Midtown, the must-see Avenue Road, for example, turns into Queen's Park Crescent, then into University Avenue as you head south, and into Oriole Parkway if you go north. My best advice: Relax and enjoy the ride.

ORIENTATION
City Layout

Toronto is laid out in a grid . . . with a few interesting exceptions. **Yonge Street** (pronounced *young*) is the main north-south artery, stretching from Lake Ontario in the south well beyond Highway 401 in the north. Yonge Street divides western cross streets from eastern cross streets. The main east-west artery is **Bloor Street,** which cuts through the heart of downtown.

"Downtown" usually refers to the area from Eglinton Avenue south to the lake, between Spadina Avenue in the west and Jarvis Street in the east. Because this is such a large area, it's been divided here into five sections. **Downtown West** runs from the lake north to College Street; the eastern boundary is Yonge Street. **Downtown East** goes from the lake north to Carlton Street (once College St. reaches Yonge St., it becomes Carlton St.); the western boundary is Yonge Street. **Midtown** extends from College Street north to Davenport Road; the eastern boundary is Jarvis Street. **The Danforth/the East End** runs east to Danforth Avenue; the western boundary is Broadview Avenue. **Uptown** is the area north of Davenport Road.

In Downtown West, you'll find many of the lakeshore attractions: Harbourfront, Ontario Place, Fort York, Exhibition Place, and the Toronto Islands. It also boasts the CN Tower, City Hall, the Four Seasons Centre for the Performing Arts, the Rogers Centre (formerly known as SkyDome), Chinatown, the Art Gallery of Ontario, and the Eaton Centre. Downtown East includes the Distillery District, the St. Lawrence Market, the Sony Centre (formerly the Hummingbird Centre), the St. Lawrence Centre for the Arts, and St. James's Cathedral. Midtown contains the Royal Ontario Museum, the Gardiner Museum, the University of Toronto, Markham Village, and chic Yorkville, a prime area for shopping and dining. The Danforth/the East End features Riverdale Farm, the historic Necropolis, and Greektown. Uptown has traditionally been a residential area, but it's now a fast-growing entertainment area, too. Its attractions include the Sunnybrook park system and the Ontario Science Centre.

Underground Toronto

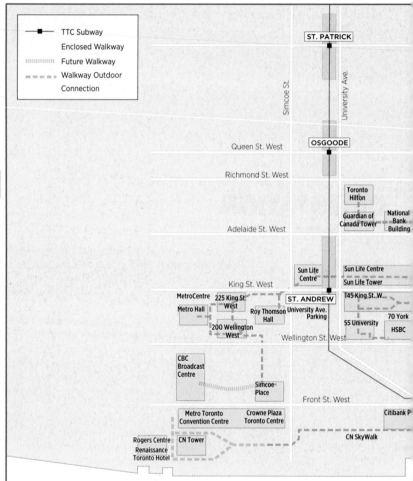

North Toronto is another developing area, with theaters such as the Toronto Centre for the Arts, galleries, and some excellent dining. It's not yet a prime tourist destination, but it is on the rise and gets a few mentions throughout this guide.

Note: Some of the primary attractions lie outside the downtown core or even the city limits. The Toronto Zoo, Paramount Canada's Wonderland, and the McMichael Canadian Art Collection are all full- or half-day trips.

FINDING AN ADDRESS This isn't as easy as it should be. Your best bet is to call ahead and ask for directions, including landmarks and subway stations. Even the locals need to do this.

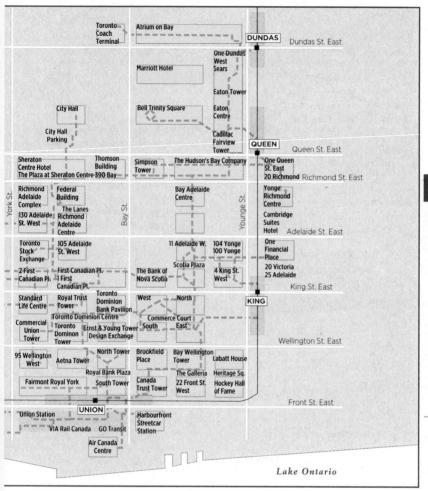

The Neighborhoods in Brief

DOWNTOWN WEST

The Toronto Islands These three islands in Lake Ontario—Ward's, Algonquin, and Centre—are home to a handful of residents and no cars. They're a spring and summer haven where Torontonians go to in-line skate, bicycle, boat, and picnic. Centre

Island, the most visited, holds the children's theme park Centreville. Catch the ferry at the foot of Bay Street by Queen's Quay.

Harbourfront/Lakefront The landfill where the railroad yards and dock facilities once stood is now a glorious playground opening onto the lake. This is home to the

TAP into TO, the Toronto Ambassador Program

Following the lead of such cities as New York and Sydney, Toronto is training some of its citizens to act as tour guides in popular neighborhoods. Tours take an hour or more, and they're free of charge. Call ✆ 416/338-2786 or head to **www.**

toronto.ca/tapto for more information. Every effort is made to match visitors and greeters by interest, so if you are particularly curious about architecture, history, food, or culture, make sure to mention that when you book your tour.

Harbourfront Centre, one of the most vibrant literary, artistic, and cultural venues in Canada.

Financial District   Toronto's major banks and insurance companies have their headquarters here, from Front Street north to Queen Street, between Yonge and York streets. Toronto's first skyscrapers rose here; fortunately, some of the older structures have been preserved. Ultramodern BCE Place incorporated the facade of an historic bank building into its design.

Entertainment District   Also known as the Theatre District, this area, dense with big-name venues, stretches from Front Street north to Queen Street and from Bay Street west to Bathurst Street. King Street West is home to most of the important venues, including the Royal Alexandra Theatre, the Princess of Wales Theatre, and Roy Thomson Hall. Just north is the Four Seasons Centre for the Performing Arts (the new home of the Canadian Opera Company and the National Ballet of Canada), and south are the Convention Centre, the CN Tower, and the Rogers Centre.

Chinatown   Dundas Street West from University Avenue to Spadina Avenue and north to College Street are the boundaries of Chinatown. As the Chinese community has grown, it has extended along Dundas Street and north along Spadina Avenue. Here, you'll see a fascinating mixture of old and new. Hole-in-the-wall restaurants share the sidewalks with glitzy shopping centers built with Hong Kong money.

Kensington Market   Just west of Spadina Avenue and north of Dundas Street West is

one of Toronto's most colorful neighborhoods. Successive waves of immigration—Eastern European Jews, Portuguese, Caribbean, and more—have left their mark. Filled with tiny but wonderful food shops, restaurants, and vintage clothing stores, it's easy to while away an afternoon here (especially on the car-free summer Sundays, when the area becomes a pedestrian-only zone).

Queen Street West   This stretch from University Avenue to Bathurst Street offers an eclectic mix of mainstream shops, funky boutiques, secondhand bookshops, and vintage-clothing emporiums. It's also packed with eateries: bistros, cafes, and gourmet food shops line the street. Despite the intrusion of mega-retailers, many independently owned boutiques still flourish.

Art & Design District   In the past, Queen Street West (see above) was considered edgy. Now, that description is more accurately applied to West Queen West, which starts at Bathurst Avenue and runs west to Gladstone Avenue and beyond. This neighborhood is one of the coolest in the city, full of art galleries; one-of-a-kind boutiques selling clothing, housewares, and antiques; and some truly great restaurants.

Ossington Avenue   Ossington is *the* hot hub of Toronto's nightlife scene with great restaurants and cafes that round out a thriving day-time culture. Combine a tour of the strip with a walk en route along Dundas Street West to see some of the hippest and newest spots the city has to offer.

Little Italy   This charming, lively area, filled with open-air cafes, *trattorias,* and shops, serves the longstanding Italian and Portuguese communities along College Street, between Palmerston Boulevard and Shaw Street. The crowds can't stay away, which has driven up traffic, especially on weekend evenings, and helped to expand the offerings to include sushi spots and hot bars.

DOWNTOWN EAST

Old Town/St. Lawrence Market During the 19th century, this area, east of Yonge Street, between the Esplanade and Adelaide Street, was the focal point of the community. Today, the market's still going strong, and attractions such as the glorious St. James Cathedral continue to draw visitors. It's also an area on the rise with fine restaurants and stellar shops.

The Beaches Communal, youthful, safe, and comfortable—these adjectives describe this neighborhood that's just 30 minutes from downtown at the end of the Queen Street East streetcar line. A summer resort in the mid-1800s, the Beaches' boardwalk and sandy beach ensure that it remains casual and family-oriented to this day. In 2006, there was a local poll to rename this area "The Beach" (a term preferred by many residents), but "The Beaches" is still the way the neighborhood is known.

Leslieville Once a down-on-its-luck stretch of Queen Street East, between Carlaw and Leslie Street, and a former industrial area, the strip has now been gentrified. There are upstart boutiques, vintage and antique stores, cafes, bars, and excellent bistros. Its borders are expanding, too—you'll see "Leslieville" signs after you cross Broadview Avenue.

Little India Gerrard Street East, between Greenwood Avenue and Main Street, is well known for its festival-like atmosphere. It's partly because of the multicolored lights that light up the street at night, but the vibrant street life is visible at any time of day. The blocks are filled with Indian restaurants, grocers, and shops that specialize in saris, beautiful textiles, and treasure-chests of trinkets.

MIDTOWN

Queen's Park and the University Home to the Ontario Legislature and many of the colleges and buildings that make up the handsome campus of the University of

UNDERGROUND TORONTO

As if it weren't enough to know Toronto's streets, in cold weather, it's best to get an understanding of the labyrinthine walkways beneath the pavement, too. This wide-ranging network is an excellent way to get around the downtown core when the weather is grim. You can eat, sleep, dance, shop, and go to the theater without even donning a coat.

You can walk from the Dundas subway station south through the Eaton Centre until you hit Queen Street; turn west to the Sheraton Centre and then head south. You'll pass through the Richmond-Adelaide Centre, First Canadian Place, and Toronto Dominion Centre, and go all the way (through the dramatic Royal Bank Plaza) to Union Station. En route, branches lead off to the stock exchange, Sun Life Centre, and Metro Hall. Additional walkways link Simcoe Plaza to 200 Wellington West and to the CBC Broadcast Centre. Other walkways run around Bloor Street and Yonge Street and elsewhere in the city. Check the "Underground Toronto" map on p. 58 or look for the large, clear underground PATH maps throughout the concourse.

This underground city even has its own attractions. First Canadian Place, in particular, is known for free lunch-hour lectures, opera and dance performances, and art exhibits.

Toronto, this leafy neighborhood extends from College Street to Bloor Street, between Spadina Avenue and Bay Street.

Yorkville Originally a village outside the city limits, this area immediately north and west of Bloor and Yonge streets became Toronto's Haight-Ashbury in the 1960s. For the past few decades, the vibe has been haute, not hippie. The pretty streets are lined with designer boutiques, galleries, cafes, and restaurants.

The Annex This largely residential neighborhood is a mix of small parks, handsome homes, and a strip along Bloor Street West that offers some good shopping for books and knick knacks, plus a few attractive restaurants and pubs, and one unique attraction, the Bata Shoe Museum. The Annex stretches from Bedford Road to Bathurst Street and from Harbord Street to Dupont Avenue. Revered urban-planning guru the late Jane Jacobs called this area home.

Koreatown The bustling blocks along Bloor Street West, between Bathurst and Christie streets, are filled with Korean restaurants; alternative-medicine practitioners, such as herbalists and acupuncturists; and shops filled with made-in-Korea merchandise.

THE DANFORTH/THE EAST END

Rosedale Meandering these quiet, tree-lined avenues offers a tour of some of Toronto's grandest homes. This residential area, comprised of snaking streets that make it easy to get lost, runs from Yonge and Bloor streets northeast to Castle Frank and the Moore Park Ravine. It's named after the residence of Sheriff William Jarvis, who is largely credited with ending the 1837 Upper Canada Rebellion.

Church Street/The Gay Village Between Gerrard Street and Bloor Street East, along Church Street, lies the heart of Toronto's original gay and lesbian community. The "ghetto" has since evolved, and gay Torontonians now live and play all around town. Still, there remains a concentration of restaurants, cafes, and shops that offer a gay

focus. Church Street is where 19th-century Toronto's grandest churches were built.

Cabbagetown Writer Hugh Garner described this as the largest Anglo-Saxon slum in North America, long before it became a gentrified neighborhood of restored, often pretty and pricey, Victorian and Edwardian homes. The boundaries run from east of Parliament Street to the Don Valley and between Gerrard and Bloor streets. The name is an historic reference: The original Irish immigrants who settled here in the late 1800s grew row upon row of cabbages on their front lawns. Riverdale, Toronto's only inner-city farm, is at the eastern edge of the district.

Greektown Across the Don Valley Viaduct, Bloor Street becomes the Danforth, which marks the beginning of Greektown. It's lined with old-style Greek tavernas and hip Mediterranean bars and restaurants that are crowded from early evening into the night. The densest wining-and-dining area starts at Broadview Avenue and runs about 8 blocks east.

UPTOWN

Christie and St. Clair Until not long ago, this was a modest residential neighborhood where Torontonians would venture for some great Italian gelato or for a street party during the World Cup. Now, the area and beyond are proving a popular place to visit for good cafes, some fine Jamaican fare, and for the Green Barns development, a mix of artists studios, farmers market, community gardens, and events space. The area runs west from Christie Street to Dufferin Street.

Eglinton Avenue The neighborhood surrounding the intersection of Yonge Street and Eglinton Avenue is jokingly known as "Young and Eligible." It's a bustling area filled with restaurants—from neighborhood favorites to fine dining destinations—as well as live-music pubs and nightclubs. To the east, it intersects with the 243-hectare (600-acre) Sunnybrook park system and with the Ontario Science Centre.

THE BEST OF TORONTO IN 1 DAY

You'd better put on your walking shoes because seeing the best of Toronto in a day means covering a lot of territory. This itinerary explores the city's most famous attractions, including the ones everyone back home will ask you about (like the CN Tower). It's a downtown walk that will take you from the city's highest point to its waterfront, from the commercial core to a handful of lofty public buildings. Take comfort: There is plenty of refreshing green space along the way. *Start: From Union Station, walk west along Front Street to Bremner Boulevard to the CN Tower.*

1 CN Tower ★

Today, you're starting at the top. Even if the famous tower isn't the tallest in the world anymore, don't overlook Toronto's most celebrated icon (plus, the glass elevator makes the ride up even more of a thrill). Beginning your tour here will give you a perspective on Toronto, its neighborhoods and general layout, even if it all seems on a model scale from the great heights. If it's a clear day, you might be able to see all the way to Niagara Falls. But even if it isn't clear out, you can check out the stomach-churning glass floor. Lie flat, I dare you, or just jump up and down on it for a vertiginous thrill. See p. 122.

2 Rogers Centre ★

This is the domed stadium formerly known as SkyDome. The formal tour is for sports fans only; otherwise, just idly appreciate the massive statues of cheering (and jeering) spectators on the facade. If you want to see the Toronto Blue Jays play ball (or the Toronto Argonauts play football, Canadian style), come back later in the day. See p. 141.

3 Toronto Music Garden ★★★

I know that getting to the waterfront is no joy, but it's entirely worth it when you reach the tranquil Toronto Music Garden. A lovely green space, it's also reached by a comfortable street-car ride and is flanked by new boardwalks and some additional, albeit less green, parks. The Music Garden was designed by world-renowned cellist Yo-Yo Ma and landscape architect Julie Moir Messervy to invoke Bach's First Suite for Unaccompanied Cello. It may sound high-falutin', but when you're wandering around the grounds, it's simply serene. See p. 143.

4 Harbourfront Centre ★★

This is the kind of place where you could easily spend a day, so you may need to tear yourself away to stay on track. There are glassblowers, potters, jewelry makers, and other artisans to watch at their work in the Craft Studio; the Artists' Gardens, a series of diverse landscapes created by local talent, is another highlight. Depending on how active you feel, this is also your chance to get out on the water: The Harbourfront Canoe and Kayak School will let you rent a boat and offers instruction. See p. 123.

5 Queen's Quay Terminal 🍴

If you want to sit outside and watch the lakefront traffic—boat and human—go for a light meal or a drink at the casual BoatHouse Grill (© 416/203-6300), on the ground floor of

Suggested Toronto Itineraries (Days 1 & 2)

DAY ONE

1 CN Tower
2 Rogers Centre
3 Toronto Music Garden
4 Harbourfront Centre
5a BoatHouse Grill ☕
5b Pearl Harbourfront Chinese Cuisine ☕
6 Air Canada Centre
7 Union Station
8 Sharp Centre for Design
9 Art Gallery of Ontario
10a FRANK ☕
10b AGO Café ☕
11 New City Hall
12a Four Seasons Centre for the Performing Arts
12b Roy Thompson Hall

DAY TWO

1 Yorkville
2 Royal Ontario Museum
3 Food Studio at ROM ☕
4 George R. Gardiner Museum of Ceramic Art
5 Victoria College
6 Queen's Park & the Ontario Legislature
7 Allan Gardens
8 Cabbagetown
9 Riverdale Farm
10 Necropolis
11 Daniel et Daniel ☕
12 Distillery District

the Queen's Quay building. A more upscale restaurant is Pearl Harbourfront Chinese Cuisine (📞 416/203-1233). The Queen's Quay complex also has a variety of cafes and food vendors just outside, if you want just a quick bite. See p. 123.

6 Air Canada Centre ★

One nice thing about walking back to the downtown core this way is that you can cross through the Air Canada Centre, which is a lot more pleasant than the other busy and often traffic-congested options. This sports complex is home to both the Raptors basketball team and the Maple Leafs hockey team, but it also hosts blockbuster music concerts; you'll see photographs of some of the acts as you walk through the passageway. See p. 215.

7 Union Station ★

This is one of the city's underappreciated wonders. Toronto's temple to trains is a Beaux Arts beauty, and it's worthwhile to walk through the main hall, even if you're not hopping aboard a train. Pop in to admire the tile ceiling designed by architect Rafael Gaustavino. Until the age of mass air travel, Union Station was often the first place new immigrants saw upon arrival in their new home of Toronto.

8 Sharp Centre for Design

Although Toronto has long suffered an out-of-date reputation for being strait-laced, when people do wacky things here, the new additions quickly fold into the accepted cityscape. For example, this relatively new addition to the city's architectural landscape delivers wonders from Will Alsop. Don't worry about going inside (you can't get in unless you're a student of the Ontario College of Art & Design); all the drama is right in front of you—and it's entirely unique. See p. 136.

9 Art Gallery of Ontario ★★★

Newly renovated—by local boy Frank Gehry, who grew up around the corner—and now blessed with the brilliant Thomson Collection, the AGO is arguably Toronto's best museum. Visit for the stellar collection of paintings by Canadian legends and European masters, the best collection of Henry Moore sculpture in the world, the photography gallery, and much more. See p. 119.

10 Art Gallery of Ontario 🍴

The AGO has two dining options: lovely FRANK, an upscale restaurant that serves creative, fine food, and the AGO Café, a low-key space in its basement that offers sandwiches, salads, baked goods, and other treats. Both good options, your choice should depend on mood, time, and budget.

11 New City Hall ★

It's an iconic piece in Toronto's history, plus a popular gathering place throughout the year. In warm weather, you get the reflecting pool and fountains, and when the mercury drops, there's the skating rink. Framing the whole scene, quite perfectly, is the modernist masterpiece of the city hall building itself; walk up toward and around it, and you'll see the Henry Moore sculpture *The Archer*. See p. 176.

12 Four Seasons Centre for the Performing Arts ★★★ or Roy Thomson Hall ★★★

Toronto's stunning opera house, the Four Seasons Centre, designed by local firm Diamond and Schmitt, is home to the Canadian Opera Company and the National Ballet of Canada. The acoustics have been described as quite perfect. Both companies are phenomenally popular, and you absolutely need to purchase tickets in advance. Roy Thomson Hall is the base of the Toronto Symphony Orchestra; Torontonians tend to book ahead and buy seasons tickets, but it's possible to get last-minute discounted "rush" seats for concerts here.

THE BEST OF TORONTO IN 2 DAYS

After you've taken in Toronto's best-known landmarks by following the tour above, it's time to get to know the city's heart a little better. Thanks to developments over the past few decades, there's more to see and do now than ever before. Particularly in the past decade, Toronto has embarked on some pretty ambitious projects with the goal of restoring and expanding upon what's already here—and the results are wonderful, as you'll see for yourself. *Start: Bay Station.*

1 Yorkville ★

Filled with chic boutiques and elegant galleries (and high-priced condo developments, some still under construction), this neighborhood that is part residential, mostly commercial, has long departed from its groovy 1960s vibe when it was home to the city's hippies; a century before that, it was a cemetery. Progress? See p. 181.

2 Royal Ontario Museum ★★

Toronto's most famous museum embarked upon a Daniel Libeskind–designed renovation a few years ago. Ambitiously titled Renaissance ROM, it was intended to expand the viewing area, largely through the addition of six crystal galleries that jut out over Bloor Street West. Where you spend your time here will depend on whether you have kids in tow: The small fry will insist on the dinosaurs and the Bat Cave. The Chinese galleries, which include a Ming tomb, are stellar. The Libeskind remains a divisive addition to the city's new architectural destinations. See p. 127.

3 Royal Ontario Museum 🍴

The Royal Ontario Museum has a wonderful—but very expensive—restaurant in C5. A great bet for lunch or a snack is the ROM's Food Studio (✆ 416/586-7926). This cafeteria-style eatery serves fresh salads, pizza, and pasta, as well as more exotic fare.

4 George R. Gardiner Museum of Ceramic Art ★★

Face-lifts are a common phenomenon among Toronto museums. Just across the street from the ROM, the Gardiner revealed its new visage in 2006. An understated gem, especially given the overwhelming behemoth across the street, this is a beautiful place to view small and carefully curated collections of ceramics and more. See p. 131.

5 Victoria College ★

This historic college is federated with the University of Toronto but maintains its own digs just east of the rest of the campus. It has a pretty college quad, bordered by imposing Romanesque architecture (there's some blocky 1960s stuff, too). See p. 82.

6 Queen's Park & the Ontario Legislature ★

This sweeping midtown park is also home to Ontario's legislative building. It's possible to do a tour on most days, though you can opt for sitting on one of the many benches, admiring the building's pink-stone facade and the flower gardens in front. See p. 137.

7 Allan Gardens ★

This was Toronto's first civic park, and the Edwardian Palm House conservatory is still a glamorous relic of the past. But it was only recently, when the University of Toronto's old greenhouses were relocated here and reborn as a conservatory for children, that Allan Gardens became a place to hang out again, free in the daytime of much of the seedier activity it had become known for. See p. 142.

8 Cabbagetown ★★

You can't walk these residential streets without getting a powerful sense of Toronto's history. Once considered a slum, Cabbagetown is now filled with beautifully restored Victorian and Queen Anne–style houses. Even the first housing project in Canada, Spruce Court (at the intersection of Sumach and Spruce streets), looks like a charming collection of cottages. For a complete tour, see p. 167.

9 Riverdale Farm ★★

For some, this farm is a sacred space. Whenever you visit, you'll find kids here, many of whom live in the area, learning about farm life, interacting with chickens and rare-breed piglets, and cuddling bunnies. Sound bucolic? It's a serene spot and well worth a visit, especially with young ones in tow. See p. 147.

10 Necropolis ★

This Victorian cemetery is not only picturesque, but also filled with monuments to famous people who played key roles in Toronto's history. And the Gothic Revival chapel, tiny though it is, is considered a great example of this style. See p. 144.

11 Daniel et Daniel 🍴

If you go to an event in Toronto and discover that Daniel et Daniel is catering it, you know that you're in excellent hands. At the shop, in addition to the divine pastries and chocolates, you can order salads and prepared meals for takeout. 248 Carlton St. ℭ 416/968-9275. See p. 168.

12 Distillery District ★★★

This is the perfect place to finish your tour. Once the home of the largest distillery in Canada, today, it's a multifaceted complex that has something for everyone. The redbrick architecture—a signature of Toronto's red-clay brick-works—is a Victorian wonder, but the art galleries, restaurants, and boutiques are all completely modern. You might want to stay well into the evening: Per-forming-arts troupes such as Soulpepper are based here, and if you're visiting in clement weather, there's probably an open-air art fair, market, or festival underway. See p. 209.

THE BEST OF TORONTO IN 3 DAYS

Spend your first 2 days following the earlier tours, and top it off with this exploration of Toronto's cultural mosaic and art scene. At its core, Toronto is a patchwork of dis-tinctive neighborhoods. This tour will take you through some of the oldest areas, which keep evolving in new ways. **Start:** *Dupont Station, and then walk 2 blocks north.*

1 Casa Loma ★★★

Casa Loma, a kitschy throw-back to locals, is a castle on a hill that offers an inspiring view of the sweep of the city (you'll see a lot more of Toronto than you did from the CN Tower the day before yesterday). But while you can admire the view for free, it's worth visiting the castle, too. The elegant rooms and period furniture are appropriately grand, though most interesting is perhaps climbing the towers (one Norman, one Scottish, both great). See p. 136.

2 Kensington Market ★★

You couldn't get farther from the Old Money refinement of Casa Loma. Kens-ington Market is a multiethnic mélange with strong smells (fish markets) and strong sounds (stores with pumping stereos, conversations in a dozen different languages on any street you cross). This was a Jewish neighborhood long ago, but successive waves of immigration have added Portuguese and West Indian flavors. If you want to bring home some great vintage finds, do some shopping in this area (check out Tom's Place, Fresh Baked Goods, and Courage My Love, all in chapter 9). See p. 142.

3 Chocolate Addict 🍫

It's not a cafe, so there's no place to sit down. But Chocolate Addict ★ (185 Baldwin St.; ✆ 416/979-5809; p. 197) is the perfect spot to get some ice cream or chocolate truffles to fuel your adventures.

4 Chinatown ★★

Toronto has a large Chinese population dispersed throughout the city, but this was home to the first great wave of Chinese immigrants. It's changed since its early days, particularly because of the infusion of Hong Kong money. It's such a large and significant area that it's a shame no official entryway exists. The recent addition of gilded statues of dragons and the like on poles in the middle of Spadina Avenue is a nice touch, however. See p. 154.

5 Queen Street West ★

Until recently, this would have been the Wild West of the downtown core. Now, it's mainly a space for some very cool boutiques (Fashion Crimes, Peach

Berserk, and the like; see chapter 9) scattered among mainstream chain stores. Still, it's a great place to park at a cafe, bar, or pub, and watch the parade go by—there's always plenty of street life to take in.

6 The Art & Design District ★★★

This is one of Toronto's most exciting neighborhoods. Until relatively recently, it was dive-y and derelict. Now, it's filled with art galleries and independent boutiques run by local designers. Mid- to late afternoon is the perfect time to check it out because everything is open (some of the shops are closed all morning) and the street is full of life. More recently, great restaurants with lively patios and some exciting live-music spots make it an appealing destination after dark. See p. 133.

7 Trinity Bellwoods ★

This site used to be the home of the precursor to the University of Toronto. The buildings have been torn down, but the impressive stone-and-wrought-iron gates that face Queen Street West still remain, and there are Victorian lampposts along the main paths. There are benches where you can rest and take in the scene, but it's more fun to wander. As you do, watch out for the legendary albino squirrels who reside in the park. See p. 143.

8 Swan ☕

You've earned a hearty meal, and you can have a proper one at Swan. Decked out like a retro soda fountain, this restaurant offers up excellent comfort food (think braised short ribs). There are also oysters and margaritas, for lighter appetites. 892 Queen St. W. ☏ 416/532-0452.

9 Museum of Contemporary Canadian Art ★★

You've already seen the iconic art of the AGO; now's your chance to see what's happening in today's art scene. MOCCA is a gallery that has a reputation for its (sometimes freaky) temporary exhibits. Edgy, good stuff. See p. 132.

10 Ossington Avenue ★★

For years, this has been a sleepy part of town, part of Toronto's Little Portugal neighborhood, where many of the houses have religious icons painted near the front door. But now, Ossington Avenue is the epicenter of Toronto nightlife. Drop in at Watusi (p. 221) for 1960s retro-cool cocktails and ambience, or at Sweaty Betty's (p. 221) for a no-fuss vibe and a great patio.

Suggested Toronto Itineraries (Day 3)

1 Casa Loma
2 Kensington Market
3 Chocolate Addict ☕
4 Chinatown
5 Queen Street West
6 The Art & Design District
7 Trinity Bellwoods
8 Swan ☕
9 Museum of Contemporary
  Canadian Art
10 Ossington Avenue

WHERE TO STAY

Toronto's hotel landscape offers plenty of choice, from idiosyncratic inns to homey B&Bs, conventional hotels to deluxe boutiques properties. The biggest news of late is the long-overdue arrival of a slate of five-star hotels: The city is midway through a rich development of luxury properties, including a Ritz Carlton, a groovy Thompson boutique, and a new Four Seasons in the city where the renowned chain is based. Chances are good, especially given the economic climate, that there will be deals at the high end as the newbies compete for heads on beds.

While proximity to central attractions such as the CN Tower, Harbourfront, Rogers Centre, and Eaton Centre can drive up the cost of a stay, there are some great budget-priced downtown options, too.

Lodgings are grouped by both price and location. Most are in the neighborhoods defined in chapter 4 as Downtown West, Downtown East, and Midtown. If you're having trouble finding a hotel, call **Tourism Toronto** (© **800/499-2514** or 416/203-2600) or visit **www.seetorontonow.com** for advice. Keep in mind that some special deals are available only through a hotel's website. The **Fairmont Royal York** (p. 76) almost always has an online deal; the **Park Hyatt Toronto** (p. 84) often does, too.

A note about Internet and Wi-Fi: Most accommodations in this chapter offer in-room or in-lobby Internet or Wi-Fi access. Some charge for it, some don't. For hotels that charge for Internet or Wi-Fi, the price ranges from C$15 to C$21 per day. When included in the room price, I've listed the services as "free."

BEST HOTEL BETS

o **Best Historic Hotel:** The hands-down winner is the **Fairmont Royal York** (100 Front St. W.; © **800/441-1414**), which has managed to seamlessly blend the timeless glory of a 1929 Canadian Pacific Railway–built hotel with a forward-thinking eco-consciousness. The roof garden, where the hotel grows its own mint for mojitos (among other herbs), is also home to several honeybee hives. See p. 76.

o **Best for Business Travelers:** It's a tie. For short trips, the **Hilton Toronto** (145 Richmond St. W.; © **800/445-8667**) offers a perfect location, amenities, and a wonderful restaurant, Tundra, for business lunches and dinners. But for a longer-term stay (more than a week), the **Cambridge Suites Hotel** (15 Richmond St. E.; © **800/463-1990**) gives you plenty of space, and staff there will even shop for you. See p. 73 and 79.

o **Best Budget Hotel:** Given the location and amenities, it's hard to beat the **Hotel Victoria** (56 Yonge St.; © **800/363-8228**) for price. The hotel is close to the Eaton Centre, some theaters, and the Financial District. Double rooms start at C$120 per night. See p. 79.

o **Best Hotel Restaurant: Lai Wah Heen** in the Metropolitan Hotel (110 Chestnut St.; © **416/977-9899**) has perfect Peking duck, great dim sum, and an impressive menu of mostly Cantonese specialties. See p. 94.

o **Best for a Stylish Stay: Thompson Toronto** (550 Wellington St.; © **416/640-7778**), the first international venture of the New York–based hotel mini-empire, has a super-cool vibe matched by smart service. A rooftop pool, restaurants, a terrace, and more all add to the very hip experience. See p. 74.

o **Best for Travelers with Disabilities:** The **Metropolitan Hotel** (108 Chestnut St.; © **416/977-5000**) pays a lot of attention to accessibility. The restaurants, bars, pool, gymnasium, and some rooms accommodate wheelchair users, as well as the visually and hearing impaired. See p. 74.

DOWNTOWN WEST
Very Expensive

Hilton Toronto ★   Across the street from the Four Seasons Centre for the Performing Arts, the 32-story Hilton has big rooms and business-minded luxuries. Because of its proximity to the Financial District, the Hilton is a great choice for business travelers. The standard rooms are spacious and clean-lined with large work spaces. Upgrading to an executive room adds personal concierge service and access to a private lounge that serves complimentary breakfast and evening snacks.

145 Richmond St. W. (at University Ave.), Toronto, ON M5H 2L2. ☎ **800/445-8667** or 416/869-3456. Fax 416/869-1478. www.toronto.hilton.com. 601 units. From C$319 double. Children 18 & under stay free in parent's room. Multi-night packages available. AE, DC, MC, V. Parking C$30. Subway: Osgoode. Pets accepted (C$75 per pet). **Amenities:** 3 restaurants; bar; babysitting; children's programs; concierge; health club; Jacuzzi; indoor & outdoor lap pools; room service; sauna. *In room:* A/C, TV, hair dryer, Internet ($12 daily fee), minibar.

The Metropolitan Hotel ★★   A sophisticated choice, and a bit artier than other upscale business digs, this property (located just off Dundas St. W. behind City Hall) caters to business and leisure travelers who shun the big chains. Rooms are spacious and styled in a serene color palette of beige and beechwood that evokes a spa. **Lai Wah Heen** (p. 94) serves some of the best dim sum in the city, and room-service meals are also of a high standard.

108 Chestnut St. (just south of Dundas St. W.), Toronto, ON M5G 1R3. ☎ **800/668-6600** or 416/977-5000. Fax 416/977-9513. www.metropolitan.com. 427 units. From C$300 double. Children 17 & under stay free in parent's room. AE, DC, DISC, MC, V. Parking C$21. Subway: St. Patrick. **Amenities:** 2 restaurants; bar; babysitting; concierge; health club; Jacuzzi; indoor pool; room service; sauna. *In room:* A/C, TV/DVD player, CD player, hair dryer, minibar, Wi-Fi ($12 daily fee).

Thompson Toronto ★★★   This swank downtown property, part of the quite perfect New York–based boutique chain, opened this, their first Canadian outpost, last year amid much hype and expectation. And the news is good: It delivers. The luxe rooms are chic yet comfortable; the service attentive but not cloying; the location a welcome launching point for seeing the groovier parts of the city, but also convenient to the theater district and beyond. The rooftop infinity swimming pool with its breathtaking views along with the rooftop's cozy fireplace lounge—pick your season—together offer a unique destination on the city's hotel scene. Ditto for the dining options, which range from a diner (very good fare; open 24/7) to an outpost of Scott Conant's upscale, and much praised, Scarpetta restaurant. Expect high-end fitness facilities, including a yoga studio; a 40-seat screening room; SFERRA linens on your bed and Carrera marble in the bathroom; floor-to-ceiling windows for a bright, open aspect onto the street life; and a serene, white-toned backdrop rich with wooden touches and creative flare.

550 Wellington St. W., Toronto, ON M5V 2V4. ☎ **888/550-8368** or 416/640-7778. www.thompson hotels.com. 102 units. From C$245 double. AE, DC, MC, V. Valet parking C$35. Subway: St. Patrick, then streetcar west to Bathurst St. **Amenities:** 2 restaurants; bar; fireplace lounge; babysitting; concierge; health club; outdoor pool; room service. *In room:* A/C, TV/DVD player, CD player, hair dryer, minibar, Wi-Fi ($10 per day).

Expensive

The Drake Hotel ★ 📖   An early convert to the boutique phenomenon, which came late to Toronto, The Drake is better known for its bars and restaurants than the tiny (from 14 to 36 sq. m [151–388 sq. ft.]) guest rooms that give it its name. However, the rooms *are* cleverly designed and have good amenities (CD/DVD players and lovely linens, for example) and it makes an ideal place to rest your head after a long night's indulgence in the hotel's public rooms. The Drake is something of a trend-setter and attracts a stylish and fashionable crowd to its restaurant and bar, rooftop lounge, and cafe. There is an exercise studio for yoga classes and a performance venue, the Underground, that features live music. An artist-in-residence program keeps the wall art changing. This is one hotel where you're far more likely to meet city residents than visitors.

Where to Stay in Downtown West

Baldwin Village Inn **14**
Delta Chelsea **1**
The Drake Hotel **13**
Fairmont Royal York **8**
The Gladstone Hotel **12**
Hilton Toronto **5**
Hôtel Le Germain **10**
Hotel Victoria **6**
The Metropolitan Hotel **3**
Sheraton Centre Toronto Hotel **4**
The Strathcona **7**
Thompson Toronto **11**
Toronto Marriott Downtown
  Eaton Centre **2**
Westin Harbour Castle **9**

1150 Queen St. W. (at Beaconsfield Ave.), Toronto, ON M6J 1J3. © **800/372-5386** or 416/531-5042. Fax 416/531-9493. www.thedrakehotel.ca. 19 units. From C$219 double. AE, MC, V. Subway: Osgoode, then streetcar west to Beaconsfield Ave. **Amenities:** 2 restaurants; cafe; 2 bars; access to local health club. *In room:* A/C, TV/DVD player, CD player, hair dryer, Internet (free), MP3 docking station.

Fairmont Royal York ★★ Built by the Canadian Pacific Railroad in 1929, this massive hotel has 1,365 guest rooms and suites, and 35 meeting and banquet rooms. Just sitting on a plush couch in the magnificent old-fashioned lobby and watching the crowd is an event. Still, you have to decide whether you want to stay under the same roof with countless business travelers, tour groups, and conventioneers. Service is efficient, if impersonal. Located across from Union Station, the hotel pays particular attention to accessibility, and some guest rooms are specially designed for wheelchair users, the hearing impaired, and the visually impaired. The hotel is also a leader in eco-friendly initiatives. The restaurants are also a good bet and eco-minded, as well, with an award for sustainable seafood and beehives on the roof that supply honey for the kitchens and your toast. Other special features include the Elizabeth Milan Day Spa, Epic restaurant, and the leather-lined Library Bar. *Tip:* Watch the website for special offers.

100 Front St. W. (at York St.), Toronto, ON M5J 1E3. © **800/441-1414.** Fax 416/368-9040. www. fairmont.com/royalyork. 1,365 units. From C$205 double. Packages available. AE, DC, DISC, MC, V. Parking C$40. Subway: Union. Pets accepted ($25 per night). **Amenities:** 5 restaurants; 2 bars/lounges; babysitting; concierge; health club; Jacuzzi; sky-lit indoor pool; room service; sauna; spa. *In room:* A/C, TV, hair dryer, Internet ($15 daily fee), minibar.

Hôtel Le Germain ★★ This Quebec-based company adds a continental touch that blends effortlessly with an edgy elegance. Elevators are "wrapped" in words of English and French poetry. The library lounge has a fireplace, a wall of objets d'art, and cozy white couches. The breakfast "room" on the second floor is like an expansive landing, and the tables are all communal. The guest rooms are beautifully designed: The ceilings are high, the desk can be moved around to your liking (it's attached to the wall on one side), and the linens and robes are by Frette. The peek-a-boo glass wall in every bathroom is a seductive touch (a blind can be lowered) and also makes everything feel more spacious. All guests have access to the exercise room on the 11th floor, which has floor-to-ceiling windows and an open-air terrace. Rooms on the north side are not as quiet, as they face a noisy strip of King Street restaurants and bars.

Note: A second Le Germain is scheduled to open in Toronto Maple Leaf Square next to the Air Canada Centre after this book goes to press.

30 Mercer St., Toronto, ON M5V 1H3. © **866/345-9501** or 416/345-9500. Fax 416/345-9501. www. germaintoronto.com. 122 units. From C$285 double. AE, DC, MC, V. Parking C$35. Subway: St. Andrew. Pets accepted (C$35 per pet). **Amenities:** Restaurant; bar; babysitting; concierge; health club; room service. *In room:* A/C, TV/DVD player, CD player, CD library, hair dryer, minibar, Wi-Fi (free).

Westin Harbour Castle ★ This convention hotel is on the lakefront, next to the Toronto Islands ferry docks. Its views are among the best in the city. The trade-off is that it's somewhat out of the way from the action north of the Gardiner Expressway. The hotel tries to compensate with shuttle-bus service; you'll also find a public-transit stop and a queue of cabs at the hotel. Recognizing the lack of things to do in the vicinity, management has wisely populated the hotel with attractions. The

Five-Star Pampering

Bucking the trend of reigning in the purse strings in tough economic times, Toronto's hotel inventory is about to go seriously upscale. With The King Edward Hotel, the grande dame of luxury properties, now being converted into a combination hotel/condo, there's room at the top for the five-star treatment. Enter the Ritz-Carlton, Trump, Shangri-La, and a new Four Seasons. Of these, only the Ritz-Carlton will open in 2011; the others will follow soon after.

rooftop Toula restaurant serves Northern Italian fare. Sports facilities include tennis, squash, indoor pool, gym, and spa, giving this monolithic hotel the feel of a resort.

1 Harbour Sq. (at Queen's Quay), Toronto, ON M5J 1A6. © **800/WESTIN-1** (800/937-8461) or 416/869-1600. Fax 416/361-7448. www.westin.com/harbourcastle. 977 units. From C$199 double. Additional adult C$30. Children stay free in parent's room. Multi-night packages available. AE, DC, MC, V. Parking C$30. Subway: Union, then the LRT to Queens Quay. **Amenities:** 2 restaurants; 2 bars; children's center; concierge; health club; Jacuzzi; indoor pool; room service; sauna; spa; 2 tennis courts; 2 squash courts. *In room:* A/C, TV, hair dryer, Internet ($15 daily fee), minibar.

Moderate

Delta Chelsea ★★ ☺ Though it doesn't look the part, the Delta Chelsea is the city's biggest hotel, based on number of rooms. Guest rooms are bright and cheery; a few have kitchenettes. Business travelers should consider a room on the Signature Club floor, which comes with many in-room comforts like cordless speakerphones, well-stocked desks, and ergonomic chairs. The hotel boasts a four-story indoor waterslide, plus grown-up amenities, such as Deck 27, a lounge with a panoramic view of Toronto. The pool and awesome slide, combined with a children's center and babysitting, make this a particularly attractive option for families. Weekend packages often combine tickets to the city's top attractions and theaters.

33 Gerrard St. W. (just west of Yonge St.), Toronto, ON M5G 1Z4. © **800/243-5732** or 416/595-1975. Fax 416/585-4362. www.deltahotels.com. 1,590 units. From C$179 double. Additional adult C$20. Children 17 & under stay free in parent's room. Multi-night packages available. AE, DC, DISC, MC, V. Parking C$29. Subway: College. **Amenities:** 3 restaurants; 3 bars; babysitting; children's center; concierge; health club; Jacuzzi; 2 pools (1 for adults only); sauna. *In room:* A/C, TV, hair dryer, Internet ($14 fee), MP3 docking station.

The Gladstone Hotel ★ ♙ This lovely Victorian redbrick hotel is the longest continually operating hotel in the city. Those first guests of the old railroad hotel probably wouldn't know what to make of the arty offerings of the Gladstone today, where each room is decorated—some quite extravagantly—by artists. Since it opened in 1889, "The Gladdy," as it's affectionately known, has seen its share of ups and downs, but artist Christina Zeidler and her architecturally-inclined family (her father, Eb, designed The Eaton Centre and Ontario Place; her sister Margie redesigned the art space 401 Richmond St. W.) took over in 2005, transforming the place while preserving its heritage features, including the birdcage elevator. The hip public rooms are now a hive of cultural activity, with offerings ranging from burlesque shows to indie bands, and the Melody Bar hosts the city's most colorful weekend karaoke. The 37 rooms are featured on the website, so you can choose decor according to your taste and mood, with everything from lumberjack chic (a four-poster bed

For Travelers in Need

If you should suddenly find yourself without a place to stay in Toronto, call the **Travellers' Aid Society of Toronto** (*C* 416/366-7788; www.travellersaid. ca). The organization will find you last-minute accommodations, and they can also assist in crisis situations. They maintain booths at the airport, as well as Union Station.

anchored by tree trunks) to a teen-idol theme, where the walls are plastered with retro posters, on offer. *Note:* If you're a light sleeper, this may not be the place for you.

1214 Queen St. W. (at Gladstone Ave.), Toronto, ON M6J 1J6. *C* **416/531-4635.** Fax 416/539-0953. www.gladstonehotel.com. 37 units. From C$195 double. AE, MC, V. Parking C$15. Subway: Osgoode, then streetcar west to Gladstone Ave. **Amenities:** Restaurant; cafe; bar. *In room:* A/C, TV/DVD player, CD player, hair dryer, Wi-Fi (free).

Sheraton Centre Toronto Hotel ☺

It's entirely possible to stay at this hotel and never venture outside—the Sheraton complex includes restaurants, bars, and a huge pool, and the building connects to Toronto's underground city. If you long for a patch of green, the hotel provides that, too: The south side of the lobby contains a manicured garden with a waterfall. It's also a good option for families due to its central location and extensive list of child-friendly features, including a children's center. Most of the guest rooms in this skyscraper-heavy neighborhood lack a serious view, though as you near the top of the 46-story complex, the sights are inspiring indeed, especially on the north side with a clear view of City Hall and Nathan Philips Square. Designed for business travelers, the Club Level rooms come with a fax/printer/copier and two-line speakerphone.

123 Queen St. W., Toronto, ON M5H 2M9. *C* **800/325-3535** or 416/361-1000. Fax 416/947-4854. www. sheratontoronto.com. 1,377 units. From C$249 double. Additional adult C$20. 2 children 17 & under stay free in parent's room. Packages available. AE, DC, MC, V. Parking C$33. Subway: Osgoode. **Amenities:** 2 restaurants; bar; babysitting; children's center; concierge; health club; Jacuzzi; gigantic heated indoor/outdoor pool; room service; sauna; spa. *In room:* A/C, TV, hair dryer, Internet ($15 fee).

The Strathcona ★★ 🍴

If you want to be in the Financial District but don't want to pay a bundle, this is a great option. For years, the Strathcona has been one of the best buys in the city, and a recent renovation has made it more attractive. It sits in the shadow of the Fairmont Royal York, a short walk from all major downtown attractions. The trade-offs aren't as extensive as you might think. The Strathcona's rooms are on the small side but are no less comfortable for their compact design. Lately, the hotel has taken some green initiatives, changing its lighting, reducing water usage, and becoming entirely smoke-free.

60 York St., (btw. Front St. W. & Wellington St. W.), Toronto, ON M5J 1S8. *C* **800/268-8304** or 416/363-3321. Fax 416/363-4679. www.thestrathconahotel.com. 194 units. From C$155 double. AE, DC, MC, V. Subway: Union. Private paid parking nearby C$16–C$38. **Amenities:** Cafe; bar; babysitting; bike rental; children's center; concierge; access to nearby health club; room service. *In room:* A/C, TV, hair dryer, Wi-Fi ($10 per day).

Toronto Marriott Downtown Eaton Centre

It's a shopaholic's dream: a hotel in a mall—and not just any mall, but downtown's mega mall, the Eaton Centre. This hotel caters to the tourist crowd: While a good concierge at any hotel can point you in the direction of, say, a hot restaurant, the Marriott has desks set up to facilitate day-trip planning and other activities. Because of its location, this is a fine choice for determined sightseers. One caveat is that the area immediately surrounding the Eaton Centre is pickpocket heaven. On the upside, it's always busy in this neighborhood, so you won't want for company. Also, in summer, nearby Yonge-Dundas Square (p. 210) offers open-air concerts and films.

525 Bay St. (at Dundas St.), Toronto, ON M5G 2L2. © **800/905-0667** or 416/597-9200. Fax 416/597-9211. www.marriotteatoncentre.com. 459 units. From C$179 double. AE, DC, DISC, MC, V. Parking C$30. Subway: Dundas. **Amenities:** 3 restaurants; bar; concierge; health club; Jacuzzi; indoor rooftop pool; room service; sauna; Wi-Fi ($15.95 daily in rooms; free in public rooms). *In room:* A/C, TV, hair dryer.

Inexpensive

Baldwin Village Inn ★   One wishes there were more small, affordable, family-run hotels in Toronto like the Baldwin. This small inn, in a converted house on colorful Baldwin Street, is very popular with visiting academics and hospital staff (both U of T and University Avenue's hospital row are nearby). Rooms are well cared for, bathrooms are shared, and there's a homey eat-in kitchen and a small garden in the back. This is a delightful cross between a B&B and a hotel. Reservations are strongly recommended.

9 Baldwin St. (at McCall St.), Toronto, ON M5T 1L1. © **416/591-5359.** www.baldwininn.com. 6 rooms. From C$85 single. Rates include continental breakfast. AE, MC, V. Subway: St. Patrick. **Amenities:** 2nd-floor lounge. *In room:* A/C.

Hotel Victoria ★ *✦*   In a landmark downtown building near the Hockey Hall of Fame, the Victoria retains the glamorous touches of an earlier age, such as crown moldings and marble columns in the lobby. It's Toronto's second-oldest hotel (built in 1909), but the facilities are upgraded annually. Because of its small size, the hotel offers an unusually high level of personal service and attention, which you normally wouldn't expect in budget accommodations. Standard rooms are on the small side but are nicely put together; deluxe rooms are larger and have coffeemakers and mini-fridges.

56 Yonge St. (at Wellington St.), Toronto, ON M5E 1G5. © **800/363-8228** or 416/363-1666. Fax 416/363-7327. www.hotelvictoria-toronto.com. 56 units. From C$160 double. Additional adult C$15. Rates include continental breakfast. AE, DC, MC, V. Parking in nearby garage C$14. Subway: King. **Amenities:** Restaurant; babysitting; access to nearby health club. *In room:* A/C, TV, hair dryer, Internet (free).

DOWNTOWN EAST

Expensive

Cambridge Suites Hotel ★★ *✦*   The emphasis at this all-suite hotel is comfortable home-away-from-home luxury, which makes it popular for extended stays. The smallest suite is a generous 51 sq. m (550 sq. ft.) and moves up to deluxe duplexes. The amenities for business travelers are solid. If you can drag yourself away from the cozy desk area, which has two two-line telephones and a fax, you can enjoy some of the comforts of home: fridge, microwave, and dining ware, plus coffee, tea, and snacks. And if you hand over your shopping list, the staff will stock the fridge, too. Penthouse suites come complete with Jacuzzi and breathtaking views.

15 Richmond St. E. (near Yonge St.), Toronto, ON M5C 1N2. ✆ **800/463-1990** or 416/368-1990. Fax 416/601-3751. www.cambridgesuitestoronto.com. 229 units. From C$240 suite. Rates include continental breakfast. AE, DC, DISC, MC, V. Parking C$25. Subway: Queen. **Amenities:** Restaurant; bar; babysitting; concierge; small health club; access to much larger health club nearby; Jacuzzi; room service; sauna; spa. *In room:* A/C, TV, fax, fridge, hair dryer, minibar, Wi-Fi ($11.95 daily).

Cosmopolitan Hotel ★★ This discrete, all-suite boutique property is tucked away on quiet Colborne Street, just off Yonge Street. No surprise then to discover it caters to a Zen sensibility of serenity in all aspects of its service, from decor to turndown service (a gemstone is placed on the pillow, not a mint). Yoga mats, incense sticks, and a guided relaxation CD round out the room experience. If you're not blissed out by all this, head for Shizen Spa for more serious soothing of the soul.

8 Colborne St., Toronto, ON M5E 1E1. ✆ **416/350-2000**. Fax 416/350-2460. www.cosmotoronto.com. 80 suites. From C$229 double. Rates include continental breakfast. AE, DC, DISC, MC, V. Valet parking C$33. Subway: King. **Amenities:** Wine bar; concierge; gym; room service; spa. *In room:* A/C, TV, DVD player, kitchen, Wi-Fi. ($12 daily fee).

Pantages Suites Hotel and Spa The Pantages plays up the fact that it's an oasis of serenity in the middle of the city. It's just a block east from the Eaton Centre, but Victoria Street is so quiet, you'd never guess that you're a short walk from many of Toronto's big attractions. Still, the tradeoff is that the area around the Eaton Centre is dodgy (it's not a dangerous area, but it's popular with petty thieves). In response, the Pantages pays careful attention to security (it's impossible to use the elevator without a valid guest room key card, for example). Guest rooms—spacious minisuites, really—are decked out in a soothing palette of neutrals, with ensuite kitchens and washers and dryers. Better yet, many rooms have a Jacuzzi tub. It's a soothing, restful hotel.

 family-friendly HOTELS

Delta Chelsea. This perennial family favorite has a Family Fun Zone, a multi-room play area with live bunnies and fish, a video arcade, and the only indoor water-slide in downtown Toronto. You can play together in the family pool here or drop off the tykes for babysitting. Kids will enjoy the in-room family movies, games, cookie jar (replenished daily), and nightly turndown gift. Some of the Delta Chelsea's restaurants have half-price kids' menus, further reducing the strain on the family purse. See p. 77.

Four Seasons Hotel Toronto. A hop and a skip from the newly renovated Royal Ontario Museum, this hotel has its own attractions. Guests can borrow free bicycles and video games, and use the indoor pool. Upon arrival, room service brings the kids complimentary cookies and milk. The concierge and housekeeping staff can arrange excellent babysitting services. See p. 83.

Sheraton Centre Toronto Hotel. The endless attractions of this complex—including restaurants with special menus for tykes, a garden waterfall, and a pool—mean there's a lot to keep the little ones entertained. There's a supervised play center, as well as on-call babysitting services. Kids also enjoy in-room video games and a welcome gift. A limited number of Family Guest Rooms boast a toy chest, some kid-size furniture, a fridge, and a microwave. See p. 78.

Where to Stay in Downtown East

Bond Place Hotel **4**

Cambridge Suites Hotel **7**

Cosmopolitan Hotel **8**

Courtyard Toronto Downtown **1**

Days Inn & Conference Centre
Toronto Downtown **2**

Holiday Inn Express
Toronto Downtown **6**

Neill-Wycik College Hotel **3**

Pantages Suites Hotel and Spa **5**

Cathedral †
Point of Interest ▣
Post Office ✉
TTC Subway —Ⓣ—

200 Victoria St. (at Shuter St.), Toronto, ON M5B 1V8. © **866/852-1777** or 416/362-1777. Fax 416/214-5618. www.pantageshotel.com. 157 units. From C$221 double. Rates include continental breakfast. AE, DC, MC, V. Parking C$28. Subway: Queen. **Amenities:** Restaurant; bar; bike rental; concierge; Jacuzzi; room service; sauna; spa. *In room:* A/C, TV, CD player, fax, hair dryer, kitchen, minibar, Wi-Fi (free).

Moderate

Courtyard Toronto Downtown ★   Most Courtyard-brand properties in the Marriott chain are usually out of the city center. This one near Yonge and College streets is an exception, convenient to get around on foot and on the subway line. The lobby, with its double-sided fireplace, has a surprisingly intimate feel, given the size of the 575-room hotel. Tour groups, which often book here, have a separate reception area. The guest rooms aren't big, but they are comfortable, with smart features such as windows that open and additional sinks outside the bathrooms. Ongoing refurbishments keep guest rooms looking fresh rather than lived in. While Courtyards are generally regarded as business hotels, this one has family-friendly facilities such as a children's wading pool.

 summer-only STAYS

From September to early May, the dorms at the University of Toronto and at Ryerson Polytechnic University are full of students. But in summer, many of these rooms are rented out to budget-minded travelers. If you don't mind your in-room amenities on the Spartan side, you can save a lot of money this way—and get a great downtown or midtown location, too.

Neill-Wycik College Hotel. During the school year, this is a Ryerson residence. Some students work here in the summer, when the Neill-Wycik morphs into a guesthouse. Rooms have beds, chairs, desks, and phones, but no air-conditioning or TVs (although there is a TV lounge). Groups of five bedrooms share two bathrooms and one kitchen with a refrigerator and stove. The hotel has two roof decks, on the 5th and 23rd floors. It's less than a 5-minute walk to the Eaton Centre.

96 Gerrard St. E. (btw. Church & Jarvis sts.), Toronto, ON M5B 1G7. © **800/268-4358** or 416/977-2320. Fax 416/977-2809. www.neill-wycik.com. 281 units, all w/shared bathroom.

C$45 single; C$80 double (2 twin beds); C$110 family (2 adults, plus children). MC, V. Limited on-site parking (C$10); private lots offsite. Subway: College. **Amenities:** Cafe; sauna.

Victoria University at the University of Toronto. This is a steal for this very expensive neighborhood (just a 2-min. walk from tony Yorkville). Victoria University offers simple rooms with plain furnishings (a bed, desk, and chair are standard), but the surroundings are splendid. Many of the rooms are in Burwash Hall, a 19th-century building that overlooks a peaceful, leafy quad. Guests are provided with linens, towels, and soap.

140 Charles St. W. (btw. Queen's Park & St. Thomas St.), Toronto, ON M5S 1K9. © **416/585-4524.** Fax 416/585-4530. www.vicu.utoronto.ca/facilities/accommodations.htm. 700 units, all w/shared bathroom. C$60 single; C$80 double (2 twin beds). Rates include breakfast. MC, V. Parking C$18/day or C$38/week. Subway: Museum. **Amenities:** Access to health club w/Olympic-size pool; tennis courts. *In room:* No phone.

475 Yonge St. (1 block north of College St.), Toronto, ON M4Y 1X7. © **800/847-5075** or 416/924-0611. Fax 416/924-8692. www.courtyard.com/yyzcy. 575 units. From C$149 double. AE, DC, MC, V. Parking C$30. Subway: College. **Amenities:** 2 restaurants; bar; health club; room service. *In room:* A/C, TV, hair dryer, minibar, Wi-Fi (free).

Inexpensive

Bond Place Hotel ★ The location is right—a block from the Eaton Centre, around the corner from the Canon and Elgin theaters—and so is the price. Perhaps that's why this hotel tends to be popular with tour groups. The rooms are on the small side. Book as far in advance as you can; the hotel is usually packed, especially in summer. ***Note:*** This hotel has partnerships with many Toronto hospitals, so if you're coming to the city to visit a sick relative, Bond Place will give you an especially low rate.

65 Dundas St. E. (at Bond St.), Toronto, ON M5B 2G8. © **800/268-9390** or 416/362-6061. Fax 416/360-6406. www.bondplace.ca. 287 units. From C$119 double. Additional adult C$15. Multi-night packages available. AE, DC, DISC, MC, V. Off-site parking C$25. Subway: Dundas. **Amenities:** Restaurant; bar; concierge; room service. *In room:* A/C, TV, hair dryer, Wi-Fi ($12.95 daily).

Holiday Inn Express Toronto Downtown The main selling point of this no-frills hotel is its location, close to the Financial District and the Eaton Centre. It often offers special promotions, so be sure to ask. Rooms tend to be small, with standard amenities.

111 Lombard St. (btw. Adelaide & Richmond sts.), Toronto, ON M5C 2T9. © **800/228-5151** or 416/367-5555. Fax 416/367-3470. www.ichotelsgroup.com. 196 units. From C$139 double. Rates include continental breakfast. AE, DC, DISC, MC, V. Parking C$20. Subway: King or Queen. **Amenities:** Breakfast bar. *In room:* A/C, TV, hair dryer, Wi-Fi (free).

MIDTOWN

Very Expensive

Four Seasons Hotel Toronto ★★ ☺ Although its days are numbered in this location, the legend lives on. The Rolling Stones call the Four Seasons home in Toronto, and during the Toronto International Film Festival, you can't get in for love or money. The hotel, in the ritzy Yorkville district, has earned a reputation for offering fine service and complete comfort. Despite the high rollers who frequent the place, this is a family-friendly hotel that really takes care of kids. Rooms tend to be on the small side (a standard is only about 30 sq. m/323 sq. ft.), but they're well designed and easy on the eye. Corner rooms have charming balconies offering great views of the street scene below. Take a window seat at the Avenue bar off the lobby for the serious sport of people-watching. You never know who might walk by. When The Four Seasons' new location is ready in 2013, at the other end of Yorkville on Bay Street, the in-crowd scene will no doubt move right along with it.

21 Avenue Rd. (at Yorkville Ave.), Toronto, ON M5R 2G1. © **800/268-6282** or 416/964-0411. Fax 416/964-2301. www.fourseasons.com/toronto. 380 units. From C$305 double. Multi-night discounts and packages available. AE, DC, DISC, MC, V. Parking C$30. Subway: Bay. **Amenities:** 2 restaurants; 2 bars/lounges; babysitting; bike rental; concierge; health club; Jacuzzi; indoor/outdoor pool; room service. *In room:* A/C, TV/DVD player, CD player, hair dryer, minibar, Wi-Fi ($15 daily).

The Hazelton Hotel ★ This luxury boutique hotel has a lot going for it. At just 77 rooms, it's the right size for Yorkville, and it has the best outdoor patio for people-watching (The Four Seasons' is indoor). Perks include heated bathroom floors and laptop-sized safes. The decor is understated masculine glamour in both public spaces and guestrooms (designed by local design whiz Yabu Pushelberg). Rooms are spacious, and bathrooms are indulgent, with a TV on the wall above the sink. The hotel also boasts a Mark McEwan restaurant, ONE, and a VIP screening room that seats 25.

118 Yorkville Ave. (at Hazelton Ave.), Toronto, ON M5R 1C2. ℂ **866/473-6301** or 416/964-6300. Fax 416/963-6399. www.thehazeltonhotel.com. 77 units. From C$480 double. AE, DC, DISC, MC, V. Parking C$35. Subway: Bay. **Amenities:** Restaurant; babysitting; concierge; health club; indoor lap pool; room service; spa. *In room:* A/C, TV/DVD player, CD player, hair dryer, minibar, MP3 docking station, Wi-Fi (free).

Park Hyatt Toronto ★★★   This venerable hotel commands a prime location opposite the Royal Ontario Museum at the corner of Bloor Street West and Avenue Road. It's glamorous and grown up, and boasts the best hotel bar in town (author Mordecai Richler famously called its 18th-floor Roof Lounge the only civilized place in Toronto). The Park Hyatt's two towers are linked by a lobby dotted with Eastern-inspired objets d'art. The guest rooms in the newer North Tower are among the most generously proportioned in town—the *smallest* is 46 sq. m (495 sq. ft.). The older, but frequently refurbished, rooms in the South Tower have spectacular, unobstructed views of downtown Toronto. The ground-floor restaurant **Annona** is a treat, as is the Stillwater Spa, which is a popular destination for locals.

4 Avenue Rd. (at Bloor St. W.), Toronto, ON M5R 2E8. ℂ **800/233-1234** or 416/925-1234. Fax 416/924-6693. www.parktoronto.hyatt.com. 346 units. From C$289 double. Multi-night packages available. AE, DC, DISC, MC, V. Valet parking C$34. Subway: Museum or Bay. No pets accepted. **Amenities:** Restaurant; 2 bars; concierge; health club; Jacuzzi; room service; sauna; spa. *In room:* A/C, TV, fax, hair dryer, Internet (free), minibar.

Expensive

The Sutton Place Hotel ★   The Sutton Place boasts the advantage of a small hotel, with detail-oriented, personalized service not often found in a 300-plus room property. In addition to hosting a galaxy of stars, the hotel draws sophisticated business and leisure travelers in search of serious pampering. Guest rooms are spacious, and a few suites have full kitchens. Not that you'd want to cook while you're here—the ground-floor **Accents** restaurant serves continental fare, and across the street, the star-studded Bistro 990 produces impeccable French cuisine. One downside is that The Sutton Place stands alone in its neighborhood. It's about a 10- to 15-minute walk to attractions such as the Royal Ontario Museum (see p. 127) and the Yorkville shopping district.

955 Bay St. (at Wellesley St.), Toronto, ON M5S 2A2. ℂ **866/378-8866** or 416/924-9221. Fax 416/924-1778. www.toronto.suttonplace.com. 311 units. From C$189 double. Additional adult C$29. Children 17 & under stay free in parent's room. AE, DC, MC, V. Parking C$25. Subway: Wellesley. **Amenities:** Restaurant; bar; babysitting; concierge; health club; indoor pool; room service; sauna. *In room:* A/C, TV, hair dryer, minibar, Wi-Fi ($16 daily).

Moderate

Clarion Hotel & Suites Selby ★ 🏨   Ornate chandeliers, stucco moldings, and high ceilings make this 1890s Victorian building a charming character property. In a predominantly gay neighborhood, the Selby attracts gay and straight couples, as well as seniors (they get special discounts). All of the rooms have private bathrooms, but only a few have old-fashioned claw-foot tubs. While there's no concierge, the staff

Where to Stay in Midtown

Clarion Hotel & Suites Selby **7**
Four Seasons Hotel Toronto **5**
The Hazelton Hotel **4**
Holiday Inn Toronto Midtown **1**
Howard Johnson Yorkville **3**
Park Hyatt Toronto **2**
The Sutton Place Hotel **8**
Victoria University
at the University of Toronto **6**

Point of Interest
TTC Subway

A B&B can be an excellent alternative to standard hotel accommodations. **Toronto Bed & Breakfast Reservation Service** (☏ **877/922-6522;** www.toronto bandb.com) has a short but wide-ranging list of accommodations in the city. The organization will make your reservation and send you a confirmation. The **Downtown Toronto Association of Bed and Breakfast Guest Houses** (☏ **416/410-3938;** www.bnbinfo.com) has listings for most of metro Toronto, not just downtown. **Bed and Breakfast Canada** (☏ **800/239-1141** or **905/524-5855;** www.bbcanada.com) has a very long list of independent B&B operators.

For a memorable, out of the ordinary stay, consider staying at one of the eight B&Bs located on the Toronto Islands. The cottage-like communities of Ward's Island and Algonquin Island are just a 10-minute ferry ride, but a world, away from the bustle of downtown. Some accommodations are summer seasonal, others have 1-week minimum stays. What they all share is the rare treat of staying in a park setting with wonderful views back to the city. Remember if you're out downtown to catch the last ferry back to Ward's Island (around 11:30pm) or you'll have to hire a water taxi. For a complete list of island accommodations, see www. torontoisland.org.

is very friendly and will provide plenty of recommendations for what to see and do. History buffs will love the fact that Ernest Hemingway lived here for a couple of years while he was on staff at the *Toronto Star* newspaper (and yes, there is a Hemingway suite).

592 Sherbourne St. (1 block south of Bloor St. E.), Toronto, ON M4X 1L4. ☏ **800/4-CHOICE** (800/424-6423) or 416/921-3142. Fax 416/923-3177. www.choicehotels.ca. 82 units. From C$155 double. Rates include continental breakfast. AE, DISC, MC, V. Parking C$20. Subway: Sherbourne. **Amenities:** Access to nearby health club. *In room:* A/C, TV, hair dryer, Wi-Fi (free).

Holiday Inn Toronto Midtown 🍴 Considering this hotel's tony location—steps from Yorkville and several museums, including the Royal Ontario Museum (see p. 127)—the price is hard to beat. The rooms are small but comfortable, and outfitted with well-lit worktables. All rooms have free high-speed Internet access, but there aren't many other amenities or services. This is a good home base for a leisure traveler who prizes location over other considerations. If you're not planning to hang out a lot in your hotel room, it's a small trade-off for the price.

280 Bloor St. W. (at St. George St.), Toronto, ON M5S 1V8. ☏ **888/HOLIDAY** (888/465-4329) or 416/968-0010. Fax 416/968-7765. www.ichotelsgroup.com. 209 units. From C$150 double. Multi-night & other packages available. AE, DC, DISC, MC, V. Parking C$22. Subway: St. George. **Amenities:** Restaurant; coffee shop; babysitting; health club; room service. *In room:* A/C, TV, hair dryer, Wi-Fi (free).

Howard Johnson Yorkville 🍴 This hotel is a bargain in a very expensive neighborhood. The Yorkville location is excellent, which compensates for small rooms (you're probably not going to want to spend much time there, as is the case with many value-priced hotels).

89 Avenue Rd. (btw. Yorkville & Webster aves.), Toronto, ON M5R 2G3. © **800/446-4656** or 416/964-1220. Fax 416/964-8692. www.hojoyorkville.com. 69 units. From C$150 double. Rates include continental breakfast. AE, DC, MC, V. Parking C$22. Subway: Bay or Museum. **Amenities:** Concierge; Wi-Fi (free). *In room:* A/C, TV, hair dryer.

AT THE AIRPORT
Expensive

Hilton Toronto Airport ★   The one convenience of staying out by Pearson International Airport is that rooms tend to be larger, and this Hilton is no exception. The 152 mini-suites each have king-size beds in the bedrooms, sofa beds in the living room, color TVs in both rooms, and three phones. Another lure is the chain's well-regarded business-oriented amenities.

5875 Airport Rd., Mississauga, ON L4V 1N1. © **866/565-4555** or 905/677-9900. Fax 905/677-7782. www.hilton.com. 419 units. From C$199 double. Additional adult C$25. Children stay free in parent's room. Multi-night packages available. AE, DC, DISC, MC, V. Parking C$15. **Amenities:** Restaurant; bar; free airport transfers; children's center; concierge; nearby golf course; health club; indoor pool; room service; sauna; spa. *In room:* A/C, TV, fax, hair dryer, Internet ($12.95 daily), minibar, MP3 docking station.

Sheraton Gateway Hotel in Toronto International Airport ★   They named this hotel right—it is both a gateway to the city and the closest sleep you'll get to the gateway to board a plane. Connected by skywalk to Terminal 3 (and a free SkyTrain to Terminal 1), this hotel offers comfortable, spacious rooms and, most importantly, soundproof windows. Club rooms have extra perks, such as ergonomic chairs, a fax/printer/copier, and access to a private lounge that serves complimentary breakfast and snacks. Some guest rooms have been tailored for visitors with disabilities.

Toronto AMF, Box 3000, Toronto, ON L5P 1C4. © **800/325-3535** or 905/672-7000. Fax 905/672-7100. www.sheraton.com. 474 units. From C$199 double. AE, DC, DISC, MC, V. Parking C$28. **Amenities:** Restaurant; bar; babysitting; concierge; health club; Jacuzzi; indoor pool; room service; sauna. *In room:* A/C, TV, fridge, hair dryer, Internet (free).

Moderate

Toronto Marriott Airport Hotel   Leisure travelers can benefit from weekend discounts here when the business crowd is not around. Rooms are comfortable and spacious, with standard amenities and no surprises. They've been spruced up a bit lately with down comforters and fluffier pillows. It's not home, but it's not bad for a short stay.

901 Dixon Rd. (at Carlingview Dr.), Toronto, ON M9W 1J5. © **800/905-2811** or 416/674-9400. Fax 416/674-8292. www.marriott.com. 424 units. From C$159 double. Additional adult C$20. Multi-night packages available. AE, DC, DISC, MC, V. Parking C$18. **Amenities:** 2 restaurants; cafe; bar; free airport transfers; babysitting; concierge; nearby golf course; health club; Jacuzzi; sky-lit indoor pool; room service; sauna; Wi-Fi ($15.95 daily in guest rooms; free in lobby). *In room:* A/C, TV, hair dryer, minibar.

WHERE TO DINE

Toronto is a good place to eat. In keeping with the city's overall character—generally agreeable, occasionally inventive, sometimes brilliant—you can expect to find plenty of decent food, as well as some truly memorable fare (fine or rustic). Lately, there's glamour in the air: Chef-driven openings and no-reservation hot-spots draw eager crowds, and there is a noticeable proliferation of restaurant-related books, shows, stars, and blogs.

The city's multicultural makeup ensures a rich banquet, and fusion here goes well beyond the realm of Asian: Many of the city's best cooks and chefs reinvent as they go, inspired by culinary cultures from around the globe or down the street. Other things Toronto's foodies love: the local movement, all manner of meat (and offal), pretty bakeries, Italian *trattorias,* bistros, thin-crust pizza, super-fresh seafood, a good cup of joe, and a lively pub scene. The only thing that's in short supply is fine dining on par with the world's great restaurants. However, hungry citizens do engage in a bit of adventure, like molecular gastronomy, new ways to savor brains, eating in the dark, wild foods like pickled spruce tips, and serious gourmet happenings such as Japanese, nine-course set menus at C$300 per person.

More good news: In comparison to other big cities, it all adds up to a fairly affordable feast. The bad news is that high taxes on food and alcohol put a dent in the budget, even though menu prices are generally fair. Other negatives: The city still holds onto outdated, Americanized versions of some cuisines, such as Mexican (with rare exceptions), and oftentimes, while the hottest spots are sizzling in the kitchen, service needs work. That said, the city has never tasted so good.

Note: This chapter includes a mere sampling of the city's best restaurants, and lately, there's been a recession-busting wave of openings, including second locations for established eateries and entirely new places. So be sure to check out one of Toronto's dining websites, such as www.dineto.com, http://martiniboys.com, www.toronto.com/restaurants, or www.torontolife.com/restaurants for updates.

And remember, the city is a good place for walking; a useful tip for working up an appetite.

DINING NOTES Whatever your budget, expect to add about 30% to the total: There's a 13% tax (HST, which stands for a "harmonized sales tax"), plus you need to leave the standard tip of 15% or more if the service has been adequate or better (20% if the service was great). Restaurants normally leave tipping to the diner's discretion; exceptions are often for parties of six or more, where 15% might be added automatically. Wine and other alcoholic beverages are pricey in part because the provincial government levies high taxes and also because restaurateurs often charge as high as a 30% markup. Some establishments let you bring your own and add a corkage fee. One more cost to keep in mind: There is a 10% tax on alcohol.

BEST DINING BETS

o **Best Patio:** If it's people-watching you crave, check out the **Diplomatico** (known as "The Dip"; 594 College St.; ℭ **416/534-4637**) in Little Italy, but not for the food, which is convenience-food-meets-Italian (frozen pizzas, etc.). See p. 102. If you're looking for fine dining in a leafy locale, try **Loire** (119 Harbord St.; ℭ **416/850-8330**) for its pretty deck, fine French fusion fare, and brilliant wine list. See p. 107.

o **Best Charcuterie:** It's a love affair with offal: Toronto has taken its sweet time to fully embrace this trend, but at last, the top spots offer good and sometimes excellent charcuterie made in-house. With more than 40 kinds of cured, dried, and otherwise prepared meat, bone, and organ dishes, **The Black Hoof & Hoof Café** (928 & 923 Dundas St. W.; ℭ **416/551-8854**) reigns supreme. See p. 99.

o **Best Tapas:** Partners Chris McDonald and Doug Penfold at **Cava** (1560 Yonge St.; ℭ **416/979-9918**) do tapas best with inventive dishes and more than 20 wines offered by the glass for pairing. See p. 116. **Torito** (276 Augusta Ave; ℭ **416/961-7373**) is a low-key, laid-back alternative.

o **Best Museum Restaurant:** The renovation at the Royal Ontario Museum brought with it the inspired **C5** (100 Queen's Park; ℭ **416/586-7928**), which some say is the best thing about the entire project. See p. 106.

- **Best Bakery Lunch:** Toronto loves its quiches, croissants, and dainty desserts: The number of fine bakery-cafes is proof. A favorite is the pioneering **Patachou** (1120 Yonge St., at Roxborough St.; ℂ **416/927-1105**), which brought true French pastries to the city back in the day and arguably still makes the best croissant in town. See p. 118.

- **Best Hotel Restaurant:** At **Lai Wah Heen** (110 Chestnut St.; ℂ **416/977-9899**), in the Metropolitan Hotel, perfect Peking duck, great dim sum, and an impressive menu of mostly Cantonese specialties make up for dismal decor. See p. 94.

- **Best for Families: Grano** (2035 Yonge St.; ℂ **416/440-1986**) is an Italian restaurant that knows how to treat the *ragazzini*. Simple pastas, delicious breads and sweets, tasty salads, and the lively, warm atmosphere combine to make it feel like you're visiting family. See p. 116.

RESTAURANTS BY CUISINE

The prices within each review refer to the cost in Canadian dollars of individual main courses, using the following categories: Very Expensive ($$$$), main courses at dinner average more than C$35; Expensive ($$$), C$25 to C$35; Moderate ($$), C$15 to C$25; and Inexpensive ($), C$15 and less. Restaurants are listed alphabetically at the end of the index in the back of this book.

AFRICAN
Lalibela (Midtown, $, p. 110)

AMERICAN
Allen's ★★★ (The East End, $$, p. 112)

Bymark ★★ (Downtown West, $$$$, p. 97)

Jump Cafe & Bar ★★ (Downtown West, $$$, p. 97)

Lolita's Lust & the Chinchilla Lounge ★ (The East End, $$$, p. 111)

Swan ★ (Downtown West, $$, p. 102)

ASIAN
Café 668 ★ (Downtown West, $, p. 103)

Foxley ★★★ (Downtown West, $$$, p. 97)

BISTRO
Biff's Bistro & Wine Bar ★★ (Downtown East, $$$, p. 104)

The Black Hoof & Hoof Café ★★★ (Downtown West, $$$, p. 99)

Brassaii ★★ (Downtown West, $$$, p. 96)

C5 ★★★ (Midtown, $$$$, p. 106)

Delux ★★★ (Downtown West, $$, p. 99)

The Drake ★★ (Downtown West, $$, p. 99)

earth ★★★ (Midtown, $$, p. 106)

Edward Levesque's Kitchen ★★ (Downtown East, $$, p. 105)

Foxley ★★ (Downtown West, $$$, p. 97)

Gallery Grill ★★ (Downtown West, $$$, p. 100)

Gilead Café and Bistro ★★★ (Downtown East, $, p. 96)

Globe Bistro ★★ (The East End, $$$, p. 111)

Le Sélect Bistro ★★ (Downtown West, $$, p. 98)

Lolo ★ (Uptown, $$, p. 116)

Messis ★ (Midtown, $$, p. 110)

Niagara Street Café ★★ (Downtown West, $$$, p. 98)

Swan ★ (Downtown West, $$, p. 102)

Key to Abbreviations: $$$$ = Very Expensive $$$ = Expensive $$ = Moderate $ = Inexpensive

Where to Dine Downtown

Cathedral ✝
Point of Interest ▢
Post Office ✉
TTC Subway —Ⓣ—

Ame **7**

Balzac's Coffee
Roastery **20**

Biff's Bistro & Wine Bar **16**

Bymark **10**

Canoe Restaurant & Bar **12**

Ematei **8**

Gilead Bistro & Café **19**

Great Cooks on Eight **13**

Hiro Sushi **18**

Jules Bistro **4**

Jump Cafe & Bar **15**

Lai Wah Heen **9**

Lee Garden **2**

Mother's Dumplings **1**

The Rivoli **3**

Rodney's Oyster House **6**

Senses Bakery **14**

Soma Chocolate **21**

Starfish **17**

Tutti Matti **5**

Vertical **11**

CANADIAN

C5 ★★★ (Midtown, $$$$, p. 106)
Canoe Restaurant & Bar ★★★ (Downtown West, $$$$, p. 93)
Cowbell ★★★ (Downtown West, $$, p. 96)
Eigensinn Farm ★★★ (Out of town, $$$$, p. 117)
RubyWatchCo ★★★ (The East End, $$$, p. 104)

CHINESE

Lai Wah Heen ★★★ (Downtown West, $$$, p. 94)
Lee Garden ★ (Downtown West, $$, p. 100)

CONTINENTAL

Ancaster Old Mill ★★★ (Out of town, $$$, p. 118)

DELI

Caplansky's (Downtown West, $, p. 110)

FRENCH

Auberge du Pommier ★★★ (Uptown, $$$$, p. 115)
Conviction ★★ (Downtown West, $$$, p. 97)
Jacques Bistro du Parc (Midtown, $$, p. 107)
Loire ★★ (Downtown West, $$$, p. 107)

GREEK

Astoria Shish Kebob House (The East End, $, p. 112)
Avli ★ (The East End, $$, p. 112)
Mezes (The East End, $, p. 114)
Myth ★ (The East End, $$$, p. 112)
Pan on the Danforth ★ (The East End, $$, p. 112)

HEALTH FOOD

Camros Organic Eatery ★★ (Midtown, $, p. 110)

INDIAN

Nataraj ★ (Midtown, $, p. 111)

INTERNATIONAL

Brassaii ★★ (Downtown West, $$$, p. 96)
Messis ★ (Midtown, $$, p. 110)
Pangaea ★★★ (Midtown, $$$, p. 96)
North 44 ★★★ (Uptown, $$$$, p. 115)
The Rivoli (Downtown West, $$, p. 101)
Scaramouche ★★★ (Uptown, $$$$, p. 115)

ITALIAN

Bar Mercurio ★★ (Downtown West, $$$, p. 107)
Bar One ★ (Downtown West, $$, p. 99)
Grano ★★ (Uptown, $$, p. 116)
The Local Kitchen and Wine Bar ★★ (Downtown West, $$, p. 100)
Mistura ★★★ (Midtown, $$$$, p. 106)
Seven Numbers ★★ (The East End, $$, p. 114)
Terroni ★★ (Downtown East, $, p. 102)
Tutti Matti ★★ (Downtown West, $$, p. 102)
Trattoria Giancarlo ★★ (Downtown West, $$$, p. 98)
Zucca Trattoria ★★★ (Uptown, $$, p. 116)

JAPANESE/SUSHI

Ame ★★★ (Downtown West, $$, p. 94)
Hiro Sushi ★★★ (Downtown West, $$$, p. 104)

LIGHT FARE

Camros Organic Eatery ★★ (Midtown, $, p. 110)
Café Diplomatico (Downtown West, $, p. 102)
Caffé Brasiliano (Downtown West, $, p. 103)

Dufflet Pastries ★ (Downtown West, $$, p. 118)

Great Cooks on Eight ★★ (Downtown West, $$, p. 100)

Hannah's Kitchen (Uptown, $, p. 117)

Pain Perdu ★ (Uptown, $$, p. 117)

Patachou ★ (Midtown, $$, p. 118)

Senses Bakery ★ (Downtown West, $$, p. 118)

Rebel House (Uptown, $, p. 117)

Soma Chocolate (The East End, $$, p. 118)

Terroni ★★ (Downtown West, $, p. 102)

MEDITERRANEAN

Chiado ★ (Downtown West, $$$, p. 94)

Myth ★ (The East End, $$$, p. 112)

Vertical ★★ (Downtown West, $$$, p. 99)

PIZZA

Conviction ★★ (Downtown West, $$$, p. 97)

Terroni ★★ (Downtown West, $$, p. 102)

SEAFOOD

Chippy's ★ (Downtown West, $, p. 103)

Oyster Boy ★★ (Downtown West, $$, p. 101)

Rodney's Oyster House ★★ (Downtown West, $$, p. 102)

SPANISH

Cava ★★★ (Uptown, $$, p. 116)

Torito Tapas Bar ★★★ (Downtown West, $, p. 104)

VEGETARIAN

Café 668 ★ (Downtown West, $, p. 103)

Camros Organic Eatery ★★ (Midtown, $, p. 110)

VIETNAMESE

Mi Mi Restaurant (Downtown East, $, p. 106)

Pho Hung (Midtown, $, p. 111)

DOWNTOWN WEST

This is where you will find Toronto's highest concentration of great restaurants. **Little Italy,** which runs along College Street, generally has better bars and cafes than restaurants; the streets of **Chinatown,** which radiate from Spadina Avenue, are lined with brightly lit, busy eateries; and lately, **West Queen West, Dundas West,** and **Ossington Avenue** are all proving to be enticing destinations for dining.

Very Expensive

Canoe Restaurant & Bar ★★★ CANADIAN   Some come for the panoramic view offered at this modern, chic dining room, but the top-quality service, sophisticated food, and fine wine cellar are what keep them coming back. Simply put, this is one of the city's—and perhaps country's—best restaurants. Executives are the main clientele at lunchtime, when the place can feel corporate; dinner, with the twinkling cityscape backdrop, is more romantic. Thanks to the passion of executive chef Anthony Walsh, menus are seasonal and offer a selection of top ingredients from local purveyors. The flavor is Canadian cuisine with rarities such as Nunavut caribou and Québec foie gras, all handled with delicacy and brilliant technique. If you're ready to splurge, tasting menus, at C$100 per person (add C$50 for paired wines), are impressive and generous. If you're on a budget, drop in at the bar for a glass of Niagara wine and a nibble.

A Note on Smoking

A provincial law came into effect in 2006 that banned smoking at restaurants in Ontario: There is no smoking indoors, and patios that have any sort of covering are also smoke-free. This has made for a great deal of confusion because tableside umbrellas that are close-set apparently count as covering, according to the law. You can smoke on uncovered patios.

54th floor, Toronto Dominion Tower, 66 Wellington St. W. © **416/364-0054.** www.canoerestaurant. com. Reservations required. Main courses C$39–C$44. AE, DC, MC, V. Mon–Fri 11:45am–2:30pm & 5–10:30pm. Subway: King.

Chiado ★★★ SEAFOOD/MEDITERRANEAN   Local Portuguese families flock here for special occasions; the atmosphere is an old-world balance of sophistication and warmth. At its core, it's a great fish restaurant, thanks in part to the fresh seafood flown in most days of the week; although you do have to ignore the carbon footprint while you tuck into that perfectly grilled sardine or pan-seared monkfish. The wine list is equally impressive, especially for those who believe Portuguese wines are plonk and are willing to learn otherwise. Upstairs is a less formal dining option: a bar with a small, but fine, menu.

864 College St. © **416/538-1910.** www.chiadorestaurant.com. Reservations recommended. Main courses C$25–C$45. AE, DC, MC, V. Mon–Fri 11am–4pm; Mon–Sat 5–10pm. Subway: College, then a streetcar to Ossington Ave.

Lai Wah Heen ★★★ CANTONESE   This is one hotel dining room where you'll find more locals than visitors. The interior is vintage Art Deco; spare pictograms dominate the walls of the two-level space. The extensive menu is mainly Cantonese, and regulars come for the excellent Peking Duck, dim sum (especially the Sunday brunch tasting menu), and delicacies such as alligator loin dumplings. There's a midtown location, too: Lai Toh Heen (629 Mount Pleasant Rd.; © **416/489-8922**).

In the Metropolitan Hotel, 110 Chestnut St. © **416/977-9899.** www.metropolitan.com/lwh. Reservations recommended. Main courses C$22–C$48. AE, DC, MC, V. Daily 11:30am–3pm; Sun–Thurs 5:30–10:30pm; Fri & Sat 5:30–11pm. Subway: St. Patrick.

Expensive

Ame ★★★ JAPANESE/LOUNGE   The Rubino brothers, Michael and Guy, are local legends for their highly stylized restaurants and serious dedication to the culinary arts. This very modern lounge and restaurant, rich with wood and fine textiles, is their latest creation: a Japanese reinvention of their acclaimed Rain restaurant. The focus is on sushi and sashimi with a Robata grill, plus an elegant dinner menu. The vegetable tempura alone exemplifies the care chef Guy takes in the kitchen. Dazzling cocktails, too. An ultra hip destination, and with the choice of eating at the bar or in the dining room, it suits a range of budgets.

19 Mercer St. (at John St.) © **416/599-7246.** www.rainrestaurant.ca. Reservations recommended. Main courses C$15–C$25. AE, DC, MC, V. Mon–Wed 5:30–10pm; Thurs–Sat 5:30–11pm. Subway: St. Andrew, then west to John St. & south to Mercer St.

Where to Dine in the West End

Point of Interest ▪

AREA OF DETAIL

| 0 | 1/4 mi |
| 0 | 0.25 km |

Bar One **16**
The Black Hoof & Hoof Café **8**
Brassaii **23**
Café 668 **6**
Café Diplomatico **2**
Caffé Brasiliano **5**
Chiado **1**
Chippy's **13**
Conviction **22**
Cowbell **18**
Delux **10**
The Drake **17**

Dufflet Pastries **12**
Ella's Uncle **7**
Foxley **9**
Le Sélect Bistro **21**
The Local Kitchen
 and Wine Bar **19**
Niagara Street Café **20**
Oyster Boy **14**
Swan **15**
Terroni **11**
Torito **4**
Trattoria Giancarlo **3**

LOCAL lovers UNITE!

Toronto is deep into a love affair with local foods. From top dining rooms to little cafes, from the new wave of pizzerias to the boom of burger joints, just about everywhere you look, cooks are tapping into local, farm-fresh sources, from unctuous cheeses to pastured meats, organic fruits and vegetables, and plenty of local wine and craft beer to wash it all down. There are even local coffee roasters in on the scene (which promises a fresher bean) and mixologists—a fancy name for cocktail creators, er, bartenders—who are embracing the trend. There are too many to list in their entirety, but here are a few of the top locavore haunts.

Allen's. Although there's currently an unofficial competition to create the next great burger in Toronto, don't overlook this venerable burger pub and restaurant, where the excellent meat, the heart of any great burger, is sourced from local farms and then ground on-site. The owners are so proud of their sources, they list the animal feed on the menu. To boot, the wine list is local. See p. 112.

Cowbell. 1564 Queen St. W. (✆ **416/849-1095**; www.cowbellrestaurant. ca). Chef Mark Cutrara is so dedicated to knowing his food, he took a year off to

learn the art of butchery before opening this nose-to-tail star. He has the same commitment to his sources: local, small-scale, and often organic farms. If you're in town, check out the monthly "Farmers Dinners" that feature a member of the Cowbell family of suppliers.

Gilead Café and Bistro. You could say star Jamie Kennedy is Toronto's original locavore chef; he's been promoting these sources for decades, and to great effect. Kennedy is a maestro at the stove, and his suppliers reflect his high standards. After years of running a small restaurant empire, he's back in the kitchen at this modest and beautiful *boîte*. See p. 105.

Pangaea. Chef Martin Kouprie has a taste for locally sourced wild foods, so expect to find seasonal menus embellished with cattail hearts, wild mushrooms, wild berries, and what is arguably the last wild meat, caribou, on offer. See p. 107.

RubyWatchCo. One prix-fixe dinner nightly with four courses and the main ingredients supplied by local purveyors. Celebrity chefs Lynn Crawford and Lora Kirk work closely with farmers, and the mutual respect is evidenced in the truly inspired results. See p. 104.

Brassaii ★★ BISTRO/INTERNATIONAL   This large, pretty space with a lovely courtyard and a magnet-of-a-bar was hot, and then it was not. Now, with a new chef (Bruce Woods, formerly of the very flashy Centro) and a new look, it's once again a good bet for a fine meal, good cocktails, and a busy vibe. The menus, grown-up enough to feature ostrich, champagne risotto, and meatballs made of Kobe beef, cover all possible daily food needs, from breakfast to lunch, dinner, and late-night snacks (at least, on weekdays). The restaurant is named for the 1920s French photographer; his prints adorn the walls.

461 King St. W. ✆ **416/598-4730.** www.brassaii.com. Reservations recommended. Main courses C$20–C$39. AE, MC, V. Mon–Fri 7:30–11am & 11:30am–midnight; Sat 10am–2:30pm & 5:30pm–midnight; Sun 10am–3pm. Subway: St. Andrew, then a streetcar west to Spadina Ave.

Bymark ★★ AMERICAN/BISTRO   In the heart of the financial district sits the most corporate of the Mark McEwan empire of swanky restaurants. Think burgers, onion rings, steaks, and snazzy seafood—all top-grade. The kitchen delivers consistently fine, if uninspired, fare. The extensive wine list, which was a draw for big expense accounts before the recession hit, now offers good value, especially with a fine selection of wines by the glass.

66 Wellington St. W. (at Bay St.). *©* **416/777-1144.** www.bymarkdowntown.com. Reservations recommended. Main courses C$32–C$47. AE, DC, MC, V. Mon–Fri 11:30am–2:30pm; Mon–Sat 5–11pm. Subway: King, then walk west to Bay St.

Conviction ★★ FRENCH/PIZZA   If you've visited Toronto before, you may have sampled some of Marc Thuet's excellent cooking at Centro, Bite Me, or Thuet. His new spot, Conviction, started with a gimmick: All of the kitchen and serving staff has served time in jail. The risk has paid off: The quality of the food and service is excellent. The concept even attracted a film crew for a reality show, "Conviction Kitchen." The restaurant has inspired the chef to return to his Alsatian roots, a welcome move for all who love Thuet's generous and rich treats such as the hearty soups, slow-braised stews, and excellent pizzas which are made with his signature dough (his family has been in the baking business for 200 years). For a sample of Thuet's irresistible baked goods, try one of the handful of Petite Thuet *boulangeries* around town (www.petitethuet.com).

609 King St. W. *©* **416/603-2777.** www.convictionrestaurant.com. Reservations required. Main courses C$23–C$37. AE, DC, MC, V. Tues–Sat 6pm–midnight; Sun 11am–2pm. Subway: St. Andrew, then a streetcar west to Portland St.

Foxley ★★ FUSION/BISTRO   It was just four years ago that this unpretentious bistro opened on Ossington Avenue, unknowingly leading a brigade of new eateries to what is now the city's must-visit strip for foodies. Chef/owner Tom Thai, long known as a top sushi chef, creates beautiful small-plate dishes such as plump dumplings, steamed (often sustainable) fish dishes, smoked pork belly, and more. The flavor is fusion: pan-Asian with European and Mexican influences. Eat what you please since there's a fresh note to this cooking—light on salt and fat—and the reasonable prices are equally encouraging. The only drawback, really, is that they don't accept reservations. So arrive early, put your name on the list, and then trundle off for a drink while you wait.

207 Ossington Ave. *©* **416/534-8520.** Reservations not accepted. Main courses C$7–C$24. Mon–Sat 5–11pm. Subway: Dundas St., then a streetcar west to Ossington Ave.; or Ossington Ave. (on Bloor line), then a bus south to Foxley St.

Jump Cafe & Bar ★★ AMERICAN   This sprawling space in Commerce Court can be tricky to find. Just follow the buzz: as the decibel level rises, you'll know you're on the right track. Yet, even with all the table-hopping and schmoozing, Jump is really about fine food. Standards such as green salads, grilled meats, and housemade fresh pastas are all handled with panache. Even the onion rings are a notch above the norm. The vibe is smart and fun with a well-curated wine list to match. Service and quality are consistently good.

1 Wellington St. W. *©* **416/363-3400.** www.jumpcafe.com. Reservations required. Main courses C$17–C$36. AE, DC, MC, V. Mon–Fri 11:45am–midnight; Sat 5pm–midnight. Subway: King.

Le Sélect Bistro ★★ BISTRO   Le Sélect is a Toronto tradition: a Parisian-style bistro that moved to Wellington Street West (a few blocks from its original home) a few years ago and has since remained as popular as ever. The patio is small but pretty in good weather, the esteemed wine cellar a draw, and the favorites, such as steak-frites, savory tarts, duck confit, and rich desserts, are all nicely done. Try the artisan cheeses from Québec.

432 Wellington St. W. ℂ **416/596-6405.** www.leselect.com. Reservations recommended. Main courses C$20–C$30; 3-course prix-fixe menu C$35. AE, DC, MC, V. Sun–Thurs 11:30am–11:30pm; Fri & Sat 11:30am–midnight. Subway: Osgoode.

Niagara Street Café ★★ BISTRO   Owner Anton Potvin has flare, as does accomplished chef Nick Liu, and together they have created a lovely little bistro with an emphasis on local, organic, and artisanal ingredients. Don't worry, there's nothing righteous or even dutiful about the experience; it's pure pleasure, from the crispy snail and lettuce salad to the duck confit, the daily wild fish special, or the bison *bavette*. Desserts, made in-house, are worth saving room for; service-with-a-smile adds another positive note. Brunch is a neighborhood draw.

169 Niagara St. (at King St.). ℂ **416/703-4222.** www.niagarastreetcafe.com. Main courses C$19–C$27. AE, DC, MC, V. Wed–Sun 6–10:30pm. Subway: St. Patrick & then King St. streetcar west to Niagara St.

Trattoria Giancarlo ★★ ITALIAN   In summer, the pretty patio in the heart of Little Italy is one of the strip's quietest. It's also where you'll find decent Italian (modern) fare, a cut above most of the food in this very touristy 'hood. Pastas are handled with particular skill, such as the bracingly fresh lemon and basil linguine, and salads and mains, such as the popular thick veal chop, are also consistently good. There's a new addition: a dark and cool little wine bar adjoining the dining room where peek-a-boo windows offer a chance to watch the parade outside without your presence being known. There's one curious thing about this longstanding spot: The wine list is much more extensive than the chalkboard lists, so you have to do a little probing to find the best match.

41 Clinton St. (at College St.). ℂ **416/533-9619.** Main courses C$18–C$35. AE, DC, MC, V. Mon–Sat 6–11pm. Subway: College, then a streetcar west to Clinton St.

Vertical ★★ MEDITERRANEAN   The prime location of Vertical in First Canadian Place is secondary to the refined cooking from chef Tawfik Shehata. The local-loving chef combines Mediterranean flavors with local sources and often organic

---

📎 Online Reservations

A number of the city's hottest restaurants don't take reservations, but if you want to be assured a table ahead of time, check out **OpenTable.com**. Relatively new to Toronto, the reservation system is nonetheless reliable, and the roster of restaurants is growing (at press time there are 235 listed). The good news is that the list includes gems such as Canoe, Cava, and Vertical. The bad news is that this American-based service includes places that are nowhere near Toronto, some as far as Ottawa, which is a 5-hour drive.

ingredients. The look, and clientele, are somewhat corporate, but the mainstream menu with a seasonal bent is treated with a surprising degree of culinary passion. Don't miss the daily seafood specials. Service is smooth, and the wine list offers plenty of excellent pairings.

In First Canadian Place, 100 King St. W. © **416/214-2252.** www.verticalrestaurant.ca. Reservations recommended. Main courses C$18–C$39. AE, DC, MC, V. Mon–Fri 11:30am–midnight. Subway: King.

Moderate

Bar One ★ ITALIAN   In-the-know locals gather at the marble bar or slide into leather booths here for good, affordable food that delivers standards and more. The ravioli filled with sunny butternut squash, pasta with tomato-and-wild-mushroom sauce or with an assortment of seafood, or one of the many different pizzas (that change often) are the best bets. Desserts, like the *semifreddo,* are delicious, too, and at brunch there are good egg dishes. Gluten-free pizza dough and pasta are also available.

924 Queen St. W. (at Shaw St.). © **416/535-1655.** www.bar-one.com. Main courses C$12–C$28. AE, DC, MC, V. Mon 5–10pm; Tues–Fri 5–11pm; Sat 9am–4pm & 5–11pm; Sun 9am–4pm & 5–10pm. Subway: Exhibition.

The Black Hoof & Hoof Café ★★★ 🏠 BISTRO   Nose-to-tail eating is taken to extremes, and to truly tasty heights, at this brilliant restaurant-bar and its sister brunch-and-bar bistro right across the street. Co-owner/chef Grant van Gameren's in-house charcuterie is the star, with the tongue sandwich drawing raves, but the pastas and soups are equally inspired. At the Café, brunch dishes include standouts like pancakes topped with rabbit confit and little bone-marrow doughnuts, all daring and beautiful. Be prepared to wait: The buzz around these two spots is deafening.

928 & 923 Dundas St. W. © **416/551-8854** or 416/792-7511. Reservations not accepted. Main courses C$10–C$24. No credit cards. Restaurant Sun–Wed 6–11:30pm, Thurs–Sat 6pm–1am; cafe Thurs–Mon 10am–2pm & 6pm–2am. Subway: St. Patrick, then a streetcar west to Grace St.

Delux ★★ CUBAN/BISTRO   Warmth and comfort come together in this small, simple bistro both in lovely touches, such as cookies made-to-order (what could be more warming?), and in the satisfying Cuban-inspired French-bistro cuisine that is the creation of chef/owner Corrina Mozo. Lovely salads, garlicky roast chicken, a good Cubano sandwich, and frites are mainstays. The desserts are standouts, especially the coffee-flavored crème brûlée.

92 Ossington Ave. (at Humbert St.). © **416/537-0134.** Reservations recommended. Main courses C$18–C$25. DC, MC, V. Tues–Thurs 6–10:30pm; Fri & Sat 6–11pm; Sun 10:30am–3pm & 6–10pm. Subway: Osgoode, then a streetcar west to Ossington Ave.

The Drake ★★ BAR/BISTRO   It's a good spot to satisfy most appetites. You can come for a busy brunch, great smoked meats and ribs, burgers, a range of bars, a hopping night-time lounge, a sidewalk patio, or a full-on dining room that's good for big parties. The Drake is a destination for music, fun, and food, and the kitchens are overseen by excellent chef Anthony Rose. Groovy yet friendly.

1150 Queen St. W. (at Beaconsfield Ave.). © **416/531-5042.** www.thedrakehotel.ca. Main courses C$14–C$37. AE, DC, MC, V. Mon–Sat 11am–2:30pm & 6–11pm; Sun 10:30am–2:30pm & 6–11pm. Subway: Osgoode, then a streetcar to Beaconsfield Ave.

Ematei ★★ JAPANESE/SUSHI   One of Toronto's most authentic sushi and *izakaya* spots, this place attracts regulars looking for fine fare who don't mind the drab decor. Don't miss the hot pots, grilled fish, tantalizing tempura, and hand-rolls. The best values are the three-course menus. Service is no-nonsense.

30 St Patrick St. ✆ **416/340-0472.** Main courses C$9–C$29. AE, DC, MC, V. Mon–Fri noon–2:30pm; daily 5pm–midnight. Subway: Osgoode.

Gallery Grill ★★ BISTRO/CONTINENTAL   This small, pretty restaurant sits perched above the University of Toronto's neo-gothic Great Hall, so the setting is stunning, with daytime-only menus to match. Chef Suzanne Baby is a local, under-the-radar treasure whose elegant fare includes soups such as cardamom-scented carrot purée, fresh pastas, poached fish fillets, and fresh veggie dishes. It's all done with a continental flare, including the excellent eggs. The wines are selected with care, and the service is pleasant yet pro. Make time for a stroll around the campus after lunch.

7 Hart House Circle (at King's College Circle). ✆ **416/978-2445.** www.harthouse.utoronto.ca. Main courses C$14–C$18. AE, DC, MC, V. Sept–June Mon–Fri 11:30am–2:30pm; Sun 11am–2pm. Closed July, Aug & holiday weekends. Subway: Museum, then walk south to Harbord St. or take Bus 94.

Great Cooks on Eight ★★ CAFETERIA/LUNCH   If you've shopped till you dropped at the Eaton Centre, take a break one big door south at this cafeteria-style cafe and restaurant on the eighth floor of the department store the Bay. It's a pleasant retreat for good lunchtime fare, and a broad selection of teas and fine sweets, all at reasonable prices. If you're feeling inspired, consider signing up for one of the cooking classes that take place in the evening.

401 Bay St. (at Queen St.). ✆ **416/861-4333.** www.greatcooks.ca. Main courses C$7–C$17. AE, DC, MC, V. Mon–Fri 11:30am–3pm. Subway: Queen.

Lee Garden ★ CANTONESE   It's been around since 1978, back when the options for Cantonese cuisine were few in Toronto, and it has since satisfied crowds with consistently good, if predictable, menus that specialize in seafood, tofu, and veggie dishes. Meats are hearty, too. The signature dish is fork-tender grandfather's smoked chicken with honey and sesame seeds. Expect a crowd: This spot remains ever popular.

331 Spadina Ave. ✆ **416/593-9524.** Reservations not accepted. Main courses C$15–C$20. AE, MC, V. Daily 4pm–midnight. Subway: Spadina, then the LRT south to Baldwin St.

The Local Kitchen and Wine Bar ★★ ITALIAN   Parkdale's latest hot number is part authentic Italian *trattoria*, part contemporary Toronto. The crowded, convivial room is idiosyncratic, the service pro yet friendly, and the food absolutely fantastic. Chef Fabio Bondi arrives pre-dawn each morning to make stunning fresh pasta like smoked gnocchi with creamy Taleggio cheese. Vegetables, fish, and meats are often on par with the noodles. The wine list is simple yet good, and each evening, there's an interesting wine highlighted, whether a rare Sicilian white or a new local vintage.

1710 Queen St. W. ✆ **416/534-6700.** Reservations not accepted. Main courses C$15–C$25. AE, DC, MC, V. Tues & Wed 5:30–10pm; Thurs–Sat 5:30–11pm. Subway: Osgoode, then a streetcar west to Triller Ave.

A second CUP

Do you love coffee? Toronto has finally moved beyond a dependence on cookie-cutter chain coffee shops and is embracing a full-on barista movement. It seems every week there's a new spot opening up. Here's a very short list of some of the best, but ask around; there's likely a great cafe just around the corner, where the espresso is dynamite and the owner can talk beans all day. *Note:* most of these spots, Euro-style, open early and close before suppertime.

Balzac's Coffee Roastery. Building 60, 55 Mill St. (© **416/207-1709**). The airy cafe invites lounging upstairs in the loft living room or downstairs near the roaster. Beans are fresh-roasted and then micro-roasted on the premises for super-freshness.

Dark Horse Espresso Bar. 682 Queen St. E. (© **647/436-3460**); 215 Spadina Ave. (© **416/979-1200**). Is it the caffeine? Everyone here buzzes—happily. Pleasant vibe, good pastries, lots of free newspapers and magazines, Wi-Fi for all . . . oh, and consistently excellent (fair-trade) joe. Who could ask for anything more?

Ella's Uncle. 916 Dundas St. W. (© **416/703-8881**). There are two great things about this little, mostly take-out spot: Great brews from local roaster Classic Coffee (bonus: the roaster is eco-friendly), plus the yummy baked goods made in the doll-house kitchen behind the bar. Really nice staff, too.

Ezra's Pound. 238 Dupont St. (© **416/929-4400**); 913 Dundas St. W. (© **647/346-8448**). You can sit down to warm croissants, a light lunch, or just plain great coffee—organic and fair-trade—where free Wi-Fi invites lingering in the pretty space. More tranquil than most coffee bars.

Sam James Coffee Bar. 297 Harbord St. (© **647/341-2572**). Some claim this tiny spot, named for owner/award-winning barista, serves the best brew in town. To be sure, the *crema* would make a mamma cry. The siphon coffee—you have to see it to understand—is a work of art. A Montreal roaster, Toi, Moi e Café, supplies the beans. Lovely pastries come from top chef J.P. Challet's catering company.

Oyster Boy SEAFOOD   Mollusc expert Adam Colquhoun runs a vibrant, fun, and very friendly bar and casual dining room where the fresh on-the-shell fare is superb and as fine as the cooked seafood, sourced mostly from Canadian suppliers. Fish and chips are excellent, pastas are generous, and the wine list features great pairings from Canada and abroad.

872 Queen St. W. (at Strachan Ave.). © **416/534-3432.** Main courses C$11–C$17. AE, DC, MC, V. Mon-Wed 5-10pm; Thurs-Sun 5-11pm. Subway: Osgoode, then a streetcar west to Strachan Ave.

The Rivoli FUSION   The Riv is better known as a club than a restaurant—the back room plays host to live music, stand-up comics, and poetry readings. The kitchen serves up jerk chicken, steamed curried mussels, salads, and a classic house burger. It's better than most bar food, for sure. Prices are fair, too.

332-334 Queen St. W. © **416/597-0794.** www.rivoli.ca. Reservations accepted only for groups of 6 or more. Main courses C$11–C$20. AE, MC, V. Daily 11:30am–2am. Subway: Osgoode.

Rodney's Oyster House ★★ SEAFOOD   Rodney is Toronto's original "Oyster-man," one of only a handful left now. This spot is a favorite with nearby condo dwellers and office workers, but is also a draw as a destination. The Maritime-inspired setting is unpretentious and includes whimsical touches such as fishing paraphernalia. The main draw is the super-fresh oysters, but chowders and pastas are very good, too. There's a new locale at 56 Temperance St. (✆ **416/703-5111**).

469 King St. W. ✆ **416/363-8105.** www.rodneysoysterhouse.com. Reservations recommended (reservations cannot be made for the patio except for groups of 10 or more). Main courses C$10–C$29. AE, DC, MC, V. Mon–Sat 11am–1am. Subway: St. Andrew.

Swan ★ AMERICAN/BISTRO   Just west of Trinity Bellwoods Park, this dining room recalls a retro soda fountain, with a counter and swirly stools on one side, booths with Formica tables on the other, and a vintage Coca-Cola cooler in the middle of the room. But the crowd that's been gathering at Swan for the past decade and more slurp up martinis and oysters (supplied by nearby Oyster Boy; see p. 101). The menu includes roasted capon with bourbon gravy and braised beef short ribs marinated in beer and marmalade. There's a nice selection of wines, almost all available by the glass. The popular weekend brunch features the usual eggy plates.

892 Queen St. W. ✆ **416/532-0452.** Reservations recommended. Main courses C$17–C$28. AE, DC, MC, V. Mon–Fri noon–10pm; Sat & Sun 10am–10pm. Subway: Osgoode, then a streetcar west to Crawford St.

Terroni ★★ 🍴 ITALIAN/PIZZA   This was Toronto's first serious venture into true Southern Italian pizza. It's since grown to be something of a mini-empire and a tried-and-true place for fine, thin-crust pies; good pastas; traditional salads made with beans, greens, and sausage (yum!); and other traditional dishes and desserts made with nonna's kitchen in mind. Great value and always popular. There are other locations at 1 Balmoral Ave. (✆ **416/925-4020**) and 106 Victoria St., Dundas Square (✆ **416/955-0258**).

720 Queen St. W. (at Claremont St.). ✆ **416/504-0320.** www.terroni.ca. Main courses C$10–C$23. AE, MC, V. Mon–Wed & Sun 9am–10pm; Thurs–Sat 9am–11pm. Subway: Osgoode, then a streetcar west to Claremont.

Tutti Matti ★★ ITALIAN   Chef/owner Alida Solomon, a native Torontonian, worked in Tuscan restaurant kitchens for years, and the results are worth a visit to her friendly restaurant. You'll find a combination of local ingredients, such as Ontario-made prosciutto and *salumi*, on the menu along with traditional bean soups, house-made fresh pastas, good braised meats, and some satisfying desserts. The small open kitchen offers a bit of drama, and the atmosphere is convivial. Expect a somewhat noisy experience, but all in good fun *alla Italiana*. The wine list reveals Solomon's intimate knowledge of great Tuscan vintages. The lunchtime prix-fixe menu offers great value.

364 Adelaide St. W. (at Spadina Ave.). ✆ **416/597-8839.** www.tuttimatti.com. Main courses C$9–C$30. AE, DC, MC, V. Mon–Fri noon–3pm; Mon–Sat 6–10:30pm. Subway: Osgoode, then any streetcar west to Spadina Ave. or Spadina streetcar to Adelaide St.

Inexpensive

Café Diplomatico ITALIAN/PIZZA   Talk about location! This is one of the best patios in Little Italy for kicking back and watching the parade go by. The scene varies from Italian grandmothers to community families and plenty of dressed-up visitors (especially on weekend nights). The food, however, is secondary: The pizzas are basic, sandwiches merely satisfying, and pastas are often poor. The Dip, as it's known, attracts long lines to secure a seat. Good fun. Eat elsewhere.

594 College St. (at Clinton St.). © **416/534-4637.** www.diplomatico.ca. Main courses C$5–$15. AE, DC, MC, V. Mon–Fri 8am–2am; Sat & Sun 8am–3am. Subway: Queen's Park, then a streetcar west to Clinton St.

Caffé Brasiliano 🍴 PORTUGUESE/CAFETERIA   Need some fuel for the day? Look no further than this busy, very affordable spot where hordes of taxi drivers go for home-cooked meals. This traditional cafe moved across the street to expanded digs, which feature comfy booths, and serves buffet (read: steam-table) fare alongside rib-sticking specials like generous sandwiches, hot lasagna, and hearty soups. For dessert: the neighborhood specialty is a Portuguese custard tart with a touch of perfectly caramelized crust.

849 Dundas St. (at Euclid St.). © **416/603-6607.** Main courses C$5–C$10. No credit cards. Mon–Sat 6am–11pm. Subway: St Patrick, then a streetcar west to Claremont St.

Café 668 ★ ASIAN FUSION   This vegetarian restaurant used to be a dingy spot at 668 Dundas West, but it has been reinvented as a sleek cafe/bistro offering the same Asian-fusion fare it won acclaim for, but in a much prettier room. Soups are a standout, as are the wide selection of noodles. Mock meats are, well, a poor stand-in. Salad rolls are fresh and worth a try. Overall, spicing can be through the roof, so take note from the friendly guide on the menu.

885 Dundas St. W. (at Claremont St.). © **416/703-0668.** www.cafe668.com. Main courses C$11–C$14. No credit cards. Tues–Fri 12:30–4pm & 6–9pm; Sat & Sun 1:30–9pm. Subway: St. Patrick, then a streetcar west to Claremont St.

Chippy's ★ FISH AND CHIPS   Great, non-greasy fish and chips are hard to find, so little wonder this shoe-box spot on Queen West is a hit with its signature light batter (Guinness beer is a key ingredient) and chunky, home-cut fries. There's halibut, cod, and haddock for frying, and an assortment of garnishes, most of them in fact not any improvement over a bit of ketchup or malt vinegar. The location, across the street from the beautiful and sprawling Trinity Bellwoods Park, calls out for a good-weather picnic. A second location is at 490 Bloor St. W., at Bathurst St. (© **416/516-7776**).

893 Queen St. W. (at Strachan Ave.). © **416/866-7474.** Sun–Wed 11:30am–8pm; Thurs–Sat 11:30am–9pm. Main courses C$9–C$13. No credit cards. Subway: Osgoode, then a streetcar west to Strachan Ave.

Jules Bistro ★★ FRENCH/BISTRO   A lunchtime hangout by day and a pretty cafe by night, this little French treasure serves up good quiches, lovely salads, crisp frites, sweet and savory crêpes, and buttery desserts. It's a simple, friendly spot with a suitably approachable wine list and price tag to match. A C$25 prix fixe menu is a steal. Regulars pack the place midday and neighborhood locals linger over candlelit tables after dark.

147 Spadina Ave. (at Queen St. W.). © **416/348-8886.** Reservations recommended. Main courses C$13–C$20; prix-fixe menu C$25. AE, DC, MC, V. Mon–Fri 11:30am–9pm; Sat noon–5pm. Subway: Osgoode, then a streetcar west to Spadina Ave.

Mother's Dumplings ★ 🍴 ASIAN   The website of this family-oriented, idiosyncratic spot proudly states: "No longer does our restaurant appear to be a hole in the wall." That's because this beloved dumpling spot has moved to a new location, a welcome improvement from the plastic tables and chairs of yore. But new polish or not, this mom-and-pop spot remains one of the best places for Chinese dumplings in town. Chefs drop by for the silken pockets made on-site, as well as fine noodles and more.

421 Spadina Ave (just north of College St.). ⓒ **416/217-2008.** www.mothersdumplings.com. Main courses C$3.50–C$8. DC, MC, V. Daily 11am–10pm. Subway: Spadina, then a streetcar south to College St.

Torito ★★ SPANISH/TAPAS   Kensington Market—and Augusta Avenue, in particular—is filled with eateries, but this one is a little gem that serves small-plate, Spanish-rooted fare that is fun and fine, like roasted quail with a pomegranate glaze, smoked trout with potato salad, and "tongue in cheek": braised tongue beside seared-and-braised cheek in a red-wine sauce. The wine list offers plenty of sherry and cava (sparkling Spanish wine), plus sangria for pairing.

276 Augusta Ave. ⓒ **647/436-5874.** www.toritotapasbar.com. Reservations not accepted. Tapas plates C$5–C$11. Mon–Sat 5:30–11pm. MC, V. Subway: Spadina, then a streetcar south to College St.

DOWNTOWN EAST

Expensive

Biff's Bistro & Wine Bar ★★ 🍴 BISTRO   The Oliver-Bonacini team that created a number of top-notch Toronto restaurants (Jump, Canoe, and Auberge du Pommier, among others) also invented this good-value, classic bistro. The setting is cozy but chic, and the menu features fine fare like pan-fried halibut covered with thinly sliced potatoes and traditional roast leg of lamb. The three-course dinner is a steal at C$33, with many choices for appetizers and mains. The good wine list focuses on Ontario. If you're heading to a Canadian Stage Company show or to the Sony Centre, you could not pick a better place to dine.

4 Front St. E. (at Yonge St.). ⓒ **416/860-0086.** www.oliverbonacini.com. Reservations strongly recommended. Main courses C$18–C$35. AE, DC, MC, V. Mon–Fri noon–2:30pm; Mon–Sat 5–10pm. Subway: Union or King.

Hiro Sushi SUSHI   Take a seat at the bar, as many sushi aficionados do, and enjoy the spectacle of watching star chef Hiro Yoshida create beauty in front of your eyes. Pick from the master chef's selection of sushi and sashimi for a memorable experience. Soups are also inspired, and tempura is light as air.

171 King St. St. E. (at Jarvis St.). ⓒ **416/304-0550.** Main courses C$20–C$30. AE, DC, MC, V. Mon–Fri noon–2:30pm; Mon–Sat 6:30–10:30pm. Subway: King.

RubyWatchCo ★★★ BISTRO   Star chef Lynn Crawford, formerly of Four Seasons in Toronto and New York, teamed with Michelin-starred chef Lola Kirk to create a unique dining experience: There's one prix-fixe dinner offered nightly with four courses—no choices—and the main ingredients are supplied by local purveyors. At C$49 a head, the price might seem high, but given that the food is stellar, the atmosphere convivial, and the chefs work attentively on all details, the risky venture is proving a hit. Don't try to visit without a reservation.

730 Queen St. E. (at Broadview Ave.) © **416/465-0100.** www.rubywatchco.ca. Reservations essential. Prix-fixe menu C$49. AE, MC, V. Tues–Sat 6–11pm. Subway: Broadview, then a streetcar south to Queen St. E.

Moderate

Gilead Bistro & Café ★★★ 👔 🎁 CAFE/BISTRO

After years of building a restaurant empire and then recently scaling back, star chef Jamie Kennedy is behind the stove at this exceptional, small, beautiful bistro. In other words, the food is sublime. Menus change daily and draw inspiration from local and seasonal ingredients. (Kennedy is a pioneering locavore.) Come for a light breakfast of fresh baked pastries and organic yogurt; at lunch, try the chef's famous, thyme-scented frites alongside impossibly light battered whitefish. At dinner, the more sophisticated menu is a showcase for Kennedy's classical French training: *gallantine* of chicken, pork confit, perfect duck breast, delicately handled vegetables, soups that sing, and fine desserts. Wines are local, including some from Kennedy's vineyard. Finding your way can be tricky: It's in a tiny alley in Corktown.

4 Gilead Place. © **647/288-0680.** www.gileadcafe.ca. Reservations accepted for dinner & for parties of 6 or more at brunch. Main courses C$6–C$26. AE, DC, MC, V. Mon 8am–5:30pm; Tues–Sat 8am–11pm; Sun 10am–3pm. Subway: King, then a streetcar east to Trinity St. & walk 1 block east to Gilead Place.

Edward Levesque's Kitchen ★★ BISTRO

An early arrival to the now-popular, once-empty Leslieville, this casual diner and bistro emphasizes local and organic products that up the quality overall. The burgers are good and are made fresh as are the generous salads; breakfasts are excellent, including eggs poached in tomato sauce and fine frittatas. Bistro fare includes succulent leg of lamb, veggie risotto, and lovely desserts, including house-made pies.

1290 Queen St. E. © **416/465-3600.** www.edwardlevesque.ca. Reservations accepted for dinner. Main courses C$15–C$24. AE, MC, V. Sat & Sun 9am–3pm; Thurs & Fri 11:30am–2:30pm; Tues–Sat 5:30–10pm. Subway: Queen, then a streetcar east to Leslie St.

Tomi-Kro MEDITERRANEAN/ASIAN

Another Leslieville neighborhood haunt, this warm and friendly spot serves up fine Mediterranean-Asian fusion fare. John Coronius, a former partner in Lolita's Lust, named this (in Greek) "the little place." A bold sense of fun greets you at the door: lamps covered in hearts, blaring music, and nonsense declarations on the menu. The food, thankfully, is usually more serious. Pairings include octopus with sake.

1214 Queen St. E. (at Leslie St.). © **416/463-6677.** Main courses C$18–C$26. AE, DC, MC, V. Mon–Wed 6–10pm; Thurs–Sat 6–11pm. Subway: Queen, then a streetcar east to Leslie St.

Starfish SEAFOOD

Toronto has a thing for bivalves: There's a wealth of excellent oyster houses around town. Owner Patrick McMurray is a world-champion oyster-shucker, and he knows his goods. Stop by for some beautiful oysters or sample the excellent fish and chips, perfect prawns, or more substantial fare like poached and grilled fish and seafood. Beers and wines are well selected, and the ambiance is cheerful.

100 Adelaide St. E. (at Church St.). © **416/366-7827.** www.starfishoysterbed.com. Main courses C$18–C$35. AE, DC, MC, V. Mon–Fri noon–3pm; Mon–Sat 5–11pm. Subway: King.

Inexpensive

Mi Mi Restaurant VIETNAMESE   Authentic Vietnamese is the name of the game at this family-run spot, where locals go for fine barbecued meats, delicate seafood, well-done rice and noodle dishes, fine *pho* soups, and inspired rice rolls. The vibe is fun and relaxed; it may take a while to get a seat or for dishes to arrive, but it's worth the wait.

688 Gerrard St. E. (at Broadview Ave.). *C* **416/778-5948.** Main courses C$5–C$17. No credit cards. Mon, Tues, Thurs & Fri 10am–10pm; Wed noon–10pm; Sat & Sun 10am–10:30pm. Subway: Broadview, then a streetcar south to Gerrard St.

MIDTOWN

Very Expensive

C5 ★★★ BISTRO/CANADIAN   The renovation of the Royal Ontario Museum remains controversial, but there's little argument that this beautiful restaurant, which is located on the top level and is headed by chef Ted Corrado, is worth a visit. The skylights and crisscrossing window segments provide a gorgeous view of the city. More importantly, the modern and chic dining room is host to fine dining with a distinct local flavor.

At the Royal Ontario Museum, 100 Queen's Park. *C* **416/586-7928.** www.c5restaurant.ca. Reservations recommended for dinner. Main courses C$26–C$45. AE, DC, MC, V. Tues–Sat 11:30am–2:30pm; Thurs–Sat 5:30–10pm. Subway: Museum or Bay.

Mistura ★★★ ITALIAN   Owner-chef Massimo Capra, with his handlebar moustache and million-watt smile, is a fixture around town. With partner Paolo Paolini he runs one of the city's best Italian restaurants. The risottos are, for starters, quite perfect, which is a testament to the kitchen's talent. There are handmade pastas, such as buckwheat noodles with pulled duck *ragu,* and entrees, including a C$56 Kobe beef steak, are top-notch. Sexy in decor, the place is great for romantic dinners, but it also caters to business clientele and family affairs. Service is pro, the wine list a lesson in fine Italian vintages (with a lot of New World wines, too). Upstairs is the more modest Sopra Supper Lounge with equally fine fare and often live music.

265 Davenport Rd. *C* **416/515-0009.** www.mistura.ca. Reservations recommended. Main courses C$22–C$56. AE, DC, MC, V. Mon–Wed 5:30–10pm; Thurs–Sat 5:30–11pm. Subway: Bay.

Expensive

earth ★★★ BISTRO   Globe Bistro's (see p. 111) team has moved to Rosedale, and the news is good: Prices are trimmed, and the attractive dining room and lounge are hopping with locals who love chef Kevin McKenna's culinary talent and owner Ed Ho's gracious touch. Together, they share a serious commitment to local foods, so produce is local and seasonal. Meats are sourced from nearby farms and butchered on-site, and you can order your flesh by the ounce. Smart. The wood-burning oven is used to cook beautiful flatbreads and more, including a scrumptious suckling pig. A long list of wines by the glass, some local, and homey desserts round out the experience.

1055 Yonge St. (at Roxborough St. E.). *C* **416/551-9890.** www.globeearth.ca. Reservations essential. Main courses C$17–C$25. AE, DC, MC, V. Mon–Fri 11:30am–11pm; Sat & Sun 11am–11pm. Subway: Rosedale.

Pangaea ★★★ INTERNATIONAL   In a neighborhood with few good places to eat—it's all about work or shopping here—this truly delightful, high-end restaurant hops with chic regulars at lunch and dinner. Open for 15 years, the chef/co-owner team of Martin Kouprie and Peter Geary deliver consistent elegance with fine food, attentive service, and a stellar cellar. The tone of the place is muted, even conservative, but behind the scenes, Kouprie's adventurous streak makes for an unusual selection of wild foods; think wild-caught fish (the restaurant is certified by Ocean Wise for its sustainable practices), wild mushrooms, wild berries—whatever is in season and inspires the chef.

1221 Bay St. ⓒ **416/920-2323.** www.pangaearestaurant.com. Reservations recommended. Main courses C$29–C$44. AE, DC, MC, V. Mon–Sat 11:30am–11:30pm. Subway: Bay.

Moderate

Bar Mercurio ★★ FRENCH   There's something quintessentially Italian about this casual *trattoria* (it's not a bar) that stays open from breakfast through to late suppers. You can come for an espresso and brioche, return for excellent pizzas made in the wood-burning oven at lunch and—why not?—stroll back for dinner and sample the signature beef medallion with crab or some fine pastas and salads. Whatever time of day, linger on the noisy patio or inside (often equally boisterous); take your time. Across the street is the stylish (and more subdued) L'Espresso, good for brunch and a great deal for lunch.

270 Bloor St. W. (at St. George St.). ⓒ **416/960-38770.** Main courses C$22–C$32. AE, MC, V. Mon–Sat 7am–11pm. Subway: St. George.

Jacques Bistro du Parc ★ FRENCH   It's a rarity: a Yorkville restaurant that has nothing trendy or pretentious about it. Husband-and-wife Jacques and Martine Sorin have been faithfully running this charming little brasserie for 33 years, and little has changed, or indeed, has needed to. The omelets are perfectly cooked and properly buttery, salads are fresh and generous (particularly the niçoise), and quiches are very good, too. On a bitter day, the French onion soup is as warm and welcoming as the place itself.

126A Cumberland St. ⓒ **416/961-1893.** www.jacquesbistro.com. Reservations recommended at lunch & on weekends. Main courses C$16–C$32. AE, MC, V. Mon–Sat 11:30am–3pm & 5–10:30pm. Subway: Bay.

Loire ★★★ FRENCH   For awhile, this pretty bistro was too hot to handle: It was tough to get in, and sometimes service came with an attitude. But things have lightened up, and it's now a convivial spot for fine and sometimes inventive French fare. Chef Jean-Charles Dupoire and top sommelier Sylvain Brissonet are clearly enjoying their hard-earned accolades. Both hail from the Loire region, so expect French classics and plenty of beautiful wines and perfect pairings. Dupoire is stretching a bit, adding fusion touches to standards, and to good ends. Lake Erie whitefish comes with a chili-cornmeal crust and a garlic confit, lemon polenta, and salsa *verde*. Regulars opt for the burgers, lamb, or beef.

119 Harbord St. ⓒ **416/850-8330.** www.loirerestaurant.ca. Reservations recommended. Main courses C$17–C$27. AE, MC, V. Tues–Fri noon–2:30pm; Tues–Sat 5:30–10pm. Subway: Spadina, then the LRT south to Harbord St.

Where to Dine in Midtown & Uptown

Heath St. W

↑ *To inset area*

Heath St. E

🔷24

Rose Park Dr.

St. Clair Ave. E.

🔷30

Briar Hill Ave. 🔷29 Sherwood Ave.

🔷28 Keewatin Ave.

Ⓣ **ST. CLAIR**

ST. MICHAELS CEMETERY

Rosehill Ave.

Glenrose Ave.

Inglewood Dr.

Erskine Ave.

Broadway Ave.

Duplex Ave.

Yonge St.

David Balfour Park

Mt. Pleasant Rd.

Garfield Ave.

Roehampton Ave.

Rosedale Heights Dr.

Yonge St.

Walker Ave.

Summerhill Ave.

SUMMERHILL

Ⓣ

Summerhill Ave.

EGLINTON Ⓣ Eglinton Ave.

🔷27

Conacher Park

Douglas Dr.

Rosedale Park

Soudan Ave.

🔷26 Hillsdale Ave.

Manor Rd.

Marlborough Pl.

🔷23

Rowanwood

Roxborough Dr.

| 0 | 200 yds |
| 0 | 200 m |

Belsize Dr.

🔷25

🔷22

🔷21

Roxborough St. E

ROSEDALE

Ramsden Park

Ⓣ

Crescent Rd.

Glen Rd.

Belmont St.

South Dr.

Craigleigh Gardens

Scollard St.

Bay St.

Church St.

Rosedale Valley Rd.

Mt. Pleasant Rd.

Sherbourne St. N.

Elm Ave.

Maple Ave.

St.

Ⓣ🔷17 Ⓣ **BLOOR-YONGE**

BAY Ⓣ

Dale Ave.

Bloor St. E

SHERBOURNE Ⓣ

🔷19 Hayden St.

Charles St.

Howard St.

🔷18

St. Mary St.

Huntley St.

Sherbourne St.

Isabella St.

St. James Ave.

Gloucester St.

Earl St.

Yonge St.

St. Nicholas St.

Jarvis St.

CHURCH AND WELLESLEY

Wellesley St. E

Ⓣ **WELLESLEY**

Bleecker St.

Parliament St.

Rose Ave.

Breadalbane St.

Maitland St.

Homewood Ave.

Grosvenor St. Alexander St.

Grenville St. Wood St.

🔷20

Maple Leaf Gardens

CABBAGETOWN

COLLEGE Ⓣ

Mutual St.

Carlton St.

Granby St.

Allan Gardens

| Point of Interest | ⬜ |
| TTC Subway | —Ⓣ— |

Gerrard St. W

Yonge St.

Church St.

Gerrard St. E

| 0 | 1/4 mi |
| 0 | 0.25 km |

◀

Elm St.

7 West Café **18**
Auberge du Pommier **30**
Bar Mercurio **10**
C5 **13**
Camros Organic Eatery **19**
Caplansky's **9**
Cava **24**
earth **22**
Ezra's Pound **5**
Gallery Grill **14**
Grano **25**
Hair of the Dog **20**
Hannah's Kitchen **27**
Jacques Bistro du Parc **16**
Lalibela **3**
Loire **8**
Lolo **29**
Messis **7**
Mistura **11**
Nataraj **6**
North 44 **28**
Pain Perdu **1**
Pangaea **17**
Patachou **2** & **23**
Pho Hung **12**
Rebel House **21**
Sam James Coffee Bar **4**
Scaramouche **15**
Zucca Trattoria **26**

Messis ★★ 🍴 BISTRO/INTERNATIONAL   Nearly 20 years old, this simple bistro is Eugene Shewchuk's vision realized: he wanted to create an accessible and pleasant spot with good food and fair prices, a place where cooks can happily eat. The menu changes frequently, keeping as its mainstays Italian pastas and Mediterranean meat dishes, and ranging into Asia, too. Thin-crust pizzas are kept simple, and mains tend to stick to a small selection of two meats, one fish. It's all very good. To boot, it was one of the first fine restaurants along the Harbord Street strip, which now has good options from one block to the next. The California-dominated wine list is as reasonably priced as the food.

97 Harbord St. ✆ **416/920-2186.** www.messis.ca. Reservations accepted. Main courses C$13–C$25. AE, MC, V. Sun–Thurs 5:30–10pm; Fri & Sat 5:30–11pm. Subway: Spadina, then the LRT south to Harbord St.

Inexpensive

Caplansky's 🎒 ☺ DELICATESSEN   Montréal's smoked meat is rightfully famous. Now, Toronto has a fantastic version to call its own. Zane Caplansky's fatty, um, marbled pastrami-on-rye is the main attraction: The hand-cut slices of pink, salty goodness are also featured in hash browns, with eggs, in a burger, and numerous other worthy ways. Choose your fat content: lean, medium, or full-on. Students and profs, foodies and families all make pilgrimages. There are other deli delights at this spacious new spot with a great patio. Try the pickled tongue, the lox, or if you're feeling sanctimonious, the salad (protein provided by only chick peas).The kids menu includes kosher hot dogs.

356 College St. W. ✆ **416/500-3852.** http://caplanskys.com. Main courses C$10–C$13. V. Sun–Tues 10am–10pm; Wed–Sat 10am–11pm. Subway: Osgoode, then the College streetcar west to Brunswick Ave.

Camros Organic Eatery 🎒 HEALTH FOOD/LIGHT FARE/VEGETARIAN Yonge and Bloor streets are a major intersection, yet the food options nearby are mostly dreadful; in other words, mostly fast-food chains. But this terrific little find is a great alternative. Saffron and cinnamon scent the air: a signal to the fact this is Persian cuisine. The emphasis is on health-conscious eating; every dish is vegetarian and made from certified organic produce. Try the cabbage roll stuffed with nutty brown rice, bright peppermint, sweet tomatoes, and tarragon; or the *ghorme sabzi,* a satisfying savory stew of kidney beans and spinach. There's more to love about this place, including comprehensive ingredient lists to help people with food allergies and takeout containers that are 100% biodegradable.

25 Hayden St. ✆ **416/960-0723.** www.camroseatery.com. Reservations not accepted. 2-item combo C$7.50. MC, V. Mon–Fri 11:30am–7:30pm. Subway: Yonge/Bloor.

Lalibela ☺ ETHIOPIAN   This is delicious Ethiopian cuisine with plenty of vegetarian options, rich with flavor and a friendly vibe, too. It's a winning combination; little wonder a second location has opened up (1405 Danforth Ave.; ✆ **416/645-0486**). If you don't know your *yemiser wat* from your *asa gulashe,* have no fear: The staff will guide you to what you're looking for and prepare custom tasting platters. It's great for kids, too, with a special menu of small tasting portions or, for fussy eaters, mac-and-cheese and fries.

869 Bloor St. W. ✆ **416/535-6615.** www.lalibelaethiopianrestaurant.com. Main courses C$5–C$12. V. Daily 10am–2am. Subway: Ossington, then walk 1 block east.

Nataraj ★ INDIAN   There's usually a bit of a wait for a table, especially at dinnertime—Nataraj's cuisine is popular with Annex residents and university students given its good value and better-than-fair Northern Indian menus. The decor is tired, but this isn't a place to linger anyway. Line up, sit down, order curries, tandoori chicken, rich veggie dishes such as the *chana masala* (chickpeas cooked with potatoes, tomatoes, onions, and spices) and the *saag paneer* (house-made cottage cheese cooked in onion and spinach), and be on your merry way. The tandoor-baked breads are good for scooping up the special relishes, such as the *kachumbor* (cucumber, tomato, and onion marinated in lime juice).

394 Bloor St. W. ✆ **416/928-2925.** Reservations not accepted. Main courses C$9–C$13. AE, DC, MC, V. Mon–Fri noon–2:30pm; daily 5–10:30pm. Subway: Spadina.

Pho Hung VIETNAMESE   Students love the generous portions and mainstream tastes of this bright Vietnamese soup-and-noodle spot. Favorites include the lemongrass-scented broth, beef noodle soup, filling rice dishes, spring rolls, and the Vietnamese milkshakes. There is a second location in Chinatown, at 350 Spadina Ave. (✆ **416/593-4274**).

200 Bloor St. W. ✆ **416/963-5080.** Main courses C$8–C$12. V. Mon–Sat 11am–10pm. Subway: St. George or Museum.

THE DANFORTH/THE EAST END

The general theme along the Danforth has long been Greek, although today there is more variety: good pubs, bars, restaurants, and lounges line the busy thoroughfare. You can still come for good and middling (but cheap) Greek, too.

Expensive

Globe Bistro ★★ BISTRO   There's a chic dining room, a cool bar, a breezy patio, and some very fine cooking at this popular neighborhood bistro. Owner Ed Ho and chef Kevin McKenna have created a go-to destination with staying power, in part due to a great wine cellar and generous deals, such as half-price bottles on Sunday. The vibe is fun, the dishes sometimes stellar, such as the Muscovy duck breast and elk loin. You can also make a meal of the many tantalizing starters. There is a definite local-and-seasonal bent that is genuine.

24 Danforth Ave. ✆ **416/466-2000.** www.globebistro.com. Reservations recommended. Main courses C$19–C$29. AE, DC, MC, V. Mon–Fri 11:30am–2pm; Sun 11am–2pm; daily 6–11pm. Subway: Broadview.

Lolita's Lust & the Chinchilla Lounge ★ BISTRO   Relaxed, fun, and accessible, this restaurant and lounge offers a break from the Danforth's Greek theme with pretty good food. Lolita's Burger has a reputation as irresistible: bacon, white cheddar, and caramelized onions top a mile-high beef patty. Desserts are popular, too, with safe bets like bread pudding with caramel and chocolate sauce. The upstairs Chinchilla Lounge is often booked for private parties, but when it's not, it's a hopping spot for martinis.

513 Danforth Ave. ✆ **416/465-1751.** www.lolitaslust.ca. Reservations recommended. Main courses C$15–C$29. AE, MC, V. Daily 5pm–2am. Subway: Chester.

Myth ★ GREEK/MEDITERRANEAN West Coast meets Mediterranean in this trendy, noisy, bar/restaurant where Greek standards are complemented with plenty of fish offerings. Pizzas—topped with spiced lamb, zucchini, and onion purée—are also on offer. But it's not all about the food: Screens play mythic movies, and as the night goes on, the crowd gathers at the bar, where a DJ starts spinning at 11pm.

417 Danforth Ave. (btw. Logan & Chester aves.). ✆ **416/461-8383.** torontomyth.blogspot.com. Reservations recommended. Main courses C$11–C$29. AE, MC, V. Mon–Wed 5–11pm; Thurs–Sun noon–11pm; bar daily till 2am. Subway: Chester.

Moderate

Allen's ★★ AMERICAN This time-honored pub, burger joint, and casual dining room takes its name and inspiration from the institution in New York City. Take note of the excellent beef, lamb, and pork—the heart of any great burger—which is sourced from local farms and then butchered and ground on-site. Pastas, salads, and mains are all consistently good. Brunch, especially when the lovely patio is open, is a treat. Desserts are comfort food: pies and homey sweets. The selection of beers—on tap and in bottles—is another draw. The fine wine list is focused on local.

143 Danforth Ave. (at Broadview Ave.). ✆ **416/463-3086.** www.allens.to. Main courses C$10–C$26. AE, DC, MC, V. Mon–Fri 11:30am–1am; Sat & Sun 11am–1am. Subway: Broadview.

Avli ★ GREEK Always noisy, occasionally raucous, this taverna serves up some of the best Greek standards on the Danforth—non-greasy, thoughtfully prepared, and carefully seasoned. *Meze* starters are de rigueur: *kopanisti* (spicy feta with peppers) and hummus, for those who want cold food; grilled octopus and steamed mussels, for those who like it hot. The half chicken stuffed with cashews, dates, apples, and rice is exquisite, and the meat *moussaka* is the best around. Like the menu, the wine list is both extensive and very reasonably priced.

401 Danforth Ave. ✆ **416/461-9577.** www.avlirestaurant.com. Reservations recommended. Main courses C$12–C$22. AE, DC, MC, V. Daily noon–midnight. Subway: Chester.

Pan on the Danforth ★ GREEK Pan feels like a spot for a celebration: Staff are friendly; weekend nights, in particular, are busy and humming; and the vibe is all Mediterranean warmth. This long-established eatery serves Greek classics—dips and starters are especially conventional—but the quality is good and often a notch above competitors on the strip. Portions are generous, and fish and lamb dominate. The well-chosen wine list favors the New World. The crowd is fairly sophisticated, which may explain the cryptic message over the bar: YOU'VE DONE IT ALREADY. On weekend evenings, diners are treated to live music: traditional Greek bouzouki on Fridays and jazz piano on Saturdays (there's also a belly dancer who turns up for performances on other evenings, too).

516 Danforth Ave. ✆ **416/466-8158.** www.panonthedanforth.com. Reservations recommended. Main courses C$16–C$25. AE, MC, V. Sun–Thurs noon–11pm; Fri & Sat noon–midnight. Subway: Chester or Pape.

Inexpensive

Astoria Shish Kebob House GREEK If you're wandering around the Danforth, choosing a restaurant will seem like a daunting task. There are so many, and their menus are very similar. This restaurant is a cut above. A casual spot popular with area residents for years, it delivers with a meat-heavy menu with a love of

Where to Dine on the Danforth & The East End

Allen's **1**
Astoria Shish Kebob House **5**
Avli **4**
Dark Horse Espresso Bar **11**
Edward Levesque's Kitchen **14**
Globe Bistro **2**
Lolita's Lust &
    the Chinchilla Lounge **9**
Mezes **7**
Mi Mi Restaurant **10**
Myth **6**
Pan on the Danforth **8**
RubyWatchCo **12**
Seven Numbers **3**
Tomi-Kro **13**

broiling—beef, lamb, chicken, and seafood all fare well under the heat. Vegetarians can try the fair souvlaki or *moussaka*. Expect a wait if you arrive after 8:30pm or so on weekends.

390 Danforth Ave. ℭ **416/463-2838.** www.astoriashishkebobhouse.com. Reservations accepted on weekdays. Main courses C$10–C$17. AE, MC, V. Mon–Wed, Fri & Sat 11am–1am; Thurs & Sun 11am–midnight. Subway: Chester.

Mezes GREEK   This sophisticated space doles out exactly what it promises. *Mezes* are light snacks meant to keep you going until it's time for dinner. Still, it's worth spoiling your appetite to indulge here (especially given the often pedestrian offerings on the strip). Choices range from grilled calamari and octopus to spicy eggplant dip and leek pie. Save room for the honey-sweet baklava. Bonus: There's a heated patio, so you can dine al fresco, even when the weather is less than balmy.

456 Danforth Ave. ℭ **416/778-5150.** www.mezes.ca. Reservations accepted till 7:30pm. Appetizers C$4–C$10. AE, MC, V. Mon–Thurs 11am–midnight; Fri & Sat 11am–1am; Sun noon–midnight. Subway: Chester.

Seven Numbers ITALIAN   This super-popular, Italian family *trattoria* began life on Eglinton Avenue West, and then took hold on the Danforth. So, whether east or west, everyone gets to enjoy the generous, well-prepared and mamma-inspired fare such as grilled veggies, fresh pastas, flavorful salads, and Italian standards like *bistecca*. Rosa Marinuzzi runs the business with her sons. The cheerful atmosphere is sincere, not a show: pure, simple fun.

307 Danforth Ave. (at Broadview Ave.). ℭ **416/322-5183.** www.sevennumbers.com. Main courses C$7–C$17. AE, DC, MC, V. Tues–Sat 5–11pm; Sun 5–10pm. Subway: Broadview.

SLEEPLESS IN TORONTO: WHAT TO DO WHEN
midnight munchies ATTACK

We've all heard of cities that never sleep. Well, Toronto isn't one of them. The city's restaurant scene starts to doze off around 10pm, even on weekends. Sure, there are 24-hour doughnut shops, but if you're looking for something more substantial, try one of the following late-night options.

Hair of the Dog. 425 Church St. (ℭ **416/964-2708**). This sounds like a bar, but it's a low-key restaurant in Toronto's Gay Village that's open every night until 2am. The eclectic menu includes plenty of seafood and Asian-inspired dishes.

Rodney's Oyster House. Open until 1am 6 nights a week, with the city's freshest oysters served in a relaxed, informal restaurant (just remember the patio closes before the rest of the restaurant does). See p. 102.

7 West Café. 7 Charles St. W. (ℭ **416/928-9041**). Open 24 hours a day. Delish sandwiches and pasta platters hit the spot. Those with serious sugar cravings can indulge in cakes and pies from several of the city's best bakers.

If you're on the Danforth, you're in luck: Many of the terrific Greek tavernas and restaurants there, such as **Myth** (p. 112), stay open until the wee hours, even on weeknights.

UPTOWN

This area is too large to be considered a neighborhood, stretching as it does from north of Davenport Road to Steeles Avenue. While it doesn't have the concentration of restaurants that the downtown area enjoys, a number of stellar options make the trip north worthwhile.

Very Expensive

Auberge du Pommier ★★★ 🎁 FRENCH Don't have time to drop by your French country house this weekend? Then this cozy, fine-dining room that exudes Provençal-style charm is a ready alternative. Chef Jason Bartenger combines classical French technique with the best of Canadian ingredients. Service is equally refined, as is the extensive wine list. Creamy lobster and white-bean soup, and baked artichokes stuffed with French goat cheese are lovely starters. Entrees, such as pan-seared scallops with braised oxtail in a cabernet *jus* keep up the pace. Crème brûlée isn't always on the dessert menu (which changes with the season, just like the regular menu), but be sure to order it when available.

4150 Yonge St. ✆ **416/222-2220.** www.oliverbonacini.com. Reservations strongly recommended. Main courses C$36–C$44. AE, DC, DISC, MC, V. Mon–Fri 11:45am–2:30pm; Mon–Thurs 5–9pm; Fri & Sat 5:30–9:30pm. Subway: York Mills.

North 44 ★★★ INTERNATIONAL The soft lighting and strategically situated mirrors wrap the dining room—and its occupants—in a lovely glow. Upscale regulars succumb to the seduction of a three-course meal. Celebrity chef Mark McEwan's menu, which changes with the seasons, borrows from Mediterranean, American, and Asian sources, with inspired results. On the list of main courses, you might find grilled veal tenderloin with orange peppercorns, toasted barley, and root veggies, or roasted Muscovy duck breast with orange-soy marinade and foie gras. There are always a few pasta and pizza choices. The wine list is loftily priced and built to suit the high-end fare. Service is seamless.

2537 Yonge St. ✆ **416/487-4897.** www.north44restaurant.com. Reservations required. Main courses C$31–C$53. AE, DC, MC, V. Mon–Sat 5–11pm. Subway: Eglinton.

Scaramouche ★★★ 🎁 INTERNATIONAL Tucked into a tony midtown apartment building with beautiful views over the city, Scaramouche isn't easy to find. But it's worth the effort. Chef Keith Froggett and maitre d' Carl Corte have been quietly perfecting one of the city's finest restaurants for more than 25 years. Understated and elegant, the menus are laden with luxe ingredients like caviar, foie gras, truffles, and oysters; main dishes include venison loin wrapped in smoked bacon and a rich, red-wine glaze. Top pastry chef Joanne Yolles has returned after years at Pangaea (see p. 107), so the sweets are equally stunning. The wine list has a broad reach, and there's a nice selection of cognacs. The formal dining room, which is best for special occasions, is complemented by the adjoining casual pasta bar and grill.

1 Benvenuto Place (off Avenue Rd.). ✆ **416/961-8011.** www.scaramoucherestaurant.com. Reservations required. Main courses C$34–C$47. AE, DC, MC, V. Dining room Mon–Sat 5:30–10pm; pasta bar Mon–Fri 5:30–10:30pm, Sat 5:30–11pm. Subway: St. Clair, then a streetcar west to Avenue Rd. & walk 4 blocks south to Edmund Ave.

Expensive

Cava ★★★ SPANISH/TAPAS Chef Chris McDonald is a local legend for his culinary prowess, which was honed at his formal (and former) Avalon restaurant. Now with partner and chef Doug Penfold, he is the driving force at Cava, where inventive, small-plate dishes—sometimes daring, but always delicious—offer Iberian-inspired menus with salt cod cakes, beef cheeks, and more. House-cured charcuterie is not to be missed: think smoky chorizo and dried salamis, plus Iberico ham hand-cut to order (a skill in itself). There are more than 20 well-selected wines offered by the glass for pairing. The vibe is delightfully low-key, although professionalism informs everything from service to sweets. And speaking of desserts, Xococava, next door, is worth a visit on its own for rich, artisan chocolates, silken ice creams, and more, all made on-site.

1560 Yonge St. ② **416/979-9918.** www.cavarestaurant.ca. Reservations strongly recommended. Tapas plates C$3.50–C$18. AE, DC, MC, V. Daily 5–10pm. Subway: St. Clair.

Moderate

Grano ★★ ☺ ITALIAN While Toronto has no shortage of Italian eateries, few spots have as much ambience as Grano. Thanks to owners Robert and Lucia Martella—he's in the front; she's in the kitchen below—this is an institution for celebrating the joys of Italian culture and Canada's inspired Italo riches. The busy *trattoria* sprawls over several dining areas, including a small and quiet courtyard at the back that is heavenly on sunny days. This high-energy spot attracts couples, friends, and families with *bambini* in tow. The cooking is hearty, with lovely pastas, breads baked on-site, tender *osso buco,* and ricotta gnocchi paired with shrimp in a white-wine sauce. A nice feature: You can order many dishes in appetizer-sized portions or more substantial portions for sharing. The desserts are a delight—you must try the white chocolate and raspberry tart at least once.

2035 Yonge St. ② **416/440-1986.** www.grano.ca. Reservations recommended. Main courses C$14–C$24. AE, DC, MC, V. Mon–Fri 9:30am–11pm; Sat 9am–11pm. Subway: Davisville or Eglinton.

Lolo ★ 🍷 BISTRO Lolo is airy and bright, with white walls and a relaxed ambience. More importantly, the menu—and the prices—are refreshingly down-to-earth. The mains are bistro classics, from the roasted Cornish hen (updated with a citrus-basil glaze) to the grilled rib-eye steak with green-peppercorn sauce and crispy frites. In addition to the a la carte menu, a prix-fixe option serves up three courses for a mere C$25. All of the desserts—including a fine lemon tart—are made on the premises.

2590 Yonge St. ② **416/483-2590.** Reservations recommended. Main courses C$15–C$25; prix-fixe menu C$25. AE, DC, MC, V. Daily noon–3pm & 5–10pm. Subway: Eglinton, then walk north 6 blocks to Albertus Ave.

Zucca Trattoria ★★★ ITALIAN Inviting in spirit and truly Italian in the kitchen, this pretty *trattoria* has been winning quiet accolades from fans for more than a decade. It's chef Andrew Milne-Allan's baby, and most nights, the chef is at the stove. Agnolotti and other fresh pastas made by the maestro are consistently great. There are meaty ragouts, poppy-seed sauces, plenty of delicate vegetables, and entrees that feature local purveyors such as the fine Cumbrae Farms. (Milne-Allan can be seen shopping at farmers markets throughout the year.) The grilled whole fish, which changes according to what's fresh, also proves a standout. Desserts are restrained and lovely.

2150 Yonge St. (at Berwick Ave.). ℂ **416/488-5774.** Reservations recommended. Main courses C$16-C$36. AE, DC, MC, V. Daily 5:30-10pm. Subway: Eglinton or Davisville.

Inexpensive

Hannah's Kitchen LIGHT FARE   National magazines and newspapers have published several of its recipes, but this cubbyhole-like eatery remains defiantly low-key. Diners seat themselves at wooden banquettes or tiny tables. The menu includes many pasta dishes, both cold (pesto *radiatore* salad with chicken and pine nuts is the top pick) and hot (the penne *arrabiata* is the spiciest in town), with three or four daily specials. Occasional forays into the exotic include a few Indonesian rice dishes and the ever-popular pad Thai. Desserts are a must, so check out the selection behind the counter on your way in.

2221 Yonge St. ℂ **416/481-0185.** Reservations not accepted. Main courses C$7-C$14. MC, V. Mon-Fri 10am-10pm. Subway: Eglinton.

Pain Perdu 🍴 BAKERY   It's a sit-down bakery and lovely daytime spot for fine quiches, cheesy sandwiches like a fine Croque Monsieur, and a wealth of lovely pastries. The owner is from the Basque region, so also expect a wicked gateaux Basque, which is a buttery, custard tart infused with anise. The namesake dish is a kind of Gallic French toast baked with cream and topped with fruit.

736 St. Clair Ave. W. (at Christie St.). ℂ **416/656-7246.** Main courses C$5-C$7. DC, MC, V. Tues-Fri 7am-7pm; Sat 7am-5pm; Sun 8am-4pm. Subway: St. Clair, then a streetcar west to Christie St.

Rebel House COMFORT FOOD/LIGHT FARE   Friendly service combines with better-than-average pub grub and an impressive selection of microbrews (almost entirely Canadian) to make for a popular neighborhood spot. In summer, the gorgeous patio is a bonus. The food isn't exotic, but it's good: The spinach and apple salad is fresh, the Québécois *poutine* fine with beer drinking, and the steak frites decent. Most main courses are priced below C$15.

1068 Yonge St. ℂ **416/927-0704.** www.rebelhouse.ca. Reservations not accepted. Main courses C$8-C$23. AE, MC, V. Restaurant Mon-Sat 11:30am-11pm, Sun 11:30am-10pm; bar Mon-Sat 11:30am-1am, Sun 11:30am-11pm. Subway: Rosedale.

OUT OF TOWN

Toronto is a sprawling city, and as it has expanded, restaurants have cropped up in formerly out-of-the-way regions. If you have a car, you might want to head out of town for some great dining just an hour or two beyond the city limits.

Very Expensive

Eigensinn Farm ★★★ 🏠 INTERNATIONAL   Michael Stadtlander is perhaps the most famous and celebrated chef working in Canada today. At this intimate dining room—which is also home to his family, including restaurant partner and wife Nobuyo—you're visiting the farmstead where much of the goods on the menu have been raised and grown. It's a singular approach (nearly 19 years running): A dozen diners gather at the table for an eight-course feast, and Michael and Nobuyo set to work on their culinary magic. Dishes include braised meats, poached fish, produce

SWEET TREATS: TORONTO'S
BEST dessert CAFES

I've got a serious sweet tooth, and to my mind, dessert should be its own food group. Here are some of the city's most delicious places to satisfy a sugar craving and do some people-watching at the same time.

Dufflet Pastries. 787 Queen St. W. ((℃ **416/504-2870**). On menus around town, you'll sometimes see mention of "desserts by Dufflet." It's an institution: popular for everything from butter tarts to berry pies or three-tiered cakes heavy with icing and rich with flavor. The cafe also serves light fare.

Patachou. 1120 Yonge St., at Roxborough St. (℃ **416/927-1105**); 835 St. Clair Ave. W. (℃ **416/927-1105**). Toronto knew little about proper French pastries when this bakery opened almost 30 years ago, but this family-owned patisserie set the bar, and it has remained unchallenged since. Croissants are chewy inside, crisp and flaky on the outside; brioche are perfect; and a range of sweets—bright fruit tarts, deep chocolate sweets like the éclair or rich opera cake—are outstanding. The

chic yet friendly cafes also serve lovely continental breakfasts and fine lunches.

Senses Bakery. 2 Queen St. E. ((℃ **416/364-7303**). The menu has some light, lunch-appropriate food, but the real draw is the divine collection of pastry confections and chocolates.

Soma Chocolate. In the Distillery District, 55 Mill St. (℃ **416/815-7662**). Owners David Castellan and wife Cynthia Leung run the best chocolatier in town. Beans are carefully sourced from far-flung locales for fair-trade and organic certifications, with taste a factor above all. Then, in this micro-factory where the process is on view, the beans are roasted, turned into paste (which is where most chocolatiers begin their work), and spun into beautiful truffles, exquisite bars, irresistible (chocolate) cakes, cookies, and more. In summer, have a gelato. In winter, don't miss the house specialty, a *bicerin* (beech-er-een) made with melted chocolate, espresso, and warm milk. There's plenty to take away, too.

rendered perfect, and more. The simplicity is deceptive; techniques are masterful. BYOB and be prepared to linger.

449357 10th Concession, Singhampton. ℃ **519/922-3128.** Reservations required; bookings need to be made months in advance. Prix fixe menu C$275. AE, DC, MC, V. Call for hours of operation.

Moderate

Ancaster Old Mill ★★ ITALIAN   The setting is lovely, so little wonder it's still a popular spot for weddings, banquets, and other events. Yet chef Jeff Crump and pastry chef Bettina Schormann have turned this old-time country spot into a go-to destination for Toronto diners who love hearty, honest fare that celebrates the best of the local season. Pigs are roasted whole, the lamb rack is quite perfect, vegetables are turned into gnocchi and rich sides, and the desserts are simply splendid.

548 Old Dundas Rd, Ancaster. ℃ **905/648-1828.** Reservations recommended. Main courses C$20–C$35. AE, MC, V. Tues–Sat 11:30am–10pm; Sun 9:30am–2:30pm & 5–9pm.

WHAT TO SEE & DO

Toronto presents a wealth of attractions, so it's best to pick a focus and stick with it. If it's simply getting to know the city, you're off to the races: There are plenty of things to do, see, and taste in the downtown core and beyond, all within reasonable reach. Many major museums, art galleries, and top attractions are downtown and situated in neighborhoods worth exploring. There's plenty in the heart of the city to keep all ages engaged, but there are day trips to consider, too: pristine waters, sublime beaches, a massive theme park, and spectacular stretches of wine country. Keep in mind that visitors in 2011 will be able to enjoy the recently renovated and expanded Art Gallery of Ontario, new five-star hotels, added attractions lakeside, and more. Other prime Toronto Attractions, such as the Royal Ontario Museum, the Gardiner Museum, and the Ontario Science Centre have already completed their renovations and are completely open to visitors again.

Some attractions can easily take up an entire day, such as the Ontario Science Centre, the Harbourfront, the Toronto Islands, and Canada's Wonderland. For less ambitious outings, explore the many parks, the thriving arts scene, or the shopping possibilities. And pack a good pair of walking shoes because the best way to appreciate Toronto is on foot.

THE TOP ATTRACTIONS

Art Gallery of Ontario ★★★ If you go to only one major attraction while you're in Toronto, let it be the AGO. Fresh from a top-to-bottom renovation—and reinvention—by Toronto son Frank Gehry, it is a

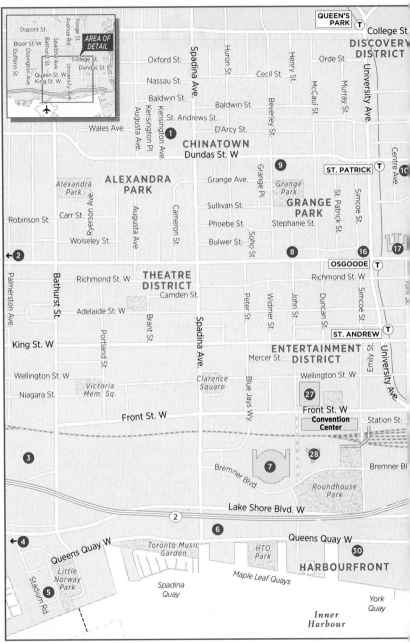

AREA OF
DETAIL

Dupont St.

Bloor St. W

Dufferin St.

Ossington Ave.

Yonge St.

Avenue Rd.

Spadina Ave.

Bathurst St.

University Ave.

College St.

Dundas St. E

Queen St. W

King St. W

Oxford St.

Spadina Ave.

Huron St.

Henry St.

Orde St.

University Ave.

QUEEN'S
PARK ⓣ

College St

DISCOVERY
DISTRICT

Nassau St.

Cecil St.

Baldwin St.

Baldwin St.

Beverley St.

McCaul St.

Murray St.

St. Andrews St.

Wales Ave.

Augusta Ave.

Kensington Pl.

Kensington Ave.

D'Arcy St.

CHINATOWN
Dundas St. W ❶

ST. PATRICK ⓣ

Centre Ave.

⑩

*Alexandra
Park*

**ALEXANDRA
PARK**

Grange Ave.

Grange Pl.

*Grange
Park*

**GRANGE
PARK**

St. Patrick St.

Simcoe St.

❾

Robinson St.

Carr St.

Ryerson Ave.

Augusta Ave.

Cameron St.

Sullivan St.

Phoebe St.

Stephanie St.

Wolseley St.

Bulwer St.

Soho St.

❽

⑯

Ⓣ

⑰

Palmerston Ave.

Bathurst St.

Richmond St. W

**THEATRE
DISTRICT**
Camden St.

Peter St.

Widmer St.

John St.

Duncan St.

OSGOODE ⓣ

Richmond St. W

Simcoe St.

❷

Adelaide St. W

Brant St.

Spadina Ave.

ST. ANDREW Ⓣ

King St. W

Portland St.

Mercer St.

**ENTERTAINMENT
DISTRICT**

Emily St.

University Ave.

Wellington St. W

*Victoria
Mem. Sq.*

*Clarence
Square*

Blue Jays Wy.

Wellington St. W

Niagara St.

❷⓻

Front St. W

Front St. W

**Convention
Center**

Station St.

❸

Bremner Blvd.

❼

❷⓼

*Roundhouse
Park*

Bremner Bl

Lake Shore Blvd. W

②

❹

Queens Quay W

*Toronto Music
Garden*

*HTO
Park*

❻

Queens Quay W

❸⓪

*Little
Norway
Park*

Stadium Rd.

❺

*Spadina
Quay*

Maple Leaf Quays

HARBOURFRONT

York
Quay

*Inner
Harbour*

Air Canada Centre **29**
Allan Gardens **11**
Art Gallery of Ontario **9**
BMO Field **4**
Campbell House **16**
Canada's Sports Hall of Fame **4**
Canadian Broadcasting
  Corporation Museum **27**
ChumCity **8**
City Hall **15**
CN Tower **28**
Design Exchange **20**
The Distillery Historic District **22**
Eaton Centre **14**
Fort York **3**
Harbourfront Centre **30**
Hockey Hall of Fame **25**
Ireland Park **5**
Kensington Market **1**
Mackenzie House **13**
Museum of Contemporary
  Canadian Art **2**
Old City Hall **18**
Ontario Place **4**
Osgoode Hall **17**
Rogers Centre **7**
Royal Bank Plaza **26**
St. James' Cathedral **21**
St. Lawrence Market **23**
St. Michael's Cathedral **12**
Sony Centre **24**
Textile Museum of Canada **10**
Toronto Dominion Centre **19**
Toronto Islands **31**
Toronto Music Garden **6**
Trinity-Bellwoods **2**

Cathedral ✝
Point of Interest ▢
Post Office ⊠
TTC Subway —Ⓣ—

0 ——— 1/4 mi
0 ——— 0.25 km

wonder. Gehry's vision is throughout; the fabulously twisted floating staircase is especially impressive. There are skylights in some rooms, adjusted every day to best display the works (to spectacular effect with Lawren Harris's paintings of the arctic). Gorgeous Galleria Italia lets you view the scene on Dundas Street down below while you take a rest from the art. Most of all, there's a dramatic increase in the amount of viewing space. Gehry's work is inspired yet practical, a tough act to follow.

Local media magnate the late Ken Thomson gave his beautiful and extensive collection of paintings, carved miniatures, medieval triptychs, and model ships to the AGO. The Thomson Collection, which includes an unparalleled collection of great Canadian art and international drawings such as Peter Paul Reubens' masterpiece, *The Massacre of the Innocents,* is a must. (One note: The late Lord Thomson believed that art should be allowed to speak for itself, in other words, unencumbered by the usual identifying labels. For some, this is an irritant, but for others, it improves the experience.)

And there's far more to see. The AGO's European collection ranges from the 14th century to the French Impressionists and beyond. The Canadian collection is strong, particularly the paintings by the Group of Seven and the extensive collection of Inuit art. The AGO is also famous for its collection of Henry Moore sculptures, which number more than 800. (The artist gave them to Toronto as a tribute to local citizens' enthusiasm for his work: Public donations brought his sculpture *The Archer* to decorate Nathan Phillips Square after politicians refused to support it.) In one room, 14 or so of his large works are displayed, while some of Moore's largest sculptures sit outside the museum, where everyone can appreciate them.

317 Dundas St. W. (btw. McCaul & Beverley sts.). ☎ **416/977-0414.** www.ago.net. Admission C$20 adults, C$16 seniors, C$11 students (w/ID) & children 6–17, free for children 5 & under; free admission Wed 6–8:30pm. Tues & Thurs–Sun 10am–5:30pm; Wed 10am–8:30pm. Closed Jan 1 & Dec 25. Subway: St. Patrick.

CN Tower ★ ☺   The CN Tower may no longer be the world's tallest freestanding structure (thanks, Burj Dubai), but Torontonians, who have long disparaged the tower, have come to admire it, partly because the new LED lights on it look glorious after sundown. However you approach Toronto, the first thing you see is this slender structure. Glass-walled elevators glide up the 553m (1,814-ft.) tower, first stopping at the 346m-high (1,135-ft.) Look Out level. (The truly fearless can ride up in the vertiginous glass-*floored* elevator, which the CN Tower opened in 2008.) Walk down one level to experience the Glass Floor, which is great for a dizzying face-plant: Through it, you can see all the way down to street level. Take comfort: The floor won't break. The glass can withstand the weight of 14 adult hippos.

 A Tiny Gem of a Gallery

The Ontario College of Art and Design (OCAD), located steps away from the AGO, has its own gallery. Called the **OCAD Professional Gallery,** it was launched in 2007 to explore the connections between art and design. So far, the tiny 111-sq.-m (1,195-sq.-ft.) space has shown work by Canadian Karim Rashid (famous for his stylish housewares and table accessories) among others. Located at 100 McCaul St., the gallery is open from Wednesday to Friday 1 to 7pm, and on weekends from noon to 6pm. There is no admission fee. For more information, call ☎ **416/977-6000** or visit www.ocad.ca.

Above the Look Out is the world's highest public observation gallery, the Skypod, 447m (1,467 ft.) above the ground. From here, on a clear day, the sweeping vista stretches to Niagara Falls, 161km (100 miles) south, and to Lake Simcoe, 193km (120 miles) north. Atop the tower sits a 102m (335-ft.) antenna mast erected over 31 weeks with the aid of a giant Sikorsky helicopter. It took 55 lifts to complete the operation.

The tower attractions are often revamped. Some perennial draws are the IMAX Theatre and the flight simulators. A series of interactive displays showcases the CN Tower, along with such forerunners as the Eiffel Tower and the Empire State Building.

301 Front St. W. ℂ **416/868-6937.** www.cntower.ca. Look Out & Glass Floor C$23 adults, C$21 seniors, C$15 children 4–12; Total Tower Experience (Look Out, Glass Floor, Skypod, IMAX & 2 rides) C$35 all ages. Daily 9am–11pm (shorter hours in winter). Closed Dec 25. Subway: Union, then walk west on Front St.

The Distillery District ★★★   Although founded in 1832, it wasn't until 2003 that this 45-building complex was reinvented as an historic district. This was once home to the Gooderham-Worts Distillery, which was Canada's largest distilling company in the 19th century. A miller named James Worts, who emigrated from Scotland in 1831, built the first building on the site: a windmill intended to power a grain mill (the millstone he brought with him is still on display). His brother-in-law, William Gooderham, soon joined him in the business. In 1834, Worts's wife died in childbirth, and in despair, Worts drowned himself in the mill's well. Gooderham took over the business and adopted Worts's son, who eventually joined the business.

Tough Enough

To resist the elements, the CN Tower is built of sturdy stuff—contoured, reinforced concrete covered with thick, glass-reinforced plastic—and designed to keep ice accumulation to a minimum. The structure can withstand high winds, snow, ice, lightning, and earth tremors.

The complex is an outstanding example of industrial design from the 19th century. Much of the construction here was done with Toronto's own red brick; you'll see it in everything from the buildings to the streets themselves. One exception is the mill building, which was built out of stone.

The Distillery District has launched an ambitious program of events throughout the year, including a blues festival, a jazz festival, and an outdoor art exhibition; also, a farmers' market takes place on summer Sundays. See chapter 10 for the performing-arts venues and troupes based in the district.

55 Mill St. ℂ **416/367-1800.** www.thedistillerydistrict.com. Free admission. Subway: King, then a streetcar east to Parliament St.

Harbourfront Centre ★ ☺   This cultural center encompasses a 38-hectare (94-acre) strip of waterfront land, once-abandoned warehouses, charming piers, and an old smoke stack. The center, which opened in 1974, is a stunning urban playground and one of the most popular destinations for locals and visitors alike—a great place to spend time strolling, picnicking, gallery-hopping, biking, shopping, and sailing.

Queen's Quay, at the foot of York Street, is the first stop on the LRT line from Union Station (you can also get there in 5 min. on foot, walking south from Front St., but that requires you to go under the Gardiner Expwy.). From here, boats depart for harbor tours and ferries leave for the Toronto Islands. In this renovated warehouse,

What to See & Do in Midtown

Bata Shoe Museum **3**

Casa Loma **1**

George R. Gardiner
Museum of Ceramic Art **9**

Justina M. Barnicke Gallery
at Hart House **4**

Necropolis **12**

Ontario Legislature **7**

Osborne Collection of
Early Children's Books **6**

Queen's Park **8**

Riverdale Farm **13**

Royal Ontario Museum
(ROM) **10**

Spadina Museum Historic
House & Garden **2**

Toronto Reference Library **11**

University of Toronto
Art Centre **5**

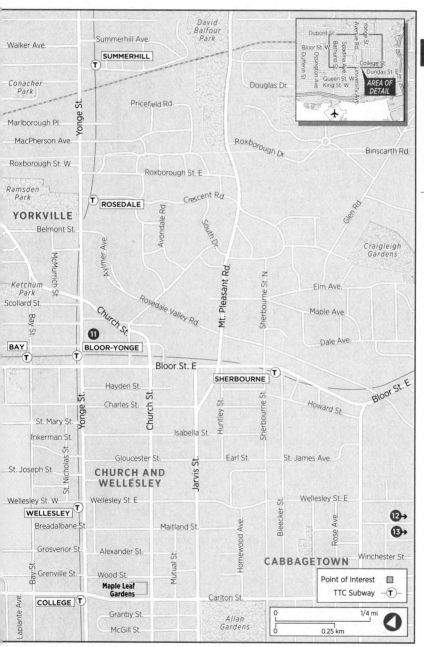

Walker Ave.

Summerhill Ave.

SUMMERHILL Ⓣ

David Balfour Park

Conacher Park

Pricefield Rd.

Douglas Dr.

Marlborough Pl.

MacPherson Ave.

Roxborough Dr.

Binscarth Rd.

Roxborough St. W

Roxborough St. E

Ramsden Park

Crescent Rd.

ROSEDALE Ⓣ

YORKVILLE

Belmont St.

Avondale Rd.

South Dr.

Craigleigh Gardens

Ketchum Park

Scollard St.

Bay St.

McMurrich St.

Aylmer Ave.

Rosedale Valley Rd.

Church St.

Mt. Pleasant Rd.

Sherbourne St. N.

Elm Ave.

Maple Ave.

Dale Ave.

Glen Rd.

BAY Ⓣ Ⓣ

Ⓣ **BLOOR-YONGE**

⑪

Bloor St. E

Bloor St. E

SHERBOURNE Ⓣ

Hayden St.

Charles St.

Church St.

Howard St.

St. Mary St.

Inkerman St.

Huntley St.

Sherbourne St.

Yonge St.

St. Nicholas St.

Isabella St.

St. Joseph St.

Gloucester St.

Jarvis St.

Earl St.

St. James Ave.

CHURCH AND WELLESLEY

Wellesley St. W

WELLESLEY Ⓣ

Wellesley St. E

Wellesley St. E

Bleecker St.

Rose Ave.

⑫→

⑬→

Breadalbane St

Maitland St.

Grosvenor St.

Alexander St.

Mutual St.

Homewood Ave.

CABBAGETOWN

Winchester St.

Bay St.

Grenville St.

Wood St.

Maple Leaf Gardens

Point of Interest ▢

TTC Subway —Ⓣ

Laplante Ave.

COLLEGE Ⓣ

Granby St.

Carlton St.

Allan Gardens

McGill St.

0 _____ 1/4 mi
0 _____ 0.25 km

Area of Detail (inset):

Dupont St.

Bloor St. W

Dufferin St.

Ossington Ave.

Bathurst St.

Spadina Ave.

Avenue Rd.

Yonge St.

University Ave.

College St.

Dundas St. E

Queen St. W

King St. W

AREA OF DETAIL

you'll find the Premiere Dance Theatre and two floors of shops. To get something to eat, you can stay at Queen's Quay's casual Boathouse Grill or walk west to **York Quay**'s Lakeside Terrace restaurant. York Quay also has a decent art gallery with rotating art installations. There's an information booth with a calendar of events, also available online (www.harbourfrontcentre.com).

Harbourfront has several venues devoted to the arts. The **Power Plant** is a contemporary art gallery with some excellent and often edgy shows; behind it is the **Du Maurier Theatre Centre.** At the **Craft Studio,** you can watch artisans blow glass, throw pots, and make silk-screen prints. You can buy their works at **Bounty Contemporary Canadian Craft Shop.** The **Artists' Gardens** features outdoor gardens created by local and visiting landscape architects, designers, and other artists.

More than 4,000 events take place annually at Harbourfront, the biggest of which are two literary gems: the **Harbourfront Reading Series** in June and the **International Festival of Authors** in October (see "Calendar of Events," in chapter 3). Other happenings include films, dance, theater, music, children's events, multicultural festivals, and marine events. Harbourfront is best in the summer but a great destination year-round, especially with the pretty skating rink and other activities for wintertime fun. In midwinter, the winds blowing off Lake Ontario can be wicked, so dress appropriately.

235 Queens Quay W. ✆ **416/973-4000.** www.harbourfrontcentre.com. Subway: Union, then LRT to Queen's Quay or York Quay.

Ontario Science Centre ★★★ ☺ Since this pioneering interactive science museum opened in 1969, generations of Toronto's kids, and their offspring, have proven loyal fans. It's not surprising: The hands-on approach to exploring the wide world of science is absolutely thrilling. With more than 800 exhibits, there is an abundance of things to touch, push, pull, or crank. Test your reflexes, or balance, or heart rate, or grip strength; watch frozen-solid liquid nitrogen shatter into thousands of icy shards; study slides of butterfly wings, bedbugs, fish scales, or feathers under a microscope; land a spaceship on the moon; see how many lights you can turn on or how high you can elevate a balloon using pedal power. The fun goes on and on.

In addition, the city's only planetarium, an Omnimax cinema, and a collection of small theaters showing assorted documentaries and slide shows are located here. A recent addition is the C$40-million Weston Family Innovation Centre, with new exhibit halls and a focus on interactive learning and problem-solving. There are also some outdoor improvements, including a music-making water garden. The food is much less exciting: Spots for hungry visitors are Galileo's Bistro, a buffet-style restaurant, and Valley Marketplace, a cafeteria. The on-site gift shop, a Mastermind outlet, has a good collection of educational toys and games. This is one Toronto

A Real Deal

You can save a lot of money visiting Toronto's attractions by purchasing a **Toronto CityPass.** See the CN Tower, Casa Loma, the Ontario Science Centre, the Royal Ontario Museum, and the Toronto Zoo for C$59 adults, C$39 kids 4 to 12. Each booklet of tickets is valid for 9 days from the time the first one is used. For a list of ticket vendors or to purchase online, visit **www.citypass.com.**

A Night at the OSC

Pack your PJs and grab your sleeping bag for a unique sleepover opportunity at the OSC. Fun for the whole family, the OSC hosts these unique pajama parties on a handful of Saturday nights each season. Sleep among the exhibits, watch a science show, do fun activities, take part in a DJ/PJ party, watch a film, and wake up to breakfast to start your Sunday. At C$54 per person, it's not surprising these special events sell out quickly. Go online and check it out: www.ontariosciencecentre.ca.

attraction that always seems to be busy (blame school groups), so arrive at 10am to see everything. Make no mistake: The OSC provides a full day's entertainment.

770 Don Mills Rd. (at Eglinton Ave. E.). ℂ **416/696-3127,** or 416/696-1000 for Omnimax tickets. www. ontariosciencecentre.ca. OSC C$18 adults, C$14 seniors & children 13–17, C$11 children 4–12, free for children 3 & under; Omnimax C$12 adults, C$9 seniors & children 13–17, C$8 children 4–12, free for children 3 & under. Combination discounts available. Daily fall–spring 10am–5pm, summer 10am–7pm. Closed Dec 25. Subway: Yonge St. line to Eglinton Ave., then 34 Eglinton bus east to Don Mills Rd. By car: From downtown, take Don Valley Pkwy. to Don Mills Rd. exit & follow signs.

Royal Ontario Museum ★★ ☺ This is Canada's largest museum, with 6 million objects in its collections. Now that the massive and controversial renovation designed by star-chitect Daniel Libeskind is complete, visitors can appreciate the results, or decry them, as many Torontonians do. The new crystal wing, which houses six galleries, hangs out over Bloor Street, hiding the main entrance. (Finding your way in is just one of the inconveniences of the design.) From the interior of the crystal, there are peek-a-boo views to the street below, but it's best to focus on the content here, rather than the playful and often irritating renovation. Fortunately, there's plenty to see, with particular strengths in natural history and world cultures.

Don't miss the Chinese galleries, which feature an intact Ming tomb, as well as the Bishop White Gallery of Chinese Temple Art, wonderful galleries exploring the ancient world (Egypt, Greece, Cyprus, and Bronze Age Aegean are standouts), dazzling dinosaurs for days, a newly improved Bat Cave (which is a very popular draw for kids), and galleries devoted to birds and mammals. Hands-on galleries invite children to play educational games such as the CIBC Discovery Gallery's "dinosaur dig" (a hit with would-be paleontologists). The totem poles are remarkable, too, as are the mummies.

You can easily spend a day here, especially if you include a meal at either the refined C5 (one of the city's top restaurants) or at the humble but delicious Food Studio in the basement.

100 Queen's Park. ℂ **416/586-8000.** www.rom.on.ca. C$24 adults, C$21 seniors & students (w/ID), C$16 children 4–14, free for children 3 & under; free admission Wed 4:30–5:30pm; half-price admission Fri 4:30–9:30pm. Sat–Thurs 10am–5:30pm; Fri 10am–9:30pm. Closed Dec 25. Subway: Museum.

The Toronto Islands ★★★ ☺ In only 7 minutes, an 800-passenger ferry takes you to 245 hectares (605 acres) of island parkland crisscrossed by shaded paths and quiet waterways—a glorious spot to walk, play tennis, bike, feed the ducks, putter around in boats, picnic, or soak up the sun. Of the 14 islands, the 2 major ones are **Centre Island** and **Ward's Island.** The first is the most popular with tourists;

SAVING ON admission costs

The major museums are pricey in Toronto, especially when compared with the smart and progressive freebie programs in cities like London. The ROM is particularly expensive, with a C$24 admission for adults and additional charges for special exhibitions. The list below will help you save on admission fees. Just keep in mind that these free or discounted times do change, so check before you visit.

o **Art Gallery of Ontario:** Free admission every Wednesday from 6 to 8:30pm.

o **Bata Shoe Museum:** Pay-what-you-can admission every Thursday

from 5 to 8pm (suggested donation is C$5).

o **Royal Ontario Museum:** Free admission every Wednesday from 4:30 to 5:30pm; half-price admission every Friday from 4:30 to 9:30pm (note that these policies do not apply to special exhibitions, which are always ticketed at the full price).

o **Textile Museum of Canada:** Pay-what-you-can admission every Wednesday from 5 to 8pm; also, the website often offers coupons for C$1 off regular-priced admissions.

Ward's is more residential (about 600 people live on the islands). Originally, the land was a peninsula, but in the 1800s, storms shattered the finger of land into islands.

On Centre Island, families enjoy **Centreville** (© **416/203-0405;** www.centre island.ca), an old-fashioned amusement park that's been in business since 1966. You won't see the usual neon signs, shrill hawkers, and greasy hotdog stands. Instead, you'll find a turn-of-the-20th-century village complete with a Main Street; tiny shops; a firehouse; and the Far Enough Farm, where the kids can pet lambs, chicks, and other barnyard animals. The kids will also love trying out the antique cars, fire engines, old-fashioned train, authentic 1890s carousel, flume ride, and aerial cars. All-day rides pass costs C$21 for those 4 feet tall and under, C$30 for those taller than 4 feet; a family pass for four is C$90. Centreville is open from 10:30am to 6pm daily from mid-May to Labour Day, and weekends in early May and September.

Centreville Amusement Park 84 Advance Road, Centre Island. © **416/392-8193.** www.toronto.ca/ parks/island/summerschedule.htm. Round-trip fare C$6.50 adults, C$4 seniors & students 15–19, C$3 children 3–14, free for children 2 & under. Ferries leave from docks at the bottom of Bay St. Subway: Union Station, then the LRT to Queen's Quay.

Toronto Zoo ★★ ☺ Covering 284 hectares (702 acres) of parkland, this unique zoological garden contains some 5,000 animals, plus an extensive botanical collection. Pavilions—including Africa, Indomalaya, Australasia, and the Americas—and outdoor paddocks house the plants and animals.

One popular zoo attraction is at the **African Savanna** project. It re-creates a market bazaar and safari through Kesho (Swahili for "tomorrow") National Park, past such special features as a bush camp, rhino midden, elephant highway, and several watering holes. It also includes the **Gorilla Rainforest,** one of the most popular sights at the zoo and the largest indoor gorilla exhibit in North America. Another hit is Splash Island, a kids-only water park that includes a replica of a Canadian Coast Guard ship.

Ten kilometers (6¼ miles) of walkways offer access to all areas of the zoo. Be prepared to walk long distances, but during the warmer months, the Zoomobile takes visitors around the major walkways to view the animals in the outdoor paddocks. The zoo has restaurants, a gift shop, first aid, and a family center. Visitors can rent strollers and wagons, and borrow wheelchairs. The African pavilion has an elevator for strollers and wheelchairs. There are several parking areas and plenty of picnic tables.

361A Old Finch Avenue, Scarborough, ON. (north of Hwy. 401 & Sheppard Ave.), Scarborough. ☏ **416/392-5900.** www.torontozoo.com. C$23 adults, C$17 seniors, C$13 children 4–12, free for children 3 & under. Summer daily 9am–7:30pm; spring & fall daily 9am–6pm; winter daily 9:30am–4:30pm. Last admission 1 hr. before closing. Closed Dec 25. Subway: Bloor-Danforth line to Kennedy, then bus no. 86A north. By car: From downtown, take Don Valley Pkwy. to Hwy. 401 east, exit on Meadowvale Rd. & follow signs.

WHERE TO eat WHEN YOU'RE GOING TO . . .

It's a growing trend that has thankfully come to Toronto: Decent food at museums, galleries, and other attractions. To make your planning easier, here are some of Toronto's top attractions where you can find inspiration for the belly, as well as the mind, all under one roof:

○ **The Art Gallery of Ontario:** The newly renovated AGO has two fine options: **FRANK** restaurant (expensive) (see p. 66) and the **AGO Café** (cheap and cheerful salads and sandwiches). Both are run by the same kitchen, which is headed by local star chef Anne Yaromovitch. The emphasis is on local, and the wine list offers a good sampling of Ontario's top wines.

○ **CN Tower:** The CN Tower's restaurant, **360,** is a little pricey and a bit of a tourist trap; but if you enjoy a panoramic view, and a rotating one at that, with your steak and foie gras, this can offer a memorable meal. The prix-fixe menus offer good value.

○ **Four Seasons Centre for the Performing Arts:** Toronto has a perfect culinary match for its sleek, modern new opera house: the neighboring **Nota Bene**. Run by the pair who steered what was Toronto's absolutely top dining room, Splendido, this is a more casual affair

with really delicious fare. Book ahead.

○ **The Hockey Hall of Fame or the Sony Centre:** You're in luck here because the stellar **Biff's** (4 Front St. E.) (see p. 104) is just across the street. You're also right by **Le Papillon** (69 Front St.) and **the Wine Bar** (9 Church St.)—well-priced places that serve impressive food. If you've got children in tow, try kid-friendly **Shopsy's** (33 Yonge St.).

○ **Ontario Science Centre:** While people who work at the OSC love to point out that it's in the geographic center of Toronto, it's Nowheresville as far as food is concerned (though the museum does have its own restaurant). But if you head north to the new Don Mills Centre, you'll find **McEwan Foods,** a tony gourmet store run by celebrity chef Mark McEwan with chairs and tables for lunch and snacks.

○ **Royal Ontario Museum:** The ROM has two good dining spots: The elegant (and expensive) **C5** (see p. 106) gets consistent raves from local critics, while the casual, cafeteria-style **Food Studio** serves up fine lunch and supper that will keep you fueled for a long day at the museum.

MORE MUSEUMS

Bata Shoe Museum ★★ Imelda Marcos—and anyone else obsessed with shoes—would love this museum, which houses the Bata family's 10,000-item collection. The building, designed by Raymond Moriyama, looks like a whimsical shoebox. The main gallery, "All About Shoes," traces the history of footwear. It begins with a plaster cast of some of the earliest known human footprints, which date to 4 million B.C. You'll come across such specialty shoes as spiked clogs used to crush chestnuts in 17th-century France, Elton John's 12-inch-plus platforms, and Prime Minister Pierre Trudeau's well-worn sandals. One display focuses on Canadian footwear fashioned by the Inuit, while another highlights 19th-century ladies' footwear. The second-story galleries house changing exhibits, which have taken on some serious topics, such as a history of foot binding in China.

327 Bloor St. W. (at St. George St.). ✆ 416/979-7799. www.batashoemuseum.ca. C$14 adults, C$12 seniors, C$8 students (w/ID), C$5 children 5–17, free for children 4 & under. Tues, Wed, Fri & Sat 10am–5pm; Thurs 10am–8pm; Sun noon–5pm. Subway: St. George.

Black Creek Pioneer Village ★ ☺ In this quaint reconstruction of a Victorian-era village, costumed interpreters happily answer questions about life in the 19th century. Dress casually because you'll be spending most of your time here outside. Life at Black Creek moves at the gentle pace of rural Ontario as it was more than a century ago. The original pioneers on this land were Daniel and Elizabeth Strong, a newlywed couple in 1816 who cleared 40 hectares (99 acres) of wilderness for farming and built a log house in their spare time. Eventually, a village developed around this site, and many of the existing buildings date from the 1860s. Every day is different here, so depending on when you visit, you might find "villagers" spinning, sewing, rail splitting, sheep shearing, or threshing. You can count on sampling the villagers' cooking, wandering through the cozily furnished homesteads, visiting the working mill, shopping at the general store, and rumbling past the farm animals in a horse-drawn wagon. The beautifully landscaped village has more than 30 restored buildings to explore.

1000 Murray Ross Pkwy. (at Steeles Ave. & Jane St.), Downsview. ✆ 416/736-1733. www.blackcreek. ca. C$15 adults, C$14 seniors & students, C$11 children 5–15, free for children 4 & under. May & June Mon–Fri 9:30am–4pm; Sat, Sun & holidays 11am–5pm. July to Labour Day Mon–Fri 10am–5pm; Sat, Sun & holidays 11am–5pm. Sept–Dec Mon–Fri 9:30am–4pm; Sat, Sun & holidays 11am–4:30pm. Closed Jan–Apr, Dec 25 & 26. Subway: Finch, then bus no. 60 west to Murray Ross Pkwy.

Canadian Broadcasting Corporation Museum ★ ☺ The CBC has been Canada's national broadcaster since 1936—and its history intersects with the country's own. But this is anything but a time capsule. The museum has interactive exhibits that are fun for kids and shows film clips (including great documentary clips) that engage all ages. Temporary exhibits explore subjects such as radio sound effects or honor much-loved programs (such as Canadian childhood favorites *The Friendly Giant* and *Mr. Dressup*).

250 Front St. W. ✆ 416/205-5574. www.cbc.ca/museum. Free admission. Mon–Fri 9am–5pm. Subway: Union.

Design Exchange Located in the old Stock Exchange Building, the Design Exchange—or DX, as it prefers to be known—has become an important Canadian design museum. It features work from disciplines as varied as architecture to fashion, and from landscape design to interactive media design. Note that the Resource Centre has been officially reopened, and its library-like collection of design books, magazines, and other materials can be viewed by appointment (Mon, Wed, and Fri afternoons).

234 Bay St. © **416/363-6121.** www.dx.org. Free admission; special exhibits C$10 adults. Mon–Fri 10am–5pm; Sat & Sun noon–5pm. Subway: King.

George R. Gardiner Museum of Ceramic Art ★★
It's a rarity: a museum dedicated to the ceramic arts. Plus, since its renovation that expanded it from 1,765 sq. m (19,000 sq. ft.) to 2,694 sq. m (29,000 sq. ft.), it is quite simply a beautiful and tranquil space to explore. Located across the street from the Royal Ontario Museum, there's plenty to see here, from pre-Columbian relics including Olmec and Maya figures, to objects from Ecuador, Colombia, and Peru. It's clearly a collection curated with passion. The majolica collection includes spectacular 16th- and 17th-century salvers and other pieces from Italy, and the Delftware collection includes fine 17th-century chargers. The 18th century is represented by Continental and English porcelain: Meissen, Sèvres, Worcester, Chelsea, Derby, and other great names. Among the highlights are objects from the Swan Service—a 2,200-piece set that took 4 years (1737–1741) to make—and a collection of commedia dell'arte figures. There are free guided tours on Tuesday, Thursday, and Sunday at noon. Popular chef Jamie Kennedy runs a pretty cafe above, so you can stay for lunch.

111 Queen's Park. © **416/586-8080.** www.gardinermuseum.on.ca. C$12 adults, C$8 seniors, C$6 students (w/ID), free for children 12 & under. Mon–Thurs 10am–6pm; Fri 10am–9pm; Sat & Sun 10am–5pm. Closed Jan 1 & Dec 25. Subway: Museum.

Justina M. Barnicke Gallery at Hart House ★
Hart House is, well, the cultural heart of the University of Toronto community, and the Justina M. Barnicke Gallery is one of its treasures. But don't be taken aback by the gallery's small size: Its extensive collection of Group of Seven paintings and other Canadian artworks, both historical and contemporary, is scattered throughout the hallways and rooms of Hart House (it's a public building, so feel free to wander and explore; just remember that the small plaques naming the work and its artist are hidden on the lower-right side of each frame or canvas). The Barnicke is a two-room gallery that features an ever-changing series of monthly exhibits. Occasionally, historical works are on show, but the focus is on works by contemporary artists working with various media.

💬 Signs & Whispers

Have you ever wandered around a neighborhood that intrigued you, wishing that you could get some inside information on the place? Now, thanks to **[murmur]**, you can—at least, in a few Toronto districts, including Kensington Market, the Art & Design District on West Queen West, the Annex around Bloor Street West, and Fort York. Look for signs that have a green ear logo and a phone number underneath; when you dial that number, you'll hear an interesting tidbit that will deepen your appreciation for what you're seeing. The project was developed as part of the city of Toronto's Culture Capital program, and its creators hope to eventually expand it throughout the city. Visit **www.murmurtoronto.ca** for details.

At Hart House, 7 Hart House Circle. ℂ **416/978-8398.** www.jmbgallery.ca. Free admission. Mon–Sat noon–5pm (shorter hours in summer; call ahead). Subway: St. George or Museum.

Museum of Contemporary Canadian Art ★ MOCCA has relocated to the very hot Art & Design District on Queen Street West. The ever-growing collection includes works by Stephen Andrews, Genevieve Cadieux, Ivan Eyre, Betty Goodwin, Micah Lexier, Arnaud Maggs, and Roland Poulin, among many others. MOCCA's mandate has been widening in recent years, and that has made this gallery increasingly a must-visit. Some of the temporary exhibits, such as 2009's collection of pulp-fiction-themed art and the 2010 exhibit on the Andy Warhol transsexual star Candy Darling, have proven show-stoppers. There is an air of irreverence and playfulness that makes this museum a delight to visit.

952 Queen St. W. ℂ **416/395-7430.** www.mocca.ca. Free admission; donation requested. Tues–Sun 11am–6pm. Closed all statutory holidays. Subway: Osgoode, then a streetcar west to Shaw St.

Textile Museum of Canada ★ This museum is internationally recognized for its collection of historic and ethnographic textiles and related artifacts; although due to its specialized nature, it's best for those with an interest in the wide world of fabrics. There are fine Oriental rugs and tapestries from all over the world, a gallery that presents the work of contemporary artists, and the museum, which is so small only a fraction of the collection is on display at any given time. The space is vibrant and interesting.

55 Centre Ave. ℂ **416/599-5321.** www.textilemuseum.ca. C$15 adults, C$10 seniors, C$6 students & children 5–14, free for children 4 & under. Thurs–Tues 11am–5pm; Wed 11am–8pm. Closed Jan 1 & Dec 25. Subway: St. Patrick.

University of Toronto Art Centre ★ 📖 This is a real find—and one that very few people outside the Toronto university community know about. You enter the center from the University College quad, an Oxford-style cloistered garden that itself is a work of art. Inside, you'll find a gallery housing the Malcove Collection, which consists mainly of Byzantine art dating from the 14th to the 18th centuries. There are early stone reliefs and numerous icons from different periods. One of the Malcove's gems was painted by a German master in 1538: Lucas Cranach the

---

 The McMichael Canadian Art Collection

If you have access to a car and happen to be a fan of Canadian landscape painters (such as the Group of Seven, David Milne, and Emily Carr), drive the 40km (25 miles) north to Kleinburg for this very beautiful gallery. The McMichael sits on 40 hectares (99 acres) of conserved land, a bucolic setting that would have inspired many of the artists featured in its collection. It was founded by Robert and Signe McMichael in 1965, when they donated their property, home, and collection to the province of Ontario. Today, the collection includes more than 6,000 works. If you intend to visit, call ahead; the McMichael does shut down some galleries while preparing new shows, and its hours (normally daily 10am–4pm) are sometimes shortened. It's located at 10365 Islington Ave., Kleinburg (ℂ **888/213-1121** or **905/893-1121;** www.mcmichael.com). Admission is C$15 adults, C$12 seniors and students with ID, free for children 5 and under; parking is C$5.

Elder's *Adam and Eve*. The rest of the Art Centre is devoted to temporary exhibitions, which may display University College's collection of Canadian art or other special exhibits.

15 King's College Circle. ☏ **416/978-1838.** www.utac.utoronto.ca. Free admission. Tues–Fri noon–5pm; Sat noon–4pm. Closed all statutory holidays. Subway: St. George or Museum.

Exploring the Neighborhoods

Toronto is a patchwork of neighborhoods, and the best way to discover its soul and flavor is to meander along its streets. On foot, you can best appreciate the sights, sounds, and smells that lend each area its particular character. Following are some of the most interesting neighborhoods.

DOWNTOWN WEST

Art & Design District ★★★ Also known as West Queen West. Queen Street west of Bathurst Street used to be a no-man's land—not because it was dangerous, but because little of importance was believed to be that far from the downtown core. How times have changed: This is one of the liveliest 'hoods in the city (one magazine dubbed it the coolest in the country). It's now home to the **Museum of Contemporary Canadian Art**, or MOCCA (p. 132); chic hotels the **Drake Hotel** (p. 74) and the **Gladstone Hotel** (p. 77); and a bounty of good cafes and restaurants.

West Queen West is all funky fun. It's got great shops for housewares and antiques, such as Quasi-Modo (p. 184), and excellent art galleries, such as the Stephen Bulger (p. 186). The clothing boutiques are exceptional: glamorous Cabaret (p. 195) for vintage, Girl Friday (p. 193) for original designs, and Delphic (p. 192) for menswear. It's also got some fine-but-affordable dining, such as Swan (p. 102). Take the subway to Osgoode and the streetcar over to Bathurst, and start walking west from there.

Chinatown ★★ Stretching along Dundas Street west from Bay Street to Spadina Avenue and north and south along Spadina Avenue, Chinatown is home to some of Toronto's 350,000 Chinese-Canadian residents. Packed with fascinating shops and restaurants, it has bilingual street signs and red-painted poles topped by dragons along Spadina.

As you stroll through Chinatown, stop in at some of the shops and teahouses. A couple of popular stores include Tap Phong (p. 185) and B&J Trading (p. 198). A walk through Chinatown at night is especially exciting—the sidewalks fill with people, and neon lights shimmer everywhere. You'll pass gleaming noodle houses, windows hung with rows of glossy-brown cooked ducks, record stores selling the top 10 in Chinese, and trading companies filled with Asian produce.

To get to Chinatown, take the subway to St. Patrick station and walk west. For more details, see "Walking Tour 1: Chinatown & Kensington Market," in chapter 8.

Little Italy ★★ Along College Street, between Euclid and Shaw, Little Italy competes with West Queen West as the hottest spot in the city. The area hums at night as people crowd the coffee bars, pool lounges, nightclubs, and *trattorias*. **The Mod Club** (p. 217) is a good live-music venue. Notable restaurants in the area include longstanding favorite **Trattoria Giancarlo** with its nice patio and its cool little adjoining wine bar, plus the new and very hot **L.A.B** and **Sottovoce,** which also has a good terrace for people watching. There's lots more, from burgers to pizzas and a nice little streetside fish eatery. Great boutiques in the area are **Sim & Jones,** which features chic, smart casual clothing for women, and **Mink** (p. 199), a glittering oasis of faux gemstones. To get here, ride any College Street streetcar west to Euclid Avenue.

Queen Street West ★ This street was once considered the heart of Toronto's avant-garde scene. That would be a serious stretch today. Sure, it's home to some clubs—such as the **Rivoli** (p. 216)—where major Canadian artists and singers have launched their careers (see chapter 10), but it's also where you'll find mainstream shops such as Club Monaco, Gap, and Le Chateau. Edgy? Not anymore. (See "Art & Design District," above, if you want a walk on the—somewhat—wilder side.)

Queen Street West officially starts at Yonge Street, but it doesn't really pick up, style-wise, till you cross University Avenue. This is prime shopping territory, with one-of-a-kind clothing boutiques such as Fresh Collective (p. 188) and Peach Berserk (p. 194). You'll also find a number of anti-quarian bookstores, antiques and/or junk shops, nostalgic record emporiums, kitchen supply stores, and discount fabric houses. To start exploring, take the subway to Osgoode and walk west along Queen Street West.

DOWNTOWN EAST

The Beaches This is one of the neigh-borhoods that makes Toronto a unique city. Here, near the terminus of the Queen Street East streetcar line, you can stroll or cycle along the lakefront boardwalk. Because of its natural assets, it has become a popular residential neighborhood for young boom-ers and their families, and Queen Street has plenty of browse-able stores, such as **Book City** (p. 187). Just beyond Waverley Road, you can turn down through Kew Gardens to the boardwalk and walk all the way past the Olympic Pool to Ashbridge's Bay Park. To get to the Beaches, take the Queen Street East streetcar to Woodbine Avenue.

Leslieville ★ Queen Street East between Broadview and Leslie Street has become the place to shop for well-priced antique and vintage furniture. Stop in at **Zig Zag** (p. 183), **G.U.F.F.** (p. 182), and **Uppity!** Vintage clothing is another Leslieville specialty: stop in at **Gadabout**

(p. 195) or **Thrill of the Find** (p. 195). This is also a great spot for lounges (such as **Bar-rio,** p. 219) and bistros (such as **Edward Levesque's Kitchen,** p. 105).

MIDTOWN

Mirvish Village One of the city's most illustrious characters is Honest Ed Mirvish, who started his career in the 1950s with a no-frills department store at the corner of Markham and Bloor streets (1 block west of Bathurst Street). Even from blocks away, neon signs race and advertisements tout-ing bargains hit you from every direction. Among his other accomplishments, Mirvish saved the Royal Alexandra Theatre on King Street from demolition; established a row of adjacent restaurants for theater patrons; and developed this block-long area with art galleries, restaurants, and bookstores. The late, great Mirvish was also responsible for saving and renovating London's Old Vic.

Stop by and browse, and don't forget to step into Honest Ed's (see "The Best Bar-gains," on p. 190). To start your visit, take the subway to Bathurst.

Yorkville ★ This area stretches north of Bloor Street West, between Avenue Road and Bay Street. Since its founding in 1853 as a village outside the city proper, Yor-kville has experienced many transforma-tions, and it's going through another right now. In the 1960s, it was Toronto's answer to Haight-Ashbury. In the 1980s, it became the hunting ground of the chic, who spent liberally at **Hermès, Chanel,** and **Cartier.** Today, new condos are going up so quickly that Yorkville feels like one big construction zone. Nevertheless, the area is still a shop-per's paradise. **Jeanne Lottie** (p. 193), **Dinah's Cupboard** (p. 197), and **Winners** (p. 191) are good for value, as is the recent arrival of the U.S. funky chain **Anthropolo-gie.** If you want to be really decadent, visit the **Stillwater Spa** (p. 150) at the Park Hyatt hotel or the **Holt Renfrew Spa** (p. 150). The Aquatic Reiki treatment at he Stillwater—which takes place in a water-filled room—is a memorable experience.

If you're an architecture buff, take a look at the redbrick building on Bloor Street at the end of Yorkville Avenue that houses the Toronto Reference Library. Step inside, and you'll find one of Toronto's most serene spots. To reach Yorkville, take the subway to Bay.

THE EAST END

Danforth/Greektown This eclectic area along Danforth Street east of the Don River is hot, hot, hot. It swings until the early hours, when the restaurants and bars are still crowded and frenetic. During the day, visitors can browse the traditional Greek stores—such as **Akropol,** a Greek bakery at no. 458 (✆ **416/465-1232**) that displays stunning multi-tiered wedding cakes in the window. The neighborhood is becoming more ethnically diverse, and its new character is reflected by stores such as **Blue Moon** (no. 375; ✆ **416/778-6991**), which sells beautiful crafts from the developing world (the store supports only producers that provide healthy working conditions and fair pay), and **El Pipil** (no. 267; ✆ **416/465-9625**), which has colorful clothing, knapsacks, and jewelry. To get to the Danforth, ride the subway to Broadview and walk east.

ARCHITECTURAL HIGHLIGHTS

Toronto is a beautiful city in spite of itself—or, rather, in spite of some of the city planners and developers who have torn down valuable parts of the city's architectural legacy in the name of progress. Toronto grew by leaps and bounds in the Victorian and Edwardian eras, which is why there are so many stunning buildings from those times (take a walk around the **University of Toronto campus** for a quick introduction to the different styles or the **Ontario Legislature** and the **old city hall**). However, much of the 20th century wasn't as kind: Clumsy planners plunked the Gardiner Expressway near the waterfront—making what should have been prime territory into a wasteland—and roughly 28,000 buildings were demolished between 1955 and 1975. A few of the buildings that went up during that era were stunners, such as Ludwig Mies van der Rohe's black-glass **Toronto-Dominion Centre** and Viljo Revell's **new city hall.** And although Toronto has its share of forgettable buildings, enough Gothic-inspired ones survived to allow the city to make a convincing stand-in for New York on-screen. The good news here and now: Toronto is in the throes of an impressive architectural renaissance, from Gehry's AGO to Libeskind's ROM (love it or hate it), Alsop's quirky OCAD building to the Four Seasons Hotel stunner, and much, much more. If you're interested in exploring Toronto's

Walk This Way

Several doors on the first story of Casa Loma open to a grand terrace that overlooks the gardens; most visitors step out, look at the gorgeous fountain and flowers below, and then proceed with the castle tour, which is truly a mistake. From the terrace, it's almost impossible to see the entrances to several winding paths that lead around the extensive grounds and command amazing views. Follow the grand staircase down and enjoy a leisurely ramble.

architectural history, the Royal Ontario Museum's **ROMwalks** programs are an excellent way to go.

Casa Loma ★★★ ☺   A kitschy glitch in the city's skyline to locals, this castle on a hill offers an inspiring view of the sweep of the city (you'll see a lot more of Toronto from here than you did from the CN Tower). But while you can admire the view for free, it's worth visiting the interior of the castle, too. The elegant rooms and period furniture are appropriately grand, though most interesting are perhaps climbing the towers (one Norman, one Scottish, both great).

Sir Henry Pellatt, who built it between 1911 and 1914, had a lifelong fascination with castles. He studied medieval palaces, and gathered materials and furnishings from around the world, bringing marble, glass, and paneling from Europe; teak from Asia; and oak and walnut from North America. He imported Scottish stonemasons to build the massive walls that surround the 2.5-hectare (6¼-acre) site.

Wander through the majestic Great Hall, with its 18m-high (59-ft.) hammer-beam ceiling; the Oak Room, where three artisans took 3 years to fashion the paneling; and the Conservatory, with its elegant bronze doors, stained-glass dome, and pink-and-green marble. The castle encompasses battlements and a tower; Peacock Alley, designed after Windsor Castle; and a 1,800-bottle wine cellar. A 244m (801-ft.) tunnel runs to the stables, where Spanish tile and mahogany surrounded the horses.

The tour is self-guided; pick up an audiocassette, available in eight languages, upon arrival (it's included in the price of admission). From May to October, the gardens are open, too. There's also a Druxy's deli (part of a local chain) on-site, which is good to know, as there aren't many dining options nearby.

1 Austin Terrace. © **416/923-1171.** www.casaloma.org. C$20 adults, C$14 seniors & children 14–17, C$11 children 4–13, free for children 3 & under. Daily 9:30am–5pm (last entry at 4pm). Closed Dec 25. Subway: Dupont, then walk 2 blocks north.

City Hall ★   An architectural spectacle, city hall houses the mayor's office and the city's administrative offices. Daringly designed in the late 1950s by Finnish architect Viljo Revell, it consists of a low podium topped by the flying-saucer-shaped Council Chamber, enfolded between two curved towers. Its interior is as dramatic as its exterior. A free brochure detailing a self-guided tour of city hall is available from its

---

   Looking Sharp

No building in Toronto is more distinctive than the **Sharp Centre for Design.** While it doesn't dominate Toronto's skyline the way that the CN Tower does, it's a work of stark originality. Designed by renowned architect Will Alsop, it opened in 2004 to near-universal shock—and acclaim—including a Worldwide Architecture Award from the Royal Institute of British Architects. The upper portion of the structure is referred to as the "table top," and its white-and-black checkerboard body stands 26m (85 ft.) above the street on 12 spindly, colorful legs. It's most dramatic at night, when it's lit by 16 large metal lights with blue bulbs. Sadly, it's open only to students of the Ontario College of Art & Design, not the public. Located on McCaul Street just south of Dundas Street West, you'll see it in the "Chinatown & Kensington Market" tour, on p. 154.

A Place in the Sun . . . with Music

While it's easy to get carried away in the shops of Eaton Centre, don't overlook Trinity Square, on the west side of the building near the Sears department store. The complex surrounds two of Toronto's oldest landmarks: **Church of the Holy Trinity,** dating to 1847, and **Scadding House** (✆ 416/598-4521), home of Trinity's rector. Concerned citizens demanded that the developers not block sunlight from reaching the buildings. They got their way—the sun continues to shine on the church's twin towers.

If you can, drop by on a Monday: Holy Trinity hosts an eclectic concert series called **"Music Mondays"** that features everything from modern jazz to Hindustani classical music (see the church's website at www.holytrinity toronto.org for the schedule, or call ✆ 416/598-4521, ext. 222). Concerts take place at 12:15pm, and there is a requested C$5 donation.

information desk; the tour can also be printed from the website below in French, Chinese, German, Italian, Japanese, Korean, Portuguese, and Spanish.

In front stretches **Nathan Phillips Square** (named after the mayor who initiated the project). In summer, you can sit and contemplate the flower gardens, fountains, and reflecting pool (which doubles as a skating rink in winter), as well as listen to concerts. Here, you'll find Henry Moore's *The Archer* (formally, *Three-Way Piece No. 2*), purchased through a public subscription fund, and the Peace Garden, which commemorates Toronto's sesquicentennial in 1984. In contrast, to the east stands the **old city hall,** a green-copper-roofed Victorian Romanesque–style building.

100 Queen St. W. ✆ **416/338-0338.** www.toronto.ca/city_hall_tour/nps.htm. Free admission. Self-guided tours Mon–Fri 8:30am–4:30pm. Subway: Queen, then walk west to Bay Street.

Eaton Centre ★ Does a mall really deserve a star? Perhaps this one does. Buttressed at both ends by 30-story skyscrapers, this urban shopping center stretches from Dundas Street south along Yonge Street to Queen Street (557,418 sq. m/6 million sq. ft.). An unusually upscale **Sears** department store anchors the north sections, and more than 285 stores and restaurants, and two garages, fill the rest. Twenty million people shop here annually.

Inside, the structure opens into the impressive **Galleria,** a 264m-long (866-ft.) glass-domed arcade dotted with benches, orchids, palm trees, and fountains; it's further adorned by Michael Snow's 60 soaring Canada geese, titled *Step Flight.* The birds are made from black-and-white photos mounted on cast fiberglass frames. But let's face it: You're probably here to shop (see chapter 9 for guidance).

Dundas & Yonge sts. ✆ **416/598-8700.** www.torontoeatoncentre.com. Mon–Fri 10am–9pm; Sat 9:30am–7pm; Sun noon–6pm. Subway: Dundas or Queen.

Ontario Legislature ★ At the northern end of University Avenue, with University of Toronto buildings to the east and west, lies Queen's Park, a lovely green place in the heart of the city. Embedded in its center is the rose-tinted sandstone-and-granite Ontario Legislature, which has stood here since 1893. Its stately domes, arches, and porte-cocheres are the work of English architect Richard Waite, who was influenced by the Richardson Romanesque style. Be sure to call ahead before you visit to make sure that the building will be open to the public that day. Try to take the Friday afternoon "Art & Architecture" tour that runs between 2 and 3:30pm (it's free, but advance reservations are required to participate). If you're interested in observing the Ontario Legislature in session, consult its schedule on the website.

111 Wellesley St. W. (at University Ave.). © **416/325-7500.** www.ontla.on.ca. Free admission. Early Sept to late May Mon–Fri; late May to early Sept daily. Call for tour information & reservations. Subway: Queen's Park.

Royal Bank Plaza   Shimmering in the sun, Royal Bank Plaza looks like a pillar of gold, and with good reason. During its construction, 70,874g (2,500 oz.) of gold went into the building's 14,000 windows as a coloring agent. More important, the structure is a masterpiece of architectural design. Two triangular towers of bronze mirror glass flank a 40m-high (131-ft.) glass-walled banking hall. The external walls of the towers are built in a serrated configuration so that they reflect a phenomenal mosaic of color.

In the banking hall, hundreds of aluminum cylinders hang from the ceiling, the work of Venezuelan sculptor Jesús Raphael Soto. Two levels below, a waterfall-and-pine-tree setting is naturally illuminated from the hall above.

Front & Bay sts. Free admission. Subway: Union.

St. James' Cathedral ★★★   This stunning early English Gothic–style Anglican cathedral owes its existence at least in part to a group of American Loyalists. They joined with a group of British immigrants to found a congregation in 1797, and they were given a plot of land, which today is bounded by Church, King, Jarvis, and Adelaide streets. They started building Toronto's first church on this site in 1803. The original frame building was enlarged in 1818 and replaced in 1831—and that burned down in 1839. The first cathedral replaced it, only to be destroyed in the great fire of 1849. The present building was begun in 1850 and completed in 1874. It boasts the tallest steeple in Canada. Inside, there's a Tiffany window in memory of William Jarvis, one of Toronto's founding fathers. All of the stained-glass windows are dazzling, but a favorite is the High Altar window—its lower panel bears a distinct resemblance to Leonardo da Vinci's painting of the Last Supper.

In addition to being a great work of architecture, St. James' is a good place to stop and rest for a bit. Unless there's a service going on, it doesn't draw much of a crowd, so it feels like a private oasis in the middle of downtown. St. James' also hosts free concerts every Tuesday at 1pm from September to June. The park-like setting and adjoining park are pretty, too.

65 Church St. © **416/364-7865.** www.stjamescathedral.on.ca. Free admission. Sun–Fri 7:30am–5:30pm; Sat 9am–3pm. Subway: King.

St. Michael's Cathedral ★★★   The principal seat of the Catholic archdiocese of Toronto, St. Michael's is another 19th-century neo-Gothic structure. Built between 1845 and 1848, it originally had a plain interior design with clear-glass windows and white walls. That changed in 1850, when Armand de Charbonnel became the second Bishop of Toronto. Charbonnel was a Frenchman who lived in Montréal, and at first, he was so opposed to his new position that he actually traveled to Rome to beg Pope Pius IX not to make him take it. The pope had other ideas and used Charbonnel's visit to consecrate him in the Sistine Chapel. However, when the new bishop finally arrived in Toronto in September 1850, he threw himself into beautifying St. Michael's. He

The Big O

The University of Toronto has some of the most eclectic architecture in the city. For an introduction, take the walking tour that begins on p. 67. Unfortunately, one of the most talked-about buildings is one that you can't get inside: the **Graduate House**, located at the campus's western edge at 60 Harbord St. (at Spadina Ave.). Designed by architect Thom Mayne, this award-winning building looks not unlike a concrete bunker, and the giant UNIVERSITY OF TORONTO sign only has the last letter visible at most viewing angles, earning the structure the nickname "The Big O." There are many more new and interesting buildings on campus, such as the Leslie Dan Faculty of Pharmacy, with a design much sexier than its name would suggest.

sold lands that he owned in France and donated the proceeds to the cathedral. He bought dazzling stained-glass windows from France, built interior chapels, and commissioned paintings; he also imported the Stations of the Cross from France (that's why they're in French). While improvements and additions have been made since Charbonnel's time, no one did more to make St. Michael's the masterpiece it is.

St. Michael's is particularly venerated for its musical tradition. It has its own boys' choir—which has won awards internationally—and of the four Masses they sing weekly, three are on Sunday.

65 Bond St. © **416/364-0234.** www.stmichaelscathedral.com. Free admission. Mon–Sat 6am–6pm; Sun 6am–10pm. Subway: Queen or Dundas.

Toronto Reference Library Step inside—a pool and a waterfall gently screen out the street noise, and the space opens dramatically to the sky. Light and air flood every corner. This 1977 six-story structure is another masterwork by Toronto architect Raymond Moriyama, who also designed the Bata Shoe Museum (see p. 130).

789 Yonge St. © **416/395-5577.** Free admission. Year-round Mon–Thurs 10am–8pm, Fri & Sat 10am–5pm; Thanksgiving–Apr also Sun 1:30–5pm. Subway: Yonge/Bloor.

HISTORIC BUILDINGS

Campbell House ★ This lovely old house has a small art gallery filled with rotating exhibitions. An 1822 mansion, it belonged to Sir William Campbell, a Loyalist and sixth chief justice of Upper Canada. The man's home has been beautifully restored (complete with a lovely collection of period furniture), even if it *was* moved several blocks from its original location in 1972. Guided tours take about half an hour and provide insight into Toronto's early history.

160 Queen St. W. (at University Ave.). © **416/597-0227.** www.campbellhousemuseum.ca. C$6 adults, C$4 seniors & students (w/ID), C$3 children 5–12. Year-round Mon–Fri 9:30am–4:30pm; May–Oct also Sat & Sun noon–4:30pm. Closed Dec 25. Subway: Osgoode.

Colborne Lodge This charming, English-style Regency cottage with a three-sided veranda was built from 1836 to 1837 to take advantage of the view of Lake Ontario and the Humber River. At the time, it was considered way out in the country and a bother to travel to during the harsh winters. In 1873, the owner, a Toronto surveyor and architect named John Howard, donated the house and surrounding land to the city in return for an annual salary. That created the impressive and expansive High Park (see "Parks, Gardens & Cemeteries," below), a great recreational area.

High Park. 𝄞 **416/392-6916.** C$6 adults, C$4 seniors & students (w/ID), C$3 children ages 5-12. Tues-Sun noon-5pm; call ahead as hours vary. Subway: High Park.

Fort York ★ ☺ For those interested in history—especially military history—this is a treat. This historic base was established by Lt. Gov. John Graves Simcoe in 1793 to defend "little muddy York," as Toronto was then known. Americans sacked it in April 1813, but the British rebuilt that same summer. Fort York was used by the military until 1880 and was pressed back into service during both world wars.

You can tour the soldiers' and officers' quarters; clamber over the ramparts; and in summer, view demonstrations of drills, music, and cooking. If you can, try to visit on Victoria Day, Canada Day, or Simcoe Day (see "Holidays," p. 28), when there are plenty of special events. These include the ever-popular Kids' Drill, in which kids get to take part in a military exercise.

100 Garrison Rd. (off Fleet St., btw. Bathurst St. & Strachan Ave.). 𝄞 **416/392-6907.** www.fortyork.ca. C$8 adults, C$4 seniors & children 13-18, C$3 children 6-12, free for children 5 & under. Mid-May to early Sept daily 10am-5pm; early Sept to mid-May Mon-Fri 10am-4pm, Sat & Sun 10am-5pm. Subway: Bathurst, then streetcar no. 911 south.

Mackenzie House This Greek Revival brick row house dates from the mid–19th century. It was once the home of William Lyon Mackenzie, a fiery orator and newspaper editor who had a most unusual career. He became Toronto's first mayor in 1836 . . . and then, in 1837, he led the Upper Canada rebellion against British rule. Mackenzie fled to the United States with a bounty on his head but returned to Toronto after influential friends arranged a pardon. Some of those same friends bought this house for him, and Mackenzie lived here from 1859 until his death in 1861. It's furnished in 1850s style, and in the back is a print shop modeled after Mackenzie's own. Mackenzie was born in Scotland, and celebrations for Hogmanay and Robbie Burns Day are always special here.

82 Bond St. 𝄞 **416/392-6915.** C$6 adults, C$4 seniors & students, C$3 children 5-12, free for children 4 & under; higher admission rates on holidays. May-Aug Tues-Sun noon-5pm; Sept-Dec Tues-Sun noon-4pm; Jan-Apr Sat & Sun noon-5pm. Subway: Dundas.

Spadina Museum Historic House & Garden ★ How do you pronounce "Spadina"? In the case of the avenue, it's Spa-*dye*-na; for this lovely landmark, it's Spa-*dee*-na. Why? Who knows! But if you want to see how the leading lights of the city lived in days gone by, visit the historic home of financier James Austin. The exterior is beautiful; the interior, even more impressive. Spadina House contains a remarkable collection of art, furniture, and decorative objects. The Austin family occupied the house from 1866 to 1980, and successive generations modified and added to the house and its decor. *Note:* At press time, the museum was undergoing a restoration, but the impressive gardens remain open while work continues inside.

285 Spadina Ave. 𝄞 **416/392-6910.** www.toronto.ca/spadinamuseum. Free admission. Gardens Mon-Fri 9am-4pm. Subway: Dupont.

FOR SPORTS FANS

Air Canada Centre ★ This sports and entertainment complex is home to the Maple Leafs (hockey) and the Raptors (basketball). Longtime fans were crushed when the Leafs moved here in 1999 from Maple Leaf Gardens—the arena that had housed the team since 1931—but the Air Canada Centre has quickly become a fan favorite; the center was designed with comfort in mind (the seats are wide and upholstered). Seating is on a steeper-than-usual grade so that even the "nosebleed" sections have decent sightlines.

40 Bay St. (at Lakeshore Blvd.). ✆ **416/815-5500.** www.theaircanadacentre.com. Subway: Union, then the LRT to Queen's Quay.

Canada's Sports Hall of Fame   In the center of Exhibition Place, this three-floor space celebrates the country's greatest male and female athletes in all major sports. Complementing the displays are touch-screen computers that tell you everything you could want to know about particular sports personalities and Canada's athletic heritage.

Park Yourself Here

Spadina House is the next-door neighbor of Casa Loma (p. 136). Between the two is a small but lovely park that is almost hidden by the trees that shade it. Many visitors don't notice it, but locals love it. Grab a bench here if you want to take a breather.

115 Princes Blvd., Exhibition Place. ✆ **416/260-6789.** Free admission. Mon–Fri 10am–4:30pm. Subway: Bathurst, then streetcar no. 511 south to end of line.

BMO Field ★   With a capacity of 20,000, it's home to Canada's National Soccer Team as well as the popular Toronto FC, Canada's first Major League Soccer team. This is Canada's first soccer-specific stadium and, despite some initial hiccups with the quality of the playing surface, it's won many plaudits for the intimate atmosphere and infectious attitude of the noisy fans, who sing cheers and chants throughout the matches.

BMO Field, 170 Princes Blvd., Exhibition Place. ✆ **416/360-GOAL** (4625). www.torontofc.ca/bmo-field. $C26–$C120. Subway: Bathurst, then streetcar no. 511 south to end of line.

Hockey Hall of Fame ★ ☺   Ice hockey fans will be thrilled by the artifacts collected here. They include the original Stanley Cup, a replica of the Montréal Canadiens' locker room, Terry Sawchuck's goalie gear, Newsy Lalonde's skates, and the stick Max Bentley used. You'll also see photographs of the personalities and great moments in hockey history. Most fun are the shooting and goalkeeping interactive displays, where you can take a whack at targets with a puck or don goalie gear and face down flying video pucks or sponge pucks.

In Brookfield Place, 30 Yonge St. (at Front St.). ✆ **416/360-7765.** www.hhof.com. C$15 adults, C$12 seniors, C$10 children 4–18, free for children 3 & under. Mon–Fri 10am–5pm; Sat 9:30am–6pm; Sun 10:30am–5pm. Closed Jan 1 & Dec 25. Subway: Union.

Rogers Centre ★   This is home to the Toronto Blue Jays baseball team and the Toronto Argonauts football team. In 1989, the opening of this stadium, then known as SkyDome, was a gala event. The stadium represents an engineering feat, featuring the world's first fully retractable roof and a gigantic video scoreboard. It is so large that a 31-story building would fit inside the complex when the roof is closed.

1 Blue Jays Way. ✆ **416/341-2770.** www.rogerscentre.com. Subway: Union, then follow the signs & walkway.

MARKETS

Toronto's markets are an important part of its heritage. The markets have traditionally been surrounded by neighborhoods that have absorbed wave after wave of immigrants into the city's fabric. Make like a local and dive into the fray. In addition to the markets listed below, check out the smaller ones at the **Distillery District** (p. 209) and at **Riverdale Farm** (p. 147), plus a wealth of farmers markets that have sprouted at Dufferin Grove, the Green Barns at Wychwood, the Brick Works, and beyond.

 Coffee Break

One Kensington Market spot that's worth a stop is **Ideal Coffee** (84 Nassau St.; *(C)* **416/362-7700**). This groovy little cafe serves organic and fair-trade beans, and roasts its own. A great cup of joe to keep you on the go.

Kensington Market ★★ This colorful, lively area should not be missed. You'll hear Caribbean, Portuguese, Italian, and other languages and dialects as merchants spread out their wares—squid and crabs in pails; chickens and pigeons; local breads; cheese from around the world; apples, pears, peppers, ginger, and West Indies mangoes; salted fish from Portuguese dories; and lace, fabrics, and other colorful remnants. There's no market on Sunday. Kensington Avenue itself is a treasure trove of vintage clothing stores. You'll see a lot of junk here, but amazing finds can be had at shops such as **Courage My Love** (14 Kensington Ave.; *(C)* **416/979-1992**) (see p. 195). Most of the shops display their wares outdoors in decent weather, adding to the color and charm of the area. Several summer Sundays are car-free in Kensington Market, making for a pedestrian paradise.

Bounded by Dundas St., Spadina Ave., Baldwin St. & Augusta Ave. No phone. Most stores Mon–Sat. noon–6pm. Subway: St. Patrick, then Dundas St. streetcar west to Kensington St.

St. Lawrence Market This handsome food market is in a vast building constructed around the facade of the second city hall, built in 1850. Vendors sell fresh meat, fish, fruit, vegetables, and dairy products, as well as other foodstuffs. The best time to visit is early Saturday morning, shortly after the farmers arrive. Don't miss the gallery on the second floor that exhibits historic shows about the city; it's free, too.

92 Front St. E. *(C)* **416/392-7219.** Tues–Thurs 8am–6pm; Fri 8am–7pm; Sat 5am–5pm. Subway: Union.

PARKS, GARDENS & CEMETERIES

Downtown

Allan Gardens ★ ☺ What a difference a few years can make. Allan Gardens used to be down at the heels and seedy, but since the University of Toronto relocated its Botany Greenhouses here in 2004, this park has been infused with new life. This was actually Toronto's first civic park, created on the 4 hectares (10 acres) donated to the city by former mayor George William Allan. Originally called the Horticultural Gardens, the city renamed the park after Allan died in 1901. The stunning glass-domed Palm House conservatory dates back to 1910 and contains six greenhouses.

It has been joined by U of T's restored and renovated greenhouses, now called the Allan Gardens Children's Conservatory.

Btw. Jarvis, Sherbourne, Dundas & Gerrard sts. ℂ **416/392-1111.** Free admission. Daily dawn–dusk. Subway: Dundas.

Ireland Park ★★ 🏛 In 1847, Toronto was a city of 20,000—until 38,000 Irish immigrants arrived that summer. On June 21, 2007, this memorial to the Irish Famine was opened at Eireann Quay by Mary McAleese, president of Ireland. The park was inspired by Rowan Gillespie's "Departure" series of famine figures, which stand on Dublin's Liffey quayside, depicting Irish emigrants looking out to sea. There are seven figures in Dublin and five in Toronto's new park, which seems appropriate given how many Irish perished on the journey. The figures in Ireland Park were also created by Gillespie, and they are called the "Arrival" series. There is also a memorial in the park to the more than 1,100 who died just after their arrival; as their names are discovered, they are inscribed in a limestone wall.

At Bathurst St. & Queens Quay W. (across from Bathurst Quay). ℂ **416/601-6906.** www.irelandpark foundation.com. Free admission. Daily dawn–dusk. Subway: Union, then the LRT to Spadina Ave. & walk west to Bathurst St.

Toronto Music Garden ★★★ Toronto is a city of gardens, but this one along Toronto's waterfront is a favorite of mine. Cellist Yo-Yo Ma and landscape designer Julie Moir Messervy created the Toronto Music Garden to invoke Bach's First Suite for Unaccompanied Cello. The prelude is represented by the undulating curves of a river-scape; the allemande by a forest grove that's filled with wandering trails; the courante by a swirling path through wildflowers; the *menuett* by a pavilion of formally arranged flowerbeds; and finally the gigue, with its giant grass steps that lead you back to the real world. It's tough to translate the experience into words, but the music garden is a don't-miss spot if you visit Toronto in warm weather.

475 Queens Quay W. ℂ **416/338-0338.** Free admission. Daily dawn–dusk. Subway: Union, then the LRT to Spadina.

Trinity Bellwoods ★ 🏛 This gorgeous neighborhood park was originally part of a military reserve when Toronto was still a small town called York and the British troops were garrisoned at Fort York (p. 140). Eventually, parcels were sold to retiring officers, but in 1851, Bishop John Strachan bought up some of the land in order to found a college. Strachan was furious at the University of Toronto's decision to become a secular school, and he founded the Anglican Trinity College in 1852 (of course, Trinity is now part of the university, though it has kept its Anglican traditions). The buildings were torn down, but the impressive stone-and-wrought-iron gates that face Queen Street West still remain, and there are Victorian lampposts illuminating the main paths at night. Given the colorful neighborhood it's located in (the Art & Design District), it's no surprise that Trinity Bellwoods has hosted some interesting events, including an anarchist book fair and drumming circles. Be on the lookout for the legendary albino squirrels who reside here—there's a coffee shop across the street named in honor of the rodent.

Btw. Dundas St. W., Crawford St., Queen St. W. & Gore Vale Ave. ℂ **416/392-1111.** Free admission. Daily dawn–dusk. Subway: Osgoode, then a streetcar west to Bellwoods Ave.

Music Alfresco

The **Toronto Music Garden** hosts some of the city's best summer concerts. From late June to mid-September, you can count on listening to live music here every Thursday at 7pm and on Sundays at 4pm. Sometimes you'll hear classical music—especially by the baroque composers—but the programs are rather eclectic. Recent offerings have included Spanish flamenco music and traditional Chinese melodies. All performances are free.

Midtown

High Park ★ ☺   This 161-hectare (398-acre) park in the far west of Midtown was architect John G. Howard's gift to the city. He lived in Colborne Lodge, which still stands in the park (p. 139). The grounds contain a large lake called Grenadier Pond (great for ice skating in wintertime); a small zoo; a swimming pool; tennis courts; sports fields; bowling greens; and vast expanses of green for baseball, jogging, picnicking, bicycling, and more. The Dream in High Park (p. 226), an annual Shakespearean offering in the open air, is staged each summer and draws crowds who often picnic on-site.

1873 Bloor St. W. (south to the Gardiner Expwy.). No phone. www.toronto.ca/parks. Free admission. Daily dawn–dusk. Subway: High Park.

Necropolis ★   If you have a fascination with historic cemeteries, definitely make a stop here. Located in Midtown East, this is one of the city's oldest cemeteries, dating to 1850. Some of the remains were originally buried in Potters Field, where Yorkville stands today.

Before strolling through the cemetery, pick up a History Tour brochure at the office. You'll find the graves of William Lyon Mackenzie, leader of the 1837 rebellion, as well as those of his followers Samuel Lount and Peter Matthews, who were hanged for their parts in the rebellion. (Mackenzie himself went on to become a member of Parliament. Go figure.) Other notables buried in the 7.2-hectare (18-acre) cemetery include George Brown, one of the fathers of Confederation; Anderson Ruffin Abbot, the first Canadian-born black surgeon; Joseph Tyrrell, who unearthed dinosaurs in Alberta; and world-champion oarsman Ned Hanlan. Henry Langley, who designed the Necropolis' porte-cochere and the Gothic Revival chapel—as well as the spires of St. James' and St. Michael's cathedrals (p. 138)—is also buried here.

200 Winchester St. (at Sumach St.). ✆ **416/923-7911.** www.mountpleasantgroupofcemeteries.ca. Free admission. Daily 8am–dusk. Subway: Castle Frank, then bus no. 65 south on Parliament St. to Wellesley St. & walk 3 blocks east to Sumach St.

Uptown & Further Afield

Edwards Gardens   This quiet, formal 14-hectare (35-acre) garden is part of a series of parks that stretch over 240 hectares (593 acres) along the Don Valley. It's not easily reached by public transit, so be prepared to make a special and long trip. Gracious bridges arch over a creek, rock gardens abound, and roses and other seasonal flowers add color and scent. The garden is famous for its rhododendrons. The

Civic Garden Centre operates a gift shop and offers free walking tours on Tuesday and Thursday at 11am and 2pm. The Centre also boasts a fine horticultural library.

777 Lawrence Ave. E. (at Leslie St.). ℂ **416/392-8188.** www.toronto.ca/parks. Free admission. Daily dawn–dusk. Subway: Eglinton, then bus no. 51 (Leslie) or 54 (Lawrence).

Mount Pleasant Cemetery ★★ This isn't as atmospheric as the Necropolis, but it's easier to get to and spread over gorgeous grounds (it's actually home to one of the finest tree collections in North America). Mount Pleasant is also the final resting place of many fascinating people, such as Glenn Gould, the celebrated classical pianist; Dr. Frederick Banting and Dr. Charles Best, the Toronto researchers who discovered insulin in 1922; golfer George Knudson; the Massey and Eaton families, whose mausoleums are impressive architectural monuments; Prime Minister William Lyon Mackenzie King; Canada's greatest war hero, Lt. Col. William Barker; and writer and editor Jim Cormier.

375 Mount Pleasant Rd. (north of St. Clair Ave.). ℂ **416/485-9129.** www.mountpleasantgroupof cemeteries.ca. Free admission. Daily 8am–dusk. Subway: St. Clair.

Scarborough Bluffs ★★ On the eastern edge of Toronto is a natural wonder that's well worth a half-day visit. The Scarborough Bluffs are unique in North America, and their layers of sand and clay offer a remarkable geological record of the great ice age. Rising up to 105m (345 ft.) above Lake Ontario, they stretch out over 14km (8¾ miles). The first 45m (148 ft.) contains fossil plants and animals that were deposited by the advancing Wisconsin Glacier 70,000 years ago. The bluffs were given their name in 1793 by Lady Elizabeth Simcoe, wife of the first Lieutenant Governor of Upper Canada (Ontario); as she sailed to York, as Toronto was then known, she was reminded of the cliffs of Yorkshire.

South of Kingston Rd. No phone. www.toronto.ca/parks. Free admission. Daily dawn–dusk. Subway: Victoria Park, then no. 12 Kingston Rd. bus to Brimley Rd. & about a 15-min. walk south along Brimley Rd. By car: From downtown, take Don Valley Pkwy. to Hwy. 401 east, exit on Brimley Rd. & drive south.

ESPECIALLY FOR KIDS

The city puts on a fabulous array of special events for children at **Harbourfront.** In February, there's **ALOUD: A Celebration for Young Readers.** Come April, **Spring Fever** welcomes the season with egg decorating, puppet shows, and more; on Saturday mornings in April, the 5-to-12 set enjoys **cushion concerts.** For information, call ℂ **416/973-4000** or visit **www.harbourfrontcentre.com**.

For more than 30 years, the **Lorraine Kimsa Theatre for Young People** (165 Front St. E., at Sherbourne St.; ℂ **416/862-2222** for box office or 416/363-5131 for administration) has been entertaining youngsters. Its season runs from August to May.

The 11th annual **Sprockets Toronto International Film Festival for Children** screens more than 100 entries from 29 countries. Like the Toronto International Film Festival in September, the screenings, to be held in April, take place around the city. Call ℂ **416/968-FILM** (416/968-3456) for details or visit **www.sprockets.ca**.

Help! We've Got Kids is an all-in-one print and online directory for attractions, events, shops, and services appropriate for kids younger than 13 in the greater

Toronto area. It doesn't provide a lot of detail about most of the entries, but the listings make a great starting point. Visit **www.helpwevegotkids.com.**

Look for the "Kids" icon in the sections above for the following Toronto-area attractions that have major appeal for kids of all ages. The best venues (at least, from a kid's point of view) are these:

o **Black Creek Pioneer Village:** For crafts, costumes, and an entertaining take on history. See p. 130.

o **Harbourfront:** Kaleidoscope is an ongoing program of creative crafts, active games, and special events on weekends and holidays. There are also a pond, winter ice skating, and a crafts studio. See p. 123.

o **Ontario Science Centre:** Kids race to be the first at this paradise of hands-on games, experiments, and push-button demonstrations—800 of them. See p. 126.

o **Toronto Zoo:** One of the best in the world, modeled after San Diego's—the animals in this 284-hectare (702-acre) park really do live in a natural environment. See p. 128.

For more specialized interests:

o **Allan Gardens Children's Conservatory:** For hands-on learning experiences about plants and ecology. See p. 142.

o **Casa Loma:** The stables, secret passageway, and fantasy rooms capture children's imaginations. See p. 136.

o **CN Tower:** Especially the simulator games and the glass floor. See p. 122.

o **Fort York:** For its reenactments of battle drills, musket and cannon firing, and musical marches with fife and drum. See p. 140.

o **High Park:** Wide-open spaces, plus the chance to hang out with llamas. See p. 144.

o **Hockey Hall of Fame:** Who wouldn't want the chance to tend goal against Mark Messier and Wayne Gretzky (with a sponge puck), and to practice with the fun and challenging video pucks? See p. 141.

o **Royal Ontario Museum:** The top hits are the Ancient Egypt Gallery, the Hands-On Biodiversity Gallery, and the Maiasaur Project. See p. 127.

o **Toronto Islands–Centreville:** Riding a ferry to this turn-of-the-20th-century amusement park is part of the fun. See p. 127.

Ontario Place ☺ For all its Space Age looks, this is really just a fun amusement park, more thrilling than Centreville on Centre Island (p. 128) but nowhere near as

---

 A Storybook Sanctuary

The **Osborne Collection of Early Children's Books** is a treasure trove for bibliophiles of all ages. Located at the Lillian H. Smith Branch of the Toronto Public Library (239 College St.; ℂ 416/393-7753), the collection includes a 14th-century manuscript of Aesop's fables, Victorian and Edwardian adventure and fantasy tales, 16th-century schoolbooks, storybooks once owned by British royalty, an array of "penny dreadfuls" (cheap thrillers from the days when a paperback book cost a penny), and Florence Nightingale's childhood library. Special exhibits at the Osborne often feature whimsical subjects. You can visit the library weekdays between 10am and 6pm or Saturdays from 9am to 5pm.

cool as Paramount Canada's Wonderland (see below). From a distance, you'll see five steel-and-glass pods suspended on columns 32m (105 ft.) above the lake, three artificial islands, and a huge geodesic dome. The five pods contain a multimedia theater, a children's theater, a high-technology exhibit, and displays that tell the story of Ontario in vivid kaleidoscopic detail. The dome houses Cinesphere, where specially made IMAX movies are shown year-round.

Ontario Place has many attractions targeted at kids, starting with the **H2O Generation Station,** a gigantic "soft play" structure with twisting slides, towers, and walkways. The **Atom Blaster**—which claims to be Canada's largest foam-ball free-for-all—is fun for the whole family. Younger children will enjoy the **MicroKids** play area with its ball pit, climbing platforms, and other tot-appropriate draws.

At night, the **Molson Amphitheatre** accommodates concert-goers in the reserved seating area under the canopy and on the surrounding grass. For concert information, call ✆ **416/260-5600;** for tickets, call **Ticketmaster** (✆ **416/870-8000**).

955 Lakeshore Blvd. W. ✆ **416/314-9811,** or 416/314-9900 for recorded info. www.ontarioplace.com. Grounds only C$18 adults, C$12 seniors & children 4–5, free for children 3 & under, separate fees for rides & events (pricing varies by month); Play All Day pass C$34 adults, C$18 seniors & children 4–5, free for children 3 & under. Park open mid-May to Labour Day daily 10am–dusk; evening events end & dining spots close later. Closed (except Cinesphere) early Sept to early May. Subway: Bathurst, then Bathurst St. streetcar south.

Paramount Canada's Wonderland ★ ☺ An hour north of Toronto lies Canada's answer to Disney World. The 120-hectare (297-acre) park features more than 200 attractions, including 65 rides, a water park, a play area for tiny tots (KidZville), and live shows. Because the park relies on a local audience for most of its business, it introduces new attractions every year. Some of the most popular have been the Behemoth, Canada's biggest, fastest, and tallest rollercoaster; the Fly, a roller coaster designed to make every seat feel as though it's in the front car (the faint of heart can't hide at the back of this one!); Sledge Hammer, a "menacing mechanical giant" that stands 24m (80 ft.) tall and hurls riders through accelerated jumps and free-falls; Cliffhanger, a "super swing" that executes 360-degree turns and makes riders feel immune to gravity; and the Xtreme Skyflyer, a hang-gliding and skydiving hybrid that plunges riders 46m (151 ft.) in a free-fall. The roller coasters range from the looping, inverted Top Gun to the track-free suspended Vortex.

The Splash Works water park offers a huge wave pool and water rides spread over 8.1 hectares (20 acres), from speed slides and tube rides to special scaled-down slides and a kids' play area. You'll also find Hanna-Barbera characters, including Scooby-Doo, strolling around the park (and ready to get their picture taken with the kids). Additional attractions include Wonder Mountain and its high divers (they take the 20m/66-ft. plunge down Victoria Falls to the mountain's base), restaurants, and shops.

9580 Jane St., Vaughan. ✆ **905/832-7000** or 905/832-8131. www.canadaswonderland.com. Pay-One-Price Passport (includes unlimited rides & shows, but not special attractions or Kingswood Music Theater) C$45 adults, free for children 2 & under; check website for specials. June 1 to June 25 Mon–Fri 10am–8pm, Fri & Sat 10am–10pm; June 26 to Labour Day daily 10am–10pm; late May & early Sept to early Oct Sat & Sun 10am–8pm. Closed mid-Oct to mid-May. Subway: Yorkdale or York Mills, then GO Express Bus to Wonderland. By car: From downtown, take Yonge St. north to Hwy. 401 & go west to Hwy. 400. Go north on Hwy. 400 to Rutherford Rd. exit & follow signs. From the north, exit at Major Mackenzie Dr.

Riverdale Farm ★★ Situated on the edge of the Don Valley Ravine, this working farm located on 3 hectares (7½ acres) right in the city is a favorite with small

Retro Thrills

With the fanfare given to the new rides Paramount Canada's Wonderland introduces each summer, many park-goers overlook the older attractions. The Wild Beast is one of the original roller coasters, and it's still one of the best. The first few times you hurtle along the track, you'll be convinced that the whole rickety structure is about to fall down at any moment. Guess what—it was designed to feel that way! Other tried-and-true favorites include the Minebuster and the Dragon Fire. A bonus: shorter queues!

tots. They enjoy watching the cows, pigs, turkeys, and ducks—and can get close enough to pet many animals, such as the rabbits. Because this really is a farm, you'll see all of the chores of daily life, such as horse grooming, cow and goat milking, egg collecting, and animal feeding. Adults should note that the farm shop has some seasonal produce and baked goods, and that there's a farmers' market on-site Tuesdays from May to October.

201 Winchester St. (at Sumach St.). © **416/392-6794.** Free admission. Daily 9am–5pm. Subway: Castle Frank, then bus no. 65 south on Parliament St. to Wellesley St. & walk 3 blocks east to Sumach St.

ORGANIZED TOURS

For summer weekends, it's always a good idea to make tour reservations in advance. At slower times, you can usually call the same day or simply show up.

Bus Tours

Try the **Hop-On Hop-Off City Tour** offered by **Gray Line** (184 Front St. E.; © **416/594-3310;** www.grayline.ca). The good thing is that it goes to such major sights as the Eaton Centre, City Hall, Casa Loma, Yorkville, Chinatown, Harbourfront, the Rogers Centre, and the CN Tower, and a ticket allows you to get on and off the bus over a 2-day period. These narrated tours, which operate daily starting at 10am, cost C$35 adults, C$31 seniors, and C$18 children 4 to 11; free for children 3 and under.

OUTDOOR ACTIVITIES

Toronto residents love the great outdoors, whatever the time of year. In summer, you'll see people cycling, boating, and hiking; in winter, they are skating, skiing, and snowboarding.

For additional information on facilities in the parks, golf courses, tennis courts, swimming pools, beaches, and picnic areas, contact **Toronto Parks and Recreation** (© **416/392-8186;** www.toronto.ca/parks). Also, see "Parks, Gardens & Cemeteries," earlier in this chapter.

Beaches

The Beaches is the neighborhood along Queen Street East from Coxwell Avenue to Victoria Park. It has a charming boardwalk that connects the beaches, starting at **Ashbridge's Bay Park,** which has a sizable marina. **Woodbine Beach** connects to

Kew Gardens Park and is a favorite with sunbathers and volleyball players. Woodbine also boasts the **Donald D. Summerville Olympic Pool.** Snack bars and trinket sellers line the length of the boardwalk.

Many locals prefer the beaches on the **Toronto Islands.** The ones on **Centre Island,** always the busiest, are favorites with families because of such nearby attractions as **Centreville.** The beaches on **Ward's Island** are much more secluded. They're connected by the loveliest boardwalk in the city, with masses of fragrant flowers and raspberry bushes along its edges. **Hanlan's Point,** also in the Islands, is Toronto's only nude beach.

Canoeing & Kayaking

The **Harbourfront Canoe and Kayak School** (283A Queens Quay W.; ℂ **800/960-8886** or 416/203-2277; www.paddletoronto.com) rents canoes and kayaks; call ahead if you are interested in taking private instruction.

You can also rent canoes, rowboats, and pedal boats on the **Toronto Islands** just south of Centreville.

Cross-Country Skiing

Just about every park in Toronto becomes potential cross-country skiing territory as soon as snow falls. Best bets are Sunnybrook Park and Ross Lord Park, both in North York. For more information, contact **Toronto Parks and Recreation** (ℂ **416/392-8186;** www.toronto.ca/parks). Serious skiers interested in day trips to excellent out-of-town sites such as Horseshoe Valley can contact **Trakkers Cross Country Ski Club** (ℂ **416/763-0173;** www.trakkers.ca), which also rents equipment.

Cycling

With biking trails through most of the city's parks and more than 29km (18 miles) of street bike routes, it's not surprising that Toronto has been called one of the best cycling cities in North America. Favorite pathways include the **Martin Goodman Trail** (from The Beaches to the Humber River along the waterfront); the **Lower Don Valley** bike trail (from the east end of the city north to Riverdale Park); **High Park** (with winding trails over 160 hectares/395 acres); and the **Toronto Islands,** where bikers ride without fear of cars. For advice, call the **Ontario Cycling Association** (ℂ **416/426-7416**), contact **Toronto Parks and Recreation** (ℂ **416/392-8186;** www.toronto.ca/parks), or visit www.toronto.ca/livegreen/greenlife_onthego_cycling. htm. Bike lanes are marked on College/Carlton streets, the Bloor Street Viaduct leading to the Danforth, Beverly/St. George streets, Jarvis Street, and Davenport Road.

 Walk/Jog/Cycle in Peace

One of the best places to walk, jog, or cycle in the city is the path that connects downtown with the Don Valley Ravine and winds up at the **Evergreen Brick Works.** There's plenty of topography and the promise of a beautiful and tranquil spot to rest at the end of the journey. On Saturdays in summer, you can also refuel at the farmers market where good prepared foods, often made with local and seasonal ingredients, make the trek back a breeze.

spas IN THE CITY

In the past decade or so, Toronto has established a reputation for superior spas, some in hotels and others stand alone facilities. Here's a short list of the best, and most unique to the city:

Elmwood Spa. 18 Elm St. (✆ **416/977-6751;** www.elmwoodspa.com). Just a stone's throw from the busy corner of Dundas and Yonge streets, and therefore a convenient respite for shoppers who have exhausted themselves at the nearby Eaton Centre, this is a favorite day spa where you can while away many serene hours of pampering, dining, and quiet play. They really have it all: massages and facials, a range of water therapies that center around a pretty pool, steam rooms, a whirlpool, and a poolside lounge where spa cuisine and herbal teas are served. The service is top-notch and the brand so highly respected they have their own line of beauty products, lotions, and potions. Facials are a highlight.

Holt Renfrew Spa. Holt Renfrew, 50 Bloor St. W. (✆ **416/960-2909;** www.holtrenfrew.com). Located in one of Toronto's most luxurious stores is, appropriately enough, one of the city's most luxurious spas. Decorated in modern-chic blond wood and glass (and with a seemingly endless number of private treatment rooms), the spa provides a good range of cosmetic services, from manicures to massage. If you've flown to Toronto, try their Jet Lag Facial, which rehydrates the skin and includes lymphatic leg therapy.

Stillwater Spa. Park Hyatt Toronto, 4 Avenue Rd. (✆ **416/924-5471;** www.stillwaterspa.com). Water is the theme at this spa in the Park Hyatt, and it undulates in streams under transparent floor panels and courses down walls in mini-waterfalls. Before you even get to the treatment rooms, you'll be dazzled by the changing areas, which include the expected whirlpool and sauna, but also have private cabana-like nooks for reclining (personal TV screens come with a headset). There's something for everyone at this lovely spot, from manicures to hair "rituals," Swedish and Reiki massage to anti-stress treatments. For a taste of Canadiana, try some of the patriotic-inspired treatments such as Canadian grain facial (with grain from Alberta) or the BC seaweed wrap. The hotel dining room, combined with the health menu at the Spa, offer culinary delights, too.

For a list of bike rental shops, contact the **Toronto Bicycling Network** (✆ **416/766-1985;** www.tbn.ca). One sure bet is **Wheel Excitement** (249 Queens Quay W., Unit 110; ✆ **416/260-9000;** www.wheelexcitement.ca). If you're interested in cycling with a group or want information about daily excursions and weekend trips, contact the Toronto Bicycling Network.

Be forewarned: Like many other North American cities, the tensions between cyclists and car drivers are mounting, so be on your guard and take it easy.

Fitness Centers

The **Metro Central YMCA** (20 Grosvenor St.; ✆ **416/975-9622;** www.ymcatoronto.org) has excellent facilities, including a 25m (82-ft.) swimming pool, all kinds of cardiovascular machines, Nautilus equipment, an indoor track, squash and racquetball courts, and aerobics classes. The **University of Toronto Athletic Centre** (55 Harbord St., at Spadina Ave.; ✆ **416/978-3436;** www.ac-fpeh.com) offers similar facilities. Guest passes to both centers are C$25 per day.

For yoga aficionados, there's no better place to stretch than **Yoga Plus** (40 Eglinton Ave. E., 8th Floor; ☎ **416/322-9936;** www.yogaplustoronto.com). A single class costs C$20; there's also a pay-what-you-can "Karma" class available. For a listing of all of Toronto's yoga studios, visit **www.yogatoronto.ca,** which covers the city and the Greater Toronto Area.

Golf

Toronto is obsessed with golf: There are more than 75 public courses within an hour's drive of downtown. Here's information on some of the best.

○ **Don Valley.** 4200 Yonge St., south of Highway 401 (☎ **416/392-2465**). Designed by Howard Watson, this is a scenic par-71 course with some challenging elevated tees. The par-3 13th hole is nicknamed the Hallelujah Corner (it takes a miracle to make par). It's considered a good place to start your kids. Greens fees are C$30 to C$63.

○ **Humber Valley.** 40 Beattie Ave., at Albion Road (☎ **416/392-2488**). The relatively flat par-70 course is easy to walk, with lots of shade from towering trees. The three final holes require major concentration (the 16th and 17th are par-5s). Greens fees are C$44 to C$52.

○ The **Glen Abbey Golf Club,** 1333 Dorval Dr., Oakville (☎ **905/844-1800;** www.glenabbey.ca). The championship course is one of the most famous in Canada. Designed by Jack Nicklaus, the par-73 layout traditionally plays host to the Canadian Open. Greens fees are C$135 to C$265.

Travelers who are really into golf might want to consider a side trip to the **Muskoka Lakes** (see chapter 11). This area, just 90 minutes north, has some of the best golfing in the country at courses such as **Taboo** and the **Deerhurst Highlands.**

Ice Skating & In-Line Skating

Nathan Phillips Square in front of city hall becomes a free ice rink in winter, as does an area at Harbourfront Centre. Rentals are available on-site. More than 25 parks contain artificial rinks (also free), including Grenadier Pond in High Park—a romantic spot, with a bonfire and vendors selling roasted chestnuts. They're open from November to March.

In summer, in-line skaters pack Toronto's streets (and sidewalks). Go with the flow and rent some blades from **Wheel Excitement** (see "Cycling," above).

Skate till You Drop?

Let's say you'd like to go skating, while your traveling companion wants to hit the shops. If you head to **Hazelton Lanes,** you can both get what you want. A central courtyard doubles as a skating rink. Better yet, the shopping center's **Customer Service Centre** (☎ **416/968-8600**) offers complimentary skate rentals. It's hard to beat a deal like that.

Jogging

Downtown routes might include **Harbourfront** and along the lakefront, or through **Queen's Park** and the University. The **Martin Goodman Trail** runs 20km (12 miles) along the waterfront from the Beaches in the east to the Humber River in the west. It's ideal for jogging, walking, or cycling. It links to the **Tommy Thompson Trail,** which travels the parks from the lakefront along the Humber River. Near the Ontario Science Centre in the Central Don Valley, **Ernest Thompson Seton Park** is also good for jogging. Parking is available at the Thorncliffe Drive and Wilket Creek entrances.

These areas are generally quite safe, but you should take the same precautions you would in any large city.

Rock Climbing

Toronto has several climbing gyms, including **Joe Rockhead's** (29 Fraser Ave.; ✆ 416/538-7670; www.joerockheads.com) and the **Toronto Climbing Academy** (100 Broadview Ave.; ✆ **416/406-5900;** www.climbingacademy.com). You can pick up the finer points of knot tying and belaying. Both gyms also rent equipment.

Snowboarding & Skiing

The snowboard craze shows no sign of abating, at least from January to March (or anytime there's enough snow on the ground). One popular site is the **Earl Bales Park** (4169 Bathurst St., just south of Sheppard Ave.), which offers rentals. The park also has an alpine ski center, which offers both equipment rentals and coaching. Call (✆ **416/395-7931**) for more information.

Swimming

The municipal parks, including High and Rosedale parks, offer a dozen or so outdoor pools (open June–Sept). Several community recreation centers have indoor pools. For **pool information,** call ✆ 416/338-7665.

Visitors may buy a day pass to use the pools at the **YMCA** (20 Grosvenor St.; ✆ **416/975-9622**) and the **University of Toronto Athletic Centre** (55 Harbord St., at Spadina Ave.; ✆ **416/978-4680**).

Tennis

There are 200 municipal parks across Toronto with tennis facilities. The most convenient are the courts in High, Rosedale, and Jonathan Ashridge parks. They are open from April to October only. Call **Toronto Parks** (✆ 416/392-1111) for information. The Toronto Parks website also has a brochure you can download; visit www.toronto.ca/parks.

SPECTATOR SPORTS

AUTO RACING   The Grand Prix of Toronto (formerly the Molson Indy; ✆ 416/588-7223; www.grandprixtoronto.com) takes place in July at the Exhibition Place Street circuit. Check the website for 2011 updates.

BASEBALL   Rogers Centre (1 Blue Jays Way, on Front St., beside the CN Tower) is the home of the **Toronto Blue Jays.** For tickets, contact the Toronto Blue Jays at ✆ **888/OK-GO-JAY** (888/654-6529) or 416/341-1234, or http://toronto.bluejays.mlb.com.

BASKETBALL   Toronto's basketball team, the **Raptors,** has its home ground in the **Air Canada Centre** (40 Bay St., at Lakeshore Blvd.). The NBA schedule runs from October to April. The arena seats 19,500 for basketball. For information, contact the **Raptors Basketball Club** (40 Bay St.; ✆ **416/815-5600;** www.nba.com/raptors). For tickets, call **Ticketmaster** (✆ **416/870-8000**).

FOOTBALL   Remember Kramer on *Seinfeld?* He would watch only Canadian football. If you're not familiar with it, here's your chance to catch a game. **Rogers Centre** (1 Blue Jays Way) is home to the **Argonauts** of the Canadian Football League. They play between June and November. For information, contact the club at ✆ **416/341-2700** or visit www.argonauts.on.ca. For tickets, call **Ticketmaster** (✆ **416/870-8000**).

GOLF TOURNAMENTS   Canada's national golf tournament, the **Bell Canadian Open,** usually takes place at the **Glen Abbey Golf Club** (✆ **905/844-1800**) in Oakville, about 40 minutes from the city. Most years, it runs over the Labour Day weekend.

HOCKEY   Hockey isn't Canada's national sport, believe it or not (that's lacrosse), but it's undoubtedly the most popular. The **Air Canada Centre** (40 Bay St., at Lakeshore Blvd.) is the home of the **Toronto Maple Leafs** (http://mapleleafs.nhl.com). The team hasn't won a Stanley Cup since 1967, but droves of fans stick with the franchise nonetheless. Though the arena seats 18,700 for hockey, tickets are not easy to come by because many are sold by subscription. The rest are available through **Ticketmaster** (✆ **416/870-8000**).

HORSE RACING   Thoroughbred racing takes place at **Woodbine Racetrack** (Rexdale Blvd. and Hwy. 427, Etobicoke; ✆ **416/675-6110** or 416/675-7223). It's famous for the Queen's Plate (usually contested on the third Sun in June); the Canadian International, a classic turf race (Sept or Oct); and the North America Cup (mid-June). Woodbine also hosts harness racing in spring and fall.

SOCCER   Toronto's new soccer club, the **Toronto FC** (http://toronto.fc.mlsnet.com), is beloved by Torontonians. It's the first non-U.S. team in Major League Soccer. They play at BMO Field at Exhibition Place; it was built for the FC, and it holds 20,195 spectators. For tickets, call **Ticketmaster** (✆ **416/870-8000**).

TENNIS TOURNAMENTS   Canada's international tennis championship, the **Rogers Cup,** takes place in Toronto *and* Montréal every August (the men's and women's championships alternate cities each year). In 2011, the women play in Toronto, the men in Montréal. For more information, call ✆ **877/283-6647** or check www.lovemeansnothing.ca.

 Stephen Colbert vs. the Raptors

Toronto's basketball team has been on Stephen Colbert's bad side since the very first episode of Comedy Central's *The Colbert Report* on October 17, 2005. At that time, Colbert put the Raptors "On Notice" for losing a game to Maccabi Tel Aviv, the Euroleague champions. Things got worse in early

2007: Because the Raptors' mascot came in ahead of the Saginaw Spirits' Steagle Colbeagle the Eagle (named after Colbert) in an online poll, Colbert demoted the Raptors to his "Dead to Me" board. Oh, the indignity of being on the same list as bowtie pasta, screw-cap wines, and men with beards!

CITY STROLLS

T oronto is a great city for walking. The patchwork of dynamic ethnic neighborhoods, the impressive architecture, and the many parks all combine to encourage visitors to lace up and hit the streets. To boot, there are small cafes and eateries for refueling along the way or for taking a lazy break. But because the city is such a sprawling place, you'll need to pick your route carefully . . . unless you're happy to wander.

The walking tours in this chapter aren't designed to provide an overview, but rather to guide you through the most colorful and exciting neighborhoods in the city, which feature worthwhile sights on almost every corner.

WALKING TOUR 1: CHINATOWN & KENSINGTON MARKET

START:	**St. Patrick subway station.**
FINISH:	**Queen's Park subway station.**
TIME:	**At least 2 hours. Depending on how long you want to linger at the Art Gallery of Ontario and at various stops, perhaps as long as 8 hours.**
BEST TIMES:	**Tuesday through Saturday during the day.**
WORST TIMES:	**Monday, when the Art Gallery is closed.**

This walk takes you through the oldest of Toronto's Chinatowns (the city's original Chinatown was on York Street between King and Queen streets, but skyscrapers replaced it long ago). Although at least four Chinatowns exist today, and most Chinese live in the suburbs, the intersection of Dundas Street and Spadina (pronounced spa-*dye*-na) Avenue is still a major shopping and dining area for the Asian community. As a new wave of immigrants has arrived from Southeast Asian countries—Thailand and Vietnam, in particular—this old but vibrant Chinatown has taken them in. Today, many businesses here are Vietnamese or Thai.

Successive waves of immigration have also changed the face of the nearby Kensington Market. From the turn of the 20th century until the 1950s, it was the heart of the Jewish community. In the 1950s, Portuguese immigrants arrived to work in the food-processing and meatpacking

Walking Tour: Chinatown & Kensington Market

1 St. Patrick's Church
2 Sharp Centre for Design
3 Art Gallery of Ontario
4 The Grange
5 Bau-Xi
6 Consulate General of Italy
7 The Herb Depot
8 J & S Arts and Crafts
9 Ten Ren Tea
10 Chinatown Centre
11 Dragon City
12 Oriental Harvest
13 Happy Seven and Lee Garden
14 Tap Phong Trading Company
15 Plaiter Place
16 Tom's Place
17 Chocolate Addict
18 My Market Bakery
19 Exile
20 Courage My Love
21 Dancing Days
22 Bellevue Square Park
23 Kiever Synagogue
24 Sasmart Smart Wear
25 Casa Acoreana
26 Perola Supermarket
27 Augusta Dining
28 Church of St. Stephen-in-the-Fields

industries, and made it their home. In the '60s, a Caribbean presence arrived. Today, this market retains traces of all these communities.

From the St. Patrick subway station, exit on the northwest corner of Dundas St. and University Ave., and walk west on Dundas St. Turn right onto McCaul St. At no. 131, you'll see:

1 St. Patrick's Church

Built in 1861 for Toronto's Irish Catholic community, this church became the base of German-speaking Catholics from 1929 to the late 1960s. Inside, you'll find some of the most beautiful stained glass in Toronto. The church is also a popular site for concerts.

Go back toward Dundas St. and walk west; looking south on McCaul St., you'll see:

2 Sharp Centre for Design

This is one of the city's more controversial contributions to the recent surge in new and bold architecture. Will Alsop's building, which is part of the Ontario College of Art & Design, looks like a checkerboard box on stilts. The Sharp Centre won a Worldwide Award from the Royal Institute of British Architects in 2004; they described it as "courageous, bold, and just a little insane." Admire the insanity from the outside; visitors are not allowed beyond the lobby.

Continue west along Dundas St. On your left is the:

3 Art Gallery of Ontario

Thanks in part to an attractive top-to-bottom renovation by architect Frank Gehry—and even more to the addition of the brilliant Thomson collection—the AGO is now Toronto's don't-miss museum. Famous for the Group of Seven canvases and Henry Moore gallery, the AGO is also home to European masterworks (including Rubens's *Massacre of the Innocents*), an eye-popping collection of carved miniatures, and a photography gallery. Lately, a new gift from local collector and philanthropist Dr. Ydessa Hendeles will add 32 Canadian and international contemporary artworks—the most significant single gift of contemporary art in the AGO's 110-year history.

Walk behind the AGO, following Beverley St. south. Behind the AGO, you'll find:

4 The Grange

This historic mansion was the original home of the Art Gallery of Ontario. Built in 1817, the Georgian mansion is still part of the AGO. The surrounding Grange Park is still a charming spot, in spite of nearby development—Village by the Grange, an apartment and shopping complex, is also tucked back here.

Retrace your steps to Dundas St. W. and cross so that you're on the north side of the street. On this block, you'll find:

5 Bau-Xi

This gallery, at 340 Dundas St. W., represents contemporary Canadian artists. It's been in business since 1965 and offers a worthwhile perspective on the national current art scene.

Walk west along Dundas St.; at the northwest corner of Beverley and Dundas sts. is the:

6 Consulate General of Italy

It doesn't look like a government building: The rambling late-19th-century mansion, with its sandy brick, quasi-Gothic windows and wrought-iron decoration, is a beauty. Too bad you can't go in.

You're now walking into the heart of Chinatown, with its grocery stores, bakeries, and emporiums selling herbs, handcrafts, and other items from Asia.

What follows are some of my favorite stops along the stretch of Dundas St. between Beverley St. and Spadina Ave. On the south side, or the left side as you go west, is:

7 The Herb Depot

At nos. 407–409, this market carries every herb under the sun. Many are a mystery, but the terrific English-speaking herbalists and acupuncturists on duty are happy to help. Several markets in Chinatown carry similar wares, but this one is the best bet for those who don't speak Chinese.

On the north side of the street is:

8 J & S Arts and Crafts

This shop, at no. 430, is a good place to pick up souvenirs, including kimonos and happy coats, kung-fu suits, cushion covers, and all-cotton Chinatown T-shirts. **Kim Moon,** no. 438, is an Asian bakery that features abalone cookies, deep-fried lotus crisps, and dim sum pork buns (my husband is a huge fan).

9 Ten Ren Tea ☕

Ten Ren Tea sells all kinds of tea—black, oolong, green—stored in large canisters at the back of the store. Charming ceramic teapots and cups are on sale here, along with gnarled root ginseng. You can break here for tea—but even if you don't want to sit down, the staff will probably urge you to sample an unfamiliar variety in a tiny cup. 454 Dundas St. ✆ 416/598-7872.

Cross Dundas St. so that you are on the south side of the street again. Turn left at Spadina Ave. and walk south to the first stoplight. Cross Spadina Ave. at this light and directly ahead of you is:

10 Chinatown Centre

This huge complex at 222 Spadina Ave. is now the go-to Chinatown mall. It has an incredible array of businesses under one roof: **Clean Slate Beauty** is here, as is **Fortune Jade** (which stocks costume jewelry, as well as real pieces), and **Kid's House,** which has great deals on clothing for children. There's also a food court and a Super 8 hotel.

Walk north on Spadina Ave.; at the southwest corner of Spadina and Dundas is:

11 Dragon City

This mall at 280 Spadina Ave. is smaller—and far quieter—than Chinatown Centre. Still, it's notable for a few things. The pet store **Downtown Pet Centre** is in the basement; they have emperor sharks, fancy *orandas,* and piranhas to watch in the aquariums, as well as a great collection of gear for your dog/cat/bird/fish at home. Dragon City also has Hui's Pharmacy, a Canada Post outlet inside Sun Wa bookstore, and free Wi-Fi throughout the building.

Cross Dundas St. and walk north on Spadina Ave.; at no. 310 is:

12 Oriental Harvest

Look at all the different provisions—chili and fish sauces, fresh meat and fish (including live tilapia in tanks), preserved plums, chrysanthemum tea and other infusions, moon cakes, and large sacks of rice. There's also a great selection of Kasugai Japanese-made gummy candies (my favorite flavor is lychee) and sweet rice snacks to keep you going.

13 Happy Seven and Lee Garden ☕

For fine, reasonably priced food, a Chinatown favorite is Happy Seven (358 Spadina Ave.; ℂ 416/971-9820). If you don't mind lining up, head for the ever-popular Lee Garden (331 Spadina Ave.; ℂ 416/593-9524; p. 100).

Continuing north, cross St. Andrews St. to reach:

14 Tap Phong Trading Company

This shop, at 360 Spadina Ave., stocks terrific wicker baskets of all shapes and sizes, as well as woks and ceramic cookware, attractive mortars and pestles, and other household items.

Cross Baldwin St., and you'll come to:

15 Plaiter Place

At 384 Spadina Ave., Plaiter Place has a huge selection of wicker baskets, birdcages, woven blinds, bamboo steamers, hats, and other fun items. **Fortune Housewares,** no. 388, carries kitchen and household items—including brand names—for prices at least 20% lower than elsewhere in the city.

Now double back to Baldwin Street. You're heading into the heart of the **Kensington Market** area, which is particularly rich with cultural diversity. Once, it was primarily a Jewish market; later, it became a Portuguese neighborhood. Today, it is largely Asian and Caribbean, but its past lives on in many ways.

Head back to Baldwin St. and walk west, you'll find:

16 Tom's Place

This traditional haberdasher—located at 190 Baldwin St.—is a place where you can still haggle for a deal on good, Italian-made men's shirts. The store also sells women's clothing, but it's mostly the men's suits and clothing that draws crowds.

Across the street is:

17 Chocolate Addict

Located at 185 Baldwin St., this tiny temple to chocolate has some tasty, unusual offerings (mmm, wasabi truffles . . .).

Across the street and down a few shops, look for:

18 My Market Bakery

At 172 Baldwin St. is one of the market's finest bakeries, with plenty of fresh goods baked on-site, plus a selection of some other small bakeries around town. Good for breads, pastries, and cookies, too.

Further down the street, at no. 64, is Tutti Frutti, a well-stocked health-oriented grocery store (great for those with food allergies or celiac disease).

As you stroll south along Kensington Ave. and pass St. Andrews St., you will find a series of secondhand- and vintage-clothing stores.

19 Exile

At 62 Kensington Ave., on the west side of the street, this store has good jeans, leather jackets, and assorted accessories.

20 Courage My Love

The best spot for cheap but chic vintage clothing is at no. 14. It stocks retro gowns and wedding dresses, suits, and accessories, as well as new jewelry and beads for do-it-yourself projects. The C$5 rack out front (in nice weather) has some unbelievable deals; if you take some of these exquisite but damaged dresses and coats to a tailor, you can end up with beautiful, original pieces for a song.

21 Dancing Days

At no. 17 (on the east side of the street), you'll find party-ready glad rags that will make you look like an extra in *Grease*.

When you reach Dundas St., turn right and walk 1 block to Augusta Ave. Turn right on Augusta Ave. As you walk north and cross Wales Ave., you'll find:

22 Bellevue Square Park

On maps, this park is often referred to as Denison Square. Either way, it's a lovely spot. While you're checking out the statue of Canadian actor Al Waxman, you may smell whiffs of marijuana in the air. Kensington Market is home to some head shops, and smoking cannabis in public—while illegal—is not uncommon in and around the park.

Stroll through the park; at the corner of Bellevue Ave. and Denison Sq., you'll find:

23 Kiever Synagogue

This building, at 28 Denison Sq., was completed in 1927. Architect Benjamin Swartz designed it with Byzantine style in mind. The most striking features are the twin domes atop the building (sadly, the building isn't open to the public). The Kiever Synagogue was the first specifically Jewish building designated an historic site by the province of Ontario.

Turn back toward Augusta Ave., and you'll see:

24 Sasmart Smart Wear

This discount store has a wacky assortment of goods, from OshKosh clothing for kids to antique china, kitchen gear (new and used) to luggage, plus plenty of gadgets. It's a weird, cluttered space, but the prices are unbeatable.

Walk north on Augusta Ave. to:

25 Casa Acoreana

An old-fashioned store at no. 235, it stocks a full range of fresh coffees, as well as great pecans and filberts.

Just up the street is:

26 Perola Supermarket

This store, at 247 Augusta Ave., is great for cassava and strings of peppers—ancho, *arbol, pasilla*—that are hung up to dry. Check out the bins of other exotic fruits and herbs, too.

27 Kensington Market 🛒

The Aspetta Caffe (207 Augusta Ave.; ✆ 416/916-8275) is a perfect perch if you want to people-watch while sipping a *caffe* and having a tasty *panini* or pasta. If you're in the neighborhood at dinnertime, try the charming La Palette (256 Augusta Ave.; ✆ 416/929-4900) or funky Torito (276 Augusta Ave.; ✆ 647/436-5874) for tapas.

Continue north along Augusta Ave. to College St. Turn west on College St., and you'll find:

28 Church of St. Stephen-in-the-Fields

This small but historically significant church has had to fight hard to ward off the condo developers circling Kensington Market. Ironically, the Anglican Diocesan Council wanted to sell its own church, and the local community—many of whom have no religious connection to the church—came together to save it. The building is a lovely example of Gothic Revival architecture, built in 1858, and contains some splendid stained-glass windows.

On College St., hop on an eastbound streetcar, which will deliver you to the Queen's Park subway station. The southbound train will take you downtown.

WALKING TOUR 2: **WYCHWOOD**

START:	**Dupont subway station.**
FINISH:	**Pain Perdu or Patachou on St. Clair West.**
TIME:	**2 to 4 hours.**
BEST TIME:	**Weekdays during business hours or Saturday mornings.**
WORST TIMES:	**Sundays, when many buildings are closed or reserved for weddings.**

This eclectic tour takes in the city archives; a castle; a stately home; a toll keeper's house; and two artist enclaves, one in a sylvan glade, the other in a former public-transit parking lot. The castle is a tale in itself: Toronto's kitschy chateau, Casa Loma, is a museum and events destination, complete with Elizabethan-style chimneys, Rhineland turrets, secret passageways, and an underground tunnel. Built about 100 years ago, it was a dream-come-true for a wealthy financier who, in the long term, had greater architectural ambitions than cash. The neighborhoods involved include busy Davenport; the magical park-like setting of Wychwood Park, with its stately homes; the pretty Hillcrest area, another residential gem; and finally, the new and very progressive development of an old "barn" for streetcars that was saved from ugly development by a brilliant partnership between Artscape, the city's primo art cooperative, and the Stop Food Community Centre, a leading activist organization that works to feed, with dignity, Toronto's poor. Any day of the week, stop by what's known as The Green Barns, and you might find there's a screening of a topical documentary on food politics, an exhibit of resident artists' work, children from the nursery school playing outside, or a bustling farmers market that runs year-round.

From the Dupont subway station, walk north on Spadina Rd. under the train bridge and to the City of Toronto Archives, at 255 Spadina Rd.

Walking Tour: Wychwood

Artscape Wychwood Barns **1**
The Baldwin Steps **3**
Casa Loma **6**
City of Toronto Archives **7**
Spadina Museum: Historic House & Gardens **5**
Tollkeeper's Park **4**
Wychwood Park **2**

1 City of Toronto Archives

This often-overlooked repository is the closest thing Toronto has to a museum of the city. Ongoing exhibits, largely photography-based, reflect events and themes in the city's past. The collection has more than 1 million images, dating from 1856.

Walk 100 meters north to the TOP of Spadina Rd., at Davenport Rd., and look up at the zigzagging flight of stairs you are about to climb:

2 The Baldwin Steps

This part of Spadina Road ends at the base of a zigzagging flight of stairs that ascends the pre–Ice Age shoreline of the ancient Lake Iroquois. A public right-of-way that dates from the 1800s, The Baldwin Steps are a rare example in the city of a thigh-burning incline. The panoramic views of downtown and Lake Ontario are worth the effort. The steps are named after Robert Baldwin, a former premier of Ontario who owned land in this well-to-do neighborhood.

Continue on the path for 50m (164 ft.), with Toronto's turreted wonder, Casa Loma, on your left. Instead of visiting, though, turn right into the lush garden setting of this more subdued stately mansion:

3 Spadina Museum: Historic House & Gardens

The historic home of financier James Austin was occupied by the family for over 100 years, from 1866 until 1980, when it became a city-run museum. In 2010, the interior was completely renovated and updated from a 19th-century setting to one focused on the inter-war years, with an emphasis on decorations from the 1920s. The grounds are as sumptuous as the interiors.

It's just a hop, skip, and a jump across the street to a more exuberant neighbor:

4 Casa Loma

Sir Henry Pellatt, who built this faux chateau between 1911 and 1914, studied medieval palaces and then gathered materials and furnishings from around the world, bringing marble, glass, and paneling from Europe; teak from Asia; and oak and walnut from North America. He then imported Scottish stonemasons to build the massive walls that surround the 2.5-hectare (6¼-acre) site. The architect was a local talent E. J. Lennox.

Wander through the majestic Great Hall, with its 18m-high (59-ft.) hammer-beam ceiling; the Oak Room, where three artisans took 3 years to fashion the paneling; and the Conservatory, with its elegant bronze doors, stained-glass dome, and pink-and-green marble. The castle encompasses battlements and a tower, and a 244m (801-ft.) tunnel runs to the stables, where Spanish tile and mahogany surrounded the horses.

5 Sir Henry's Café 🍽

Situated on the lower level in what was originally designed as Sir Henry's private exercise room, Sir Henry's Café is just a cafeteria-style coffee shop and feels pretty down-market from the surroundings. But if you're in need of some quick fuel, this is the only stop around. (✆ 416/913-3247).

From Casa Loma, walk down Walmer Rd., then turn right along Davenport Rd. to Bathurst St. The northwest corner of the intersection is home to one of the oldest structures in the city, a toll keeper's cottage:

6 Tollkeeper's Park

This little home built in 1835 is where hapless toll keepers tried to extract pennies from passing horse-drawn traffic along Davenport Road until tolls were abolished in 1890. It's also a rare example of vertical (rather than horizontal) wood planking. The simple living conditions in the two-bedroom home attest to the terms of the office: Any uncollected tariffs were deducted from their pay. A small interpretive center, where costumed docents regale visitors with stories of life in Muddy York, is connected to the house.

Continue west on the north side of Davenport Rd. until you reach the sign for Wychwood Park Private Grounds:

7 Wychwood Park

Don't let the "private" sign deter you: Step through the stone gate to enter another world tucked into the heart of the city. The fortunate residents of this secret enclave like to keep the wooded setting to themselves; another sign just inside the gate—"Danger Deep Water Quicksand"—is merely a ruse to deter visitors. Immediately ahead is a pond (often featuring the resident swan) and a fork in the road. The route to the left is a little shorter, but both are pleasant, taking you past many English-style Arts and Crafts homes designed by Toronto architect Eden Smith. Marmaduke Matthews envisioned an artist colony when he built the first home here in 1874, naming it after Wychwood Forest in Oxfordshire, England. This early example of a planned community retains its natural landscaping and bucolic setting.

Exit Wychwood Park at the north end and walk north on Wychwood Ave. 2 blocks until you get to:

8 Artscape Wychwood Barns

It's hard to imagine, as you come out at the top of these winding, tree-lined roads, that a TTC streetcar repair barn operated here until the 1990s. Now, it's one of the city's most successful transformations of industry into arts space. Artscape Wychwood Barns opened in 2009; attractions include studios for the 2 dozen artists-in-residence, ongoing exhibits of new work, and archival images of the old Barns. The Stop Food Community Centre, a leading activist organization that fights poverty and pushes political agendas on the food front, runs the food side of the space with a bake oven, greenhouse, community kitchen, and classroom on site. There are lots of events to check out, from movies to fab dinners/fundraisers. (www.thestop.org). A bustling Saturday farmers market is complete with picnic-like prepared foods, such as butternut squash empanadas and some of the best fish tacos anywhere. If the weather cooperates, sit outside with a bite to eat and watch the parade of dogs, kids, farmers, and shoppers. Kick back: You've earned it.

Walk 2 blocks north to St. Clair Ave. W., where there are plenty of great cafes and restaurants.

9 Pain Perdu or Patachou ☕

Try Pain Perdu (736 Saint Clair Ave. W.; ℂ 416/656-7246) for great quiches and *croque monsieur,* or Patachou (833 St Clair Ave W.; ℂ 416/782-0122) for buttery croissants and lovely pastries.

**ST. LAWRENCE &
DOWNTOWN EAST**

START:	**Union Station.**
FINISH:	**King subway station.**
TIME:	**2 to 3 hours.**
BEST TIME:	**Saturday, when the St. Lawrence Market is in full swing.**
WORST TIME:	**Sunday, when it's closed.**

At one time, this area was at the center of city life. Today, it's a little off center, yet it has some historic and modern architectural treasures and a wealth of history in and around the St. Lawrence Market.

1 Union Station

Check out the interior of this classical revival beauty, which opened in 1927 as a temple to and for the railroad. The shimmering ceiling, faced with vitrified Guastavino tile, soars 27m (89 ft.) above the 79m-long (259-ft.) hall.

Across the street, at York and Front sts., stands the:

2 Fairmont Royal York

The venerable railroad hotel is a longtime gathering place for Torontonians. It's the home of the famous Imperial Room cabaret and nightclub, which used to be one of Eartha Kitt's favorite venues. The hotel was once the tallest building in Toronto and the largest hotel in the British Commonwealth. Check out the lobby, with its coffered ceiling and opulent furnishings. One floor up on the mezzanine is a new **gallery** of black-and-white photographs that cover the hotel's long and illustrious history.

3 The Royal York ☕

Okay, you're just getting started, but it would be a missed opportunity to not stop in for a bite at one of the many good dining options at the Royal York (✆ 416/368-2511; p. 76), whether a tasty breakfast at the York Bakery or a special meal at the Epic dining room. At least try a refreshing libation at the Library Bar.

As you leave the hotel, turn left and walk east on Front St. At the corner of Bay and Front sts., look up at the stunning:

4 Royal Bank Plaza

The two triangular gold-sheathed towers rise 41 floors and 26 floors, respectively. A 40m-high (131-ft.) atrium joins them, and 68kg (150 lb.) of gold enhances the mirrored glass. Webb Zerafa Menkes Housden designed the project, which was built between 1973 and 1977.

Cross Bay Street and continue east on Front Street. On the south side of the street is the impressive sweep of **One Front Street,** the main post office building (okay, not an exciting-sounding sight, but an attractive one).

On the north side of the street is:

5 Brookfield Place

Go inside to view the soaring galleria. Skidmore, Owings, and Merrill, with Bregman & Hamann, designed it in 1993. The twin office towers connect through a

Walking Tour: St. Lawrence & Downtown East

1 Union Station
2 Fairmont Royal York
3 The Royal York 🍴
4 Royal Bank Plaza
5 Brookfield Place
6 Bank of Montreal
7 Flatiron or Gooderham Building
8 The Sony Centre
9 Beardmore Building
10 St. Lawrence Market
11 St. Lawrence Market 🍴
12 St. Lawrence Hall
13 St. James Cathedral
14a Le Meridien King Edward 🍴
14b La Maquette 🍴
14c Biagio 🍴

huge glass-covered galleria five stories high, spanning the block between Bay and Yonge streets. Designed by artist-architect Santiago Calatrava of Bregman & Hamann, it links the old Midland Bank building to the twin towers.

On Front St., turn left and continue to the northwest corner of Yonge and Front sts., stopping to notice the:

6 Hockey Hall of Fame

The ornate old building may be a surprise—built in 1885, it used to be a Bank of Montreal. Inside, the banking hall rises to a beamed coffered ceiling with domed skylights of stained glass. If you're a hockey fanatic, this is your shrine (p. 141).

From here, you can look ahead along Front St. and see the weird mural by Derek M. Besant that adorns the famous and highly photogenic:

7 Flatiron or Gooderham Building (1892)

This building was the headquarters of George Gooderham, who expanded his distilling business into railroads, insurance, and philanthropy. At one time, his liquor business was the biggest in the British Empire, and he was also president of the Bank of Toronto. The five-story building occupies a triangular site, with the windows at the western edge beautifully curved and topped with a semicircular tower. The design is by David Roberts.

At the southwest corner of Yonge and Front sts., you can stop in at:

8 The Sony Centre

The Sony Centre for the Performing Arts sits across Scott Street from the **St. Lawrence Centre.** In 1974, when the Sony was called the O'Keefe Centre, Mikhail Baryshnikov defected from the Soviet Union after performing here.

Continue east along Front St. to the:

9 Beardmore Building

At 35–39 Front St. E., this and the many other cast-iron buildings lining the street were the heart of the late-19th-century warehouse district, close to the lakefront and railheads. It lost some of its charm, though, when the **Winners** store moved in (I'm not saying that I haven't shopped there, just that the sign isn't so attractive). At no. 45 is **Nicholas Hoare,** one of the coziest bookstores in the city.

Continue east along Front St., crossing Church St. and then Market St., to the:

10 St. Lawrence Market

The old market building on the right holds this great market hall, which was constructed around the city's second city hall (1844–1845). The elegant pedimented facade that you see as you stand in the center of the hall was originally the center block of the city hall. Today, the market abounds with vendors selling fresh eggs, Mennonite sausage, seafood, meats, cheeses, and baked goods. From Thursday to Saturday, in the north building across the street, a farmers' market starts at 5am.

11 St. Lawrence Market 🍴

Don't forget the famous peameal (Canadian) bacon sandwiches at the Carousel Bakery. There's also Chris the Cheesemonger and Alex Farms for great cheeses and more. Other nearby choices include Le Papillon (69 Front St. E.; ✆ 416/367-0303; p. 129), which features savory and dessert crêpes, and HotHouse Cafe (35 Church St.; ✆ 416/366-7800).

Exit the market where you came in. Cross Wellington St. and cut through Market Lane Park and the shops at Market Sq., past the north market building. Turn right onto King St. to:

12 St. Lawrence Hall

This was the focal point of the community in the mid–19th century. This hall was the site of grand city occasions, political rallies, balls, and entertainment. It was here that Frederick Douglass delivered an antislavery lecture; Jenny Lind and Adelina Patti sang in 1851 and 1860, respectively; Gen. Tom Thumb appeared in 1862; and George Brown campaigned for Confederation. William Thomas designed the elegant Palladian-style building, which boasts a domed cupola.

Cross King Street and enter the 19th-century garden. It has a cast-iron drinking fountain for people, horses, and dogs, and flowerbeds filled with seasonal blooms.

If you like, rest on a bench while you admire the handsome proportions of St. Lawrence Hall and listen to the chimes of:

13 St. James' Cathedral

Adjacent to the garden on the north side of King Street, this is a beautiful Gothic church that is open to the public. The graceful building and its surrounding park make a serene setting to rest and gather one's thoughts, although the park can be a gathering place for some of the city's rougher citizens.

From here, you can view one of the early retail buildings, built when King Street was the main commercial street. **Nos. 129–35** was originally an Army and Navy Store; cast-iron, plate-glass, and arched windows allowed the shopper to see what was available in the store. Also note nos. 111 and 125. The **Toronto Sculpture Garden** (115 King St.; ✆ **416/485-9658**) is a quiet corner for contemplation.

14 King Street East 🚇

From St. James', the venerable Le Meridien King Edward (37 King St. E.; ✆ 416/863-9700) is only a block away. You can stop for afternoon tea in the lobby lounge, or light fare or lunch in the Café Victoria ([tel]416/364-6363). Both La Maquette (111 King St. E.; ✆ 416/366-8191) and Biagio (157 King St. E.; ✆ 416/366-4040), have appealing courtyards.

From St. James' Cathedral, go south on Church St. for 1 block and turn right into Colbourne St. From Colbourne St., turn left down Leader Lane to Wellington St., where you can enjoy a fine view of the mural on the Flatiron Building and the rhythmic flow of mansard rooflines along the south side of Front St. Turn right and proceed to Yonge St.; then turn right and walk to King St. to catch the subway to your next destination.

WALKING TOUR 4: **CABBAGETOWN**

START:	**Allan Gardens.**
FINISH:	**Sumach and Gerrard streets (for streetcar to College Station).**
TIME:	**2 to 3 hours.**
BEST TIME:	**Tuesdays from May through October, when the Farmers' Market is open in Riverdale Park West.**
WORST TIME:	**There is no worst time; all of the other attractions on this tour can be seen on weekdays and weekends.**

Cabbagetown, one of the city's oldest neighborhoods, has gone from rags to riches more times than most can count. Built up in the 1840s by Irish immigrants fleeing the Great Famine, the name of the district comes from the cabbage plants they grew in their front yards. It has been both a wealthy enclave and a slum, but today, the residential streets have been gentrified, and the surrounding commercial streets are on an upswing.

1 Allan Gardens

This was Toronto's first civic park. For many years, it ran to the seedy side, but since the University of Toronto took over the care of the greenhouses in 2004, it has become a charming place to visit again (but not at night). The Children's Conservatory is well worth a look, but the crown jewel of the garden is the Edwardian Palm House.

At the corner of Carlton and Sherbourne sts., you'll see:

2 St. Luke's United Church

Known as Sherbourne Street Methodist when the first sermon was preached here in 1887, this is one of Toronto's most beautiful examples of religious architecture. From the outside, the imposing stonework and turrets make it look like a castle. Inside, the sanctuary has been completely refurbished in the past few years. The glorious stained-glass windows are the pièce de résistance (the church once had a wealthy congregation, and you'll see that the windows were all "dedicated" by businessmen trying to outdo one another).

On the north side of Carlton St. is:

3 St. Peter's Anglican Church

This parish was originally based in a cemetery chapel. In 1866, John Strachan, the Aberdeen-born Bishop of Toronto, opened this church. It's a pretty example of High Victorian Gothic, and later additions are in keeping with its original style.

Walk east along Carlton St. to:

4 Daniel et Daniel

This food shop at 248 Carlton St. (© **416/968-9275**) is a good place for simple but tasty fare, like meat pies and generous sandwiches. There are freshly baked pastries, pâtés, tarts, cakes, and other treats made in-house.

You're now at the intersection with:

5 Parliament Street

Parliament Street got its name because the first Upper Canada government buildings in "muddy little York" (as Toronto was then known) were built at its southern end in 1793. Today, it's the main commercial artery of Cabbagetown. This isn't exactly trendy (at press time, Starbucks had yet to set up an outpost on this stretch), but you can make some great finds. At no. 480 is a branch of **Planet Aid,** the secondhand-clothing store that raises money for projects in the developing world. **Sharon's,** at no. 503, is a small but glamorous boutique with clothing and accessories. **Green's Antiques,** at no. 529, is a true gem, with plenty of great chairs, ottomans, and sofas, many of which have been newly upholstered by the talented staff.

Walking Tour: Cabbagetown

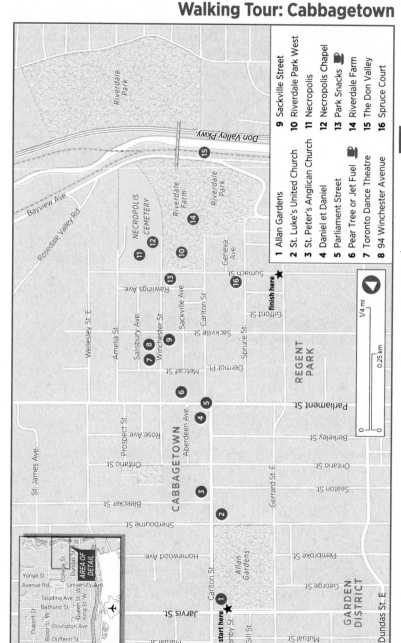

1 Allan Gardens
2 St. Luke's United Church
3 St. Peter's Anglican Church
4 Daniel et Daniel
5 Parliament Street
6 Pear Tree or Jet Fuel 🍽
7 Toronto Dance Theatre
8 94 Winchester Avenue
9 Sackville Street
10 Riverdale Park West
11 Necropolis
12 Necropolis Chapel 🍽
13 Park Snacks 🍽
14 Riverdale Farm
15 The Don Valley
16 Spruce Court

6 Pear Tree or Jet Fuel ☕

One reliable place to grab a bite is the Pear Tree (507 Parliament St.; ✆ 416/962-8190), which serves hearty salads such as the goat cheese and spinach. Another great spot is Jet Fuel (519 Parliament St.; ✆ 416/968-9982), a coffee shop that has become a local landmark (bike couriers love this place). Everything here is made with espresso, so be prepared for a good jolt.

Turn right at Winchester St. (at the corner, you'll pass the Laurentian Room), and walk east. At the northeast corner of the intersection of Winchester and Metcalfe sts., you'll see:

7 Toronto Dance Theatre

The former St. Enoch's Presbyterian Church was built in 1891 in a Romanesque Revival style. Oddly, the redbrick exterior makes the building (almost) blend in with the rest of the neighborhood (quite a feat, given its size).

Continue east to:

8 94 Winchester St.

This was once the home of magician Doug Henning. You can't go inside (it's someone else's home now), but a plaque at the front commemorates his life (1947–2000) and immortalizes him as "magician, teacher, politician." The first two are easy to get, but the last requires some explanation. In 1994, Henning stood for election to Parliament as a member of the Natural Law Party, an organization memorable mainly for its belief in levitation.

Continue walking east on Winchester St. and turn south onto:

9 Sackville Street

This quiet street had some of the loveliest homes in Cabbagetown. While the architecture is an eclectic mix, you'll mostly see variations on Victorian and Queen Anne styles. Walk down to Sackville Place (the street will be only on your left side). Across from it is Pine Terrace, a series of Victorian redbrick town houses built in 1886.

Walk north back to Winchester Ave. and follow it east to Sumach St., where you'll find:

10 Riverdale Park West

This is a lovely park that's a favorite with neighboring families. While you stop to enjoy the scenery, you can learn more about Cabbagetown's history. Look for the large maps and plaques in the park's northwestern corner, and you can learn all about many of the fascinating people who once called the neighborhood theirs. (Hint: Doug Henning fit in very well.) Depending on when you visit, you may find a farmers' market operating in the park, too.

Across from the park, on the north side of Winchester Ave., is the:

11 Necropolis

Walk under the Gothic-inspired porte-cochere to enter Toronto's city of the dead. This is the prettiest cemetery you could hope to find, and if you stop at the office (on the right side as you step under the archway), you can pick up a free map that will guide you to the final resting places of some of Toronto's famous inhabitants. Check out the imposing stone Celtic cross that marks the grave of William Lyon

Mackenzie, the leader of the Upper Canada rebellion who later became the mayor of Toronto (see the entry for **Mackenzie House,** p. 140, for more details).

When you finish here, exit through the porte-cochere; on your right is the:

12 Necropolis Chapel

This small chapel is a stunning example of High Victorian Gothic style. Architect Henry Langley built it in 1872 (he's the same person who designed the eye-catching towers at St. James' Cathedral, p. 138, and St. Michael's Cathedral, p. 138). The chapel and the adjoining porte-cochere are widely considered to be two of the finest pieces of Gothic Revival architecture in Canada. (Langley is buried in the Necropolis, and his grave is on the map mentioned above in stop 11.)

13 Park Snacks or Riverdale Farm 🍴

You won't find many places to grab a snack within the residential heart of Cabbagetown. The exception is Park Snacks (no phone), a take-out-only spot at the southwest corner of Winchester and Sumach sts. In summer, you can buy drinks, ice cream, or sandwiches here. Riverdale Park West provides many benches that are well shaded by trees. Year-round, you can buy snacks at Riverdale Farm (see stop 14, below).

On the eastern edge of the park, you'll see the entrance to:

14 Riverdale Farm

It's a rarity: a working farm in the heart of downtown. The grounds are clean and the animals very well cared for. It's a charming place to visit, particularly if you have children in tow, but even if you don't, you can appreciate the chicks, bunnies, cows, horses, rare-breed pigs, goats, and other animals. Watch out for baby animals, too.

When you leave the farm, turn to the left and follow its perimeter; this will give you a good view of:

15 The Don Valley

There's been a big movement to "Bring Back the Don" in Toronto, and the valley has been revitalized by it. The Don River is no longer a mighty force, but at least its valley is green. If you look to the north, you'll see the **Bloor Street Viaduct** (one of the best viewing points in the city).

Walk west along Spruce St. to Sumach St.; on the northwest corner, you'll see:

16 Spruce Court

This was the first public-housing project in Canada. This utopian collection of two- and three-story cottages was built in 1913 by the appropriately named architect Eden Smith. All face either onto the street or one of the leafy private courtyards. Many, though not all, of the housing blocks were designed in English Cottage style, which was intended to evoke the bucolic splendor of country life. You can't see the interiors—since 1980, these have been private family homes run by a co-op—but from the street, you can appreciate the half-timbered gables, the tall chimneys, and arched brick porches.

Walk south along Spruce St. to Gerrard St.; from here, you can catch any westbound streetcar, which will take you to College Station.

START:	**The CN Tower, near the corner of John and Front streets.**
FINISH:	**A Queen Street West watering hole.**
TIME:	**2 to 4 hours.**
BEST TIME:	**Weekdays during business hours.**
WORST TIMES:	**Weekends, when the stock market is closed and the Financial District is dead.**

Toronto's answer to Wall Street is a mix of old-fashioned—and very grand—bank buildings and modern towers that stretch to the sky.

8

CITY STROLLS | The Financial District

Start by going up the:

1 CN Tower

Although it has become a symbol of the city, the CN Tower drew a great deal of criticism when it was built in 1975. It has since been recognized as an important symbol of a city trying to forge a new identity. Robert Fulford writes in *Accidental City* (Houghton Mifflin): "In the 1970s [Toronto] was struggling to shake off the dowdy self-image that was part of its heritage as a colonial city. . . . Torontonians were starting to consider, with shy pleasure, the novel idea that their city might be attractive, even enviable. . . . At that happy moment, the tower reinforced local exuberance and asserted the city's claim to even more attention." However you view it, the most enjoyable thing is the view *from* it. If you dare, lie down on the glass floor for a unique vertiginous experience.

Once you're back down at the base, exit at the corner of John and Front streets. From here, look to the right along Front Street to see the glistening golden Royal Bank towers (part of the Royal Bank Centre). The CBC Centre stretches along the north side of Front Street for a whole long block. Inside, you can peek at the lobby radio studios and take a nostalgic radio-TV trip in the free museum.

Walk north on John St. (with the CN Tower behind you) to King St. Turn right and walk 1 block to:

2 The Princess of Wales Theatre

Princess Diana opened it in 1993. Constructed for a production of *Miss Saigon,* the theater was the brainchild of impresario Ed Mirvish and his son, David. Try to pop inside for a peek at the 929 sq. m (10,000 sq. ft.) of murals created by Frank Stella. There's one on the exterior back of the building that's worth walking around to see.

Exit the theater and continue along King Street past a cluster of restaurants owned by Ed Mirvish. (Drop in to one to check out the larger-than-life decor Ed has purchased at antique closeouts.) You'll also pass a wall of newspaper clippings about this gutsy Torontonian. Booster and benefactor of the city, he started out in bleak circumstances as owner of a bankrupt store during the Depression. He paid off the debt and launched **Honest Ed's** (see chapter 9), a discount store at Bloor and Bathurst streets that brought him fame and fortune. He saved the Royal Alex (see next stop) from demolition, and he and his son have become theater impresarios in Toronto and in London, where Ed outbid Andrew Lloyd Webber in 1982 for the Old Vic.

Walking Tour: The Financial District

1 CN Tower
2 Princess of Whales Theatre
3 Royal Alexandra
4 Roy Thompson Hall
5 St. Andrew's Presyterian Church
6 Sun Life Centre
7 2 First Canadian Place
8 First Canadian Place
9 Jump Café and Bar
10 Toronto Dominion Centre
11 Canadian Imperial Bank of Commerce
12 Scotia Tower
13 National Club Building
14 Canadian Permanent Trust Building
15 The Bay
16 Old City Hall
17 New City Hall
18 The Sheraton Centre
19 Osgoode Hall
20 Campbell House
21 Canada Life Insurance Building

3 The Royal Alexandra

John M. Lyle built this beloved theater in 1906 and 1907 at a cost of C$750,000. In 1963, it was scheduled for demolition, but Ed Mirvish bought it for C$200,000 and refurbished it. Named after Queen Alexandra, wife of Edward VII, the magnificent beaux-arts structure is Edwardian down to the last detail. It abounds with gilt and velvet, and green marble lines the entrance foyer.

Across the street from these two theaters stands the new **Metro Hall** (55 John St.), designed by Brisbin Brook Beynon. This building is pretty much a white elephant these days—it was constructed when Toronto had six separate municipal governments and a Metro Council for joint projects and concerns. On occasion, there are art installations on the first floor.

Also on the south side of the street, at the corner of King and Simcoe sts., is:

4 Roy Thomson Hall

The hall bears the name of newspaper magnate Lord Thomson of Fleet (a Canadian press baron who wound up taking a seat in the British House of Lords). Built between 1972 and 1982 and designed by Arthur Erickson, the building's exterior looks very space age. Inside, the mirrored effects are dramatic.

(A recent renovation fixed the once-poor acoustics, and the hall now justifiably hosts many of the city's top concerts.)

Continue walking east on King Street. You'll pass through the heart of the Financial District, surrounded by many towers owned and operated by banks and brokerage, trust, and insurance companies.

On the northeast corner of King and Simcoe sts. rises the first of the towers that make up the Sun Life Centre; on the southeast corner stands:

5 St. Andrew's Presbyterian Church

The church (1874–1875) is a quietly inviting retreat from the city's pace and noise. It was designed by the city's premier architect of the time, W. G. Storm, in an inspired picturesque Scottish Romanesque style. Sun Life paid C$4.3 million for the church's air rights. The doors are often locked, but if they're open, duck inside to check out the gorgeous stained-glass window of a highlander in full regalia.

Continue along King St. to University Ave. Opposite, on the northeast corner, is the:

6 Sun Life Centre's second tower

A Sorel Etrog sculpture marks this tower. Farther along the block, you'll find another sculpture, *Parent I*, by British sculptor Barbara Hepworth. It's in a courtyard setting, complete with a splashing fountain, at the northwest corner of York and King streets.

On the northeast corner stands:

7 2 First Canadian Place

The north corner of the structure is the **Toronto Exchange Tower,** at the corner of Adelaide and York streets. The Sculptor's Society Gallery, which always has an interesting free show, is in 2 First Canadian Place.

Continue along King St. past:

8 First Canadian Place

It sits on the north side, and the **Standard Life** and **Royal Trust buildings** (part of the Toronto Dominion Centre) are on the south. At the end of this block, you'll reach Bay Street. The Standard Life building is the work of New York architect Edward Durell Stone with Bregman & Hamann; the marble facing contrasts with the TD Centre, which is black. Again, there are views of the magnificent towers of the Royal Bank Centre from here.

The intersection of Bay and King streets was once considered the geographical center of Toronto's financial power. During the mining booms in the 1920s and 1950s, Bay Street was lined with offices that were filled with commission salesmen peddling penny stocks.

If it's near lunchtime and your stomach is rumbling, this isn't a bad place to take a break:

9 Jump Café and Bar 🍴

Your best bet for a leisurely lunch in this neighborhood is a block south and a block east of Bay and King sts., at Jump Café and Bar. 1 Wellington St. W. ((℃ 416/363-3400). See p. 97.

Our next stop, at King and Bay sts., is the:

10 Toronto Dominion Centre

Built between 1963 and 1969, the center was designed by Mies van der Rohe in his sleek trademark style. The black steel and dark-bronze-tinted glass tower rises from a gray granite base. Step inside and walk through the Royal Trust and Toronto Dominion Towers. Exit the TD Centre on Wellington Street and walk right; you'll come to a small staircase that leads to the courtyard behind the Toronto Dominion Bank Tower. Here, you'll find a patch of grass that holds half a dozen lazing bronze cows. Artist Joe Fafard's *Pasture* reminds the bankers and stockbrokers that Toronto's wealth derived from other stock, too.

Walk through the Centre to the King St. exit. Exit onto King St. and turn right to continue east. Cross Bay St. On the south side of King St., you'll come to the entrance to Commerce Court. Architecture buffs will want to go into the:

11 Canadian Imperial Bank of Commerce

Visit this building (built 1929–1931) if only to see the massive banking hall— 44m long (144 ft.), 26m wide (85 ft.), and 20m high (66 ft.)—with its coffered ceiling, gilt moldings, and sculpted friezes. Squirrels, roosters, bees, bears, and figures representing industry, commerce, and Mercury decorate the main entrance. For years, this 34-story building dominated the Toronto skyline. New Yorkers York and Sawyer, with Darling and Pearson, designed it. Note the carved heads on the top of the building depicting courage, observation, foresight, and enterprise. In the early 1970s, I. M. Pei was asked to design a new complex while preserving the old building. He set the new mercury-laminated stainless-steel bank tower back from King Street, creating Commerce Court.

Opposite, on the north side of King St., note the:

12 Scotia Tower

It's a red-granite building, designed by Webb Zerafa Menkes Housden between 1985 and 1988.

Walk back to Bay St. and turn right. You're now going north. At no. 303, on the east side, is the:

13 National Club Building

In 1874, the nationalist Canada First Movement, which had started in Ottawa in 1868, became centered in Toronto. It established a weekly, *The Nation,* entered politics (as the Canadian National Association), and founded the National Club, which moved here in 1907. Today, it's a prestigious private club.

Across the street on the west side, at the corner of Bay and Adelaide sts., stands the:

14 Canada Permanent Trust Building (1928)

Enter this structure, at 7 King St. E., to view the beautifully worked Art Deco brass and bronze—particularly the elevator doors, which are chased and engraved with foliage and flowers.

Cross Adelaide St. As you walk up Bay St., the magnificent Old City Hall is clearly in view. First, on the east side of Bay St., between Richmond and Queen sts., look at— or stop in to:

15 The Bay

This is one of Canada's venerable retailers. The Bay, along with its arch-rival, Eaton's, has influenced the development of the downtown areas of most major Canadian cities. (See chapter 9, "Shopping," for listings.)

Across Queen St. looms:

16 Old City Hall

Its reflection appears dramatically in the Cadillac Fairview Office Tower at the corner of James and Queen streets. This solid, impressive building, designed by Edward James Lennox, was built out of Credit River Valley sandstone. The magnificent Romanesque Revival style shows the obvious influence of H. H. Richardson. Begun in 1885, it opened in 1899, and for years, its clock tower was a skyline landmark. Today, the building houses the provincial criminal courts. Go in to see the impressive staircase, columns with decorative capitals, and mosaic floor. The stained-glass window (1898) by Robert McCausland depicts the union of Commerce and Industry watched over by Britannia. Note the carved heads on the exterior entrance pillars—supposedly portraits of political figures and citizens of the period, including the architect.

Exit along Queen St. and turn right. Pause at the intersection of Queen and Bay streets. Bay, Toronto's equivalent of Wall Street, curves at this intersection, offering a good view north and south. Cross Bay St., and you'll find yourself in Nathan Phillips Sq., with New City Hall looming above.

17 New City Hall

The city's fourth, it was built between 1958 and 1965 in modern sculptural style. It's the symbol of Toronto's postwar dynamism, although not everyone felt that way when it was built. According to Pierre Berton, Frank Lloyd Wright said of it, "You've got a headmarker for a grave and future generations will look at it and say: 'This marks the spot where Toronto fell.'" The truth is quite the opposite—this breathtaking building was the first architectural marker of an evolving metropolis. Finnish architect Viljo Revell won a design competition that drew entries by 510 architects from 42 countries, including I. M. Pei. The building has a great square in front with a fountain and pool; people flock here in summer to relax, and in winter to skate. The square's namesake, Nathan Phillips, was Toronto's first Jewish mayor.

City Hall also has some art worth viewing. Look just inside the entrance for *Metropolis,* which local artist David Partridge fashioned from more than 100,000 common nails. You'll need to stand well back to enjoy the effect. Henry Moore's sculpture *The Archer* stands in front of the building—thanks to Mayor Phil Givens, who raised the money to buy it through public subscription after city authorities refused. The gesture encouraged Moore to bestow a major collection of his works on the Art Gallery of Ontario (see chapter 7). Two curved concrete towers, which house the bureaucracy, flank the Council Chamber. From the air, the whole complex supposedly looks like an eye peering up at the heavens.

For some light refreshment, stop in at one of several dining spots in:

18 The Sheraton Centre ☕

The Sheraton Centre restaurants include the Traders pub. 123 Queen St. W.

From City Hall, walk west along Queen St. On your right, behind an ornate wrought-iron fence that once kept out the cows, you'll see:

19 Osgoode Hall

Since the 1830s, this has been the headquarters of the Law Society of Upper Canada, a professional association. Named after the first chief justice of Upper Canada, the building was constructed in stages. It started with the East Wing (built 1831–1832), then the West Wing (built 1844–1845), and the center block (built 1856–1860). The last, designed by W. G. Storm with a Palladian portico, is the most impressive. Inside is the **Great Library**—34m long (112 ft.), 12m wide (39 ft.), and 12m high (39 ft.)—with stucco decoration and a domed ceiling. The Ontario Supreme Court is across Queen Street.

Walk west 1 block to University Ave. On the northwest corner, you can visit:

20 Campbell House

This elegant Georgian residence was home to Sir William Campbell, a Scot who moved to York in 1811 and rose to become chief justice of Upper Canada. A handsome piece of Georgian architecture, it was moved to this location from a few miles farther east.

Stretching northward behind Campbell House, on the northwest side of University Ave., is the:

21 Canada Life Assurance Building

Atop the tower a neon sign provides weather reports—white flashes for snow, red flashes for rain, green beacon for clement weather, red beacon for cloudy weather. If the flashes move upward, the temperature is headed that way, and vice versa.

At University Ave. and Queen St., you can end the tour by boarding the subway at Osgoode station to your next destination, or continue walking west along Queen St. to explore its many shops and cafes.

SHOPPING

From shopaholics to casual browsers, Toronto offers plenty to interest everyone who likes to shop. As usual in this town, the wide range of choices is most easily broken down by neighborhood. The quaint, sometimes junky shops of Yonge Street deal in touristy trinkets, antiques, and local book chains like **Book City,** while Kensington Market is all vintage racks, most of them loaded down with clothing. Top labels like Gucci and Chanel line Mink Mile along Bloor Street, just a few blocks from tony Yorkville and its boutiques and shops such as **MO851,** a Canadian-owned leather store selling beautiful bags and cool jackets. Further west leads to locally designed and generally hip finds like **Fresh Baked Goods** (knitwear, not pastries), **Lilliput Hats,** and **Preloved** on Queen Street West.

That said, the economic crisis has had a visible impact in Toronto these past 2 years, and there are many empty storefronts downtown. Another challenge is the mess of construction along Mink Mile: It's all part of a plan to improve the strip and widen the sidewalks into a boulevard, but in the meantime, the work is making it hard for pedestrian and motorized traffic to gain access. And the business of selling books and music continues to decline: The closing of veteran Pages Bookstore on Queen Street West was a real loss for the city's edgier brand of pop culture. Nonetheless, business is robust enough to nurture small, new chains like **Type**—with two stores—and sustain great indie music stores such as **Soundscapes** on College Street, where you can buy CDs and hot tickets to live shows.

The **Eaton Centre** is Toronto's most famous shopping arcade, with hundreds of chain stores like Banana Republic, Pottery Barn, and the Gap, and two department stores at

Midtown Shopping: Bloor/Yorkville

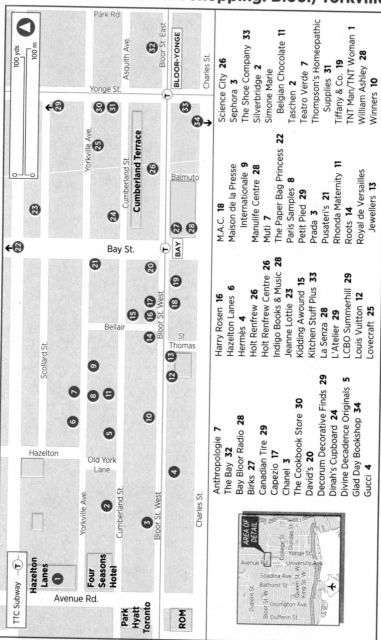

Anthropologie **7**
The Bay **32**
Bay Bloor Radio **28**
Birks **27**
Canadian Tire **29**
Capezio **17**
Chanel **3**
The Cookbook Store **30**
David's **20**
Decorum Decorative Finds **29**
Dinah's Cupboard **24**
Divine Decadence Originals **5**
Glad Day Bookshop **34**
Gucci **4**

Harry Rosen **16**
Hazelton Lanes **6**
Hermès **4**
Holt Renfrew **26**
Holt Renfrew Centre **26**
Indigo Books & Music **28**
Jeanne Lottie **23**
Kidding Awound **15**
Kitchen Stuff Plus **33**
La Senza **28**
L'Atelier **29**
LCBO Summerhill **29**
Louis Vuitton **12**
Lovecraft **25**

M.A.C. **18**
Maison de la Presse
  Internationale **9**
Manulife Centre **28**
Muti **7**
The Paper Bag Princess **22**
Paris Samples **8**
Petit Pied **29**
Prada **3**
Pusateri's **21**
Rhonda Maternity **11**
Roots **14**
Royal de Versailles
  Jewellers **13**

Science City **26**
Sephora **3**
The Shoe Company **33**
Silverbridge **2**
Simone Marie
Belgian Chocolate **11**
Taschen **2**
Teatro Verde **7**
Thompson's Homeopathic
  Supplies **31**
Tiffany & Co. **19**
TNT Man/TNT Woman **1**
William Ashley **28**
Winners **10**

either end of the block-long mall. In other words: convenient and boring. Be adventurous and check out neighborhood shops to score deals on unique clothing, housewares, and antiques (see "Great Shopping Areas," below).

THE SHOPPING SCENE

While you may want to investigate the impressive array of international retailers, don't forget the local talent. If your passion is fashion, there are great Canadian labels such as Anne Hung, Mercy, Lida Baday, Lydia K, Ross Mayerand, and Comrags, for starters.

Toronto also has a bustling arts-and-crafts community, with many galleries, custom jewelers, and artisans. Some of the best buys are on native and Inuit art. Artwork can be imported into the United States duty-free.

Stores usually open around 10am from Monday to Saturday. Closing hours change depending on the day. From Monday to Wednesday, most stores close at 6pm; on Thursday and Friday, hours run to 8 or 9pm; on Saturday, closing is quite early, usually around 6pm. Most stores are open on Sunday, though the hours may be restricted—11am or noon to 5pm is the norm.

All Toronto retailers charge shoppers for plastic bags; the minimum charge for a plastic bag is C5¢; I haven't encountered any retailers who are charging more, but by law, they are allowed to. While the move was intended to boost Toronto's eco-friendliness, the fact that the bag tax doesn't go into any environmental fund (in fact, the "tax" money is kept by the shops) has caused consternation among some shoppers.

Almost every establishment accepts MasterCard and Visa, and a growing number take American Express.

Great Shopping Areas

DOWNTOWN

Chinatown The city's original Chinatown (there are three and counting) is in the heart of the city, steps away from Kensington Market and other shopping destinations, and is well worth a visit for its collection of touristy junk, such as cheapo plastic toys and jewelry, fine rosewood furniture, exquisite ceramics, homeopathic herbs, and a bounty of exotic foodstuffs. But don't try driving here: This is traffic purgatory and best navigated on foot.

The Eaton Centre Okay, you're short on time, but you still want to fit in all your shopping. Head to the Eaton Centre. With hundreds of shops—including an Apple Store, Browns, Danier, Birks, Nine West, La Vie en Rose, Femme de Carriere, Williams Sonoma, Banana Republic, Mendocino, Laura Secord, H&M, and Indigo—you'll be sure to find something.

Queen Street West Queen Street West, between University Avenue and Bathurst Street, was once a collection of hip boutiques but is now a mix of chain stores like the Gap and neighboring Canadian-based Le Chateau for budget fashions, M.A.C. Cosmetics, Kiehls (originally of New York), and some fine local designer fare like Boomer (for men), and the groovy design store Urban Mode, which has moved just west of Bathurst. It's still a great stomping ground for fashionistas in need of a fix.

The Underground City Subterranean Toronto is a hive of shopping activity for the multitudes working in the Financial District. While you won't find many shops down here that don't have an aboveground location, the Underground City is a popular retreat for winter's coldest days and for summer heat waves, and it's convenient for those who have little time to explore beyond the neighborhood.

West Queen West Playing down its grittier roots, this hot neighborhood has earned the cutting-edge reputation once held by Queen Street West. The city has dubbed it the "Art & Design District." Starting at Bathurst Avenue and running west to Ossington Avenue and beyond, this is where you'll find a great selection of fashion talent, art galleries, and some of the best new restaurants. While you're at it, walk north to the next major street, Dundas Street West, which is on the avant-garde of all fronts, from fashion to food.

MIDTOWN

The Mink Mile, Bloor Street West This strip of real estate, known as Mink Mile, is bordered by Yonge Street to the east and Avenue Road to the west, and is where most of the top international names in fashion set up shop. If you're in the mood to see what Karl Lagerfeld is designing or to pick up a glittering bauble from Cartier or Tiffany, this is your hunting ground. Be prepared to side-step construction sites while the strip undergoes a long, drawn-out facelift.

Yorkville One of Toronto's best known—and most expensive—shopping neighborhoods, it's where you'll find art galleries of note, designer boutiques, major outlets such as Toronto's only downtown Anthropologie and Whole Foods locations, and boutiques such as the Papery for curated stationary and more.

SHOPPING A TO Z
Antiques, Furniture & Housewares
ANTIQUES

Decorum Decorative Finds If you're going on an ocean voyage, can you resist a vintage Louis Vuitton trunk? The wares here range from tables and chaise lounges to oil paintings and old books. Wares are expensive, but also top of the line. 1210 Yonge St. ✆ **416/966-6829.** Subway: Summerhill.

 Antiques Roadshow

Seven times each year, more than 70 antiques dealers from Ontario and Québec descend on Centrepoint Mall for the **Heritage Antique Market.** The goods up for grabs include 19th- and 20th-century porcelains, jewelry, silver, furniture, and paintings. If you're in town when the market is on, you're in luck. Be sure to call ahead or check the website (www. heritageantiqueshows.com) for the schedule. The market takes place on statutory holidays. Centrepoint Mall is located at 6464 Yonge St. (at Steeles Ave.) and is accessible by TTC (take the subway to Finch and board any northbound bus to Steeles). Call ✆ **416/483-6471** for more details.

Downtown Shopping: Queen Street West & West Queen West

G.U.F.F. 🖉   The name stands for "good used furniture finds," and this Leslieville store delivers on the promise. Much of the stock consists of wood pieces, often with a natural finish (not just tables and chairs, but cabinets and bed frames, too). There are also framed prints and mirrors. 1142 Queen St. E. 📞 **416/913-8025.** Subway: Queen, then a streetcar east to Bertmount Ave.

L'Atelier   This is all about glamour. Napoleon III side tables share space with chrome bar stools and rococo Italian lamps. Many of the price tags hit four digits, but there are lovely accoutrements for moderate budgets, too. 1224 Yonge St. 📞 **416/966-0200.** Subway: Summerhill.

Mostly Movables Inc.   This well-established shop is in new digs on the western fringe of Queen Street West. The early- and mid-20th-century Canadian and European furnishings are generally in fine form, and the prices are somewhat lower than those at many Yorkville and Rosedale competitors—a tradeoff for its remote location. 1684 Queen St. W. 📞 **416/531-3565.** Subway: Osgoode, then a streetcar west to Triller Ave.

Tap Phong Trading Co. **24**

Ten Thousand Villages **13**

Tom's Place **21**

Type Books **6**

Umbra **37**

The World's Biggest Bookstore **41**

Ydessa Hendeles Art
Foundation **18**

Zig Zag ★ 🛍 This shop stocks a mélange of styles, but the specialty is early Modernist pieces. The names to watch out for are Eames, Saarinen, Arne Jacobsen, and Warren Platner. This is one store that's popular with some uptown antiques dealers. 985 Queen St. E. ✆ **416/778-6495.** Subway: Queen, then any streetcar east to Carlaw Ave.

FURNITURE

The Art Shoppe This veteran furniture store, more than 75 years old, deals in top-notch furniture that is laid out like set designs on a soundstage. In other words, a dollhouse for adults. A wide range of styles is on display, from gilt baroque to streamlined Art Deco. The price tags are high, but the store is well worth browsing. 2131 Yonge St. ✆ **416/487-3211.** www.theartshoppe.com. Subway: Eglinton.

Kiosk A dynamic furniture and design spot known among the pros as a leading source for innovative, creative, and top-quality goods. Look for the latest from B&B Italia, Ligne Roset, and Poltrona Frau. The company's collection is steered by the owner's superlative eye for fine design. The collection of chairs alone is worth a visit. 288 King St. E. ✆ **416/539-9665.** www.kioskdesign.ca. Subway: King, then streetcar to Sherbourne St.

Go Where the Dealers Go

There are plenty of gorgeous antiques stores in **Rosedale**, on that stretch of Yonge Street from the Rosedale subway station to St. Clair Avenue. True bargain hunters gravitate to **Leslieville**, the stretch of Queen Street East between Carlaw and Coxwell, where small antiques shops offer great finds that need a little bit of fixing up. **Parkdale** also offers a good selection of used-furniture and other brick-a-brack shops, especially along the stretch where Queen Street West ends and meets King Street. Stop for a brilliant pasta at the Local Kitchen (see p. 100) once the shopping is done.

MADE Smart and more than a little sassy, this small showroom of furniture and accessories is a retail gallery featuring works by artists, industrial designers, and other craftspeople. The pitch? Contemporary Canadiana with cheek, and an eco-bent, to boot. A sampling includes bookends that celebrate the iconic work of Group of Seven artist Lauren Harris, modular shelves, felt stools, and funky lamps. Even if you're not a shopper, it's worth a browse to admire the clever, often handmade, goods. 867 Dundas St. W. © **416/607-6384.** www.madedesign.ca. Subway: Dundas, then streetcar west to Manning Ave.

Quasi-Modo Modern Furniture With offerings for both home and office, this shop showcases some of the best of streamlined 20th-century design. Many of the items are European imports, such as the tables and chairs by Sweden's Bruno Mathsson. 789 Queen St. W. © **416/703-8300.** Subway: Osgoode, then a streetcar west to Claremont St.

Umbra The screaming pink exterior is the award-winning work of a Toronto design firm, which is fitting for this "concept store" of a bold, global company. The two floors, brightly lit and sleek, carry the air of an art gallery, and each item features the designer's name, from a whimsical candelabra to a sleek desk, a round table to a neat tape dispenser. Designers are selected from around the world, and teams partner with design schools, such as the nearby Ontario College of Art & Design. Truly cool stuff. 165 John St. (just north of Queen St.). © **416/299-0088.** Subway: Osgoode, then a streetcar or walk west to John St.

HOUSEWARES, GLASS & FINE CHINA

Bergo Designs The selection here is a mix of international high-end standards like Alessi and Georg Jensen, and local finds like the Brothers Dressler, twin woodworkers who make beautiful pieces in their Toronto studio. There's also some architecturally inspired jewelry and watches by Frank Gehry. Prices veer to the high side, in keeping with the quality of goods. In the Distillery District, 55 Mill St. © **416/861-1821.** www.bergo.ca. Subway: King, then a streetcar east to Parliament St.

Kitchen Stuff Plus This housewares shop sells brand-name goods from the likes of Umbra (see above) at discount prices. It offers a good selection of picture frames, wine racks, area rugs, candles, painted ceramics, and kitchen accessories. There are 11 locations around town. 703 Yonge St. © **416/944-2718.** www.kitchenstuffplus.com. Subway: Yonge/Bloor.

Muti   Murano glass designs and cheery ceramics from Italy dominate this store. Look a little closer, and you'll find a few French tapestries and tablecloths, too. 88 Yorkville Ave. ✆ **416/969-0253.** Subway: Bay.

Nella Cucina   Feel like playing chef? This sleek, two-story destination for pros and home cooks alike has all you need, from Roos butcher blocks and cutting boards to top-of-the-line knives, grills, and assorted accessories. Open racks are lined with plastic condiment dispensers, 12-quart measuring cups, Le Creuset Dutch Ovens, and more. You also might want to sign up for one of the popular, one-off cooking classes led by popular local chefs. 876 Bathurst St. (just north of Bloor St. W.). ✆ **416/922-9055.** Subway: Bathurst.

Nikolau Restaurant Equipment   The name might lead you to believe that this is the place to go if you're on the hunt for a Hobart mixer or chef's whites, but in fact, this tiny, absolutely crammed store is a great place for home cooks to buy myriad quality kitchenware, from pro copper pans to Global knives and more. It's always busy, and the owners are sometimes grumpy dealing with amateur questions, so be prepared to take some time for exploring on your own. The effort usually pays off. 629 Queen St. W. (at Bathurst St.). ✆ **416/504-6411.** Subway: Osgoode, then a streetcar or walk west to Bathurst St.

Tap Phong Trading Co. 🎁   If you have only a few minutes in Chinatown, spend them here. You'll find beautiful hand-painted ceramics, earthenware, decorative items, kitchen utensils, and small appliances. Best of all, just about everything is inexpensive and of reliable quality. 360 Spadina Ave. ✆ **416/977-6364.** Subway: Spadina, then the LRT to Baldwin St.

William Ashley China   All the top brands are here—Wedgwood, All-Clad, Baccarat, Lenox—and, as the weekly ads promise, all at amazing discount prices! This place, a popular spot for wedding registries, deals in huge volume. A Mink Mile staple, right across from Holt Renfrew, it's all service and smiles. Very traditional. Manulife Centre, 55 Bloor St. W. ✆ **416/964-2900.** Subway: Bloor at Yonge or Bay on the Bloor line & a short walk.

Art

Bau-Xi Gallery   After viewing the masterworks at the Art Gallery of Ontario, you can head across the street and buy your own. Founded in 1965 in Vancouver, Bau-Xi features contemporary works by artists from across the country. 340 Dundas St. W. ✆ **416/977-0600.** www.bau-xi.com. Subway: St. Patrick.

Corkin Gallery ★   Most items here are historical or contemporary fine-art photographs from around the world. They include works by André Kertész, Nan Goldin, Irving Penn, and Brett Weston, plus a small collection of modernist painting and sculpture. In the Distillery District, 55 Mill St. ✆ **416/979-1980.** www.corkingallery.com. Subway: King, then a streetcar east to Parliament St.

Eskimo Art Gallery ★★   This award-winning gallery has the largest collection of Inuit stone sculptures in Toronto. The focus is on contemporary, and especially emerging, artists. At any given time, it shows more than 500 pieces, including prints. 12 Queens Quay W. (opposite Westin Harbour Castle). ✆ **416/366-3000.** www.eskimoart.com. Subway: Union, then the LRT to Queen's Quay.

Olga Korper Gallery Established in 1973, this gallery houses contemporary Canadian and international works. Artists represented include Averbuch, John Brown, Sankawa, and the estate of Louis Comtois. 17 Morrow Ave. (off Dundas St. W.). 🕿 **416/538-8220.** Subway: Dundas West.

Sandra Ainsley Gallery ★★ Specializing in glass sculpture, this renowned gallery represents Canadian, American, and international artists, including Dale Chihuly, Jon Kuhn, Peter Powning, Tom Scoon, Susan Edgerley, and David Bennett. The one-of-a-kind pieces have big price tags, but you can also find some affordable items, such as paperweights, vases, and jewelry. In the Distillery District, 55 Mill St. 🕿 **416/214-9490.** www.sandraainsleygallery.com. Subway: King, then a streetcar east to Parliament St.

Stephen Bulger Gallery ★★ 🎁 If you're interested in fine-art photography, especially in the documentary tradition, this is the place to go in Toronto. The Gallery displays Canadian and international photography, both by established artists and up-and-comers, from Ruth Orkin to Pete Doherty. It is one of the driving forces behind CONTACT, Toronto's Annual Celebration of Photography, which has helped launch many careers. Artists represented include Robert Burley, Ruth Kaplan, Vincenzo Pietropaolo, and Alex Webb. This is also a place locals go for some of the city's best photography exhibits. 1026 Queen St. W. 🕿 **416/504-0575.** www.bulgergallery.com. Subway: Osgoode, then a streetcar west to Ossington Ave.

Susan Hobbs Gallery 🎁 This small gallery in an unprepossessing warehouse far from the Yorkville crowd has been a major player in Canadian contemporary art since 1993. Hobbs represents some of Toronto's best artists, including Ian Carr-Harris, Shirley Wiitasalo, Robin Collyer, and Sandra Meigs. 137 Tecumseth St. (at Queen St.). 🕿 **416/504-3699.** www.susanhobbs.com. Subway: Osgoode, then any streetcar west to Tecumseth St.

Ydessa Hendeles Art Foundation ★ This is one of the most interesting contemporary art collections in the city. Hendeles features installations by international artists. Works on display include paintings, photography, and multimedia projects. Hours are limited, so call ahead to see if they're open when you're in town. 778 King St. W. 🕿 **416/603-2227.** Subway: St. Andrew, then any streetcar west to Bathurst St.

Audiovisual & Electronic Goods

Apple Store ★★★ Mac geeks, take note: Toronto has *four* Apple stores. One is at the Yorkdale shopping center, one is at Fairview Mall, and one is at Sherway Gardens, all remote from the downtown core, but the Eaton Centre location provides easy access. Eaton Centre. 🕿 **647/258-0801.** Subway: Dundas or Queen.

Bay Bloor Radio This 1,208-sq.-m (13,003-sq.-ft.) store carries the latest and greatest audio equipment, from portable units to in-home theater systems. Manulife Centre, 55 Bloor St. W. 🕿 **416/967-1122.** www.baybloorradio.com. Subway: Bay.

Canadian Tire Don't be fooled by the name—this megastore carries far more than auto parts. This is where I head when Father's Day approaches. The endless aisles overflow with gadgets for home, yard, office, car, and any place in between. There's another branch just north of Bloor, at 839 Yonge St. (🕿 **416/925-9592**). 65 Dundas St. W. 🕿 **416/979-9056.** www.canadiantire.ca. Subway: Dundas.

Henry's ★ This bi-level shop deals in analog and digital photography. The first floor has electronic equipment, darkroom supplies, and a photo-processing lab.

Upstairs, a wide selection of secondhand cameras and gear is available. 119 Church St. ☎ **416/868-0872.** Subway: Queen.

Books, Magazines & Newspapers
BOOKS

Book City ★ 🖋 For a small chain, Book City offers big discounts—many tomes are discounted by 10% to 30%. The selection of international magazines is particularly good. Book City also has several branches around the city, including 716 Queen St. W. (☎ **416/964-1167**), 1950 Queen St. E. (☎ **416/698-1444**), and 348 Danforth Ave. (☎ **416/469-9997**). 501 Bloor St. W. ☎ **416/961-4496.** www.bookcity.ca. Subway: Bathurst.

Chapters ★★ While Indigo (see below) now owns and operates the Chapters bookstores, they retain their own charm. Browse-worthy and well stocked, these are comfortable stores where, pre-purchase, you can pick up a few titles, slide into a big chair, and sip a Starbucks latte. The stores are open late, usually until 10 or 11pm on weeknights and midnight on weekends. 142 John St. ☎ **416/595-7349.** www.chapters. indigo.ca. Subway: Osgoode.

The Cookbook Store ★ In a world where neighborhood bookstores are too often on life support, this gem, 20-plus years and running, stands out for its fine selection of cookbooks, food memoirs, and the best in food writing. If you're lucky enough to be in town for one of their many book launches, book the date—Julia Child, for one, was once here. 850 Yonge St. ☎ **416/920-2665.** www.cook-book.com. Subway: Yonge/Bloor.

David Mason This well-established store has moved into a new location. It stocks many travel books and a number of first editions of Canadian, American, and British works. The collections of 19th- and 20th-century literature are vast. 366 Adelaide St. W. ☎ **416/598-1015.** www.davidmasonbooks.com. Subway: St. Andrew.

Glad Day Bookshop ★ This was the first gay-oriented bookstore in Canada, and it remains one of the best. The shelves hold a sizable collection of gay and lesbian fiction, biography, and history books, and the offerings have expanded to include magazines, CDs, videos, calendars, posters, and cards. 598A Yonge St., 2nd floor. ☎ **416/961-4161.** Subway: Wellesley.

Indigo Books Music & More ★★ ☺ This Canadian-owned chain offers an excellent selection of books, magazines, and a smaller selection of music. Like Chapters, Indigo comes complete with coffee shops and comfy seating. A favorite with night owls, they're open until 11pm or midnight every day. You'll find branches at the Eaton Centre (☎ **416/591-3622**) and at 2300 Yonge St., at Eglinton Ave. (☎ **416/544-0049**). Manulife Centre, 55 Bloor St. W. ☎ **416/925-3536.** www.chapters.indigo.ca. Subway: Yonge/Bloor or Bay.

Mabel's Fables ★ ☺ This charming shop is stocked with every book a child could possibly want—and a lot more. Offerings are grouped by age, going up to early adolescence. On weekends, author visits and other special events take place. 662 Mount Pleasant. ☎ **416/322-0438.** www.mabelsfables.com. Subway: Eglinton, then bus no. 34 to Mount Pleasant & walk 2 blocks south.

Nicholas Hoare ★ This shop has the cozy feel of an English library, with hardwood floors, plush couches, and a fireplace. There's an extensive selection of Canadian and international fiction, as well as heavyweight art books and a small but good selection of children's titles. 45 Front St. E. ✆ **416/777-2665.** Subway: Union.

Silver Snail ★ ☺ Remember those comic books you read as a kid? Well, they're all here, along with adult-oriented comics such as the *Sandman* series. You'll see a sizable section of imported editions, and posters and movie memorabilia, too. 367 Queen St. W. ✆ **416/593-0889.** www.silversnail.com. Subway: Osgoode.

Sleuth of Baker Street ★★ If you love a good mystery (as I do), you need to make a pilgrimage to Toronto's only crime-focused bookshop. Check the website before you visit so that you can take advantage of one of the shop's many author readings. Closed Mondays. 1600 Bayview Ave. (at Manor Rd. E.). ✆ **416/483-3111.** Subway: Eglinton, then bus no. 34 east to Mount Pleasant & walk 3 blocks south.

Type Books ★ 📚 This small, smart bookstore is run by a couple of English literature grads. Hip but not too cool, the selection includes serious fiction, fine books on food and art, a healthy collection of poetry, traditional and contemporary children's literature, and a lot of indie stuff that you'd have a hard time finding elsewhere. The mix proved so popular, there is now a second location on Spadina north of St. Clair Avenue (427 Spadina Rd.). 883 Queen St. W. ✆ **416/366-8973.** Subway: Osgoode, then a streetcar west to Trinity-Bellwoods.

University of Toronto Bookstore ★ 📚 This is one of the best-stocked independent booksellers in town. It also hosts its own Reading Series, which has featured authors such as Ann-Marie MacDonald and Roddy Doyle; check the website for details about upcoming events. In the Koffler Centre, 214 College St. ✆ **416/978-7900.** www.uoftbookstore.com. Subway: Queen's Park.

The World's Biggest Bookstore ★ Whether or not it is indeed the world's biggest, the 27km (17 miles) of bookshelves do contain a broad selection, as you'd expect, and a lot of remaindered stuff, too. The magazine racks alone seem endless. There's a lot to peruse, but the overly bright, bare-bones space doesn't make for a pleasant browse. 20 Edward St. ✆ **416/977-7009.** Subway: Dundas.

MAGAZINES & NEWSPAPERS

Maison de la Presse Internationale Although this store fills up fast on weekends, drawing expats and locals alike, it's still a great place to browse. The many international magazines and newspapers are as current as you'll find. The second floor is devoted to paperback novels *en français*. 99 Yorkville Ave. ✆ **416/928-2328.** Subway: Bay.

Department Stores

The Bay The Hudson's Bay Company started out as a fur-trading business when the first French-speaking settlers came to Canada. Today, the Bay boasts excellent midrange selections of clothing and housewares. Of the several Toronto locations, here are the two best. 176 Yonge St. (at Queen St.). ✆ **416/861-9111.** www.thebay.com. Subway: Queen. 2nd location at 2 Bloor St. E. (at Yonge St.). ✆ **416/972-3333.** Subway: Yonge/Bloor.

Holt Renfrew Designers such as Donna Karan, Christian Lacroix, and Yves St. Laurent figure in Holt Renfrew's four levels of merchandise. You'll also find the excellent Holt Renfrew Spa (p. 150) and the Holt Renfrew Café (which serves great sandwiches and salads). The basement connects with an underground mall and features a gourmet food department and another cafe. Holt Renfrew Centre, 50 Bloor St. W. ✆ **416/922-2333.** www.holtrenfrew.com. Subway: Yonge/Bloor.

Sears If you visited Toronto before 2000, you'll remember the gorgeous Eaton's department store, which anchored the Eaton Centre complex. Sears Canada bought the Eaton's name and opened this department store in its place. It's more upscale than your average Sears. Eaton Centre. ✆ **416/343-2111.** www.sears.ca. Subway: Dundas.

Fashion

Let's get this out of the way first: Toronto has all of the requisite big-name European boutiques along Bloor Street West, between Yonge Street and Avenue Road. You'll find **Louis Vuitton** at no. 111; **Gucci** and **Hermès** at no. 130; and **Prada** and **Chanel** at the Colonnade shopping arcade at no. 131. The listings below focus on shops particular to Toronto (with just a few exceptions). Also see "Hunting for Vintage" (p. 195) and "Shoes" (below).

CLOTHING FOR CHILDREN

Fashion Crimes ★ Toronto designer Pam Chorley's store looks like a princess's dressing room, complete with Venetian glass and ornate chandeliers. There are clothes for women here, too, but her Misdemeanors line makes gossamer gowns and ruby slippers for little girls who dream they're really princesses. 322½ Queen St. W. ✆ **416/351-8758.** Subway: Osgoode.

Kol Kid   West Queen West isn't just for grown-ups, you know. This charming boutique carries Canadian- and European-made clothing for kids, plus toys and furnishings. 674 Queen St. W. ✆ **416/681-0368.** Subway: Osgoode, then a streetcar west to Palmerston Ave.

Psst . . . Want a Free Yoga Class?

If you're in Toronto on a Wednesday or Sunday morning and feel an overwhelming urge to exercise, here's a secret you need to know: Lululemon Athletica offers **free hour-long classes** (Wednesday yoga is at 8am; Sunday is "Pilates-yoga fusion" at 9:30am). There's absolutely no charge or obligation to buy anything (though you may be tempted by the stylish workout gear that lines the walls). The classes take place at the store at 342 Queen St. W. (✆ **416/703-1399**). You should call the day before to make sure that the class is scheduled, but you can't make an advance reservation—participation is limited to the first 25 people to show up.

9

SHOPPING | Shopping A to Z

Maybe you can't get something for nothing . . . but you can score some pretty fab finds on the cheap in Toronto. It's a treasure hunt of sorts, and the spoils are anything but certain. But when you find that perfect piece marked down to next to nothing, it makes it all worthwhile. Many Toronto retailers, including luxurious Holt Renfrew, have their own outlet shops. Here's my little black book of favorite foraging grounds. Happy hunting!

Dixie Outlet Mall ★   Ten minutes from Pearson International Airport is the answer to bargain-shoppers' prayers. It's hard to beat the Dixie Outlet Mall for number of bargains per square foot. You can shop at more than 120 outlet shops here, including Jay Set (which carries Peter Nygard fashions), La Vie en Rose lingerie, and chocolatier Laura Secord, so you're bound to find something. There's also a large Winners store (see below). 1250 S. Service Rd., Mississauga. ✆ **905/278-7492.** Gardiner Expwy./Queen Elizabeth Way (QEW) west to Dixie Rd. exit; turn left & follow Dixie Rd. south to S. Service Rd.

Grreat Stuff   An awful lot of men's clothes are jammed into this small retail space, but if you're not troubled by claustrophobia, dig in for some amazing deals. Business casual is this shop's mainstay, though you can find *grreat* prices on Italian silk ties and brand-name suits. 870 Queen St. W. ✆ **416/533-7680.** www.grreatstuff.com. Subway: Osgoode, then a streetcar west to Shaw St.

Honest Ed's World Famous Shopping Centre ★   Ed's is a Toronto institution; it's been in business for more than 60 years. The store is framed with flashing red and yellow lights both outdoors *and* indoors. "Don't just stand there, buy something!" blurts out one brazen sign. This idiosyncratic store has a deal on everything from housewares to carpets, clothing to toys. Crazy-making as shopping here can be, the bargains are unbeatable. In case you need to refuel after weaving through the maze of aisles, there's a **Lettieri** (p. 224) tucked into the corner at Bloor and Bathurst streets. 581 Bloor St. W. ✆ **416/537-1574.** Subway: Bathurst.

Marilyn's 👗   Here's a rare thing: knockdown prices paired with attentive service. The specialty is Canadian fashions for women, from sportswear to glamorous

---

Lovechild   A favorite with tiny tots who are already developing fashion savvy, Lovechild offers a selection of groovy clothes in a rainbow of colors. 2523 Yonge St. ✆ **416/486-4746.** www.lovechild.ca. Subway: Eglinton.

CLOTHING FOR MEN & WOMEN

Danier 🦌   This Canadian chain carries suede and leather coats for men and women, as well as ladies' pants, skirts, and handbags. Most of the prices are very reasonable, and regular sales events knock the prices down 20% to 50%. Eaton Centre. ✆ **416/598-1159.** www.danier.com. Subway: Queen.

Lululemon Athletica ★   The athletically inclined—especially yoga devotees—will delight in this shop. In addition to the Canadian house label's nicely designed workout wear, you'll find Ayurvedic skin care products by Christy Turlington, yoga mats, and other accessories. 342 Queen St. W. ✆ **416/703-1399.** www.lululemon.com. Subway: Osgoode, then a streetcar west to Spadina Ave.

gowns. You can also attend in-store seminars on fashion-forward topics like traveling with just one suitcase. 200 Spadina Ave. © 416/504-6777. Subway: Spadina, then the LRT to Queen St. W.

Paris Samples This store snaps up designers' samples and marks them down 20% to 75%. The clothes range from wool pants to velvet dresses to micro-miniskirts. *Be forewarned:* The sizes are all under 14, and many clothes come only in the smallest sizes. 101 Yorkville Ave. © 416/926-0656. Subway: Bay.

The Shoe Company This is every foot fetishist's dream: great men's and women's shoes, from Unisa, Nine West, and others, marked down to low prices. You'll find lots of trendy styles that won't be stylish for long, but it won't hurt your pocketbook to splurge. Outlets are around the city, including one at First Canadian Place. 711 Yonge St. © 416/923-8388. Subway: Yonge/Bloor.

Tom's Place ★★ After more than 40 years in business, Tom's Place looks sharper than ever. While the shop devotes an entire floor to women's wear, the best buys are in the men's department: You'll find brand-name merchandise by the likes of Armani and Valentino. Tom's Place stocks sizes from 36 short to 50 tall. 190 Baldwin St. © 416/596-0297. Subway: Spadina, then the LRT to Baldwin St.

Winners This northern outpost of the U.S.-owned T.J. Maxx chain offers great deals on clothes for men and women (think Jones New York, Tommy Hilfiger, and Liz Claiborne), and top-name togs for the kiddies. There's also an ever-changing selection of housewares, cookware, linens, toiletries, and toys. The 3,716-sq.-m (40,000-sq.-ft.) outlet at College Park is always packed, but its large, airy space is filled with deals (© 416/598-8800; subway: College). Winners has a smaller but longstanding location in the Fashion District, which is another good bet (57 Spadina Ave.; © 416/585-2052; subway: Spadina, then the LRT to King St. W.). Its new location in Scotia Plaza, in Toronto's Underground City, will hold purchases for shoppers till closing time (so lunchtime shoppers can keep their secrets, I guess; 40 King St. W.; © 416/360-8162). The outpost on tony Bloor Street West outraged some of its high-priced neighbors, but deal-obsessed shoppers love it. 110 Bloor St. W. © 416/920-0193. www.winners.ca. Subway: Bay.

Roots ★ This is one Canadian retailer that seems to be universally loved. The clothes are casual, from hooded sweats to fleece jackets, and there's a good selection of leather footwear. Don't overlook the tykes' department, which has the same stuff in tiny sizes. Other locations include the Eaton Centre (© 416/593-9640). 95A Bloor St. W. © 416/323-9512. www.roots.ca. Subway: Bay.

Tilley Endurables ★ ◢ The Tilley hat may not be Canada's greatest style moment, but it certainly is one of the most recognizable. Tilley now offers a full range of men's and women's clothing, as well as belts, socks, and other travel gear. Everything is well made and incredibly durable. Note that Tilley has branched out into travel underwear (it admits that "sexy they may not be" but claims that two sets of its underclothes will get you around the world—*now* I'm curious). The store at Queen's Quay (207 Queens Quay W.; © 416/203-0463) is the most convenient, but the flagship store on Don Mills is unbeatable for choice. 900 Don Mills Rd.

📞 **800/363-8737** or 416/441-6141. www.tilley.com. Subway: Eglinton, then bus no. 34 east to Don Mills & walk 2 lights north to Barber Greene Rd.

TNT Man/TNT Woman 👜   The acronym stands for "The New Trend," and this small chain offers just that, with fashions from Betsey Johnson and Plein Sud for *les femmes,* and Diesel and Iceberg jeans for *les hommes.* There are also locations uptown at 368 and 388 Eglinton Ave. 87 Avenue Rd. 📞 **416/975-1960** (men's shop) or 416/975-1810 (women's shop). Subway: Bay.

CLOTHING FOR MEN

Boomer ★   Ever wonder where Barenaked Ladies or Moist get the glad rags they wear in their videos? Look no further than Boomer, a hip boutique that stocks such staples as Hugo Boss and Cinque, as well as the latest from Swedish trendsetter J. Linderberg. 309 Queen St. W. 📞 **416/598-0013.** Subway: Osgoode.

Decibel   This trendy shop is a terrific spot to pick up the latest and greatest in casual wear. Labels range from well-known brands such as Kenneth Cole to up-and-comers such as Psycho Cowboy or Pusch (from Denmark and Calgary, respectively). 200 Queen St. W. 📞 **416/506-9648.** Subway: Osgoode.

Delphic   Don't like trendy? Then don't shop here. If you do, you'll be confronted by fashion favorites such as Evisu Jeans, which are imported from Japan. 706 Queen St. W. 📞 **416/603-3334.** Subway: Osgoode, then a streetcar west to Manning Ave.

Harry Rosen ★   Designed like a mini–department store, Harry Rosen carries the crème de la crème of menswear designers, including Hugo Boss, Brioni, and Versace. There are also a good selection of work-worthy footwear and a famous "Great Wall of Shirts." Now the flagship store also claims Canada's only Tod's Place, the luxe international brand of shoes and leather accessories. 82 Bloor St. W. 📞 **416/972-0556.** www.harryrosen.com. Subway: Bay.

Korry's   This neighborhood favorite carries the latest from lines such as Canali, Canadian designer Copley, Pal Zileri, and Hugo Boss, as well as its own house brand of suits, Roberto, made with Italian wool. A great selection of samples, plus excellent ties at good prices, makes it a bargain-hunter's treasure trove, as well. 569 Danforth Ave. 📞 **416/463-1115.** Subway: Pape station.

Moores 🏷️   There's something for everyone at this spacious shop that specializes in formal wear. Most of the suits, sport coats, and dress pants are Canadian-made, and such international designers as Oscar de la Renta are represented, too. Sizes run from extra-short to extra-tall and oversize. The prices tend to be reasonable, and bargains abound. 100 Yonge St. 📞 **416/363-5442.** www.mooresclothing.com. Subway: King.

CLOTHING FOR WOMEN

Anthropologie   This American-based women's clothing store chain has grown to hundreds of locations in less than 20 years, including one in downtown Toronto. Two floors of pretty florals, sexy dresses, skinny pants, whimsical jewelry, bags, dishes, and more all add up to a pleasant, if middle-of-the-road, shopping experience. It's hard to leave empty-handed. 80 Yorkville Ave. 📞 **416/964-9700.** Subway: Bay, then walk 2 blocks north to Yorkville Ave.

Brian Bailey ★   This Canadian designer creates glamorous gowns, cocktail dresses, and smart suits. The shop is located in an edgy neighborhood, but the look is classic and feminine. 878 Queen St. W. ✆ **416/516-7188.** Subway: Osgoode, then a streetcar west to Shaw St.

Comrags Designers Judy Cornish and Joyce Gunhouse create retro-inspired clothing that looks great on a variety of body types. 654 Queen St. W. ✆ **416/360-7249.** www.comrags.com. Subway: Osgoode, then a streetcar west to Palmerston Ave.

Ewanika 🎁 The designs here are smart, modern, and generally good for work and play. Designer Trish Ewanika creates tailored suits, dresses, and more that are perfect for women who like a polished but understated look. 1083 Bathurst St. ✆ **416/927-9699.** Subway: Bathurst, then walk or take the bus north to Dupont St.

Fashion Crimes ★★ These glamorous dresses, designed by shop owner Pam Chorley, are a tribute to playful femininity and whimsical imagination. Many of the fabrics are made for Chorley in Paris, and you won't find them anywhere else. In addition to the elegant gowns, there are plenty of original accessories, including opera-length gloves, feathery boas, and glittering handbags. (Little girls have their own Misdemeanors line; see p. 189.) 322½ Queen St. W. ✆ **416/351-8758.** Subway: Osgoode.

Femme de Carriere ★ For a dose of Québécois savoir-faire, look no further than this elegant emporium. While the name translates as "career woman," the offerings range from shapely suits to evening-appropriate dresses and chic separates. Branches in shopping centers around town include First Canadian Place, Holt Renfrew Centre, and Fairview Mall. Eaton Centre. ✆ **416/595-0951.** Subway: Dundas or Queen.

Fresh Baked Goods ★ 🎁 Surprise—this *isn't* a bakery. Owner Laura Jean, "the knitting queen," features a line of flirty knitwear made of cotton, mohair, wool, or lace. The staff is friendly and incredibly helpful; if you like a sweater but not its buttons, they'll sew on different ones from their sizeable collection free of charge. They also do custom orders. 274 Augusta Ave. ✆ **416/966-0123.** www.freshbakedgoods.com. Subway: Spadina, then the LRT to Baldwin St. & walk 2 blocks west to Augusta Ave.

Girl Friday ★★ 🎁 Local designer Rebecca Nixon creates feminine dresses, suits, and separates for her shop under the name Girl Friday. The store also carries pieces from hip labels Nougat and Dish, but many come for Nixon's elegant yet affordable pieces. 740 Queen St. W. ✆ **416/364-2511.** www.girlfridayclothing.com. Subway: Osgoode, then a streetcar west to Claremont St.

Jeanne Lottie ★ 🔑 Can you make a fashion statement with a handbag? Canadian designer Jane Ip thinks so—and she's made a convert out of me. Purses for all occasions, from zebra-patterned boxy bags for day to glittering sequin-encrusted numbers for a night out, fill her boutique. Beaded shoes and sparkly accessories are also sold. Occasionally open by appointment only, so call ahead. 32 Scollard St. ✆ **416/975-5115.** www.jeannelottie.com. Subway: Yonge/Bloor.

Lilliput Hats ★ 🎁 If you're a hat fan, then Lilliput's is a must-visit for stunning designs made by the owner, Karyn Gingras. Her creations have been worn by Celine Dion and Whoopi Goldberg, among others. 462 College St. ✆ **416/536-5933.** www.lilliputhats.com. Subway: Queen's Park, then a streetcar west to Bathurst St.

Maxi Boutique Variety is the name of the game at this long-established boutique in the heart of Greektown. Labels include homegrown talent such as Lida Baday, as well as international brands such as Naf Naf, Miss Sixty, and Betsey Johnson. 575 Danforth Ave. ✆ **416/461-6686.** Subway: Pape.

Peach Berserk ★ 💼   Toronto designer (and local legend) Kingi Carpenter creates dramatically printed silk separates, dresses, and coats. Don't look for demure florals—prints range from bold martini glasses to the ironic "Do I Look Fat in This?" logo. 507 Queen St. W. ✆ **416/504-1711.** www.peachberserk.com. Subway: Osgoode, then a streetcar west to Spadina Ave.

Preloved ★★   The original Toronto boutique was destroyed by a fire in 2008. Since then, Preloved has reopened in a storefront across from Trinity-Bellwoods Park. The store's pieces really *are* one of a kind: The shop's owners breathe new life into vintage clothing and cast-off jeans and T-shirts by changing the shapes and adding details such as vintage lace. The roster of celeb fans includes Alanis Morissette. 881 Queen St. W. ✆ **416/504-8704.** Subway: Osgoode, then a streetcar west to Trinity-Bellwoods Park.

Rhonda Maternity   Red-hot mamas-to-be should check out this glamorous boutique. The stylish suits, sweater sets, and sportswear are this store's exclusive designs. 110 Cumberland St. ✆ **416/921-3116.** www.rhondamaternity.com. Subway: Bay.

Trove ★ 💼   Trove started out primarily as a jewelry store, but expanded both in size and goods to now include groovy shoes, fun hats and other accessories, and good selection of handbags. 793 Bathurst St. (at Bloor St. W.). ✆ **416/516-1258.** www.trove.ca. Subway: Bathurst.

LINGERIE

La Senza 🖊   This Montréal-based chain carries moderately priced but eye-catching bra-and-panty sets, nighties, plush unisex robes, and patterned boxers. An assortment of slippers, candles, bath mousse, and picture frames rounds out the offerings. Holt Renfrew Centre, 50 Bloor St. W. ✆ **416/972-1079.** www.lasenza.com. Subway: Yonge/Bloor.

La Vie en Rose   You'll find quite the eclectic collection of undies here, from sensible cotton briefs to marabou-trimmed teddies, retro PJs to the latest in cleavage enhancers. The items at the front of the store are inexpensive; the farther back you go, the pricier they get. Eaton Centre. ✆ **416/595-0898.** Subway: Queen.

Linea Intima ★ 💼   While there's no shortage of fabulous undergarments at this boutique, the real reason to visit is owner Liliana Mann's encyclopedic knowledge of what suits the female form. This extends to prosthetics and bras that are designed for women who have had mastectomies. 1925 Avenue Rd. ✆ **416/780-1726.** www.lineaintima. com. Subway: York Mills, then a bus west along Wilson Ave. to Avenue Rd. & walk 6 blocks south to Brooke Ave.

Secrets From Your Sister ★ 💼   Thanks to Oprah, we know that the vast majority of women in North America are wearing the wrong bra size. That won't be true of you if you visit this store, which carries a terrific selection of bras to suit figures as dissimilar as Audrey Hepburn and Jayne Mansfield, and everything in between. 560 Bloor St. W. ✆ **416/538-1234.** www.secretsfromyoursister.com. Subway: Bathurst.

SHOES (MEN'S, WOMEN'S & CHILDREN'S)

Browns ★   To treat your feet to fabulous footwear by Cesare Paciotti or Stuart Weitzman, beat a path to this shoe shop for both men and women. While you're here, check out Browns' own house label, which is well designed and less pricey. There's also athletic footwear from Puma and Adidas, and a good selection of handbags.

HUNTING FOR vintage

In-the-know shoppers will tell you that Toronto has had a truly great vintage-shopping scene since the 70s. From couture and designer finds to simple smocks, collectibles to impulse buys, if you're prepared to rummage, you can find it at the treasure troves below.

Cabaret ★★ Sally Bowles was right: Come to Cabaret, old chum. The shop features glamorous eveningwear of bygone eras—all in prime condition. Cabaret employs a seamstress to make repairs, and all clothing is dry-cleaned before it hits the sales floor. Be prepared to pay, though; this isn't one of the cheaper sources for vintage, unless you can find something in the bargain basement. 672 Queen St. W. 416/504-7126. Subway: Osgoode, then a streetcar west to Palmerston Ave.

Courage My Love ★★ With its mix of vintage clothing and new silver jewelry, Courage is a Kensington Market favorite. Dresses run from '50s velvet numbers to '80s jersey, with a few bias-cut 1930s gowns appearing once in a blue moon. There are also cashmere sweaters and handbags worthy of a night at the Stork Club. The owners' cat makes an occasional furtive appearance. 14 Kensington Ave. 416/979-1992. Subway: Spadina, then the LRT to Dundas St. W.

Divine Decadence Originals ★ The price tags at this glamorous shop are sky high, but the dresses are so magnificent and well-maintained that Divine Decadence feels like a couture museum. Take a look at the Lanvins and Balenciagas of years gone by. 128 Cumberland St., 2nd floor 416/324-9759. Subway: Bay.

Exile Secondhand jeans, leather jackets, and classic T-shirts line the racks in this Kensington Market stalwart. Bargains turn up in odd places, such as the Anne Klein scarf at the bottom of a last-chance bin. 62 Kensington Ave. 416/595-7199. Subway: Spadina, then the LRT to Baldwin St.

Gadabout Whether you're channeling Jacqueline Kennedy or Marilyn Monroe, you'll find an outfit to match your mood at this jam-packed Leslieville shop. The quality is good, and pieces are dry-cleaned before they make it onto the racks. But everything is packed in so tight that shopping here can feel exhausting after a while. There's also menswear and a wide selection of accessories and memorabilia. 1300 Queen St. E. 416/463-1254. www.gadabout.ca. Subway: Queen, then a streetcar east to Alton Ave.

I Miss You ★★ This gorgeous shop on Ossington bills itself as "modern vintage fashion," which means more emphasis on pieces from the '60s and '70s (though my favorite find here has been a dress from the '50s). The quality is excellent, and the clothes have been repaired (or lovingly preserved), so you can wear your find straightaway. 63 Ossington Ave. 416/916-7021. Subway: Osgoode, then a streetcar west to Ossington Ave.

The Paper Bag Princess ★ L.A. has had a Paper Bag Princess boutique for several years, but only recently did its owner, Toronto native Elizabeth Mason, decide to open a location in her hometown. This store is a treasure trove, and its boudoir-like setting makes it a sexy place to shop. The mint-condition Chanel and Pucci outfits cost a bundle, but what else would you expect? 287 Davenport Rd. 416/925-2603. www.thepaperbag princess.com. Subway: Bay.

Thrill of the Find Actually, this isn't as much of a hunt as the name implies. This airy shop has well-organized women's clothing on a few racks, with designer names such as Chanel featured in a separate couture section. 1172 Queen St. E. 416/461-9313. Subway: Queen, then a streetcar east to Jones Ave.

Browns has several branches around town. Eaton Centre. ℂ **416/979-9270.** www.browns shoes.com. Subway: Queen.

Capezio   Whether you're looking for the perfect pair of ballet slippers or an up-to-the-minute design from Steve Madden or Guess, you'll find it here. All the shoes and other leather goods are for women. 70 Bloor St. W. ℂ **416/920-1006.** Subway: Bay.

David's   For serious shoppers only. This high-end store stocks elegant footwear for men and women—from Bruno Magli, Bally, and Sonia Rykiel, as well as the store's own collection—but prices are accordingly steep. 66 Bloor St. W. ℂ **416/920-1000.** Subway: Bay.

Getoutside   The store doesn't look like much, with its utilitarian shelving and lighting, but it stocks an amazing variety of sneakers from manufacturers around the world. Moccasins made by Laurentian Shoes, a Québec-based company, are also on show. 437 Queen St. W. ℂ **416/593-5598.** www.getoutsideshoes.com. Subway: Osgoode.

John Fluevog ★★★   Famous for his Goth footwear, this Vancouver designer also creates shoes and boots in a kaleidoscope of colors. These shoes aren't for shrinking violets, but their funky chic will get you attention without having to stomp your feet. 242 Queen St. W. ℂ **416/581-1420.** www.fluevog.com. Subway: Osgoode.

Mephisto   These shoes are made for walking—particularly because they're made from all-natural materials. Devotees of this shop, now in its third decade, swear that it's impossible to wear out Mephisto footwear. 1177 Yonge St. ℂ **416/968-7026.** Subway: Summerhill.

Petit Pied ★ ☺   This elegant shop carries children's shoes from newborns to adolescents. Many of the brands are European, including Minibel and Elefanten, but there are also sporty designs from Nike and Reebok. 890 Yonge St. ℂ **416/963-5925.** Subway: Rosedale.

Food & Wine
FOOD

The Big Carrot   Who says health food can't be fun? This large-scale emporium stocks everything from organic produce to vitamins to all-natural beauty potions. Stop in at the cafe for a vegetarian snack or light meal. 348 Danforth Ave. ℂ **416/466-2129.** www.thebigcarrot.ca. Subway: Chester.

The Bonnie Stern School   Crammed to the rafters with cooking accoutrements (such as stovetop grills) and exotic books, this store also features the raw ingredients you need to produce fine cuisine. It carries top-notch olive oil, balsamic vinegar, Asian sauces, and candied flower petals. If you take a course or seminar, you get a 10% discount on everything you buy. 6 Erskine Ave. ℂ **416/484-4810.** www.bonniestern.com. Subway: Eglinton.

The Cheese Boutique   Cheese reigns supreme here, and any serious lover of fine *fromage* will want to visit the city's most notable aging cave. But the selection of top-end goods goes well beyond dairy: meats, charcuterie, spices, oils, teas, breads, even fresh produce, are all in stock. It's a little out of the way, so best to make it an excursion, perhaps en route for picnic fixings to nearby High Park. 45 Ripley Ave. ℂ **416/762-7292.** Subway: Jane, then a bus south on the Kingsway to Ripley Rd.

Chocolate Addict ★ 🎁 Do you know anyone who *isn't* a chocolate addict? This shop is good for a fix. Choices go well beyond the usual caramel and mint to a tangy wasabi truffle, or others infused with lavender or lemon-basil. 185 Baldwin St. *©* **416/979-5809.** Subway: Spadina, then a streetcar to Baldwin St.

Dinah's Cupboard A charming neighborhood shop stocked with fine teas, coffees, spices, pastas, exotic rice, and plenty of biscuits, this is also a favorite stop for quick lunch fare, such as excellent salads and soups. There are also plenty of delicious dishes for take-away, from rich and creamy mac-and-cheese to more sophisticated stuffed chicken and roasted vegetables. There are a few tables, too, for dining in. 50 Cumberland St. (at Bay St.). *©* **416/921-8112.** Subway: Bay, then a short walk to Cumberland St.

House of Tea Visitors to this shop can drink in the heady scent of more than 150 loose teas. And the selection of cups, mugs, and tea caddies runs from chic to comical. 1017 Yonge St. *©* **416/922-1226.** Subway: Rosedale.

Pusateri's 🎁 The Pusateri's store up at Lawrence Avenue and Avenue Road is a Toronto institution—and this younger Yorkville sibling is becoming one. The store stocks high-end sweets, meats, produce, and groceries. Travelers will appreciate the gourmet prepared meals that can be eaten on the go. 57 Yorkville Ave. *©* **416/785-9100.** www.pusateris.com. Subway: Bay.

Senses Bakery ★★★ The pastries and chocolates here are simply exquisite. The bottles of maple syrup come from an Ontario family-run operation, so they're a particularly good souvenir. In the Maritime Life Tower, 2 Queen St. E. *©* **416/364-7303.** www. senses.ca. Subway: Queen.

Simone Marie Belgian Chocolate All of the rich truffles, colorful almond dragées, and fruit jellies in this shop are flown in from Belgium. 126A Cumberland St. *©* **416/968-7777.** Subway: Bay.

Soma Chocolatemaker ★★★ 🎁 There are a mere handful of great chocolatiers in the world that compare with this artisan shop. Co-owners Cynthia Leung and David Castellan source cocoa beans from around the world and make their chocolate on-site. The open-lab design of the place allows you to watch the process, from bean to bar, and it's also an inviting place to hang out and savor one of the house specialties, like the warm coffee-and-chocolate drink *bicerin* (bee-cha-reen) or a cool, rich gelato. Don't forget to buy some to take home. In the Distillery District, 55 Mill St. *©* **416/815-7662.** www.somachocolate.com. Subway: King, then a streetcar east to Parliament St.

Sugar Mountain Confectionery Remember Pez, candy necklaces, and lollipop rings? Sugar Mountain carries the tooth-aching sweets of youth, several of which have been elevated to cult status. Teens are drawn to this store, but the biggest customers are nostalgic boomers. 2291 Yonge St. *©* **416/486-9321.** Subway: Eglinton.

Xococava If you've got an adventurous palette, this place offers exquisite chocolates and fine ice creams with plenty of exotica on the side. Sure, you can get pure chocolate—and it's heavenly—but you might be tempted by wild stuff like bacon and caramel ice cream or black mushroom truffles. The coffee is brilliant, too. 1560 Yonge St. *©* **416/979-9918.** Subway: St. Clair, then a short walk north to Delisle Court.

WINE

In Ontario, Liquor Control Board of Ontario (LCBO) outlets and small boutiques at upscale grocery stores sell wine; no alcohol is sold at convenience stores. The best deals are on locally produced wines—especially the ice wine, a sweet dessert wine that has won awards the world over. There are LCBO outlets all over the city, and prices are the same at all of them. The nicest shop is the **LCBO Summerhill** (10 Scrivener Sq.; ✆ **416/922-0403;** subway: Summerhill). Built out of a former train station, this outpost hosts cooking classes, wine and spirits tastings, and party-planning seminars. Other locations are at the Manulife Centre (55 Bloor St. W.; ✆ **416/925-5266**), 20 Bloor St. E. (✆ **416/368-0521**), the Eaton Centre (✆ **416/979-9978**), and Union Station (✆ **416/925-9644**). See **www.lcbo.com** for information about products and special in-store events.

Gifts & Unique Items

B&J Trading 🎁 This Chinatown store stocks a wide assortment of goods, but its claim to fame is the gift wrap department. The store has unusual wrapping papers, bows, and bags—but best of all are the beautiful presentation boxes that could almost be gifts themselves. 378 Spadina Ave. ✆ **416/586-9655.** Subway: Spadina, then a streetcar south to Nassau St.

The Paper Place ★ 🎁 In addition to being popular with artists, this shop has all the boxes, papers, and handmade cards you could ever need to create exquisite gift-wrappings. Better yet, it stocks instruction books! 887 Queen St. W. ✆ **416/703-0089.** www.thepaperplace.ca. Subway: Osgoode, then any streetcar west to Ossington Ave.

Teatro Verde ★★ Life is drama, so why should the items you fill your home with be dull? That seems to be the question at Teatro Verde, where even table coasters are things of beauty. In 2009, the owners moved to a renovated Georgian mansion on Yorkville Avenue, so there are even more statuettes, table linens, art books, and other delights on show now. 100 Yorkville Ave. ✆ **416/966-2227.** www.teatroverde.com. Subway: Bay.

Ten Thousand Villages ★★ Everything at these stores arrived via fair-trade programs, so the artisans who make the items benefit directly from the sale of their work. In addition to hand-crafted housewares, there's jewelry, toys, Palestinian olive oil, Shea-butter skin-care products, and outstandingly good Brazil nuts. There are branches at 474 Bloor St. W. (✆ **416/533-8476**) and 362 Danforth Ave. (✆ **416/462-9779**). 709 Queen St. W. ✆ 416/703-2263. www.tenthousandvillages.com. Subway: Osgoode, then a streetcar west to Bathurst St.

Health & Beauty

Lush This clever U.K.-based emporium stocks a selection of fizzy bath bombs, skin lotions and potions, and an ever-changing variety of soaps stacked in jagged, jewel-colored slabs. All products are sold by weight. 312 Queen St. W. ✆ **416/599-5874.** www.lush.com. Subway: Osgoode.

M.A.C. ★ M.A.C. was founded in Toronto and is now owned by Estée Lauder. This flagship store is perpetually packed, especially on weekends, but if you call ahead, you can schedule an appointment for a makeup lesson. In addition to cosmetics, the store carries skin- and hair-care supplies. 89 Bloor St. W. ✆ **416/929-7555.** www.maccosmetics.com. Subway: Bay.

Noah's 🏃 This is a Mecca for health nuts. Noah's boasts aisle after aisle of vitamins and dietary supplements, organic foods and "natural" candies, skin-care and bath products, and books and periodicals. The staff is well informed and helpful. A smaller but more centrally located outlet is at 667 Yonge St. (at Bloor; ✆ **416/969-0220**). 322 Bloor St. W. ✆ **416/968-7930**. Subway: Spadina.

Sephora This French chain of cosmetic and beauty shops is a one-stop destination for any makeover, with hair products, make-up, skincare, fragrance, and more. There are many locations around town. The one on the Mink Mile is particularly attractive. 131 Bloor St. W. ✆ **416/531-1100**. Subway: Bay Station or Queen's Park, then a short walk.

Thompson's Homeopathic Supplies 📖 This is just like an old-fashioned apothecary, with endless rows of potions behind a wooden counter. It has a homeopathic remedy for everything from the common cold to dermatitis to conjunctivitis. The staff is friendly and knowledgeable. 844 Yonge St. ✆ **416/922-2300**. Subway: Yonge/Bloor.

Jewelry

Birks ★ This Canadian institution, founded in 1879, is synonymous with top quality. Among the silver, crystal, and china is an extensive selection of fine jewelry, including exquisite pearls and knockout diamond engagement rings (the diamonds themselves were mined in northern Canada). A children's section is filled with such keepsakes as Royal Doulton Bunnykins china and whimsical picture frames by Nova Scotia's Seagull Pewter. My personal favorite is the showcase of antique estate jewelry. A smaller branch is at the Eaton Centre (✆ **416/979-9311**). Manulife Centre, 55 Bloor St. W. ✆ **416/922-2266**. www.birks.com. Subway: Bay.

Mink 📖 In gangster-speak, a "mink" is a sexy woman—exactly the type who would love the fabulous fakes at this boutique. Many of the necklaces, bracelets, and rings are Canadian-designed, but a few are Euro imports. 550 College St. ✆ **416/929-9214**. Subway: Queen's Park, then a streetcar west to Euclid Ave.

Royal de Versailles Jewellers This shop carries an eye-catching assortment of pearls, gold, and platinum. The designs range from classic to funkier, playful styles. There are also watches by the likes of Piaget, Cartier, Rolex, and Tag Heuer, as well as a Bulgari boutique. 101 Bloor St. W. ✆ **416/967-7201**. Subway: Bay.

Silverbridge Most of the necklaces, bracelets, rings, and earrings here are silver, but a few are in 18-karat gold and platinum. Designer Costin Lazar has a modern sensibility, and he will also take on custom work. Watches by Georg Jensen and Ole Mathiesen are also available. 162 Cumberland St. ✆ **416/923-2591**. www.silverbridge.com. Subway: Bay.

Tiffany & Co. Diamonds are still a girl's best friend at this Art Deco–style shop. Precious gems and designs by Elsa Peretti and Paloma Picasso are on the first level; the second floor holds silver jewelry, stationery, and housewares. 85 Bloor St. W. ✆ **416/921-3900**. www.tiffany.com. Subway: Bay.

Leather Goods

Taschen! Exclusive designer handbags, luggage, wallets, and other accessories are mainstays here. Many are European imports, and quality is high. 162 Cumberland St. ✆ **416/961-3185**. Subway: Bay.

Malls & Shopping Centers

Atrium on Bay   This two-level complex has more than 60 shops selling clothing, jewelry, furniture, and more. Bay & Dundas sts. ✆ **416/980-2801.** Subway: Dundas.

Bayview Village ★ 💼   Think that you hate malls? Visit this one before you swear off them. Elegantly designed and moderately sized, Bayview Village is home to several independent boutiques, as well as some chain stores (such as Chapters bookstore). It's also a place to come for excellent food: The Oliver & Bonacini restaurant is here. 2901 Bayview Ave. (at Sheppard Ave.). ✆ **416/226-0404.** Subway: Bayview.

College Park   This shopping center was under renovation forever, but now it houses a giant Winners store (see "The Best Bargains," on p. 190). 444 Yonge St. ✆ **416/597-1221.** Subway: College.

Eaton Centre ★   It's odd that one of urban Toronto's main attractions is a mall—but oh, what a mall. More than 285 shops and restaurants spread over four levels in the Eaton Centre, which takes up 2 entire city blocks. 220 Yonge St. ✆ **416/598-2322.** www.torontoeatoncentre.com. Subway: Dundas or Queen.

Fairview Mall   This massive shopping complex, with its 260 stores, has been around for years, but until the Sheppard subway line opened, it wasn't easily accessible by public transit. Now that the subway brings you right to the door, you can easily shop at Toronto's first H&M store, as well as the Bay, Sears, Birks, Femme de Carriere, La Senza, Harry Rosen, and Danier. 1800 Sheppard Ave E. ✆ **416/491-0151.** www.fairviewmall.com. Subway: Don Mills.

First Canadian Place ★   A piece of the labyrinth of the underground city, this complex houses 120 shops and restaurants, and stages free noontime events each week, with performances as diverse as Opera Atelier's Handel recital and the dancing monks of the Tibetan Drikung Monastery. Ongoing art exhibitions are also featured. King & Bay sts. ✆ **416/862-8138.** Subway: King.

Hazelton Lanes ★   A byword for elegance and extravagance, Hazelton is a two-level complex with about 90 shops, including the Whole Foods Market. The charming courtyard at the center transforms into an ice-skating rink in winter. 55 Avenue Rd. ✆ **416/968-8602.** www.hazeltonlanes.com. Subway: Bay.

Holt Renfrew Centre   Anchored by the chic Holt Renfrew department store, this small underground concourse is more down to earth, price-wise. It connects with the Manulife Centre and the Hudson's Bay Centre. 50 Bloor St. W. ✆ **416/923-2255.** Subway: Yonge/Bloor.

Manulife Centre ★   More than 50 posh shops—including William Ashley, Indigo Books Music & More, and a top-notch LCBO outlet (Liquor Control Board of Ontario)—occupy this complex. The Manulife connects to the Holt Renfrew Centre underground. 55 Bloor St. W. ✆ **416/923-9525.** Subway: Bay.

Royal Bank Plaza   Part of Toronto's underground city, the Royal Bank Plaza connects to Union Station and the Royal York Hotel. Its 60-plus outlets include a variety of shops, two full-service restaurants, and a food court. The building above is worth a look, too. See p. 138. Bay & Front sts. ✆ **416/974-5570.** Subway: Union.

Shops at Don Mills   Toronto's latest mall is a truly suburban affair: outdoor, but made for cars, not pedestrians. But there are some unique shops, such as McEwan (a food emporium created by top chef Mark McEwan), and Canada's first Anthropologie store. Worth a stop if you're already out at the Ontario Science Centre. 1090 Don Mills Rd. (at Lawrence Ave. E.). ☎ **416/447-6087.** www.shopsatdonmills.ca. Subway: Pape, then Don Mills bus no. 25; alternatively, go to Eglinton, then take the Lawrence 54 bus; either way, the bus ride will take roughly 20 min.

Markets

Kensington Market ★★★   This neighborhood has changed dramatically over the years. Originally a Jewish community, it became home to Portuguese and other European immigrants, and then evolved into a community bordering Chinatown with shopkeepers who hail from the Caribbean, the Middle East, and elsewhere. There are several Asian herbalists and grocers, as well as West Indian and Middle Eastern shops. Kensington Avenue has the greatest concentration of vintage clothing stores in the city, as well as some good grub and excellent cafes for refueling. For a full description, see "Walking Tour 1: Chinatown & Kensington Market," in chapter 8. Along Baldwin, Kensington & Augusta aves. No phone. Subway: Spadina, then the LRT to Baldwin St. or Dundas St. W.

St. Lawrence Market ★   This market is a local favorite for fresh produce, and it even draws people who live a good distance away. The peameal-bacon sandwiches are famous. Check out the gallery on the second floor, a quiet retreat from the busy market, where exhibits about the city are mounted, with free admission. Hours are Tuesday through Thursday from 8am to 6pm, Friday from 8am to 7pm, and Saturday from 8am to 5pm. On Saturday, there is also the farmers market from 5am, when the farmers arrive, to 1pm. See p. 142 for a complete description. 92 Front St. E. ☎ **416/392-7219.** www.stlawrencemarket.com. Subway: Union.

Music

HMV   This is the flagship Toronto store of the British chain. (You'll find smaller outlets throughout the city.) The selection of pop, rock, jazz, and classical music is large. Best of all, you can listen to a CD before you buy it. 333 Yonge St. ☎ **416/586-9668.** Subway: Dundas.

The Music Store   On the Toronto Symphony Orchestra's home turf, this attractive shop includes several TSO CDs in its collection of classical and choral music. Roy Thomson Hall, 60 Simcoe St. ☎ **416/593-4822.** Subway: St. Andrew.

  An Outlet for People Who Hate Outlets

Vaughan Mills is a massive shopping complex 32km (20 miles) north of Toronto (close to Canada's Wonderland; p. 147). This clean, modern mall is home to **Holt Renfrew Last Call** (the only Holt Renfrew discount center in the province), the world's largest **Tommy Hilfiger** store, and Canada's largest **Toys R Us/Babies R Us.** Most of the stores in Vaughan Mills aren't outlets, but there are just enough to make sure you get an easy deal (plus, there's a massive **Winners** store—do you really need more?). The only catch is that you do need to drive to get here (take Hwy. 401 to Hwy. 400, then drive north and exit at Bass Pro Mills Dr., which leads directly to the mall). For more information, call ☎ **905/879-2110** or visit www.vaughanmills.com.

Rotate This ★ 🎁 Low-key but well stocked, this is an excellent bet if you're interested in the local indie scene. In addition to CDs (new and used), there's plenty of vinyl, with countertop turntables you can use as listening stations. 801 Queen St. W. ✆ **416/504-8447.** Subway: Osgoode, then a streetcar west to Claremont Rd.

Soundscapes This neighborhood shop carries an excellent selection of new and local talent, indie bands, essential standards, eclectic finds, and more. You can also buy tickets for hot shows around town. The staff is helpful and knowledgeable. Definitely worth a look. 572 College St. ✆ **416/537-1620.** Subway: College, then a streetcar west to Manning Ave.

Wild East ★★ 🎁 This is a great source for new and secondhand CDs and DVDs. Wild East is a strong supporter of both local talent and international indie acts, so you'll find music here that you won't get anywhere else. 360 Danforth Ave. ✆ **416/469-8371.** Subway: Chester.

Sex Toys

Lovecraft ★ Believe it or not, Lovecraft is downright wholesome. Sure, there are the requisite bad-girl (and -boy) lingerie and toys, but much of the shop stocks joke gifts, T-shirts with suggestive slogans, and an impressive collection of erotic literature (no porn mags). The staff is friendly and the atmosphere playful. 27 Yorkville Ave. ✆ **877/923-7331** or 416/923-7331. www.lovecraftsexshop.com. Subway: Bay.

Toys

Kidding Awound ☺ 🎁 Wind-up gadgets are the specialty here—hundreds of 'em. There are also some antique toys (which you won't let the kids near) and gag gifts. 91 Cumberland St. ✆ **416/926-8996.** Subway: Bay.

Mastermind Toys ☺ This Canadian-owned chain stocks toys for all ages, sizes, and quirks. The stores are well laid out and staff is helpful. With dozens of major brands and some of the top lines—like Playmobil, Plan Toys, and Lamaze—it's one of the best options in Toronto, especially if you want to avoid the big-box stores. There are many locations, although they tend to be on the city's outskirts. There's also a location in the Ontario Science Centre. 2134 Queen St. ✆ **416/699-3797.** www. mastermindtoys.com. Subway: Queen, then a streetcar east to Glen Manor.

Science City ★★ ☺ Kids and adults alike will love this tiny store filled with games, puzzles, models, kits, and books—all related to science. Whether your interest is astronomy, biology, chemistry, archaeology, or physics, you'll find something here. Holt Renfrew Centre, 50 Bloor St. W. ✆ **416/968-2627.** www.sciencecity.ca. Subway: Yonge/Bloor.

TORONTO AFTER DARK

You're not going to lack for things to do after the sun goes down in Toronto. The city is a genuine Mecca for top-notch theater, with some acclaimed productions actually premiering in Toronto before heading to Broadway or London's West End. Notable local performing arts organizations include the Canadian Stage Company, the Canadian Opera Company, the National Ballet of Canada, Soulpepper (which has earned a reputation as one of North America's most creative theater companies), the Tafelmusik Baroque Orchestra and Chamber Choir, and the Toronto Symphony Orchestra.

Toronto's many dance and music venues also host the crème de la crème of Canadian and international performers. Some of the best entertainment is in Toronto's comedy clubs, which have served as training grounds for stars such as Jim Carrey, Mike Myers, Dan Aykroyd, and John Candy.

The Sony Centre for the Performing Arts—formerly known as the Hummingbird Centre—reopened in October 2010 after a major renovation and restoration. There's plenty going on at the Four Seasons Centre, Roy Thomson Hall, Massey Hall, the new and impressive Koerner Hall, and at other theaters around town.

The hottest news on the nightlife front is Ossington Avenue. This used to be a quiet stretch, but it's now *the* place to go for the coolest watering holes. The action has spilled onto the adjacent Dundas Street West strip, too. Some spots to look for: The Communist's Daughter, Dakota Tavern, Watusi, Reposado, and Sweaty Betty's.

10

Molson Amphitheatre **14**
National Ballet of Canada **23**
Native Earth
  Performing Arts Theatre **33**
Princess of Wales Theatre **19**
Rogers Centre **15**
Roy Thomson Hall **17**
Royal Alexandra Theatre **18**
Sony Centre for the
  Performing Arts **28**
St. James Cathedral **34**
The St. Lawrence
  Centre for the Arts **29**
St. Michael's Cathedral **36**
St. Patrick's Church **41**
Soulpepper **33**
Theatre Passe Muraille **5**
Toronto Dance Theatre **26**
Toronto Mendelssohn Choir **17**
Toronto Symphony Orchestra **17**
Yonge-Dundas Square **40**

CLUBS, MUSIC & BARS
Balzac's Coffee **33**
The Ben Wicks **42**
Byzantium **44**
Comedy Bar **1**
The Communist's Daughter **4**
Crews, Tango and The Zone **44**
Crocodile Rock **20**
The Dakota Tavern **4**
The Drake Lounge **6**
The Drake Underground **6**
Foundation Room **31**
The Garrison **4**
The Horseshoe Tavern **9**
The Irish Embassy **27**
The Library Bar **24**
The Melody Bar **6**
Mill Street Brew Pub **33**
Motel **6**
Pegasus Bar **46**
Phoenix Concert Theatre **43**
Reservoir Lounge **30**
The Rex Hotel Jazz & Blues Bar **22**
The Rivoli **10**
Sailor **44**
Second City **13**
Slack's **44**
Sneaky Dee's **2**
Supermarket **3**
Sutra Tiki Bar **1**
Sweaty Betty's **6**
This is London **11**
Watusi **6**
Wheat Sheaf Tavern **8**
Woody's **44**
Yuk Yuk's Supper Club **21**
Zelda's **44**

PERFORMING ARTS
Air Canada Centre **25**
Buddies in Bad Times Theatre **46**
Canadian Opera Company **23**
Canadian Stage Company **29**
Canon Theatre **39**
The Carlu **45**
Cinematheque Ontario **12**
Dancemakers **33**
Distillery District **33**
The Elgin and Winter Garden Theatre Centre **39**
Factory Theatre **7**
Fleet Dance Theatre **26**
Four Seasons Centre for the Performing Arts **23**
Glenn Gould Studio **16**
Lorraine Kimsa Theatre for Young People **32**
Massey Hall **37**

MAKING PLANS For listings of local performances and events, check out *Where Toronto* (www.where.ca/toronto) and *Toronto Life* (www.torontolife.com), as well as the *Toronto Star* (www.thestar.com). For up-to-the-minute lists of hot-ticket events, check out the free weeklies (and their informative websites) *Now* (www.nowtoronto.com) and *Eye* (www.eyeweekly.com), available around town in newspaper boxes and at bars, cafes, and bookstores. The city website www.toronto.com also boasts lengthy lists of performances. Events of particular interest to the gay and lesbian community are listed in *Xtra!* (www.xtra.ca), another free weekly available in newspaper boxes and many bookstores. The Torontoist blog (www.torontoist.com) is also a great source for upcoming performances, while www.martiniboys.com covers the bar and club scene thoroughly.

GETTING TICKETS For almost any theater, music, or dance event, you can buy tickets from Ticketmaster (© **416/870-8000;** www.ticketmaster.ca). To avoid the service charge on each ticket (not just each order) sold over the phone, head to a ticket center. They're scattered throughout the city; call the information line for the lengthy list of locations.

THE PERFORMING ARTS

Toronto's arts scene offers something for every taste year-round. The city's arts institutions are widely renowned, and top-notch international performers regularly pass through town.

Theater

Big-budget musicals—think *Cats* and *Mamma Mia!*—continue to dominate Toronto's larger theaters, but a number of excellent boutique companies also exist. Many of the smaller troupes have no permanent performance space, so they move from venue to venue. The best time to capture the flavor of Toronto's theater life is during the Fringe Festival (© **416/966-1062;** www.fringetoronto.com), usually held for 12 days starting in early July and featuring more than 100 casts from Canada and beyond.

LANDMARK THEATERS & PERFORMANCE VENUES

Canon Theatre ★ This beautiful venue has had a tumultuous history. It got its start as the Pantages Theatre in 1920, and its opulent design (by the famous theater

 discount TICKETS

Want to take in a show, but don't want to spend a bundle? Drop by the T.O. Tix booth ★ (© **416/536-6468,** ext. 40), which sells half-price day-of-performance tickets. The booth is in Yonge-Dundas Square, just across the street from the Eaton Centre. T.O. Tix accepts cash, debit cards, Visa, and MasterCard, and all sales are final. The booth is open Tuesday to Saturday from noon to 6:30pm; it's closed Sunday and Monday (tickets for performances on those days are sold on Sat). You can also buy tickets via the website www.totix.ca, but be warned that not all tickets are available online. Also available on the website are hip-TIX, where students between the ages of 15 and 29 can score C$5 tickets for certain shows.

After Dark from Chinatown to Bloor Street

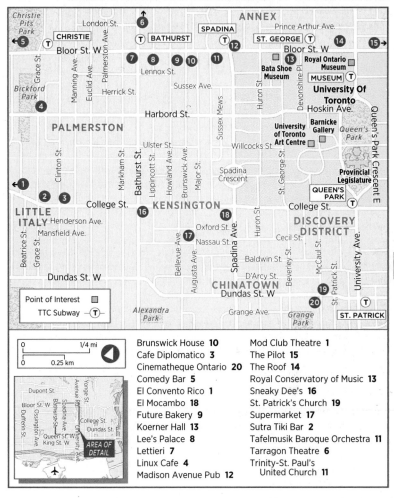

Brunswick House **10**	Mod Club Theatre **1**
Cafe Diplomatico **3**	The Pilot **15**
Cinematheque Ontario **20**	The Roof **14**
Comedy Bar **5**	Royal Conservatory of Music **13**
El Convento Rico **1**	Sneaky Dee's **16**
El Mocambo **18**	St. Patrick's Church **19**
Future Bakery **9**	Supermarket **17**
Koerner Hall **13**	Sutra Tiki Bar **2**
Lee's Palace **8**	Tafelmusik Baroque Orchestra **11**
Lettieri **7**	Tarragon Theatre **6**
Linux Cafe **4**	Trinity-St. Paul's
Madison Avenue Pub **12**	United Church **11**

architect Thomas Lamb) was widely admired. However, the theater's fortunes sank in 1929—not because of the stock-market crash, but because its owner was embroiled in a legal battle. Eventually, the gorgeous space was carved into six cinemas. It was rescued and dramatically renovated by the Livent production company, which also brought back its original name, and the new 2,250-seat Pantages Theatre was home for many years to Andrew Lloyd Webber's lavish *The Phantom of the Opera*. But after Livent collapsed, the theater went dark for a long time. Fortunately, its current owners—who have renamed it the Canon—have turned over the theater's management and programming to Mirvish Productions, Toronto's leading theater promoters and owners of the Royal Alex and the Princess of Wales Theatre (both listed below). In recent years, it has hosted such shows as *Spamalot* and *The Harder They Come.* 244 Victoria St. ☎ **416/872-1212.** www.mirvish.com. Subway: Dundas or Queen.

The Elgin and Winter Garden Theatre Centre ★   These landmark theaters first opened their doors in 1913, and the Centre is now a designated National Historic Site, owned and operated by the Ontario Heritage Trust. Both the Elgin and the Winter Garden have been restored to their Edwardian gilded glory and the theaters vie with the Royal Alexandra and the Princess of Wales Theatre (see below for both) for major shows and attention. The Centre has been termed the last operating double-decker theater in the world. The downstairs Elgin is larger, seating 1,500 and featuring a lavish domed ceiling and gilded decoration on the boxes and proscenium. Hand-painted frescoes adorn the striking interior of the 1,000-seat Winter Garden. Suspended from its ceiling and lit with lanterns are more than 5,000 branches of beech leaves, which have been preserved, painted, and fireproofed. Both theaters offer everything from Broadway musicals and dramas to concerts and opera performances, with the Toronto International Film Festival utilizing the Elgin as a cinema. 189 Yonge St. ☎ **416/872-5555** for tickets or 416/314-2901 for administration. Subway: Queen.

Farther Afield

Don't forget that two major theater festivals—the Shaw Festival (www. shawfest.com) in Niagara-on-the-Lake and the renowned Stratford Festival (www.stratfordfestival.ca) in Stratford— are only an hour or two away. See chapter 11 for details.

Four Seasons Centre for the Performing Arts ★★★   Toronto's opera house, which opened in 2006, is a stunner. Designed by architect Jack Diamond of the renowned Toronto firm, Diamond and Schmitt, it has a simple exterior, resembling a house of glass. Inside, in the tradition of truly grand opera houses, there are three stages: main, rear, and side. But the masterstroke in the Four Seasons Centre's design is its perfect acoustics. No small feat given that the structure is set on not one but two major thoroughfares, and a subway line rumbles beneath it. This is home to both the Canadian Opera Company (p. 212) and the National Ballet of Canada (p. 214). 145 Queen St. W. ☎ **416/363-8231** for tickets or 416/363-6671 for administration. www.fourseasonscentre.ca. Subway: Osgoode.

Princess of Wales Theatre ★   This spectacular 2,000-seat, state-of-the-art facility was built for the Toronto run of *Miss Saigon,* with a stage large enough to accommodate the landing of the helicopter in that production. Later, it was home to *The Lion King, Hairspray,* and the ill-fated stage adaptation of the epic *The Lord of the Rings.* More recently, it has featured *The Sound of Music.* Frank Stella, who painted 929 sq. m (10,000 sq. ft.) of colorful murals, decorated the exterior and interior walls. People in wheelchairs have access to all levels of the theater (not the norm in Toronto). 300 King St. W. ☎ **416/872-1212.** www.mirvish.com. Subway: St. Andrew.

Royal Alexandra Theatre ★★   The 1,495-seat Royal Alex is a magnificent spectacle, never mind the show! Constructed in 1907, it owes its current health to discount-store czar and impresario Ed Mirvish, who refurbished it (as well as the surrounding area) in the 1960s. Inside, it's a riot of plush reds, gold brocade, and

TORONTO AFTER DARK | The Performing Arts

baroque ornamentation. Recent productions here have included *Dirty Dancing,* a musical based on the movie, and *Rock of Ages.* Avoid the vertigo-inducing second balcony and the seats "under the circle," which don't have the greatest sight lines. Be forewarned that legroom is very limited here. 260 King St. W. ℰ **416/872-1212.** www. mirvish.com. Subway: St. Andrew.

Roy Thomson Hall ★★★   This important concert hall is home to the Toronto Symphony Orchestra (p. 213), which performs here from September to June, and to the Toronto Mendelssohn Choir (p. 213). Since it opened in 1982, it has also hosted an array of international musical artists, including Yo-Yo Ma, Jessye Norman, and Kiri Te Kanawa. The hall was designed to give the audience a feeling of unusual intimacy with the performers—none of the 2,812 seats is more than 33m (108 ft.) from the stage. This is one of the few venues where you can feel happy in the "nose-bleed" seats. With Roy Thomson's perfect acoustics, who cares about sightlines? 60 Simcoe St. ℰ **416/872-4255** for tickets or 416/593-4822 for administration. www.roythomson.com. Subway: St. Andrew.

The St. Lawrence Centre for the Arts ★★   For 3 decades, the St. Lawrence Centre has presented top-notch theater, music, and dance performances. The facade of the building is unattractive, but the theaters inside are comfortable (and there's more legroom than, say, the Royal Alex). The Bluma Appel Theatre is home to the Canadian Stage Company (p. 211), and the smaller Jane Mallet Theatre features the Toronto Operetta Theatre Company, among others. This is a popular spot for lectures, too. 27 Front St. E. ℰ **416/366-7723.** www.stlc.com. Subway: Union.

MAJOR CONCERT HALLS & AUDITORIUMS

The Carlu   Located on the seventh floor of College Park, this was considered one of the grandest concert halls in Canada when it opened in 1931. Like so many other venues in Toronto, the Carlu was shuttered in the 1970s. Now, the 1,200-seat concert hall is back in favor, and its architecture is believed to be one of the best surviving examples of Art Moderne in the world (it was created by Jacques Carlu, the architect also responsible for New York's Rainbow Room). The concerts here tend to be charity benefits, with hefty price tags for tickets. College Park, 444 Yonge St., 7th floor. ℰ **416/597-1931.** www.thecarlu.com. Subway: College.

Distillery District ★★★   This was once the home of the Gooderham-Worts Distillery, Canada's largest distilling company in the 19th century. The 45-building complex is an outstanding example of industrial design from the Victorian age (p. 123). In 2003, it was reinvented as the Distillery District, which includes galleries, restaurants, and shops. The district also houses several performing-arts venues, including the Case Goods Theatre and the state-of-the-art Young Centre for the Performing Arts. The Dancemakers (p. 214), Soulpepper (p. 212), and Native Earth (p. 212) troupes now perform here. 55 Mill St. ℰ **416/367-1800.** www.thedistillerydistrict.com. Subway: King, then a streetcar east to Parliament St.

Fleck Dance Theatre   Part of the sprawling Harbourfront Centre (p. 123) by the waterfront, this 446-seat theater (formerly the Premiere Dance Theatre) is specifically designed for dance performances and is where you can catch some of Toronto's leading contemporary dance companies. Queen's Quay Terminal, 207 Queens Quay W. ℰ **416/973-4000.** www.harbourfrontcentre.com. Subway: Union, then the LRT to York Quay.

Glenn Gould Studio ★   Located on the main floor of the Canadian Broadcasting Centre, this 341-seat radio concert hall offers chamber music, jazz, roots music, and spoken-word performances. Its name celebrates the great, eccentric Toronto pianist whose life was cut short by a stroke in 1982. 250 Front St. W. ✆ **416/205-5555.** www.glenngouldstudio.cbc.ca. Subway: Union.

Koerner Hall   Opened in 2009, this is a new jewel on Toronto's performing arts scene. Designed by the renowned KPMB Architects group, the concert hall seats 1,135 patrons. The centerpiece of The Royal Conservatory of Music's TELUS Centre for Performance and Learning, it has received rave reviews for its acoustics and has attracted such international stars as Steve Reich, Frederica von Stade, Ravi Shankar, and Baaba Maal in genres ranging from jazz to blues to world music to classical. 273 Bloor St. W. ✆ **416/408-2825.** www.rcmusic.ca. Subway: St. George or Museum.

Massey Hall   This landmark 1892 building is one of Canada's premier music venues. Its 2,753 seats are not the most comfortable in town, but the flawless acoustics will make you stop squirming. It has hosted now-legendary concerts from the likes of Charlie Parker and Neil Young, and its programming runs the gamut from classical to pop to rock to jazz. Recent visitors have included Norah Jones, Diana Krall, Jimmy Cliff, and Pat Metheny. This is also a popular stop for lectures. 178 Victoria St. ✆ **416/872-4255** for tickets or 416/593-4822 for administration. www.masseyhall.com. Subway: King.

Sony Centre for the Performing Arts   If you visited Toronto before 1997, you might remember this as the O'Keefe Centre; if you visited before 2007, it was the Hummingbird Centre. Now known as The Sony Centre for the Performing Arts, it reopened in October 2010 after a C$30-million renovation and restoration, in time to celebrate the building's 50th anniversary. Artists who have appeared in this storied venue range from Richard Burton and Liz Taylor to Bob Dylan, the Clash, and Radiohead. Star architect Daniel Libeskind, the man responsible for the Royal Ontario Museum's controversial crystal galleries (p. 127), has designed a residential tower that will loom over the theater. 1 Front St. E. ✆ **416/872-2262.** www.sonycentre.ca. Subway: Union.

Toronto Centre for the Arts   Built in 1993, this gigantic complex is home to the Toronto Philharmonia, an acclaimed classical orchestra. It also hosts international performers and shows such as a long and successful run of *Jersey Boys*. The Toronto Centre is a half-hour subway ride from downtown and located in a neighborhood with generally lame food options. Best advice: Have a really early pre-theater dinner before making the trek (see the "Uptown" section in the dining chapter for ideas). 5040 Yonge St. ✆ **416/733-9388.** www.tocentre.com. Subway: North York Centre.

Yonge-Dundas Square ★   Toronto's open-air entertainment venue is across the street from the Eaton Centre. Summer is its liveliest season: Events include a Tuesday-night film series, a "Serenades In The Square" series featuring local musicians every Wednesday at lunchtime, and Global Grooves concerts on Friday evenings. When not in use for events, this is a public square where you can stroll or sit by the fountains. This is also the home of the T.O. Tix discount-tickets booth (p. 206). Yonge & Dundas sts., southeast corner. ✆ **416/979-9960.** www.ydsquare.ca. Subway: Dundas.

MORE THAN church MUSIC

Everyone knows that a church is where you go to listen to choir music—but in Toronto, several churches double as performance spaces for classical or opera ensembles. **Trinity-St. Paul's United Church** (427 Bloor St. W.; ℭ **416/964-6337**; www.trinitystpauls.ca) is home to Toronto's acclaimed Tafelmusik Baroque Orchestra & Chamber Choir (p. 213). **St. James' Cathedral,** at 65 Church St. (ℭ **416/364-7865**; www.stjames cathedral.on.ca), hosts everything from solo performances of classical cellists to youth choirs from abroad, as well as its own high-quality 18-voice Cathedral Choir. **St. Patrick's Church** (141 McCaul St.; ℭ **416/483-0559**) is where the Tallis Choir of Toronto (ℭ **416/286-9798**; www.tallischoir.com) often performs (its repertoire is mostly Renaissance and Tudor music). And if you happen to love real church music, stop in at **St. Michael's Cathedral** (65 Bond St.; ℭ **416/364-0234**; www.stmichaels cathedral.com). Its internationally-acclaimed Boys Choir regularly sings at three weekend masses.

THEATER COMPANIES & SMALLER THEATERS

Buddies in Bad Times Theatre ★   Proudly provocative, this not-for-profit company has been dedicated to gay, lesbian, and queer theatrical expression since its founding in 1979. Their edgy work is not for everyone (the list of upcoming productions identifies shows that are "not for the faint of heart," and they mean it), but Buddies produces shows that you simply won't see anywhere else. The theater has also staged Canadian adaptations of some well-known works, such as Ibsen's *Hedda Gabler*. Controversial playwright Sky Gilbert helped build the theater's cutting-edge reputation. 12 Alexander St. ℭ **416/975-8555**. www.artsexy.ca. Tickets C$20–C$30; pay-what-you-can admission to some performances. Subway: Wellesley.

Canadian Stage ★★★   Formerly known as CanStage, this company performs an eclectic variety of Canadian (from the likes of Michel Tremblay and Robert Lepage) and international plays. Their productions are often ground-breaking. They perform at the Bluma Appel Theatre, which seats 875, and the Berkeley Theatre, a more avant-garde, intimate (240-seat) space. Bluma Appel Theatre (St. Lawrence Centre): 27 Front St. E.; Berkeley Theatre: 26 Berkeley St. ℭ **416/368-3110**. www.canadianstage.com. Tickets C$30–C$75; Mon pay-what-you-can admission. Senior & student discounts may be available 30 min. before performance. Subway for St. Lawrence Centre: Union; for Berkeley Theatre: King, then any streetcar east to Berkeley St.

Factory Theatre ★   Since it opened in 1970, the Factory Theatre has focused on presenting Canadian plays, from political dramas to over-the-top comedies. The theater likes to call itself "the home of the Canadian playwright." Performances showcase up-and-coming scribes, as well as such established playwrights as the internationally-acclaimed George F. Walker, who has had 23 shows produced here. The options veer from experimental to traditional. 125 Bathurst St. ℭ **416/504-9971**. www.factorytheatre.ca. Tickets C$15–C$37. Subway: St. Andrew, then any streetcar west to Bathurst St. and walk south to Adelaide St.

Lorraine Kimsa Theatre for Young People ★★ ☺ Toronto's such a theater town that even tiny tots (and the rest of the family) get their own performance center. For more than 30 years, the always-enjoyable Lorraine Kimsa Theatre (formerly known as the Young People's Theatre) has mounted whimsical productions such as *Jacob Two-Two Meets the Hooded Fang* (by the late, great Mordecai Richler) and children's classics like *You're a Good Man, Charlie Brown*. This theater company is particularly committed to diversity in its programming and in its artists. 165 Front St. E. ℂ **416/862-2222** for tickets or 416/363-5131 for administration. www.lktyp.ca. Tickets C$15–C$30. Subway: Union, then a streetcar east to Jarvis St.

Native Earth Performing Arts Theatre This small company is dedicated to performing works that express and dramatize the native Canadian experience and to encouraging the use of theater as a form of communication within the Native community. Playwright Tomson Highway, author of *Dry Lips Oughta Move to Kapuskasing*, was one of the company's founders. The company also performs at other theaters around town. Performing at the Case Goods Theatre in the Distillery District, 55 Mill St. ℂ **416/367-1800.** www.nativeearth.ca. Tickets C$15–C$30. Subway: King, then a streetcar east to Parliament St.

Soulpepper ★★ Founded in 1997, this artist-created classical repertory company presents theatrical masterpieces of the 20th century, under the able artistic direction of Albert Schultz Theatre. Education and youth outreach are key parts of their mandate. The highly respected—and award-winning—group recently staged *Glengarry Glen Ross* and the Canadian classic *Billy Bishop Goes To War*. Performing at the Young Centre in the Distillery District, 55 Mill St. ℂ **416/866-8666.** www.soulpepper.ca. Tickets C$40–C$75; C$20-C$22 for ages 21–30 available through www.stageplay.ca. Subway: King, then a streetcar east to Parliament St.

Tarragon Theatre ★ The Tarragon Theatre opened in 1971. It produces original works by such famous Canadian literary figures as Michel Tremblay, Michael Ondaatje, and Judith Thompson, alongside works from the likes of David Hare and David Mamet, as well as the occasional classic. There are two small theaters on-site—or three, if you count the 60-seat rehearsal hall, which is occasionally used for performances. 30 Bridgman Ave. (near Dupont & Bathurst sts.). ℂ **416/531-1827** for tickets, or 416/536-5018 for administration. www.tarragontheatre.com. Tickets C$21–C$39. Subway: Bathurst.

Theatre Passe Muraille This theater started in the late 1960s, when a pool of actors began experimenting and improvising original Canadian material. It continues to produce innovative, provocative theater by such contemporary Canadian playwrights as John Mighton, Daniel David Moses, and Wajdi Mouawad. There are two stages—the Mainspace seats 220; the more intimate (if rather uncomfortable) Backspace seats 70. 16 Ryerson Ave. ℂ **416/504-7529.** www.passemuraille.on.ca. Tickets C$15–C$35. Subway: Osgoode, then any streetcar west to Bathurst St.

Classical Music & Opera

Canadian Opera Company ★★★ Canada's largest opera company, the sixth-largest in North America, was founded in 1950. Performances take place at the Four Seasons Centre for the Performing Arts (p. 208), a venue built with opera aficionados in mind. To give you an idea of how popular the Canadian Opera Company is, its performances have been at 99% capacity for the past four years. More than

opera **OBSESSED**

It was big news back in 2006 when Toronto's opera house—the Four Seasons Centre for the Performing Arts—opened its doors. The irony was that Toronto, a city that had never had an opera house, was already a North American magnet for opera lovers. **The Canadian Opera Company** (see above) is just one reason to visit. Others include **Opera Atelier** (📞 416/703-3767; www.operaatelier.com), a renowned company that produces baroque operas (Monteverdi, Mozart, and Gluck are perennially popular). The **Toronto Opera Repertoire** (📞 416/698-9572; www.toronto-opera.com) is dedicated to making classic opera accessible to all, using supertitles in English and keeping ticket prices democratically low. **Tapestry New Opera Works** (📞 416/537-6066; www.tapestrynewopera.com) is dedicated to the production of original works of Canadian opera and musical theater. For a provocative and fantastical take on chamber opera, check out the **Queen of Puddings Music Theatre** (📞 416/203-4149; www.queenofpuddingsmusictheatre.com). The company has performed in London's Convent Garden. Further

evidence of Toronto's passionate love of opera has been the enthusiastic response to the Metropolitan Opera's Live in HD series, in which opera is screened in movie theaters around the globe. Go to www.metopera.org/hdlive for ticket info.

Toronto Mendelssohn Choir ★
This world-renowned group first performed in Massey Hall in 1895. Today, it calls Roy Thomson Hall home. Its repertoire ranges from Verdi's Requiem, Bach's St. Matthew Passion, and Handel's Messiah to the soundtrack of Schindler's List. TMC has recorded for Naxos and EMI. 60 Simcoe St. 📞 **416/598-0422.** www.tmchoir.org. Tickets C$30–C$100. Subway: St. Andrew.

Toronto Symphony Orchestra ★★★
The TSO has been revitalized under the direction of Peter Oundjian and the improved acoustics of their home venue. They perform anything from classics to jazzy Broadway tunes to new Canadian works at Roy Thomson Hall from September to June. 60 Simcoe St. 📞 **416/593-4828.** www.tso.on.ca. Tickets C$33–C$99. Subway: St. Andrew.

three-quarters of the tickets are held by subscribers, making this a tough "get" for visitors—so plan ahead. The COC is now headed by new music director Johannes Debus. Their 2010–2011 season includes productions of *Aida* and *The Magic Flute.* 145 Queen St. W. 📞 **416/363-8231** for tickets or 416/363-6671 for administration. www.coc.ca. Tickets C$62–C$292. Subway: Osgoode.

Tafelmusik Baroque Orchestra & Chamber Choir ★★ This internationally acclaimed ensemble plays baroque compositions by the likes of Handel, Bach, and Mozart on authentic period instruments. Their annual *Messiah* concerts always sell out. Visiting musicians frequently join the 19 permanent performers. It gives a series of concerts at Trinity-St. Paul's United Church (47 Bloor St. W.) and stages other performances in Massey Hall (p. 210) and the Toronto Centre for the Arts (p. 210). 427 Bloor St. W. 📞 **416/964-6337.** www.tafelmusik.org. Tickets C$32–C$82. Subway for Trinity-St. Paul's: Yonge/Bloor; for Massey Hall: King; for Toronto Centre for the Arts: North York Centre.

GREAT music ON A BUDGET

As the cost of concert tickets spirals ever upward, it can be frustrating to budget for an evening out. But there are some places you can count on scoring a deal. One best bet is **University of Toronto's Faculty of Music** (✆ **416/978-3744;** www.music.utoronto.ca), which offers a full range of instrumental and choral concerts and recitals. They are held at various locations around the St. George Campus, including Walter Hall, and many performances are free of charge. It's also worth checking out who's performing at the **Royal Conservatory of Music** (273 Bloor St. W.; ✆ **416/408-2825;** www.rcmusic.ca). There are concerts by well-known jazz vocalists or international ensembles, as well as free recitals given by faculty members and students.

Dance

Dancemakers   Now under the artistic direction of choreographer Michael Trent, Dancemakers has, over the past four decades, gained international recognition for its provocative mix of stylized physical movement and theater. It is based in the Distillery District, in a state-of-the-art 98-seat performance venue. Performing at the Case Goods Theatre in the Distillery District, 55 Mill Street. ✆ **416/367-1800.** www.dancemakers.org. Tickets C$20–C$25.

National Ballet of Canada ★★★   Perhaps the most beloved and famous of Toronto's cultural icons is the National Ballet of Canada. English ballerina Celia Franca launched the company in Toronto in 1951 and served as director, principal dancer, choreographer, and teacher. Over the years, the company has achieved great renown. The legendary Canadian ballerina Karen Kain became its artistic director in 2005. The company shares the Four Seasons Centre for the Performing Arts (p. 208) with the Canadian Opera Company. Its repertoire includes the classics (you can always count on *The Nutcracker* every December) and works by luminaries such as George Balanchine, as well as from some Canadian choreographers. 145 Queen St. W. ✆ **866/345-9595** or 416/345-9595 for tickets, or 416/345-9686 for administration. www.national. ballet.ca. Tickets from C$45–C$200. Subway: Osgoode.

Toronto Dance Theatre   The city's leading contemporary-dance company was founded in 1968, bringing an inventive spirit and original Canadian dance to the stage. Christopher House has been the company's director since 1994. House's choreography is widely acclaimed and has earned him multiple awards. TDT tours internationally and often performs at Fleck Dance Theatre, Queen's Quay Terminal, 207 Queens Quay W. Office: 80 Winchester St. ✆ 416/973-4000 for tickets or **416/967-1365** for administration. www.tdt.org. Tickets C$30–C$45.

Cinema

Cinematheque Ontario ★ 📷   A division of the Toronto International Film Festival, Cinematheque Ontario has been showing the best in world cinema for the past 20 years. The programs include directors' retrospectives, plus new films from France, Germany, Japan, Bulgaria, and other countries that you won't find in the first-run theaters around town. Screenings at the Art Gallery of Ontario, 317 Dundas

The Performing Arts | TORONTO AFTER DARK

St. W. ☎ **416/968-FILM (416/968-3456).** www.cinemathequeontario.ca. Tickets C$12 adults, C$8 seniors & students. Subway: Dundas and streetcar west to McCaul St.

Pop & Rock Music Venues

Everyone comes to Toronto, a city known for possessing one of the most active live music scenes in the world. Tickets are available through Ticketmaster (☎ **416/870-8000;** www.ticketmaster.ca). In addition to the previously mentioned Roy Thomson Hall and Massey Hall, these are the major pop and rock music venues. Ticket prices vary widely depending on both the venue and the act.

Air Canada Centre   Better known as a sports venue (it's home to the Maple Leafs and the Raptors), the Air Canada Centre also hosts popular musical acts. Neil Young has performed here, as have Tom Petty, Michael Buble, and Mariah Carey. 40 Bay St. (at Lakeshore Blvd). ☎ **416/815-5500.** www.theaircanadacentre.com. Subway: Union, then the LRT to Queen's Quay.

Molson Amphitheatre ★   This is a favorite summer spot because you can listen to music by the side of Lake Ontario. The amphitheatre seats 9,000, the cheaper lawn section, another 7,000. It regularly draws some of the biggest names in rock, pop, and country. Ontario Place, 909 Lakeshore Blvd. W. ☎ **416/260-5600.** www.livenation.com/venue/molson-canadian-amphitheatre-tickets. Subway: Bathurst, then the Bathurst streetcar south to Exhibition Place (last stop).

Rogers Centre   The biggest venue in the city, it is not used regularly for music but occasionally draws superstar like U2 and AC/DC. This venue is about as intimate as a parking lot. If you're seated in the 400 or 500 levels, you'll be watching the show on the JumboTron unless you bring your binoculars. Steer clear of the seats next to the JumboTron, or you won't see anything at all. 1 Blue Jays Way. ☎ **416/341-3663.** www.rogerscentre.com. Subway: Union.

THE CLUB & MUSIC SCENE

A few hints before you head out for the evening. The drinking age in Ontario is currently 19, and most establishments enforce the law. Expect long queues on Friday and Saturday after 10pm at downtown clubs. Bars and pubs are open daily from 11am to 2am. During such special events as The Toronto International Film Festival, the North By Northeast Music Festival (NXNE), and Pride, a number of downtown bars are allowed to stay open until 4am. If you're out at closing time, you'll find the subway shut down, but late-night buses run along Yonge and Bloor streets. Major routes on streets such as College, Queen, and King operate all night. To find out what's on, see "Making Plans," earlier in this chapter.

Comedy Clubs

Toronto must be one heck of a funny place. How else to explain why a disproportionate number of comedians, including Jim Carrey and Mike Myers, hail from here. The annual Just For Laughs festival delivers laughs every July, and the city's comedy clubs are thriving.

Comedy Bar   This new kid on the comedy block has quickly proved popular. It stresses sketch and improv comedy over stand-up (it's co-owned by Gary Rideout of sketch troupe the Sketchersons). 945 Bloor St. W. ☎ **416/238-7337.** www.comedybar.ca. Cover: free to C$12. Subway: Ossington.

The Rivoli ★ While the Riv is also known for its music performances, the Monday-night ALT.COMedy Lounge and Tuesday-night Sketch! Comedy Lounge are its biggest draws. The Riv features local and visiting stand-ups, and is best known as the place where the Kids in the Hall got their start. Shows take place in the intimate 125-seat back room. See p. 101 for a restaurant review. 332-334 Queen St. W. ✆ **416/597-0794.** www.altcomedylounge.com. Pay-what-you-can admission. Subway: Osgoode.

Second City ★ This was where Mike Myers received his formal—and improvisational—comic training. Over the years, the legendary Second City nurtured the likes of John Candy, Dan Aykroyd, Bill Murray, Martin Short, Andrea Martin, and Eugene Levy. It continues to turn out talented young actors. The shows are always funny and topical, though the outrageous post-show improvs usually get the biggest laughs. 51 Mercer St. ✆ **800/263-4485** or 416/343-0011. www.secondcity.com. Show only C$24-C$29; dinner & show C$39-C$56. Reservations required. Subway: St. Andrew.

Yuk Yuk's Toronto Yuk Yuk's is Canada's original home of stand-up comedy. Comic Mark Breslin founded the place in 1976, inspired by New York's Catch a Rising Star and Los Angeles's Comedy Store. Famous alumni include Jim Carrey, Howie Mandel, and Norm MacDonald. Jerry Seinfeld, Robin Williams, Sandra Bernhard, and Bill Hicks have all headlined here. Tuesday is amateur night and correspondingly cheap. Another Yuk Yuk's is in Mississauga, not far from Pearson International Airport (5165 Dixie Rd.; ✆ **905/434-4985**). 224 Richmond St. W. ✆ 416/967-6425. www.yukyuks.com. Show only C$12-C$20; dinner & show C$38-C$56. Subway: Osgoode.

Live Music Venues

The Drake Underground In the basement of the Drake Hotel, this venue was designed with flexibility in mind. It's a good thing, too, because the performers who appear here range from local and visiting musical acts in a wide variety of genres to burlesque artists. At the Drake Hotel, 1150 Queen St. W. ✆ **416/531-5042.** Cover C$5-C$20. Subway: Osgoode, then a streetcar west to Beaconsfield Ave.

El Mocambo ★ This world-renowned rock-'n'-roll institution hosted an infamous Rolling Stones show in the '70s, while the likes of U2 and Elvis Costello graced its stage in their early years. Its famous neon sign blinked no more when the club closed for a few years, but the venue is now back. A top-to-toe renovation has resulted in quite a different look, and it now welcomes acts from genres as diverse as indie rock, hip-hop, and roots. 464 Spadina Ave. ✆ **416/777-1777.** Cover C$5-C$20. Subway: Spadina, then a streetcar south to College St.

The Garrison Since opening in 2009, this club has quickly become a valued member of Toronto's live music scene. A mid-sized venue (capacity 350), it sports good sightlines and sound, and has a separate bar area up front if your ears need a break. It is co-owned and booked by scene veteran (Sneaky Dee's) and former rocker Shaun Bowring, and concentrates on local and visiting indie rock bands. 1197 Dundas St. W. ✆ **416/**519-9439. Cover free to C$20. Subway: St. Patrick, then a streetcar west to Ossington Ave.

The Horseshoe Tavern Since 1947, this much-loved honky-tonk has played a crucial role in Toronto's music community. The country and blues sounds it showcased in the '60s and early '70s gave way to punk and new wave, while its current booking policy primarily concentrates on modern rock and roots music styles. The

The Performing Arts

TORONTO AFTER DARK

Stones had a secret gig here in 1997, and the likes of Los Lobos, Wilco, and local heroes Blue Rodeo have also graced its stage. For 16 years, the free Nu Music Night every Tuesday has presented some real gems. The expanded room now holds 520, and a friendly and unpretentious atmosphere has remained constant. 368 Queen St. W. ✆ **416/598-4753.** www.horseshoetavern.com. Cover free to C$25. Subway: Osgoode.

Hugh's Room Call this a folk supper club for baby boomers. Around since 2001, the 200 seat venue has good sound and sightlines (except at the bar) and decent food. The booking policy ranges from folk legends like Judy Collins and the Strawbs to emerging roots singer/songwriters. 2261 Dundas St. W. ✆ **416/531-6604.** Cover C$10–C$50 Subway: Dundas W.

Lee's Palace Versailles this ain't, but ignore Lee's patina of grunge and focus instead on the excellent sightlines, high stage, and good sound. Such alternative-rock icons as Nirvana and Red Hot Chili Peppers have played the 600-capacity club, and indie rock is the primary focus these days. Alt-rock DJs spin in the upstairs room, the Dance Cave. 529 Bloor St. W. ✆ **416/532-1598.** www.leespalace.com. Cover C$5–C$15; for international touring acts, cover up to C$30. Subway: Bathurst.

The Melody Bar ★★ 🖋 This is Toronto's favorite karaoke bar, and sessions moderated by Peter Styles pack the place Friday and Saturday nights. During the rest of the week, you'll find local musicians (roots music is especially prominent), DJs, and open-mic events. Wednesday is queer night. At the Gladstone Hotel, 1214 Queen St. W. ✆ **416/531-4635.** www.gladstonehotel.com. No cover. Subway: Osgoode, then a streetcar west to Gladstone Ave.

The Mod Club Theatre ★★ One of Toronto's best mid-sized live-music venues, it's co-owned by Mark Holmes, former frontman of '80s rock faves Platinum Blonde. The Killers, Amy Winehouse, and Canadian favorites like Metric and Stars have all performed here; the concert hall morphs into a dance club later at night. 722 College St. ✆ **416/588-4MOD (416/588-4663).** www.themodclub.com. Cover up to C$15; higher prices for major concerts. Subway: Queen's Park, then a streetcar west to Crawford St.

Phoenix Concert Theatre The Phoenix is an old-school rock venue—shows are standing-room-only—and it has a loyal local following. It has showcased such legends as New York Dolls, Patti Smith, and Gang of Four, while newer stars such as Neko Case and The Raveonettes have also gigged here. On the weekends, it gets the crowds dancing with a mix of retro, Latin, alternative, and funk. 410 Sherbourne St. ✆ **416/323-1251.** Tickets C$10–C$40. Subway: College, then any streetcar east to Sherbourne St.

Reservoir Lounge ★ This joint feels like a modern-day speakeasy. The cramped space—it seats only 100—is below street level, yet feels intimate rather than claustrophobic. Live jazz, whether Dixieland, vocal jazz, or swing, belts out 7 nights a week. Defunct elsewhere, the swing dance craze lives on here, as well-dressed hepcats show their moves. 52 Wellington St. E., lower level. ✆ **416/955-0887.** www.reservoirlounge.com. Cover Tues–Sat C$5–C$7; no cover Sun & Mon. Subway: King.

The Rex Hotel Jazz & Blues Bar ★ The busiest jazz club in the city, it presents two or even three different acts daily, 7 days a week. A casual watering hole lacking the pretensions of some jazz joints, it has been drawing jazz fans since it opened in 1951. The decor hasn't changed much since the old days, but the sounds here range from the traditional to the cutting edge. The Rex features the city's best players and

Harbourfront Centre is the hub of Toronto's literary scene. It hosts the world renowned **Authors at Harbourfront Centre** (AUTHORS) program, featuring a weekly reading series (Sept–June), as well as the annual **International Festival of Authors** (IFOA) held every October. Over the past 36 years, AUTHORS has welcomed more than 5,000 writers from over 100 countries, including 17 Nobel laureates. IFOA (created in 1980) is widely recognized as one of the most important writers' events in the world, drawing a virtual Who's Who of contemporary literature. Over 10 days, more than 100 authors from at least 20 countries present their work to Toronto audiences. For more information on both programs, visit www.readings.org.

sometimes attracts international talent. 194 Queen St. W. ☎ **416/598-2475.** www.therex.ca. Cover up to C$12. Subway: Osgoode.

The Rivoli ★   Not quite the mainstay of the local music scene it once was, the Riv's back room now hosts an eclectic mix of performances, including roots, rock, jazz, comedy, and poetry reading. Tori Amos and Norah Jones made their Toronto debuts here, and Toronto comedy legends The Kids in the Hall got their start here, too. Shows begin at 8pm and continue until 2am. Upstairs, there's a comfortable billiards room and a bar. 332-334 Queen St. W. ☎ **416/596-1908.** Cover pay-what-you-can admission to C$20. Subway: Osgoode.

Supermarket ★★   Kensington Market is famous for its grocery stores, so maybe it's appropriate that this new club is playing on the name. It offers a wide assortment of live jazz, soul, roots, and rock. Earlier in the evening, Supermarket is an affordable Asian fusion restaurant, and it occasionally hosts author readings and art events. 268 Augusta St. ☎ **416/840-0501.** www.supermarkettoronto.com. Cover C$5–C$12. Subway: Spadina, then a streetcar south to College St.

DANCE CLUBS

Dance clubs come and go at an alarming pace in Toronto, with the groundbreaking, and mammoth, CiRCA a recent casualty. Be sure to check out the club listings in the free weeklies *Now* (www.nowtoronto.com) and *Eye* (www.eyeweekly.com), or at www.martiniboys.com or www.torontolife.com, to keep up with the currently cool (or hot) spots. Those listed below have survived the ultra-competitive scene by presenting a consistent music policy and lively atmosphere. Most clubs don't have rigid dress codes, though "no jeans" rules are not uncommon. And remember, it's always easier to get in earlier rather than later in the evening, when lines start to form. Several primarily gay and lesbian clubs attract a sizable hetero contingent; one notable destination is El Convento Rico (p. 223).

Crocodile Rock   There's something sweet about the fact that a club as untrendy and blue-collar as Crocodile Rock can survive in the heart of ever-changing clubland. It caters to a slightly older crowd for whom '80s pop will never die. 240 Adelaide St. W. ☎ **416/599-9751.** Cover C$5. Subway: St. Andrew.

Guvernment A popular fixture on the Toronto dance club scene for almost a quarter-century now thanks to its mandate of serving up something for just about everyone. Multiple rooms accommodate up to 3,000 club goers on always-crammed Saturday nights. Top-ranked DJs from around the world are often featured, and sounds range from house to trance, disco to hip-hop. 131 Queen's Quay E. ✆ **416/869-0045.** Cover C$10–C$15. Subway: Union.

Lula Lounge Want to sip a well-mixed mojito or caipirinha, feast on fine Latin cuisine, and catch some great music without leaving your table? If so, make a date with Lula. Located on the outskirts of Little Portugal, this vibrant and spacious room is well worth the trek. It has the feel of a nightclub in pre-Castro Havana or New Orleans, while excellent sightlines and sound, and a capacity of 250, make it one of the city's best live music clubs. Latin sounds are a specialty, but a wide variety of world music is presented here. Country, jazz, rock, and classical artists have also performed here, including Norah Jones, Jonathan Richman, and Canadian rock heroes Sloan. 1585 Dundas Street W. ✆ **416/538-7405.** Cover free to C$30. Subway: St. Patrick, then a streetcar west to Dufferin St.

Sneaky Dee's ★ The antidote to the glut of posh clubs that have been proliferating in Toronto, this long-established oasis of dive-bar boasts pool tables, Mexican food, and alternative rock (from live bands or spun by a DJ) in the club upstairs until 2am. Downstairs, the bar is open until 3am on weekdays, 4:30am on weekends. 431 College St. ✆ **416/603-3090.** Cover up to C$10. Subway: Queen's Park, then any streetcar west to Bathurst St.

The Social The first dance club to make a mark on the West Queen West strip, it continues to draw large crowds on the weekend. An eclectic mix of music styles is played, and a rotating cast of international star DJs is featured on Saturday nights. 1100 Queen St. W. ✆ **416/532-4474.** Cover from C$10. Subway: Osgoode, then a streetcar west to Dovercourt Ave.

This Is London ★ This club is more sophisticated and less frenzied than most of its peers—you might even manage a conversation. It is reminiscent of an old-fashioned gentlemen's club with its Oriental rugs and comfortable armchairs, though the dance floor is pretty hot. The music ranges from house to R&B to Top 40 and rock, and the dress code can be strict. The club's amazing ladies room features a makeup artist and hairstylist to help femmes fatales primp. 364 Richmond St. W. ✆ **416/351-1100.** Cover C$15–$20. Subway: Osgoode.

THE BAR SCENE

The current highly competitive night scene encompasses a flock of attractive bistros with diverse cuisine. You can enjoy cocktails, a reasonably priced meal, and in some, a game of pool in comfortable, aesthetically pleasing surroundings. Compared to dance clubs, the bars and lounges in Toronto are a pretty stable bunch.

Bars & Lounges

Barrio 🍴 The name is Spanish for neighborhood, and this charming and friendly lounge has been a popular fixture of the rapidly gentrifying Leslieville 'hood for almost a decade. It serves up a long list of microbrews and cocktails (try the

Blueberry Hill, a mix of blueberry vodka, cranberry juice, and lime cordial). 896 Queen St. E. ✆ **416/572-0600.** Subway: Queen, then a streetcar east to Logan Ave.

The Communist's Daughter ★ 🎁 Not the easiest place to find (look for the Nazare Snack Bar sign), but well worth the quest. A tiny laid-back spot with Formica tables, it possesses one of the city's best jukeboxes. There's excellent live music on Saturday and Sunday afternoons (jazz and country, respectively). 1149 Dundas St. W. ✆ **647/435-0103.** Subway: St. Patrick, then a streetcar west to Ossington Ave.

The Drake Lounge ★ The bar at the Drake Hotel (see p. 74) is a perfect perch for sipping martinis and envisioning yourself in a glamorous bygone era. The Lounge is designed to evoke a mid-20th-century feel. It's dressed-up, grown-up fun, and it attracts a crowd of devoted locals and suburbanites. At the Drake Hotel, 1150 Queen St. W. ✆ **416/531-5042.** Subway: Osgoode, then a streetcar west to Beaconsfield Ave.

Foundation Room 🎁 Half the fun with subterranean clubs is knowing how to find them. But the Foundation Room has far more going for it than just that: The room is decked out in glorious Moroccan style, with plush lounges, hammered-brass chandeliers, and plenty of mirrors. The vibe is very sexy—and the pomegranate martinis are delicious. 19 Church St. ✆ **416/364-8368.** Subway: Union.

The Dakota Tavern 📷 This basement honky-tonk has quickly turned into a Mecca for roots, bluegrass, and country rock in Toronto. High-profile singer/song-writers like Ron Sexsmith (a local resident), Serena Ryder, and John Doe (of X) have graced the small stage under the disco ball. Excellent Mexican and Southern-accented food is on offer, and the bar stools fashioned from wine barrels are a fun touch that pay homage to the Little Portugal locale. 249 Ossington Ave. ✆ **416/850-4579.** Subway: St. Patrick, then a streetcar west to Ossington Ave.

The Legendary Library Bar ★ This is one of the most romantic settings in town. This intimate, wood-paneled bar is the best place in the city to order a top-quality martini, served in a generous "fishbowl" glass. With its leopard-print couches and wingback chairs, it has an old-fashioned, almost colonial feel. At the Fairmont Royal York, 100 Front St. W. ✆ **416/863-6333.** Subway: Union.

Motel The recently opened Motel has quickly drawn hipsters into the heart of still-burgeoning Parkdale, just west of the Drake/Gladstone hub. Historic art pieces grace the wall, the Britpop and local content on the jukebox impresses, and the cozy place (capacity just 40) exudes a laid-back vibe. Guest bartenders and DJs will take care of your beverage and aural needs. Too bad you can't book a room. 1235 Queen St. W. ✆ **647/381-6246.** Subway: Osgoode, then a streetcar west to Gwynne Ave.

Reposado 🎁 The increased fashionableness of premium tequila is reflected in this chic little tequila bar on the scorching hot Ossington strip. It sports a relaxed vibe, the largest selection of tequilas in the city, and cool music from local combos and guest DJs on some nights. 136 Ossington Ave. ✆ **416/532-6474.** Subway: Osgoode, then a streetcar west to Ossington Ave.

The Roof ★★★ Author Mordecai Richler called this the only civilized spot in Toronto. It's an old literary haunt, with comfortable couches in front of a fireplace and excellent drinks. The walls sport caricatures of members of Canada's literary establishment. The James Bond martini—vodka with a drop of Lillet—is a popular choice. The south-facing view from the outdoor terrace is one of the best in the city. At the Park Hyatt Toronto, 4 Avenue Rd. ✆ **416/924-5471.** Subway: Museum or Bay.

TORONTO AFTER DARK | The Bar Scene

Sutra Tiki Bar   Summer never ends at this sexy, intimate bar that's long been a Little Italy favorite. The drink list is composed of the usual hot-weather suspects (mojitos, caipirinhas) and lush champagne cocktails (try the house specialty, the Sutra). Sip to the strains of soul music. In warm weather, there's a patio out back with real sand. 612 College St. © **416/537-8755.** Subway: Queen's Park, then any streetcar west to Clinton St.

Sweaty Betty's ★   This low-key, unpretentious place won't be to everyone's taste—a good thing, since the seating capacity is limited to roughly 60 people (and that includes the patio). Famous for its snarky bartenders, this is a great spot for meeting others, since the close quarters means you'll hear everyone else's conversations. Absinthe is a trendy choice here, and the jukebox is superb. 13 Ossington Ave. © **416/535-6861.** Subway: Osgoode, then a streetcar west to Ossington Ave.

Watusi ★★ 🎁   The popularity of "Mad Men" has been well-timed for Watusi, a swanky cocktail lounge exuding retro '60s cool. Located on the now hip Ossington Avenue, the place is littered with pop art, and as the clock ticks toward midnight, furniture is swept aside to make way for a long, lean dance floor. 11 Ossington Ave. © **416/533-1800.** Subway: Osgoode, then a streetcar west to Ossington Ave.

Pubs & Taverns

Allen's   Allen's sports a great bar that offers more than 150 beer selections and 278 single malts. Guinness is the drink of choice on Tuesday and Saturday nights, when folks reel and jig to the Celtic entertainment. 143 Danforth Ave. © **416/463-3086.** Subway: Broadview.

The Ben Wicks Restaurant and Pub 🎁   Around since 1980, this is a much-loved fixture of the Cabbagetown neighborhood. It is named for and was opened by the late Ben Wicks, a popular local cartoonist whose artwork still adorns the walls. Reliable pub grub (think Guinness-battered fish and chips), a convivial atmosphere, and a revamped patio are other attractions. 424 Parliament St. © **416/961-9425.** Subway: College, then a streetcar east to Parliament St.

Brunswick House   Affectionately known as the Brunny, this cavernous historic tavern (it dates back to 1876) is a favorite of University of Toronto students, even after an extensive upgrade in 2005. It boasts 10 draughts on tap, and the joint is jumping on Thumpin' Thursdays, thanks to cut-price pitchers. "We dare you to party where your Dad did" is their clever tagline. Upstairs, the Champions lounge broadcasts live horse racing simulcasts and offers off-track betting. In its former life as Albert's Hall, it was the city's best blues club, featuring legendary gigs by the likes of Stevie Ray Vaughan and Jeff Buckley. 481 Bloor St. W. © **416/964-2242.** Subway: Spadina.

Ceili Cottage   World-famous oyster shucker Patrick McMurray has opened a pearl with his new Irish pub, located in Leslieville. He has transformed a former garage into a totally charming cottage, one with an authentic late 1800s look. A 5.1cm-thick (2-in.) Kilkenny limestone bar top shipped over from Ireland is the highlight of the bar area in which the owner can often be found shucking away. A separate dining room area and a pleasant patio complete the pretty picture. 1301 Queen St. E. © **416/406-1301.** Subway: Queen, then a streetcar east to Leslie St.

Dora Keogh   Comfortable and friendly, with a decidedly authentic atmosphere, this is a good spot for a hearty meal and a pint. But the real reason to come is the music. Saturday afternoons feature top-notch jazz, while traditional Celtic melodies are served up on Thursdays at 9pm and Sundays at 5pm by some of the city's best players. The sessions are becoming legendary, especially since famous fiddler Natalie McMaster and members of the Chieftains have joined in. 141 Danforth Ave. © **416/778-1804.** Subway: Broadview.

Irish Embassy ★   Located in a stunning 1873 bank building in the Financial District, this pub fills up after the closing bell rings at the Toronto Stock Exchange. Guinness is just one of the many brews on tap, and there's an excellent pub-grub menu to tide you over. 49 Yonge St. © **416/866-8282.** Subway: King.

Madison Avenue Pub   This is another favorite haunt of University of Toronto students, but older patrons will also feel welcomed. Beer is the beverage of choice here, with more than 150 varieties available on tap. The original pub at 14 Madison Ave. has gobbled up its neighbors at 16 and 18, and now this spot is a huge complex with six separate British-style pubs and a capacity nearing 2,000 people. 14 Madison Ave. © **416/927-1722.** Subway: Spadina.

Mill Street Brew Pub ★   Situated in the historic site of an old brewery, this pub features an award-winning array of beers brewed in small batches (some are available only seasonally). The Tankhouse Pale Ale is a constant, with its five malts blended for a particularly complex flavor. It's a top pick of local hipsters. In the Distillery District, 55 Mill St. © **416/681-0338.** Subway: King, then a streetcar east to Parliament St.

The Pilot   This comfortable watering hole dates back to 1944, and it claims to be Toronto's longest continuously operating bar. Long-time regulars mingle with the suited after-work crowd, while local jazz fans love their Saturday and Sunday afternoon matinees in the Stealth Lounge. A lovely rooftop patio is another draw. 22 Cumberland St. © **416/923-5716.** Subway: Yonge/Bloor.

Wheat Sheaf Tavern   Designated an historic landmark, this is the city's oldest tavern, in operation since 1849. It draws sports fans with 13 screens and fine chicken wings. The jukebox features 1,200 choices, and there are two pool tables and a popular outdoor patio. 667 King St. W. © **416/504-9912.** Subway: St. Andrew, then any streetcar west to Bathurst St.

THE GAY & LESBIAN SCENE

Toronto's gay and lesbian community is one of the largest of any city in North America, so the nightlife scene is diverse. It remains largely concentrated in the Gay Village, around Church and Wellesley streets, but popular new locales have recently opened in Parkdale. The free weekly newspaper *Xtra!* (www.xtra.ca) lists events, seminars, and performances, geared to the gay and lesbian community; also check out Gay Toronto (www.gaytoronto.com) and the Gay Toronto Tourism Guild (www.gaytorontotourism.com) for listings. Some mostly-straight nightspots, such as the Melody Bar (p. 217), have one night a week that's gay night.

The Beaver   The name probably tells you most of what you need to know. Located between the Gladstone and the Drake, and blessed with a great patio, this cozy watering hole is famous for its girl-on-girl Sunday parties. Good food and knowledgeable DJs are other attractions. 1192 Queen St. W. © **416/537-2768.** Subway: Osgoode, then a streetcar west to Gladstone Ave.

Byzantium ★★ 🍸 An attractive but low-key bar/restaurant, Byzantium attracts an affable and affluent gay and straight crowd. The cocktails are excellent (try either the Red Velvet or the Black Orchid—they are as delicious as the names are dramatic). You can follow drinks with dinner in the adjacent top-notch dining room. The place gets packed when DJs spin on the weekend. 499 Church St. ℂ **416/922-3859.** Subway: Wellesley.

Crews, Tango, and the Zone ★ Located in two adjoining Victorian houses, this recently-reopened three-in-one club promises something for everyone. Crews is a gay bar for men, and it is known for its pubby atmosphere and its drag shows, which start at 11pm Wednesday to Sunday. The upstairs Tango bar draws a lesbian crowd to its dance floor and lounge. Then there's the Zone, which offers karaoke, drag queen and drag king shows, and dancing. 508 Church St. ℂ **416/972-1662.** Subway: Wellesley.

El Convento Rico ★★ 🏳️ The Latin beat beckons one and all—straight, gay, and otherwise—to this lively club. It has welcomed a diverse crowd for nearly 20 years now. If you don't know how to salsa, meringue, or cha-cha, you can pick up the basics at the Friday night dance lessons, but if you don't learn, no one on the jam-packed dance floor will notice. There's a substantial hetero contingent that comes out just to watch the fabulous drag queens—and don't be surprised if you encounter a bachelorette party in progress. Post-midnight shows, Friday and Saturday, are big draws. 750 College St. ℂ **416/588-7800.** www.elconventorico.com. Subway: Queen's Park, then a streetcar west to Shaw Ave.

Henhouse A new spot in Little Portugal, it's owned by two members of the Organ, a now-defunct Canadian new-wave rock band. Funky decor, a friendly atmosphere, cheap and cheerful food, and tasteful jukebox selections add up to a real success story. 1532 Dundas St. W. ℂ **416/534-5939.** Subway: St. Patrick, then a streetcar west to Dufferin Street.

Pegasus Bar ★ This relaxed pub draws a gay and lesbian crowd with its four professional-size billiard tables, trivia nights, video games, pinball machines, and gigantic TV (tuned to gay dramas). The staff is warm and welcoming. 489B Church St. ℂ **416/927-8832.** Subway: Wellesley.

Sailor This bar is attached to Woody's (see below) but has a livelier atmosphere; unlike Woody's, you won't see many women here. Every Thursday, there's a Best Chest competition; every Friday, the prize is for Best Ass. In the evening, a DJ spins an assortment of dance and alternative tunes. 465 Church St. ℂ **416/972-0887.** Subway: Wellesley.

Slack's Formerly known as Slack Alice, it's the leading lesbian bar/restaurant in the village. It draws a more mixed crowd earlier in the week and occasionally hosts live jazz. The straightforward menu is well-executed. 562 Church St. ℂ **416/969-8742.** Subway: Wellesley.

Woody's ★ A local institution, also immortalized in the television series *Queer As Folk*. Still the reigning men's bar in the village, it welcomes women and heteros. Best Chest contests, drag shows, and DJs are all featured on different nights. It's a popular meeting spot, especially for weekend brunch. 467 Church St. (south of Wellesley St.). ℂ **416/972-0887.** www.woodystoronto.com. Subway: Wellesley.

Zelda's Living Well ★ 🎁   A long-time Gay Village favorite (known just as Zelda's), it recently moved to Yonge Street but still remains popular. Zelda's has great food; fun, tacky decor (including pink flamingos); and a great sense of humor. Ideally, you'll be there for one of the many theme nights, with Dirty Bingo, drag entertainment, and talent shows all served with a smile. 692 Yonge. ✆ **416/922-2526.** Subway: Wellesley.

COFFEE HOUSES

Starbucks has certainly staked out plenty of territory in Toronto, but there are two Canadian chains that are just as popular: the **Second Cup,** which charges less for a latte, and the donut-and-coffee destination **Tim Horton's** (also known as Tim Ho's). Another chain with fewer locales is **Timothy's.** In addition to the late-night stops listed below, there's a growing barista movement in Toronto where the joe is strictly a daytime commodity—and often offers truly top brew (see p. 101).

Balzac's Coffee ★   If you're in the Distillery District (see p. 123), this is the place to stop for coffee. Not only is the setting dramatic (soaring ceilings, redbrick walls, and elaborate chandelier), but the in-house roasted coffees are deservedly famous. There's also a location in Liberty Village. In the Distillery District, 55 Mill St. ✆ **416/207-1709.** Subway: King, then a streetcar east to Parliament St.

Café Diplomatico ★ 🎁   You can come for the coffee, but it's not the main draw. Instead, crowds flock to this traditional cafe for the big patio and often for the beer on tap. It's a great hangout to watch the parade of passersby in Little Italy. 594 College St. ✆ **416/534-4637.** Subway: Queen's Park, then a streetcar west to Clinton St.

Future Bakery   This rambling cafe attracts students and those looking for a good, cheap bowl of borscht alongside a decent mug of brew. There's also a good selection of breads, buns, and pastries. A neighborhood favorite. 483 Bloor St. W. ✆ **416/922-5875.** Subway: Spadina or Bathurst.

Lettieri ★   The house rule at this small local chain is that after 7 minutes, a pot of coffee is no longer fresh. This place takes the bean seriously. In addition to the wide range of coffees, you can order focaccia sandwiches, tarts, cookies, and pastries. There are outposts at **441 Queen St.** (at Spadina Ave.; ✆ **416/592-1360**) and at the corner of Bloor and Bathurst streets, tucked into the beloved **Honest Ed's** emporium (p. 190). 94 Cumberland St. ✆ **416/515-8764.** www.lettiericafe.com. Subway: Bay.

Linux Caffe   Located near the University of Toronto campus and a short walk from College Street, this cool little cafe serves a fine brew using beans from local roaster Ideal Coffee and specializing in organic and fair-trade. There's also a fairly good simple menu. 326 Harbord St. ✆ **416/534 2116.** Subway: Spadina, then walk south 3 blocks to Harbord St.

SIDE TRIPS FROM TORONTO

Toronto has plenty to offer visitors, so it might seem a bit much to add a side trip. But if you can afford the time, there are some truly worthwhile excursions to consider. Keep in mind that distances can mean a good 2 days for a road trip. Many of the top attractions in this region are within a 2-hour drive of Toronto, making them easily accessible. The bad news: If you're trying to shoehorn all of the sights into a short stay . . . you've got some decisions to make. This chapter describes four of the best-known destinations—the theater town of Stratford; the wine region of Niagara-on-the-Lake, along with well-known Niagara Falls; the great outdoors of Muskoka Lakes; and the rich culinary destination of Prince Edward County.

For information about the areas surrounding Toronto, contact **Ontario Tourism** (© **800/ONTARIO** [800/668-2746]; www.ontariotravel.net) or visit its travel information center in the Atrium on Bay (street level) at 20 Dundas St. W.—it's just across Dundas Street from the Sears store at the northern edge of the Eaton Centre. It's open daily from 8:30am to 4:30pm; hours are extended during the summer, often to 8pm.

A note about Internet and Wi-Fi: Most accommodations in this chapter offer in-room or in-lobby Internet or Wi-Fi access. Some charge for it, some don't. For hotels that charge for Internet or Wi-Fi, the price ranges from C$15 to C$21 per day. When included in the room price, I've listed the services as "free."

STRATFORD ★

145km (90 miles) SW of Toronto

For those who care: This is the hometown of Justin Bieber. But its real claim to fame is the great Stratford Festival. Plus, it's a charming, friendly, and very pretty place to amble before and after taking in a show. The grand Stratford Festival has humble roots. The idea of a theater was launched in 1953, when director Tyrone Guthrie lured the great Sir Alec Guinness to the stage. Whether Sir Alec knew the "stage" was set up in a makeshift tent is another question, but his acclaimed performance gave the festival the push—and press—it needed to become an annual tradition. Since then, the Stratford Festival has grown to become one of the most famous in North America, and its four theaters have put this scenic town on the cultural map. It's also a lovely place to eat, cycle, walk, and relax. Even the local library is lovely.

Essentials

VISITOR INFORMATION For first-rate visitor information, go to the **Visitors' Information Centre** by the river, on York Street at Erie Street. From May to early November, it's open Sunday through Wednesday 9am to 5pm and Thursday through Saturday 9am to 8pm. At other times, contact **Tourism Stratford** (✆ **800/561-SWAN** [800/561-7926] or 519/271-5140; www.welcometostratford.com).

GETTING THERE Driving from Toronto, take Highway 401 west to Interchange 278 at Kitchener. Follow Highway 8 west onto Highway 7/8 to Stratford. (Hwy. 7/8 turns into Ontario St., Stratford's main drag, once you enter city limits.)

For me, nothing beats the train, and Stratford is a small and very walkable town, so unless you're planning to tour the surrounding area, call **VIA Rail** (✆ **800/VIA-RAIL** [800/842-7245] or 416/366-8411; www.viarail.ca). Canada's national rail company operates several trains daily along the Toronto-Kitchener-Stratford route. The toll-free number works within North America; if you're traveling from overseas, you can book your rail travel in advance through one of VIA's general sales agents (there's a long list of local agents on www.viarail.ca).

The Stratford Festival ★★★

On July 13, 1953, *Richard III,* starring Sir Alec Guinness, was staged in a huge tent. From that modest start, Stratford's artistic directors have built on the radical, but faithfully classic, base established by Tyrone Guthrie to create a repertory theater with a glowing international reputation.

Stratford has four theaters. The **Festival Theatre** (55 Queen St.) has a dynamic thrust stage (a modern re-creation of an Elizabethan stage). The **Avon Theatre** (99 Downie St.) has a classic proscenium. The **Tom Patterson Theatre** (111 Lakeside Dr.) is an intimate 500-seat theater. The **Studio Theatre** (34 George St. E.) is a 278-seat space used for new and experimental works.

World-famous for its Shakespearean productions, the festival also offers classic and modern theatrical masterpieces. Recent productions have included *West Side Story, Cyrano de Bergerac,* and *Three Sisters;* from the Bard, there's an encyclopedia of productions including *Macbeth* and *A Midsummer Night's Dream.* The bill always presents an impressive line-up that is designed to suit tastes from the contemporary to the historic, the comedic to the tragic.

Side Trips from Toronto

The season usually begins in early May and continues through mid-November, with performances Tuesday through Sunday. Ticket prices range from C$25 to C$120, with special deals for students and seniors. For tickets, call ℭ **800/567-1600** or 519/273-1600, fax 519/273-3731, or visit **www.stratfordfestival.ca.** Tickets are also available in the United States and Canada at Ticketmaster outlets. The box office opens for the new season in mid-January.

Behind The Festival Curtain ★

The Stratford Festival offers several behind-the-scenes tours that will thrill theater buffs. There are **backstage tours of the Festival Theatre,** which take about an hour, and tours of the **costume and props warehouse** at 350 Douro St., which run roughly 45 minutes. Tours cost C$8 adults, C$6 seniors and students, and should be scheduled in advance by calling the box office at ℭ **800/567-1600** or 519/273-1600.

Some performances have **preshow lectures** or **post-performance discussions.** These are free of charge but need to be reserved in advance via the box office. There are also free "Meet the Festival" events with members of the acting company and a series of special lectures about the major plays of the season. For details, dates, and times, check out **www.stratfordfestival.ca.**

Exploring the Town

Stratford was founded in 1832, and much of its historic heart has been preserved. Wandering through its pristine residential street—lined with historic homes decorated with turrets, wraparound verandas, and stained-glass windows—is a little like stepping back in time. The Visitors' Information Centre by the Avon River has maps for self-guided tours. You can also download several free audio-tour podcasts about Stratford's gardens, landmarks, and downtown from **www.welcometostratford.com.**

Paddleboat, kayak, and canoe rentals are available at the **Boathouse,** behind the information center. In summer, it's open daily from 9am until dusk. Contact **Avon Boat Rentals** (40 York St.; ℭ **519/271-7739**). There's also a boat, the *Juliet III,* that offers scenic half-hour tours.

The **Shakespearean Gardens**—a pretty, formal English garden—is a great place to relax and contemplate the flowerbeds and tranquil river lagoon, and muse on a bust of Shakespeare by Toronto sculptor Cleeve Horne. For a picnic-friendly patch of green, visit **Queen's Park,** a stone's throw from the Festival Theatre.

And speaking of picnics, Stratford is in the heart of an agricultural belt, and the abundant food options reflect the city's pride in its regional culinary riches. There are farmers markets; big seasonal food fares such as Savour Stratford in September; loads of restaurant, farm, and dairy tours; and more. Check out www.welcometo stratford.com/savour-stratford.php.

Stratford also has a good art museum, the **Gallery Stratford** (54 Romeo St.; ℭ **519/271-5271;** www.gallerystratford.on.ca). Located in an historic building on the fringes of Confederation Park, the museum exhibits contemporary and historical works by Canadian artists. Its hours change with the seasons, but mid-May through late September, it's open Tuesday through Sunday from 10am to 5pm (call ahead for hours Oct to mid-May).

ACCOMMODATIONS ■
The Annex Room **8**
Lofts at 99 **7**
Stewart House Inn **6**
The Swan Motel **16**

DINING ◆
Bentley's **7**
The Church **14**
Down the Street **11**
Keystone Alley Cafe **15**
The Old Prune **13**
Rundles **11**
York Street Kitchen **10**

ATTRACTIONS ●
Avon Boat Rentals **5**
Avon Theatre **12**
Festival Theatre **3**
Gallery Stratford **1**
Queen's Park **2**
Studio Theatre **12**
Tom Patterson Theatre **4**

An Open-Air Art Gallery

Museums are grand, but who wants to spend a glorious summer day indoors? Thanks to the **Art in the Park** (www.art intheparkstratford.com), you can have both. On Wednesdays, Saturdays, and Sundays from June to September, regional artists gather at Lakeside Drive and Front Street, and put on a show from 9am to 5pm, weather permitting. The artists and artisans work in various media, so you'll find paintings, sculptures, ceramics, jewelry, and glass, among other things. While many of the works are for sale, this isn't just a market: The artists are selected through a juried process.

A Couple of Excursions from Stratford

Only half an hour or so from Stratford, the twin cities of **Kitchener** and **Waterloo** have two drawing cards: the **Farmers' Market** and the famous 9-day **Oktoberfest** (📞 **888/294-HANS** [888/294-4267] or 519/570-HANS [519/570-4267]; www. oktoberfest.ca). The cities still have a large population of descendents of German settlers, and many are also Mennonites. On Saturday, starting at 6am, you can sample shoofly pie, apple butter, birch beer, summer sausage, and other Mennonite specialties at the market in the Market Square complex, at Duke and Frederick streets in Kitchener. For additional information, contact the **Kitchener-Waterloo Area Visitors and Convention Bureau** (2848 King St. E., Kitchener; 📞 **519/748-0800;** www.explorewaterlooregion.com). It's open in winter from 9am to 5pm weekdays only, daily in summer.

Eight kilometers (5 miles) north of Kitchener is the town of **St. Jacobs.** It has close to 100 shops in venues such as a converted mill, silo, and other factory buildings. The **Meetingplace** (33 King St.; 📞 **519/664-3518**) runs a short film about the Amish-Mennonite way of life (daily in summer, weekends only in winter). There's also the **St. Jacobs Outlet Mall** at 25 Benjamin Rd. E.; its offerings include Levi's, Lego, Reebok, Corningware, Liz Claiborne, and Paderno. The mall is open Monday through Friday 9:30am to 9pm, Saturday 8:30am to 6pm, and Sunday noon to 5pm (closed Jan 1 and Dec 25). Call 📞 **519/888-0138** for more information.

Where to Stay

When you book your theater tickets, you can book your accommodations at no extra charge. Options range from guest homes for as little as C$75 to first-class hotels charging more than C$200. Call the **Stratford Tourism Alliance** at 📞 **800/561-7926** for information (note that some accommodations are open only to festival-goers, and these can be booked only through the Accommodation Bureau). You can also book a room via **Tourism Stratford's website** (www.welcometostratford.com); for extensive bed-and-breakfast listings, check out **www.bbcanada.com**. Rooms in Stratford are most expensive in June, July, and August; it's easier to get a discount from fall to spring. In winter, even the most opulent properties deeply discount their rates. Keep in mind that most accommodations here are smoke-free.

The Annex Room ★   This small, centrally located hotel is quaint, yet luxurious: Each room has a whirlpool tub and a fireplace. The rooms are airy and bright, and elegantly decorated. Because of the hotel's tiny size, you can count on personal, considerate service. The one drawback is that there is no elevator, so guests need to be able to climb stairs.

38 Albert St., Stratford, ON N5A 3K3. ✆ **800/361-5322** or 519/271-1407. Fax 519/272-1853. www. bentleys-annex.com. 6 units. C$225 double; off-season C$125 double. Additional adult C$25. AE, DC, MC, V. Free parking. **Amenities:** Restaurant. *In room:* A/C, TV, fridge, hair dryer, minibar, Wi-Fi (free).

 ## shopping IN STRATFORD

I know, we're all here for the theater scene, but don't miss out on Stratford's excellent shopping options. If you were expecting touristy, overpriced, and kitschy, you're in for a pleasant surprise. Many of the stores downtown sell clothing and housewares that rival what you'll see in the best boutiques in Toronto. Prices tend to be quite reasonable. Here are some of my favorite spots.

○ **Art: Gallery Indigena** (69 Ontario St.; ✆ **519/271-7881;** www.galleryindigena.com) is filled with wonderful finds. They specialize in works by the Inuit, Iroquois, Cree, Plains, Woodland, and North Pacific Coast peoples. In business for more than 3 decades, the gallery hosts several "Meet the Artist" events throughout the summer, and it ships artwork all over the world.

○ **Books: Callan Books** (15 York St.; ✆ **519/273-5767**) is a charming spot with an eclectic collection that will particularly please history buffs. **Fundamentals** (52 Ontario St.; ✆ **519/273-6440**) is targeted at the small fry and has a particularly wonderful collection of illustrated storybooks.

○ **Clothing: Elizabeth Noel** (26 Ontario St.; ✆ **519/273-4506**)

sells beautiful dresses and other ladylike pieces, many of which are by Canadian labels such as Sweet Chemise and Girl Friday. **The Green Room** (40 Ontario St.; ✆ **519/271-3240**) is actually several rooms, all jam-packed with women's accessories. For men, there's **Gruv** ("groove") at 10 Ontario St. (✆ **519/273-1116**).

○ **Gift Items:** The fair-trade company **Ten Thousand Villages** (14 Ontario St.; ✆ **519/272-0700**) sells crafts, jewelry, housewares, and toys from artisans in developing countries. **Rheo Thompson Candies** (55 Albert St.; ✆ **519/271-6910**) is a local institution that makes lovely chocolates, mints, jellies, and other candies.

○ **Housewares:** You'll find both locally made cranberry glass and objects from Indonesia and Uzbekistan at **Watson's Chelsea Bazaar** (84 Ontario St.; ✆ **519/273-1790**). **White Oleander** (136 Ontario St.; ✆ **519/271-5616**) sells lovely linens, bedding, and tableware. The venerable **Bradshaws** (129 Ontario St.; ✆ **519/271-6283**) has been in business since 1895 selling crystal and china.

Lofts at 99 ★★   For convenience, you can't beat this spot at the center of town formerly known as Bentley's (the on-site restaurant still goes by that name; see p. 234). Recent renovations have turned it into a modern, chic inn with a stream-lined look. The rooms are elegant duplex suites with kitchenettes; five units have skylights. The split-level feature makes it great for families with young children. Like most Stratford accommodations, Lofts at 99 doesn't have an elevator. This is a smoke-free hotel.

99 Ontario St., Stratford, ON N5A 3H1. ⓒ **800/361-5322** or 519/271-1121. www.bentleys-annex.com. 12 units. From C$295 double. Additional adult C$25. Children 11 & under stay free in parent's room. AE, DC, MC, V. Free parking. **Amenities:** Restaurant. *In room:* A/C, TV, fridge, hair dryer, minibar, Wi-Fi (free).

Stewart House Inn ★ 🛍   This house was built in 1870, and the owners have decorated it with a suitably opulent Victorian style. There's also old-fashioned guest service: In the morning, coffee is delivered to your room; if you want to swim in the backyard saltwater pool, you'll be supplied with robes, towels, and tumblers for drinks. A full breakfast is served every morning between 8 and 10am in what used to be the ballroom. The guest rooms are nicely appointed, with each one themed to play up the romantic atmosphere. Still, the modern conveniences (flat-screen TVs, DVD players, and Wi-Fi) aren't spared. House policies are no smoking, no children, and no pets (there are, however, two small dogs in residence).

62 John St. N., Stratford, ON N5A 6K7. ⓒ **866/826-7772** or 519/271-4576. Fax 519/273-1746. www.stewarthouseinn.com. 7 units. From C$199 double. Rates include full breakfast. MC, V. Street parking. No children allowed. **Amenities:** Outdoor pool. *In room:* A/C, TV/DVD player, CD player, hair dryer, Wi-Fi (free).

The Swan Motel 🎣   The simple rooms here are typical, if high-end, motel fare, but the grounds are more like a small estate garden. Located 3km (1¼ miles) from downtown Stratford, the setting offers a tranquil escape. The property has been run by the same family for more than 40 years, and it has a warm, gracious atmosphere. The rooms are simple and clean. The grounds are the real drawing card, with a sweet Victorian gazebo, beds of perennial flowers, and an outdoor pool. This is a smoke-free hotel.

960 Downie St. S., Stratford, ON N5A 6S3. ⓒ **519/271-6376.** Fax 519/271-0682. www.swanmotel.ca. 24 units. From C$102 double. Additional adult C$15. Rates include continental breakfast. MC, V. Free parking. **Amenities:** Outdoor pool. *In room:* A/C, TV, fridge, hair dryer, Wi-Fi (free).

A NEARBY PLACE TO STAY & DINE

Langdon Hall ★★   Less than an hour's drive from Stratford, this elegant house stands at the head of a curving, tree-lined drive. Eugene Langdon Wilks, a great-grandson of John Jacob Astor, completed it in 1902. It remained in the family until 1987, when it was transformed into a beautiful country-house hotel. Today, Langdon Hall is a Relais & Châteaux property with Ontario's first restaurant to earn the much-vaunted Relais Gourmands status (a title held by the French Laundry and Fat Duck, among others). Its 81 hectares (200 acres) is a pleasing mix of manicured lawns, English gardens, and rustic woodlands. What's more, there's a balance of comfort and refinement that, combined with top-notch service, puts it on a par with Canada's truly great inns. You can choose to stay in the original house, in the converted stable suites, or in one of the rooms surrounding the cloister garden. There is an on-site spa, a small swimming pool, a network of cross-country ski trails, and a small billiards room. The generous public rooms are great gathering places, with wood-burning fires in winter and lush garden views in summer. Many come for the dining alone: Seasonal ingredients are turned into exquisite fare under the direction of chef Jonathan Gushue, and the wine list is extensive. Tea is served on the canopied veranda.

R.R. 3, Cambridge, ON N3H 4R8. ℂ **800/268-1898** or 519/740-2100. www.langdonhall.ca. 52 units. From C$329 double. Rates include full breakfast. AE, DC, MC, V. Free parking. From Hwy. 401, take exit 275 south, turn right onto Blair Rd. & follow signs. Pets accepted at no additional cost. **Amenities:** Dining room; bar; babysitting; bike rental; concierge; health club; Jacuzzi; outdoor pool; room service; sauna; spa; tennis courts. *In room:* A/C, TV, CD player, hair dryer, Wi-Fi (free).

Where to Dine

EXPENSIVE

The Church ★★ FRENCH   The Church is simply stunning. The organ pipes and the altar of the 1873 structure are intact, along with the vaulted roof, carved woodwork, and stained-glass windows. You can sit in the nave or the side aisles, and dine to appropriate music—usually Bach. Appetizers might include asparagus served hot with black morels in their juices, white wine, and cream; or sauté of duck foie gras with leeks and citron, mango, and ginger sauce. The menu is brief and to the point: classic meats with Canadian twists, such as caribou with port-and-blackberry sauce and cream-braised cabbage with shallots and glazed chestnuts; or lobster salad with green beans, new potatoes, and truffles scented with caraway. Desserts are equally dramatic. The upstairs Belfry, a more modest affair, is a popular pre- and post-theater gathering place and is open for lunch and dinner. To dine here during the festival, make reservations as soon as you buy your tickets.

70 Brunswick St. (at Waterloo St.). ℂ **519/273-3424.** www.churchrestaurant.com. Reservations required. Main courses C$38–C$44. AE, DC, MC, V. The Church: Tues–Sat 5–8:30pm, Sun 11:30am–1:30pm & 5–8pm; off-season hours vary; closed Dec to mid-Apr. The Belfry: Tues–Sat 11:30am–midnight; off-season hours vary.

The Old Prune ★ CONTINENTAL   Situated in a lovely Edwardian home, the Old Prune has three dining rooms and an enclosed garden patio. Former Montréalers, the proprietors demonstrate Québec flair in both decor and menu. The menu changes based on what's fresh and what's in season (much of the produce comes from the region's organic farms). Goods from local dairies, cheese makers, and other artisans are prominent on the menu. Among the main courses, you might find Perth County pork loin grilled with tamari and honey glaze, and served with shiitake mushrooms, pickled cucumbers, and sunflower sprouts; steamed bass in Napa cabbage with curry broth and lime leaves; or rack of Ontario lamb with smoky tomatillo-chipotle pepper sauce. Desserts, such as rhubarb strawberry Napoleon, are inspired.

151 Albert St. ℂ **519/271-5052.** www.oldprune.on.ca. Reservations required. 3-course prix-fixe menu C$66. AE, MC, V. Fri–Sun 11:30am–1pm, Tues–Sun 5–9pm; call for winter hours.

Rundles ★ 🍴 INTERNATIONAL   Rundles provides a premier dining experience in a serene dining room overlooking the river. Proprietor James Morris eats, sleeps, thinks, and dreams food. The prix-fixe dinner offers palate-pleasing flavor combinations. Appetizers might include shaved fennel, arugula, artichoke and Parmesan salad, or warm seared Québec foie gras. Typical main dishes include poached Atlantic salmon garnished with Jerusalem artichokes, wilted arugula, and yellow peppers in a light carrot sauce; or pink roast rib-eye of lamb with ratatouille and rosemary aioli. For dessert, try glazed lemon tart and orange sorbet, or hot mango tart with pineapple sorbet. In 2008, Rundles opened the Sophisto-Bistro, a more casual dining room, with a less-expensive (yet incredibly delicious) prix-fixe menu.

9 Cobourg St. ✆ **519/271-6442.** www.rundlesrestaurant.com. Reservations required. Rundles 3-course prix-fixe dinner C$80; Sophisto-Bistro 3-course prix-fixe menu C$50. AE, DC, MC, V. Apr–Oct Sat & Sun 11:30am–1:15pm; Tues & Sat 5–7pm; Wed–Fri 5–8:30pm. Closed Nov–Mar.

MODERATE

Bentley's CANADIAN/ENGLISH   Located in the Lofts at 99 hotel (see p. 232), Bentley's is *the* local watering hole and a favorite theater-company gathering spot. In summer, you can sit on the garden terrace and enjoy the light fare—grilled shrimp, burgers, pizza, fish and chips, shepherd's pie, and pastas. The dinner menu features more substantial stuff, including lamb curry, sirloin steak, and salmon baked in white wine with peppercorn-dill butter. The bar offers 15 drafts on tap.

99 Ontario St. ✆ **519/271-1121.** www.bentleys-annex.com. Reservations not accepted. Main courses C$15–C$18. AE, DC, MC, V. Daily 11:30am–1am.

Down the Street ★ ▮▮ INTERNATIONAL   This charming bohemian spot is a welcome sight, given Stratford's delicious but often pricey food scene. The menu offers selections from around the globe: Mexican guacamole and corn tortillas, Vietnamese-style pork chops in a spicy chili-honey glaze, French Dijon chicken supreme. The dessert list is short but good; try the bittersweet chocolate tart with raspberry sorbet.

30 Ontario St. ✆ **519/273-5886.** Reservations recommended. Main courses C$18–C$28. AE, DC, MC, V. Tues–Sat 11:30am–3pm & 5–9pm (bar open till 1am).

Keystone Alley Cafe ★ ASIAN/CONTINENTAL   The food here is better than at some pricier competitors. Working thespians often stop in for lunch options that may include a maple-grilled chicken-and-avocado club or a cornmeal-crusted Mediterranean tart. At dinner, entrees include breast of Muscovy duck with stir-fried Asian vegetables and egg noodles in honey-ginger sauce, as well as escallops of calf's liver with garlic potato purée and creamed Savoy cabbage with bacon. The short wine list is reasonably priced.

34 Brunswick St. ✆ **519/271-5645.** Reservations recommended. Main courses C$15–C$27. AE, DC, MC, V. Mon–Sat 11:30am–2:30pm; Tues–Sat 5–9pm.

INEXPENSIVE

York Street Kitchen ECLECTIC   This small restaurant is a fun, funky spot that serves reasonably priced, high-quality food. It's a favorite with locals, especially the arts and media set. Grub is up all day, from breakfast burritos and other morning fare to build-your-own sandwiches at lunch and, in the evenings, good comfort foods such as meatloaf and mashed potatoes, or barbecued chicken and ribs.

41 York St. ✆ **519/273-7041.** www.yorkstreetkitchen.com. Reservations not accepted. Main courses C$14–C$16. AE, V. Apr to early Oct daily 8am–8pm; early Oct–Mar daily 8am–3pm. Closed Dec 24 to Jan 5.

NIAGARA-ON-THE-LAKE & NIAGARA FALLS

130km (81 miles) SE of Toronto

Never mind that Oscar Wilde called it "a bride's second great disappointment," the honeymoon capital of Niagara Falls is worth the 2-hour drive from Toronto just to witness the majesty of the falls themselves. The tacky shops, motels, attractions—it's an unabashed tourist trap—can either be ignored or enjoyed, depending on your sensibility. Then take a scenic drive about a half-hour back toward Toronto, along the **Niagara Parkway** (p. 246), to Niagara-on-the-Lake, a quiet and pretty19th-century village that offers a welcome retreat after the carnival atmosphere of Niagara Falls. Many travelers prefer to stay at NOTL, where the food and wine offerings go well beyond the fast-food chains of the Falls and can be quite sophisticated for a tourist region. (You're now in the heart of Niagara wine country.) This is also home to the **Shaw Festival,** a theater event on par with Stratford's festival and another reason to visit, or even stay for a day or two.

Essentials

VISITOR INFORMATION The **Niagara-on-the-Lake Chamber of Commerce** (26 Queen St., Niagara-on-the-Lake; ✆ **905/468-1950;** www.niagaraon thelake.com) provides information and can help you find accommodations. It's open daily from 9am to 7:30pm from April through October, and from 10am to 5pm during the rest of the year.

For Niagara Falls travel information, contact **Niagara Falls Tourism** (5515 Stanley Ave., Niagara Falls; ✆ **800/56-FALLS** [800/563-2557] or 519/356-6061; www.niagarafallstourism.com) or the **Niagara Parks Commission** (✆ **877/NIA-PARK** [877/642-7275]; www.niagaraparks.com).

GETTING THERE Niagara-on-the-Lake is best seen by **car.** From Toronto, take the Queen Elizabeth Way (signs read QEW) to Niagara via the cities of Hamilton and St. Catharine's, and exit at Highway 55. The trip takes about 1½ hours.

Amtrak and **VIA** (✆ **416/366-8411**) operate **trains** between Toronto and New York, but they stop only in Niagara Falls and St. Catharine's, not in Niagara-on-the-Lake. Call ✆ **800/361-1235** in Canada or **800/USA-RAIL** (800/872-7245) in the United States. From either place, you'll need to rent a car. Rental outlets in St. Catharine's include **Hertz** (350 Ontario St.; ✆ **905/682-8695**). In Niagara Falls, **Avis** is at 5734 Valley Way (✆ **905/357-2847**).

The Shaw Festival

Founded in 1962, the Shaw was known for many years for presenting the dramatic and comedic works of George Bernard Shaw and his contemporaries. However, since Jackie Maxwell became artistic director, the mandate has changed: the Shaw now features forgotten plays from Shaw's era (often penned by women writers), as well as classics and new works by Canadian playwrights. As impressive a destination for theater-goers as Stratford, it runs from April until the first weekend of November

 A Great Green Initiative

Driving through Niagara-on-the-Lake by car is a delight, but many would argue that the region is best viewed by bicycle. VIA Rail offers the **Toronto-Niagara Greenbelt Express** for cyclists. These passenger trains have a bike cargo car, and you can hop aboard— for C$62 per person round trip—and get to Niagara Falls in less than 2 hours. From there, you can bike to your hotel (if you're a light traveler) or arrange for pick-up for an extra fee. Call ✆ **888/619-5984** or visit **www. biketrain.ca** for more details.

and plays in the historic **Court House Theatre,** the exquisite **Shaw Festival Theatre,** the **Royal George Theatre,** and the **Studio Theatre.** Recent performances have included *Born Yesterday, Star Chamber,* and Shaw's *In Good King Charles's Golden Days.*

Free chamber concerts take place at various locales Sunday at 11am. Chats introduce performances on Friday evenings in July and August, and question-and-answer sessions follow Tuesday-evening performances.

The Shaw announces its festival program in mid-January. Prices range from C$30 to C$110; there are some "special matinees" that offer tickets for C$40 seniors and C$25 students. For more information, contact the **Shaw Festival** (℗ **800/511-7429** or 905/468-2172; www.shawfest.com).

Exploring the Town

Niagara-on-the Lake is small, and most of its attractions are along one main street, making it easy to explore on foot. In 1792, it briefly served as the capital of Upper Canada (though the town was then called Newark). The town was burned down during the War of 1812 but quickly rebuilt afterwards.

SIGHTS

Fort George National Historic Site ★ ☺ The fort played a central role in the War of 1812: It was headquarters for the British Army's Centre Division. The division was comprised of British regulars, local militia, Runchey's corps of former slaves, and aboriginal forces. The fort was destroyed by American artillery fire in May 1813. After the war, it was partially rebuilt, but it was abandoned in 1828 and not reconstructed until the 1930s. You can view the guardroom (with its hard plank beds), the officers' quarters, the enlisted men's quarters, and the sentry posts. The self-guided tour includes interpretive films. The fort is one of Ontario's favorite "haunted" sites (ghost-hunting tours are available throughout the summer and in October).

26 Queen Street, Niagara Pkwy. ℗ **905/468-4257.** www.parkscanada.ca or www.friendsoffortgeorge. ca. Admission C$12 adults, C$10 seniors, C$6 children 6–16, free for children 5 & under. Apr–Oct daily 10am–5pm; Nov–Mar Sat & Sun 10am–5pm.

Niagara Historical Society Museum For history buffs, this museum has more than 8,000 artifacts pertaining to local history. The collection includes possessions of United Empire Loyalists who first settled the area at the end of the American

---

 Ooh, Scary

For those who believe in ghosts, Fort George is one of Ontario's favorite "haunted" sites. Reported "sightings" include a soldier patrolling its perimeter and a young damsel who appears in an 18th-century mirror. Whether you're a believer or a skeptic, the Ghost Tours are fun for the family. They run evenings from May through September, with bonus dates around Halloween. The cost is C$12 adults and children 12 and up, and C$5 children 11 and under. Contact the **Friends of Fort George** at ℗ **905/468-6621,** or visit **www.friends offortgeorge.ca** for a schedule and for more details.

ACCOMMODATIONS ■
Harbour House **15**
Moffat Inn **20**
Oban Inn **1**
The Old Bank House **2**
Prince of Wales Hotel & Spa **19**

DINING ◆
Angel Inn **11**
Epicurean **5**
Niagara Home Bakery **8**
Shaw Café and Wine Bar **3**
Stagecoach Family Restaurant **10**

ATTRACTIONS & SHOPPING ●
Court House Theatre **12**
Festival Theatre **21**
Fort George National
   Historic Site **22**
Greaves Jam **9**
Irish Design **7**
Maple Leaf Fudge **17**
Niagara Apothecary **18**
Niagara Historical
   Society Museum **16**
The Owl & the Pussycat **13**
Royal George Theatre **4**
Scottish Loft **14**
Shaw Shop **6**
Studio Theatre **21**

Revolution. So, if branding irons, portraits, maps, and other artifacts are your thing, take a few hours to peruse the museum.

43 Castlereagh St. (at Davy St.). ✆ **905/468-3912.** Admission C$5 adults, C$3 seniors, C$2 students (w/ID), C$1 children 5–12, free for children 4 & under. May–Oct daily 10am–5pm; Nov–Apr daily 1–5pm.

A SHOPPING STROLL

It's a pleasant pastime to stroll along the town's main artery, Queen Street, and check out some entertaining, albeit touristy, shops. The **Niagara Apothecary,** at no. 5 (✆ **905/468-3845**), dates to 1866 and is a store and also a bit of a museum, with the original, gold-leaf and black-walnut counters, and glass and ceramic apothecary ware, on display. At no. 13 is the **Scottish Loft** (✆ **905/468-0965**), which is filled with tartans, Celtic memorabilia, candy, books, and other assorted Scottish-themed notions. **Maple Leaf Fudge** (no. 14; ✆ **905/468-2211**) is a tooth-aching stop: You can watch as the aproned staff makes 20-plus flavors on marble slabs. At no. 16 is a charming toy store, the **Owl and the Pussycat** (✆ **905/468-3081**). At no. 35 is **Greaves Jam** (✆ **905/468-7331**), run by fourth-generation jam makers—truly good stuff. **Irish Design,** at no. 38 (✆ **905/468-7233**), sells hand-knit sweaters, traditional gold and silver jewelry, and other treasures from the Emerald Isle. The **Shaw Shop** (✆ **800/511-7429**), no. 79, next to the Royal George Theatre, carries GBS memorabilia and more. A Dansk outlet and several galleries selling contemporary Canadian and ethnic crafts round-out the mix.

TOURING NIAGARA-ON-THE-LAKE WINERIES

Visiting a local winery is one of the most delicious ways to pass an hour or two in this region. You'll also see some of the best in new and innovative wine design, architecture, and viticulture. As with any major wine region, there are the big, commercial enterprises and the small, artisan ones. Lately, celebrities have joined the club (here as elsewhere), so you can try wines with names such as Mike Weir, Wayne Gretzky, or Dan Aykroyd; mostly for the novelty, not the nose. Look for the VQA label: It identifies wines made with locally grown grapes. For maps of the area and information about vintners, contact the **Wine Council of Ontario** (✆ **905/684-8070;** www.winesofontario.org). The wineries listed below are close to the town of Niagara-on-the-Lake. Tours are free. Prices for tastings vary with the winery and the wine you're sampling, but are usually about C$10.

If you turn off Highway 55 and go down York Road, you'll reach **Château des Charmes,** west of the town of St. David's (✆ **905/262-4219;** www.chateaudescharmes.com). The winery was built to resemble a French manor house, and its architecture is unique in the region. One-hour tours are given daily. It's open from 10am to 6pm year-round.

To reach **Stratus** (2059 Niagara Stone Rd.; ✆ **905/468-1806;** www.konzelmann.ca), one of the region's more cutting-edge wineries with a focus on sustainable practices and eco-design, take Niagara Stone Road out of Niagara-on-the-Lake. This vintner is famous for its award-winning blends. Reservations are not required for tastings, but if you're traveling in a group of six or more, it's best to call in advance. Tours of the modern winery are by appointment only.

JET-BOATING THRILLS

Jet-boat excursions leave from the dock across from 61 Melville St., at the King George III Inn. Don a rain suit, poncho, and life jacket, and climb aboard. The boat takes you out onto the Niagara River for a trip along the stonewalled canyon to the whirlpool downriver. The ride starts slow but gets into turbulent water. Trips, which operate from May to October, last an hour and cost C$57 adults and C$48 children 13 and under. Reservations are required, and if you make your booking online, you'll get a discount of C$5 per ticket. Call the **Whirlpool Jet Boat Company** at ✆ **888/438-4444** or 905/468-4800, or visit **www.whirlpooljet.com**.

Where to Stay

In summer, hotel space is in high demand. If you're having trouble nailing down a room, contact the **Niagara-on-the-Lake Chamber of Commerce** (✆ **905/468-1950;** www.niagaraonthelake.com), which provides information about accommodations, from luxurious hotels to charming bed-and-breakfasts. B&Bs can also be located and booked via **www.bbcanada.com**. The prices listed below are for the peak summer season; deep discounts are available at all of these properties in early spring, late fall, and winter.

IN TOWN

Harbour House ★★★   Tucked away on a quiet street that's close to the marina, this hotel offers serenity and tranquility from the moment you step through the front door. The focus is on comfort with understated luxury, from the Frette robes to the flickering fireplaces. The beds are particularly cozy, with king-sized mattresses topped by a layer of hypoallergenic duck feathers. (For those with allergies, alternative bedding is available.) Service is thoughtful and efficient, and guests are treated to lavish breakfasts and late afternoon wine-and-cheese receptions. The hotel is entirely nonsmoking.

85 Melville St., Niagara-on-the-Lake, ON L0S 1J0. ✆ **866/277-6677** or 905/468-4683. Fax 905/468-0366. www.harbourhousehotel.ca. 31 units. From C$299 double. Rates include breakfast. AE, DC, MC, V. Free parking. **Amenities:** Bike rental; concierge; room service. *In room:* A/C, TV/DVD player, CD player, hair dryer, minibar, Wi-Fi (free).

Moffat Inn ⬧   This is a fine budget-conscious choice in a convenient location. Most rooms have brass-framed beds, and eight have fireplaces. Guests tend to congregate on the patio, which is set in a beautiful flower garden. But if you have trouble climbing stairs, this hotel is not a good choice since most of the guest rooms are on the second floor, and there's no elevator and no porter to handle luggage.

60 Picton St. (at Queen St.), Niagara-on-the-Lake, ON L0S 1J0. ✆ **905/468-4116.** www.moffatinn.com. 24 units. From C$125 double. AE, MC, V. Free parking. **Amenities:** Restaurant. *In room:* A/C, TV, hair dryer, Wi-Fi (free).

Oban Inn ★   In a prime location overlooking the lake, the Oban Inn is a lovely place to stay. The town's first real country inn, it's in a charming, sizeable white Victorian house with a large veranda. The gorgeous gardens provide the fragrant bouquets throughout the house. A complete renovation updated the pretty rooms with modern amenities, including LCD plasma televisions, Bose sound systems, and individual temperature controls in all rooms. The spa is also a popular attraction.

160 Front St. (at Gate St.), Niagara-on-the-Lake, ON L0S 1J0. © **866/359-6226** or 905/468-2165. www.obaninn.ca. 26 units. From C$260 double. AE, DC, DISC, MC, V. Free parking. **Amenities:** Restaurant; lounge; babysitting; bike rental; concierge; room service; spa. *In room:* A/C, TV, CD player, hair dryer, Internet ($10 daily fee).

The Old Bank House ★ Beautifully situated down by the river, this two-story Georgian was built in 1817 as the first branch of the Bank of Canada. In 1902, it hosted the Prince and Princess of Wales, and today, it's a charming bed-and-breakfast inn. Several tastefully decorated units have private entrances, and one also has a private trellised deck. If you're planning a romantic weekend away, you'll love the Rose Suite, with its cathedral ceiling and private balcony.

10 Front St., Niagara-on-the-Lake, ON L0S 1J0. © **877/468-7136** or 905/468-7136. www.oldbankhouse. com. 9 units. From C$189 double. Rates include breakfast. AE, MC, V. Free parking. **Amenities:** Restaurant (in high season); Jacuzzi. *In room:* A/C, TV, Wi-Fi (free).

Prince of Wales ★★ This is one of Niagara-on-the-Lake's most luxurious hotels, and you could say it has it all: a central location across from the lovely gardens of Simcoe Park; recreational facilities, including an indoor pool; a full-service spa; lounges, bars, and restaurants; and conference facilities. If you're adverse to floral fabrics and overstuffed furniture, this is not the place for you. However, if you're looking to be seriously pampered in a faux-Victorian setting, it's a good bet. Also, it's one of the rare hotels in town with a wheelchair-accessible room. Pets are welcome. This is a smoke-free hotel.

6 Picton St., Niagara-on-the-Lake, ON L0S 1J0. © **888/669-5566** or 905/468-3246. www.vintage hotels.com. 110 units. From C$275 double. AE, DC, DISC, MC, V. Free parking. Small pets accepted ($35 per pet). **Amenities:** Dining room; cafe; bar; lounge; bike rental; concierge; health club; Jacuzzi; indoor pool; room service; spa. *In room:* A/C, TV, CD player, hair dryer, Wi-Fi ($10 daily fee).

ALONG THE WINE ROUTE

Inn on the Twenty and the Vintage House ★ Cave Spring Cellars, one of Niagara's best known wineries, offers modern, well-equipped, and generous suites. Each one has an elegantly furnished living room with a fireplace and a Jacuzzi in the bathroom. Seven are duplexes—one of them, the deluxe loft, has two double beds on the second level—and five are single-level suites with high ceilings. All of the suites are nonsmoking. The inn's eatery, On the Twenty Restaurant & Wine Bar (p. 240), is across the street and is a great place to dine. The inn's spa offers a full range of services for men and women, and has special packages for couples. Next door is the **Vintage House,** an 1840 Georgian mansion with three suites, all with private entrances. All rooms are nonsmoking.

3845 Main St., Jordan, ON L0R 1S0. © **800/701-8074** or 905/562-5336. www.innonthetwenty.com. 30 units. From C$259 suite. MC, V. Free parking. From QEW, take the Jordan Rd. exit south; at the 1st intersection, turn right onto 4th Ave., then right onto Main St. **Amenities:** Restaurant; concierge; nearby golf course; health club, spa. *In room:* A/C, TV, hair dryer, Internet (free).

Where to Dine

IN TOWN

The stylish **Shaw Cafe and Wine Bar** (92 Queen St.; © **905/468-4772**) serves lunch and light meals, and has a patio. The **Epicurean** (84 Queen St.; © **905/468-3408**) offers hearty soups, quiches, sandwiches, and other fine dishes in a sunny, Provence-inspired dining room. Service is cafeteria style. Half a block off Queen

Street, the **Angel Inn** (224 Regent St.; ✆ **905/468-3411**) is a delightfully authentic English pub. For an inexpensive down-home breakfast, go to the **Stagecoach Family Restaurant** (45 Queen St.; ✆ **905/468-3133**). It also serves basic family fare, such as burgers, fries, and meatloaf, but it doesn't accept credit cards. **Niagara Home Bakery** (66 Queen St.; ✆ **905/468-3431**) is the place to stop for sweet treats like chocolate-date squares and pastries, and savories such as individual quiches.

ALONG THE WINE ROAD

Hillebrand Estates Winery Restaurant ★ CANADIAN/CONTINEN-TAL   This dining room is light and airy, and its floor-to-ceiling windows offer sweeping views over the vineyards to the distant Niagara Escarpment and more intimate peeks into wine cellars that bulge with oak barrels. The seasonal menus feature such dishes as poached Arctic char with shellfish ragout, or prosciutto-wrapped pheasant breast atop linguine tossed with mushrooms, roasted eggplant, and shallot. The starters are equally luxurious. In case the food isn't enticing enough (and it should be), the restaurant also hosts special events throughout the year, many featuring jazz musicians.

1249 Niagara Stone Road, btw. Niagara-on-the-Lake & Virgil. ✆ **905/468-7123**. www.hillebrand.com. Reservations strongly recommended. Main courses C$36–C$40. AE, MC, V. Daily spring–fall noon–11pm (closes earlier in winter).

Inn on the Twenty Restaurant & Wine Bar ★ CANADIAN   This warm and friendly restaurant is a favorite among foodies for good service, and a small but well-chosen selection of Ontario wines (with a few international additions)—but mostly for the cuisine that features ingredients from many local producers. There's the added advantage that the food is created with wine pairings in mind; especially rich desserts are made to enjoy with ice wines and late-harvest wines. Inn on the Twenty Restaurant is associated with **Inn on the Twenty** (p. 241), across the street.

At Cave Spring Cellars, 3836 Main St., Jordan. ✆ **905/562-7313**. www.innonthetwenty.com. Reservations recommended. Main courses C$22–C$35. MC, V. Daily 11:30am–3pm & 5–10pm.

The Restaurant at Vineland Estates ★★★ CANADIAN/CONTINEN-TAL   Situated in a renovated 1845 farmhouse with a sprawling patio that offers beautiful views, this restaurant serves some of the most innovative food along the wine trail. Start with a plate of mussels in a ginger broth. Follow with Canadian Angus tenderloin with a risotto of truffles and morel mushrooms; or pan-seared sweetbreads with a celeriac and potato mash, and confit of mushrooms glazed with ice wine. For dessert, try the tasting plate of Canadian farm cheeses, including Abbey St. Benoit blue Ermite; sweet-tooths can indulge in the maple-walnut cheesecake in a biscotti crust.

3620 Moyer Rd., Vineland. ✆ **888/846-3526** or 905/562-7088. www.vineland.com. Reservations strongly recommended. Main courses C$32–C$38. AE, MC, V. Daily noon–2:30pm & 5–9pm.

Along the Niagara Parkway ★★

The Niagara Parkway, on the Canadian side of the falls, is a lovely, scenic drive. Unlike the American side, there is plenty of natural beauty, including vast tracks of parkland. You can drive along the 56km (35-mile) parkway all the way from Niagara-on-the-Lake to Niagara Falls, taking in attractions en route. Here are the major ones, listed in the order in which you'll encounter them:

○ **The White Water Walk** (4330 River Rd.; ℂ **905/374-1221**): The boardwalk runs beside the raging white waters of the Great Gorge Rapids. Stroll along and wonder at your leisure how it must feel to challenge this mighty torrent, where the river rushes through the narrow channel at an average speed of 35kmph (22 mph). Admission is C$8.75 adults, C$5.15 children 6 to 12, free for children 5 and under. Open daily from 9am to 5pm (closes at 7pm or 8pm from mid-May till Labour Day).

○ **The Whirlpool Aero Car** (ℂ **905/354-5711**): This red-and-yellow cable-car contraption whisks you on a 1,097m (3,599-ft.) jaunt between two points on the Canadian side of the falls. High above the Niagara Whirlpool, you'll enjoy excellent views of the surrounding landscape. Admission is C$12 adults, C$6.80 children 6 to 12, free for kids 5 and under. Open daily May to the third Sunday in October. Hours are from 10am to 5pm (closes at 7pm or 8pm from mid-May till Labour Day).

○ **The Niagara Parks Botanical Gardens and School of Horticulture** (ℂ **905/356-8119**): Stop here for a free view of the vast gardens and a look at the 12m-diameter (39-ft.) **Floral Clock,** made up of 25,000 plants. The gorgeous **Butterfly Conservatory** is also in the gardens. In this lush tropical setting, more than 2,000 butterflies (50 international species) float and flutter among such nectar-producing flowers as lantanas and *pentas.* The large, bright-blue, luminescent Morpho butterflies from Central and South America are particularly gorgeous. Interpretive programs and other presentations take place in the auditorium and two smaller theaters. The native butterfly garden outside attracts the more common swallowtails, fritillaries, and painted ladies. Visitors are encouraged to wear brightly colored clothing to attract the butterflies. Admission is C$12 adults, C$6.80 children 6 to 12, free for children 5 and under. Open daily September to June 9am to 5pm, July and August 9am to 7pm.

○ **Queenston Heights Park:** This is the site of a famous War of 1812 battle, and you can take a walking tour of the battlefield. Picnic or play tennis in the shaded arbor before moving to the **Laura Secord Homestead** (Partition St., Queenston; ℂ **905/262-4851**). This heroic woman threaded enemy lines to alert British authorities to a surprise attack by American soldiers during the War of 1812. Her home contains a fine collection of Upper Canada furniture from the period, plus artifacts recovered from an archaeological dig. Stop at the candy shop and ice-cream parlor. Tours run every half-hour. Admission is C$4.75 adults, C$3.65 children 6 to 12, free for children age 5 and under. It's open summer daily 11am to 5pm, fall to spring Wednesday to Sunday 11am to 5pm.

○ **Fruit Farms and Wineries:** This is home to some of Canada's best stone fruit and other orchards, so you'll find peaches, apples, pears, nectarines, cherries, plums, and strawberries at **Kurtz Orchards** (ℂ **905/468-2937**) and elsewhere; you can tour the 32 hectares (79 acres) at Kurtz on a tractor-pulled tram. **Inniskillin Winery** (Line 3, Service Rd. 66; ℂ **905/468-3554** or 905/468-2187), the pioneering winery behind Canada's famous ice wine, is open June to October daily from 10am to 6pm, November through May Monday through Saturday from 10am to 5pm. The self-guided free tour has 20 stops that explain the winemaking process. A free guided tour, offered daily in summer and Saturdays only in winter, begins at 2:30pm.

● **Old Fort Erie** (350 Lakeshore Rd., Fort Erie; ☏ **905/871-0540**): It's a recon-
struction of the fort that was seized by the Americans in July 1814, besieged later by the British, and finally blown up as the Americans retreated across the river to Buffalo. Guards in period costume stand sentry duty, fire the cannons, and demonstrate drill and musket practice. Open from the first Saturday in May to mid-September daily from 10am to 5pm, and weekends only mid-September to Canadian Thanksgiving (U.S. Columbus Day). Admission is C$9.25 adults, C$5.15 children 6 to 12, free for children 5 and under.

Seeing Niagara Falls

You simply cannot come this far and not see the falls, which are one of the seven *natural* wonders of the world. When you arrive, step up to the low railing that runs along the road, and take in the spectacular view over Horseshoe Falls. Then consider climbing aboard the ***Maid of the Mist*** ★★ (5920 River Rd.; ☏ **905/358-5781;** www.maidofthemist.com). The sturdy boat takes you right in to the basin—through the turbulent waters around the American Falls; past the Rock of Ages; and to the foot of the Horseshoe Falls, where 159 million L (35 million imperial gal.) of water tumble over the 54m-high (177-ft.) cataract each minute. You'll get wet, and your glasses will mist—but that just adds to the thrill. Boats leave from the dock on the parkway just down from the Rainbow Bridge. Trips operate daily from mid-May to mid-October. Fares are C$15 adults, C$8.90 children 6 to 12, free for children 5 and under.

Go down under the falls using the elevator at the **Table Rock Centre,** which drops you 46m (151 ft.) through solid rock to the tunnels and viewing portals of the **Journey Behind the Falls** (☏ **905/354-1551**). You'll receive—and appreciate—a rain poncho. Admission is C$13 adults, C$7.50 children 6 to 12, free for children 5 and under. Another attraction at the Table Rock Centre (which has just completed a C$32-million renovation) is **Niagara's Fury.** Visitors "experience" the creation of the falls in a chamber that swirls visual images over a 360-degree screen. It's a sense-surround ride, complete with shaking ground underfoot, an enveloping blizzard, and a temperature drop in the room from 75° to 40°F degrees (24°–4°C) in 3 seconds.

 The Honeymoon Capital of the World

Seeing Niagara Falls as it is today—in all of its loud, neon, tacky glory—you might wonder how anyone would have thought it a romantic destination for a honeymoon. But back in 1801, when the falls was simply a natural wonder of the highest order, Aaron Burr's daughter, Theodosia, chose it as the perfect place for her honeymoon. Napoleon's brother Jerome Bonaparte followed in her footsteps with his bride a few years later, and then suddenly everybody thought Niagara Falls was *the* place for newlyweds. Well, not *everybody.* Oscar Wilde visited Niagara Falls in 1881 and then quipped: "Every American bride is taken there, and the sight of the stupendous waterfall must be one of the earliest if not the keenest disappointments in American married life."

SIDE TRIPS FROM TORONTO

Niagara-on-the-Lake & Niagara Falls

It's an intense experience, and not appropriate for young children. Fares are C$15 adults, C$9 children 6 to 12, free for children 5 and under. (*Warning:* The operators advise that Niagara's Fury may not be appropriate for children 6 and under, as they might find it too scary. Also, adults with a history of heart disease or back/neck injuries may want to pass on this attraction.) Open daily 9am to 9pm.

If you can't get enough of the falls, ride the external glass-fronted elevators 159m (522 ft.) to the top of the **Skylon Tower Observation Deck** (5200 Robinson St.; ✆ **905/356-2651;** www.skylon.com). The observation deck is open from June to Labour Day daily from 8am to midnight; hours vary the rest of the year, so call ahead. Adults pay C$13, children 12 and under C$7.55. It's pricey for an elevator ride.

The falls are equally dramatic in winter, when ice formations add a certain beauty to it all and the crowds of high summer are wonderfully absent.

WHERE TO STAY & DINE NEAR THE FALLS

My honest recommendation is for visitors to stay in scenic and charming Niagara-on-the-Lake and take in the carnival-like Niagara Falls during the day. But I know some people will enjoy the bright lights—and the casino scene—of Niagara Falls after dark. If you do, one high-end hotel is the **Niagara Fallsview Casino Resort** (6380 Fallsview Blvd.; ✆ **888/325-5788;** www.fallsviewcasinoresort.com), which opened in 2004. It has its own 18,580-sq.-m (199,993-sq.-ft.) casino, a performing-arts theater, a spa, and 10 dining spots. Another good hotel bet is the **Sheraton on the Falls** (5875 Falls Ave.; ✆ **888/234-8410** or 905/374-4445), which offers rooms with a truly gorgeous view of the falls; many have balconies. There's also the **Skyline Inn** (5685 Falls Ave.; ✆ **800/263-7135** or 905/374-4444), which is right by Casino Niagara.

Niagara Falls likes to boast about its newly invigorated dining scene, but it's a challenge to find good food that doesn't cost a small fortune. The **Pinnacle Restaurant** (6732 Fallsview Blvd.; ✆ **905/356-1501**) offers a Continental menu and

A FAMILY ADVENTURE

Niagara Falls has plenty of family attractions. A popular choice is **MarineLand ★**, 7657 Portage Rd. (✆ **905/356-9565;** www.marinelandcanada.com). Its multiple aquariums have a walrus mascot, dolphins, sea lions, and freshwater fish. Friendship Cove, a 17-million-L (4.5-million-gal.) breeding and observation tank, lets the little ones see killer whales up close.

MarineLand also has rides, including a Tivoli wheel (a fancy Ferris wheel), Dragon Boat rides, and Dragon Mountain, a roller coaster that loops, double-loops, and spirals through 305m (1,001 ft.) of tunnels. Admission is C$40 adults

and children 10 and over, C$33 children 5 to 9, free for children 4 and under. It's open daily mid-May to June and September to mid-October 10am to 5pm, July and August 9am to 6pm; it's closed mid-October through mid-May.

A new attraction at the falls is Canada's first **Great Wolf Lodge** (3950 Victoria Ave.; ✆ **905/354-4888** or 800/605-9653). Part of an American chain of family resorts known for the quality of services, rooms, and activities, Great Wolf is probably best known for its massive indoor water park. But wait, there's more, including a four-story interactive tree-house water fort.

Niagara Falls

ACCOMMODATIONS ■
Niagara Fallsview
  Casino Resort **14**
Sheraton on the Falls **3**
The Skyline Inn **5**

DINING ◆
Edgewaters Tap & Grill **16**
Elements on the Falls **12**
The Keg **11**
Lucky's **6**
Pinnacle Restaurant **15**
Queenston Heights Restaurant **1**
Rainforest Café **7**
Whirlpool Restaurant **1**

ATTRACTIONS ●
American Falls **10**
Casino Niagara **4**
Great Wolf Lodge **1**
Horseshoe
  (Canadian) Falls **13**
Maid of the Mist **9**
MarineLand **17**
Niagara's Fury **12**
Skylon Tower
  Observation Deck **8**
Table Rock Centre **12**
White Water Walk **2**

NIAGARA PARKWAY COMMISSION RESTAURANTS

The Niagara Parkway Commission has commandeered the most spectacular scenic spots for its restaurants. These used to be reasonably priced places serving lunch and dinner, but recent renovations have focused on creating more upscale settings, with prices to match. **Table Rock Centre,** right across from the falls, has had a complete renovation, and its new restaurant, **Elements on the Falls** (✆ 905/354-3631) is expensive but delicious. Also close to the falls is **Edgewaters Tap & Grill** (✆ 905/356-2217), a more casual restaurant that's appropriate for the whole family (there's a special menu for kids).

Whirlpool Restaurant (✆ 905/356-7221), at the Whirlpool Golf Course near Queenston, is open to the public while the course is open (May–Dec). My favorite of the Niagara Parkway Commission's eateries is the **Queenston Heights Restaurant** (14184 Niagara Pkwy.; ✆ 905/262-4274). Set in the park among firs, cypresses, silver birches, and maples, the restaurant affords a magnificent view of the lower Niagara River and the lush, abundant land through which it flows. The restaurant also serves up an excellent duck confit and boasts a great wine list.

a remarkable view from the top of the Konica Minolta Tower. **The Keg** (5950 Victoria Ave.; ✆ 905/353-4022) is a reliable steakhouse chain. Over at Casino Niagara, **Lucky's** (5705 Falls Ave.; ✆ 888/946-3255) serves up hearty portions of prime rib, as well as burgers and pizza. The **Rainforest Café** (5875 Falls Ave.; ✆ 905/374-2233) is a family favorite with its animatronic gorillas and serpents, and its tried-and-true menu of pizzas, burgers, and sandwiches. The **Skylon Tower** (✆ 905/356-2651) revolving restaurant is the top choice in town at 236m (775 ft.) above the ground and overlooking the falls, with menus featuring Caesar salads, filet mignon, lobster tails, and more fancy classics.

THE MUSKOKA LAKES

Just a 90-minute drive north of Toronto, the Muskoka region has been a magnet for visitors since the 19th century. Though the area proved futile for farming (it's located on the Canadian Shield, where you need dig only a foot or two in some places to come up against sheets of granite), its more than 1,600 lakes, unspoiled wilderness, and laid-back attitude made it an excellent place for a retreat. In the past decade, Muskoka's charms have expanded to include excellent golf courses, soothing spas, and top-notch restaurants. While the region is most popular in summer, when families congregate at the resorts and Hollywood celebrities such as Goldie Hawn and Tom Hanks lounge at their lakefront "cottages," this is a great area to visit at any time of the year.

Once accessible only by water, Muskoka is still a boater's dream. The region also has several towns of note: Gravenhurst, Bracebridge, Port Carling, Huntsville, and Bala. It's well worth devoting a day or two to explore the area, the quaint towns and most of all, the dazzling waterways. Be forewarned: This is not the Great White

The Muskoka Lakes Region

North. Particularly in summer, the area is busy with crowds. If you're looking for wide open wilderness, you have to travel further north to Algonquin Park or to some of the more remote stretches of Georgian Bay.

Essentials

GETTING THERE   You can drive from the south via Highway 400 to Highway 11, from the east via highways 12 and 169 to Highway 11, and from the north via Highway 11. It's about 160km (99 miles) from Toronto to Gravenhurst, 15km (9¼ miles) from Gravenhurst to Bracebridge, 25km (16 miles) from Bracebridge to Port Carling, and 34km (21 miles) from Bracebridge to Huntsville. **VIA Rail** (© **416/366-8411;** www.viarail.ca) services Gravenhurst, Bracebridge, and Huntsville from Toronto's Union Station. An airport about 18km (11 miles) from Gravenhurst is used mainly for small aircraft. Several other landing strips and a helicopter landing pad are at the Deerhurst Resort in Huntsville.

VISITOR INFORMATION   For information on the region, contact **Muskoka Tourism** (© **800/267-9700** or 705/689-0660; www.discovermuskoka.ca).

GETTING AROUND   While you won't need a car if you plan to stay close to your resort while you're here (an entirely reasonable proposition), you will need a car if you're planning to do a lot of sightseeing in the area. You could take the train to Bracebridge and then rent a car at **Budget** (1 Robert Dollar Dr.; ✆ **705/645-2755**). Huntsville has an **Enterprise** car rental center at 197 Main St. W. (✆ **705/789-1834**).

Exploring the Towns

Gravenhurst and Huntsville are scenic, and they also have enough shops, restaurants, parks, and public squares to make them worth a visit. Unless you have kids and plan to visit Santa's Village (see below), there's not much of a reason to linger in Bracebridge.

GRAVENHURST

Gravenhurst is Muskoka's first town—the first you reach if you're driving from Toronto and the first to achieve town status.

The **Norman Bethune Memorial House** (235 John St. N.; ✆ **705/687-4261**) is the restored 1890 birthplace of Dr. Norman Bethune. In 1939, this surgeon, inventor, and humanitarian died tending the sick in China during the Chinese Revolution. Tours of the historic house include a modern exhibit on Bethune's life. In summer, the house is open June through October daily from 10am to 4pm, November through May weekdays only from 1 to 4pm. Admission is C$4 adults, C$2.50 children 6 to 16, free for children 5 and under.

Sailing is one of Muskoka's greatest summer pastimes. Gravenhurst is home to the Muskoka Fleet, which includes a lovingly restored coal-powered 1887 steamship, the **RMS *Segwun.*** There are many options for cruising, such as a 1-hour tour; a 2½-hour lunch cruise; and a 4-hour late-afternoon tour of **Millionaire's Row,** where the real estate is as dazzling as the natural beauty. Reservations are required for all tours; call ✆ **866/687-6667** or 705/687-6667, or visit **www.realmuskoka. com** for more information. Tour prices start at C$18 adults, C$11 children 12 and under.

Year-round, there are theater performances at the **Gravenhurst Opera House** (✆ **705/687-5550**), which celebrated its 109th anniversary in 2010. In summer, there are shows at the **Port Carling Community Hall** (✆ **705/765-5221**).

BRACEBRIDGE: SANTA'S WORKSHOP

Halfway between the equator and the North Pole, **Bracebridge** bills itself as Santa's summer home, and **Santa's Village** (✆ **705/645-2512;** www.santasvillage.ca) is an imaginatively designed fantasyland full of kiddie delights: pedal boats and bumper boats on the lagoon, a roller-coaster sleigh ride, a Candy Cane Express, a carousel, and a Ferris wheel. At Elves' Island, children can crawl on a suspended net and over or through various modules—the Lunch Bag Forest, Cave Crawl, and Snake Tube Crawl. Mid-June through Labour Day, it's open daily from 10am to 6pm. Admission is C$27 children 5 and over, C$22 seniors and children 2 to 4, and free for children under 2.

PORT CARLING

As waterways became the main means of transportation in the region, **Port Carling** grew into the hub of the lakes. It became a boat-building center when a lock was installed connecting Lakes Muskoka and Rosseau, and a canal between Lakes Rosseau and Joseph opened all three to navigation. The **Muskoka Lakes Museum,** at 100 Joseph Street (📞 **705/765-5367**), captures the flavor of this era. July and August, it's open Monday through Saturday from 10am to 5pm and Sunday noon to 4pm; June, September, and October, hours are Tuesday through Saturday from 10am to 4pm and Sunday from noon to 4pm. Admission is by donation, with a suggested C$2 minimum.

HUNTSVILLE

Starting in the late 1800s, lumber was the name of the game in Huntsville, which is today Muskoka's biggest town. You can see some of the region's early history at the **Muskoka Heritage Place,** which includes **Muskoka Pioneer Village** (88 Brunel Rd., Huntsville; 📞 **705/789-7576;** www.muskokaheritageplace.org). It's open from mid-May to mid-October daily from 11am to 4pm. Admission is C$10 adults, C$7 children 3 to 12, free for children 2 and under. Muskoka Heritage Place also features the **Portage Flyer Steam Train.** Once part of the world's smallest commercial railway (running from 1904–1958), it's been reborn as a tourist attraction and reopened in 2010 after a thorough renovation.

Robinson's General Store on Main Street in Dorset (📞 **705/766-2415**) is so popular, it was voted Canada's best country store. Wood stoves, dry goods, hardware, pine goods, and moccasins—you name it, it's here.

Where to Stay

Muskoka is famous for its lakes, and also for its resorts. Bed-and-breakfast and country-inn choices also abound. Contact **Muskoka Tourism** (📞 **800/267-9700** or 705/689-0660; www.discovermuskoka.ca). The prices listed below are for the peak summer season; deep discounts are available at all of these properties in early spring, late fall, and winter.

RESORTS

Deerhurst Resort ★★★ ☺   The Deerhurst is a perfect spot for a family vacation. This stunning resort complex rambles over 320 hectares (791 acres), and it offers everything from two 18-hole golf courses (part of the Muskoka Golf Trail) to a golf academy; a full-service Aveda spa; endless kilometers of nature trails for hiking (or snowmobiling or cross-country skiing in winter); canoeing, kayaking, and all manner of watersports; an ambitious musical revue that runs all summer; and horseback riding. The accommodations here are spread out among several buildings on the property and range from high-ceilinged hotel rooms in the Terrace and Bayshore

The Shania Connection

The Deerhurst has many charms to recommend it, and whether or not you stay there, you must check out the pro song-and-dance stage show. Now in its 28th year, it's famous in part because Shania Twain performed in it for 3 years (1988–1990). Twain has kept up her connection with the Deerhurst since, even having her wedding there. In 2002, she brought Katie Couric and a NBC film crew to reminisce about her days here on stage. Twain continues to visit the resort—and rumor has it that when she does, she always checks out the show.

buildings to fully appointed one-, two-, or three-bedroom suites, many with fireplaces and/or whirlpools.

1235 Deerhurst Dr., Huntsville, ON P1H 2E8. ✆ **800/461-4393** or 705/789-6411. Fax 705/789-2431. www.deerhurstresort.com. 388 units. From C$197 double. AE, DC, DISC, MC, V. Free parking. Take Canal Rd. off Hwy. 60 to Deerhurst Rd. **Amenities:** 2 restaurants; 2 bars; children's programs; concierge; 2 18-hole golf courses; indoor sports complex; 11 Jacuzzis; 5 pools (2 indoor, 3 outdoor); room service; sauna; spa; tennis courts; 3 squash courts; racquetball court. *In room:* A/C, TV, hair dryer, Internet (free), minibar.

Delta Grandview Resort ★ ☺ If the Deerhurst is for the folks on the fast track, the Delta Grandview is for those looking for a more measured pace. This smaller resort retains the natural beauty and contours of the original farmstead, even while providing the latest resort facilities. Eighty accommodations are traditional hotel-style rooms, but most units are suites in a series of buildings, some down by the lake and others up on the hill with a lake view. The main dining room, the Rosewood Inn, is located in one of the resort's original buildings and overlooks Fairy Lake. In the summer, snacks are served at the Dockside Restaurant right on the shores of the lake, and the free Kidzone program provides supervision—and plenty of fun—for kids 4 to 12 from 8am to 4pm.

939 Hwy. 60, Grandview Drive, Huntsville, ON P1H 1Z4. ✆ **888/472-6388** or 705/789-4417. www. deltahotels.com. 123 units. From C$230 double. AE, DC, DISC, MC, V. Free parking. **Amenities:** 2 restaurants; babysitting; children's programs; 2 golf courses (18-hole & 9-hole); health club; indoor & outdoor pools; 3 tennis courts. *In room:* A/C, TV, Internet ($12 daily fee).

Taboo Resort ★★★ ☺ Near Gravenhurst in the southern Muskoka region, Taboo stands out for sleek sophistication in a leafy setting. Known until May 2003 as Muskoka Sands, the resort's new name may suggest a hedonistic adults-only retreat. The truth is anything but: Taboo is a family-friendly zone, with a kids' club that schedules activities for every day of the week during the high season in summer. And the fact that the resort is so willing to take care of the children means that many adults can soak up spa treatments or dine at one of the on-site restaurants without a second thought. One of my favorite things about Taboo is that every single room, large and small alike, has its own deck or balcony. While all of the sophisticated offerings at the resort are excellent, nothing beats taking in the utterly serene setting it enjoys. The hotel is entirely nonsmoking.

1209 Muskoka Beach Rd., Gravenhurst, ON P1P 1R1. ✆ **800/461-0236** or 705/687-2233. www.taboo resort.com. 157 units. From C$229 double. AE, DC, MC, V. Free parking. **Amenities:** 2 restaurants; bar; children's programs; concierge; 2 golf courses (18-hole & 9-hole); health club; Jacuzzi; 4 pools (3 outdoor, 1 indoor); room service; sauna; spa; 5 tennis courts; squash court. *In room:* A/C, TV, fridge, hair dryer, Wi-Fi (free).

Windermere House Resort ★ This traditional lakeside resort was destroyed by fire in 1996 but was rebuilt according to the original 1870s design. Well-manicured lawns sweep down to the lovely Lake Rosseau, while a broad veranda furnished with Adirondack chairs sets the leisurely mood. You can take in the water sports or just kick back with a book and a beverage. Rebuilding post-fire allowed the guest rooms to incorporate modern conveniences (including air-conditioning) while retaining old-fashioned charm. Most of the rooms have gorgeous views (the best ones overlook the lake), and a few have balconies or decks. This is a smoke-free hotel.

2508 Windermere Road, off Muskoka Rte. 4 (P.O. Box 68), Windermere, ON P0B 1P0. © **888/946-3376** or 705/769-3611. Fax 705/769-2168. www.windermerehouse.com. 70 units. From C$220 double. Rates include breakfast. Weekly rates also available. AE, MC, V. Free parking. **Amenities:** Restaurant; lounge; children's programs; golf course; outdoor pool; room service; tennis courts. *In room:* A/C, TV, Internet (free), minibar.

A COUNTRY INN

Inn at the Falls ★ 🎁 This attractive "inn" is actually a group of seven Victorian houses on a quiet cul-de-sac overlooking Bracebridge Falls and the Muskoka River. Inviting floral gardens surround an outdoor heated pool, patios, and lawns for relaxing. Some units have fireplaces, Jacuzzis, and balconies; others have views of the falls. The Fox & Hounds is a popular local gathering place. In winter, the fire crackles and snaps; in summer, the terrace is filled with umbrella-shaded tables. The more elegant Carriage Room serves upscale continental fare. Quite the perfect getaway-from-it-all spot, and easy on the budget, too. This is a smoke-free hotel.

1 Dominion St. (P.O. Box 1139), Bracebridge, ON P1L 1V3. © **877/645-9212** or 705/645-2245. www.innatthefalls.net. 39 units. From C$155 double. Additional adult C$16. Rates include breakfast. AE, DC, MC, V. Free parking. **Amenities:** 2 restaurants; nearby golf course; outdoor pool; Wi-Fi (free). *In room:* TV.

Where to Dine

VERY EXPENSIVE

Elements Restaurant, Culinary Theatre & Lounge ★★★ 🎁 CANADIAN The fact that the chefs here have cooked at some of Toronto's most famous kitchens draws gourmets from far and wide. The restaurant's floor-to-ceiling windows face west, so that you can take in the glorious sunset over the lake. The a la carte menu includes Nova Scotia lobster with charred-corn-and-crab bread pudding.

The Culinary Theatre offers another kind of dining experience. Only 18 seats are available at a time for this culinary school/live cooking show mix. Guests participate

---

THE ROCKY ROAD FOR GOLFERS

Muskoka attracts golfers by the droves. Many of the region's resorts offer pro-designed courses, created by the likes of Nick Faldo, Mike Weir, and Mark O'Meara. The greens here truly are different. Muskoka is located on the **Canadian Shield,** a bedrock layer just a few feet below the surface. The granite thwarted farmers who tried to work the land, but it makes an excellent setting for golfers. The landscape is filled with natural rock outcroppings. Not only does the locale make for a stunning landscape, but it also heightens the challenge. Add in the primeval forests and plenty of pristine water, and you'll understand why the term "magical" is so often applied to Muskoka.

The Muskoka Tourism website (**www.discovermuskoka.ca**) has information about great local golf courses. Another good resource is **www.teeingitup.com/ontario**. You'll also find information on resort websites: **Taboo** (p. 250) has a course that's considered one of the best in Canada; the **Delta Grandview** (p. 250) has the first course designed by Mark O'Meara; and **Deerhurst** (p. 249) has two 18-hole courses, including the famous **Deerhurst Highlands.** Another big draw is the **Rock** (www.therockgolf.com), a course designed by Nick Faldo on the shores of Lake Rosseau.

by selecting ingredients. Each meal—a tasting menu of three, five, or seven courses—is cooked as you watch and learn.

At Taboo Resort, 1209 Muskoka Beach Rd., Gravenhurst. ✆ **705/687-2233.** www.tabooresort.com. Reservations required. Main courses C$21–C$41; Culinary Theatre menu C$90, higher for special events. AE, DC, MC, V. Daily 6–10pm.

EXPENSIVE

Eclipse ★★ CANADIAN/INTERNATIONAL The spacious dining room with a soaring ceiling of Douglas fir beams offers an expansive view over hills and lakes. The lengthy dinner menu has plenty of vegetarian options and fare for carnivores, too. A favorite appetizer is the baked phyllo pastry filled with forest mushrooms and goat cheese. The Sizzle—the signature dish—is tiger shrimp sautéed in garlic, dried chilies, and white wine, and baked under mozzarella. Filling stuff. Entrees include breast of pheasant filled with wild rice and cranberries, and a rack of lamb rubbed with fresh herbs and served with an apple-maple compote. The wine list, with 300-plus selections, offers plenty of pairings.

1235 Deerhurst Dr. (at the Deerhurst Resort), Huntsville, ON P1H 2E8. ✆ **705/789-6411.** www.deerhurst resort.com. Reservations recommended. Main courses C$24–C$45. AE, DC, MC, V. Daily 5–11pm.

3 Guys and a Stove ★★ ☺ INTERNATIONAL This is a family restaurant with a special menu for kids. But don't let the unpretentious atmosphere and the casual name fool you—the cooking is *very* fine. The curried pumpkin-and-sweet potato soup is an absolute must when it's on the menu; the spicy chicken stew is another winner. This restaurant is also a terrific choice for vegetarians: The list of pasta and rice main-course dishes is substantial.

143 Hwy. 60, Huntsville. ✆ **705/789-1815.** www.3guysandastove.com. Main courses C$20–C$38. AE, MC, V. Daily 11am–9:30pm.

MODERATE

Blondie's ★ 🍴 COMFORT FOOD/DELI/SEAFOOD This family-run restaurant is a rare find in Muskoka: a mix of the area's typical comfort foods—fish and chips, prime rib, eggs Benedict, smoked-meat sandwiches—plus more exotic fare, such as sushi. Blondie's is also the official caterer to the Gravenhurst Opera House. The setting is like a country kitchen, with round wooden tables and cheery decorations, and the service is just as warm.

151 Brock St., Gravenhurst. ✆ **705/687-7756.** Reservations recommended for dinner. Main courses C$12–C$21. MC, V. Mon & Tues 9:30am–3pm; Wed–Sat 9:30am–8pm.

PRINCE EDWARD COUNTY

75km (47 miles) SW of Toronto

Culinary tourism is on the rise everywhere, and Ontario is definitely in on the game. Traveling to eat has turned Prince Edward County (PEC), a once-remote island on Lake Ontario a couple of hours' drive east of Toronto, into a very hot spot.

Originally settled by Mohawk Indians, the United Empire Loyalists moved into the area known as "the County" and soon turned it into a wealthy region rich in barley. As demand for beer grew across North America, so did the County's barley-baron mansions. Today, a handful of these beauties have been transformed into luxury inns. For most of the past century, PEC was a quiet, sometimes poor, agricultural

Prince Edward County

ACCOMMODATIONS ■
Angeline's Restaurant Inn **1**
isaiah tubbs **12**
The Merrill Inn **4**

DINING ◆
Angeline's Restaurant Inn **1**
Barley Days Brewery **2**

The Bean Counter Coffee Co.
  & Gelaterie **6**
Buddha Dog **3**
Harvest Restaurant **7**
isaiah tubbs **12**
The Merrill Inn **4**
Miss Lily's Café **5**
Slickers **11**

ATTRACTIONS ●
Fifth Town Artisan Cheese **10**
Lake on the Mountain **9**
Norman Hardie Wines **13**
Prince Edward County
  Chamber of Tourism
  & Commerce **8**
Sandbanks National Park **12**

area with just one small town, the struggling Picton. It still has one main town, but now Picton is thriving. And a number of smaller towns and villages, such as Bloomfield, Wellington, Milford, and Waupoos, have distinguished themselves with food-related attractions such as a craft brewery, a stellar ice-cream shop, or a unique cheese dairy.

A couple of decades ago, a back-to-the-land movement started attracting painters, artisans, glass blowers, and organic-minded farmers. Aspiring vintners came next, then chefs, bakers, even gourmet hot-dog makers. Now, the place is a hot culinary spot, especially for Torontonians. Given the pristine sand dunes, inland lakes, the Sandbanks Provincial Park, and a mysterious lake that sits perched 62m (203 ft.) up above Lake Ontario, the County is worth a day or two to take in the sights and senses. Keep in mind that this area is best explored during warm months, from spring through fall. A number of shops, galleries, and restaurants close, or seriously cut back hours, during the winter months.

Essentials

VISITOR INFORMATION **Prince Edward County Chamber of Tourism & Commerce** is at 116 Main St., Picton (✆ **800/640-4717;** or 613/476-2421; www. pecchamber.com). It has a wealth of information about what to see and do, as well as where to dine and sleep. Hours change with the seasons, but it's generally open 9am to 5pm, with some added hours in summer and through autumn.

To help you choose from the range of culinary vacations, visit the **Savour Ontario** website (www.savourontario.ca; the site is a bit obtuse—start by clicking "Find a Restaurant," and you're on your way). There's also the **Ontario Culinary Tourism Alliance** website (www.ontarioculinary.com); although the organization serves the trade, the site has a lot of useful information for tourists.

GETTING THERE Prince Edward County is easy to reach by car. From Toronto, take Highway 401 east to exit 525 (before Trenton), then take Highway 33 to Picton. The drive takes about 2½ hours.

What to See & Do

The County is best explored by car, although it's also a great place to bike once you've arrived. You can visit wineries and restaurants on cycling tours or map your own itinerary. In fact, most of the tours in the region, from art to wine, are self-directed. It's in keeping with the region's independent, off-the-beaten-path character.

Arts Trail The County is a busy community of artists, in addition to food and wine pros, and this initiative equips visitors with the information and routes they need to discover more than 30 artists, artisans, and galleries. You can expect to find beautiful paintings, sculpture, contemporary photography, pottery, blown glass, hand-crafted jewelry, and more. There are eight galleries that represent multiple artists, as well; the Oeno is particularly cutting edge. Like most things in the County, this is a seasonal program; the 2010 kick-off was late May and ran through autumn. ✆ **866/845-664.** www.artstrail.ca.

 SIPPING SPOTS

Barley Days Brewery With a nod to the County's barley-rich past, this craft brewery is an entirely modern enterprise. Stop by for a taste and a tour. 13730 Loyalist Parkway, Picton. ✆ **613/476-7468.** www. barleydaysbrewery.com.

Norman Hardie Wines This small estate makes excellent wines from grapes grown in the area and in Niagara. The acclaimed results are putting the County on the wine map. Stop by for a tasting: There are a handful of vintages to choose from and always someone on hand to guide you through the experience. A little taste of Burgundy in Ontario. 1152 Greer Rd., Wellington. ✆ **613/399-5297.**

More Cheese, Please

Fifth Town Artisan Cheese (4309 County Rd. 8, Picton; ✆ 613/476-5755; www.fifthtown.ca) is the world's first LEED-certified dairy, meaning it has outstanding eco-practices. It's worth a visit and tour just to see the process, which includes recycling clean water for the property's wetlands, and to check out the ultra-modern building design. All very new. More importantly, the cheeses are works of art—and definitely good enough to eat. They also offer wine and cheese tastings from June to September. Call ahead to check on hours and tours.

Lake on the Mountain It's a small, sometimes turquoise-hued lake perched 62m (203 ft) above the great Lake Ontario and a local legend because its source remains a mystery to this day. Surrounded by a pretty park, a popular pub, some lovely country homes, and a small inn, the lake offers a grand view across the Bay of Quinte. Bring a picnic lunch and watch the ferries below as they cross the 1km (½-mile) channel to the mainland. It's a great place to bid farewell to the County before hopping aboard the car ferry below at Glenora. C.R. 7 (off Hwy. 33, near Glenora). www.ontario parks.com/english/lakem.html. Daily vehicle permit C$10–$18. Daily 9:30am–dusk. From Hwy. 401, take Hwy. 49 south to Picton.

Sandbanks National Park ★ It's a short drive to this spectacular provincial park that includes the West Lake formation, claimed to be the largest freshwater baymouth sand-dune system in the world. In other words: It's an amazing beach. The water is shallow, the sand clean, and the dunes—many between 12m (39 ft.) and 25 meters (82 ft.) high—provide a bit of topography that's good for hiking and also for sheltered picnic areas on blistering days. In fact, this camping ground and natural water-park features plenty of picnic areas and day-use programs like campfires and other activities. So, you can come for the day or stay overnight—but the latter only if you've planned well ahead since these campground sites are booked months in advance. R.R. 1, Picton. ✆ 613/393-3319. www.ontarioparks.com/english/sand.html. Daily vehicle permit C$10–$18. Daily 9:30am–dusk.

Taste Trail If you're interested in exploring wineries, cafes, restaurants, breweries, and more, this self-guided route through the County has a lot to offer. There's a free booklet that lists 31 participating businesses as well as route maps and brief listings on each destination. Once on the road, you'll find there are signs identifying the Taste Trail, too. Along the way, there are plenty of tastings and tours to consider. Take your time; this is slow food—anything but fast. ✆ 866/845-6644. www.tastetrail.ca.

Where to Stay

There are many good options for staying a night or two, from homey B&Bs to lakeside self-catering cottages to very pretty inns. The County's inns are some of the best choices if you're looking for good dining and lodging all in one locale.

Angéline's Restaurant Inn ★★★ ☺ The heart of this modest but pretty property is the original Victorian house, where the dining room serves up local ingredients with sophisticated flare under the guidance of chef Sebastien Schwab. There are three dining areas, including the Victorian Room for small private parties. The cozy rooms are mostly situated in a separate building; a new suite has been added to the main house. There are gardens and public rooms for all to enjoy, too. Angéline's is known also for its workshops, which range from on-site pottery classes to well-being seminars (think: feng shui and numerology).

433 Main St. (Hwy. 33), Bloomfield, ON K0K 1G0. ✆ **877/391-3301.** or 613/393-3301. angelinesrestaurant inn.com. 10 units. C$80–C$135 double. AE, DC, DISC, MC, V. Free parking. Take Hwy. 401 East & exit at number 522. Proceed South on Wooler Rd. to Hwy. 33 south (Loyalist Pkwy.).Turn left on C.R. 1 (Prince Edward Rd. 1), then turn right on Hwy. 62 south & drive directly to Bloomfield. **Amenities:** Restaurant; cafe. *In room:* TV, DVD player, Wi-Fi (free).

isaiah tubbs   This is the biggest resort around these parts, with acres of gardens and woodlands very close to Sandbanks Park. The rooms range from simple ones in the restored 1820s home to more spacious suites in outlying lodges; best of all are the Beach House Suites, which give you a taste of the exceptional location. The food is pretty standard but better than many family-style resorts.

1642 County Rd. 12, Picton. ✆ **800/724-2393.** www.isaiahtubbs.com. 88 units. From C$169 double. AE, DC, MC, V. Take Hwy. 401 east to exit 522 (Wooler Rd.), then go south on Wooler Rd. to Hwy. 33. Turn right onto Hwy. 33, then turn right at County Rd. 32 in Bloomfield. Turn right onto County Rd. 12 & follow it for approximately 9km (5½ miles). **Amenities:** 2 restaurants; bar; fitness center; heated pool (seasonal); sauna; tennis courts. *In room:* A/C, TV, fridge, hair dryer, Wi-Fi (free).

Merrill Inn ★   Simply one of the nicest inns in the area, the Merrill has a great location in the center of Picton. Housed in an impressive Victorian manse, the rooms are elegant yet comfortable, and attention to detail is evident throughout, from the good linens to tasteful antique decorations and pretty bathrooms. The food is another top draw, whether you're staying the night or not. The stellar dining room led by chef Michael Sullivan (who has a passion for local and fresh ingredients) is a leader in regional cuisine. There's also a good wine bar and a sunny patio. In between hot breakfasts with homemade breads, a picnic lunch, and a three-course a la carte dinner, there's time for one of the Merrill's 1-hour walking tours of Picton. Choose between the "Graveyards and Gallows" tour or the less grim option of the town's historic architecture. Either way, a good way to get a little exercise in between meals.

343 Main St., Picton. ✆ **866/567-5969** or 613/476-7451. www.merrillinn.com. 13 units. From C$179 double. Rates include breakfast. AE, MC, V. Free parking. **Amenities:** Restaurant; wine bar; spa. *In room:* A/C, TV, Wi-Fi (free).

Where to Dine

Food is a major attraction here, so unless you stay and stay, there are more places to feast than your belt can comfortably accommodate. Road trips around the region will lead you to discoveries like a beautiful little winery, or you can opt for staying in Picton, where you can choose from the many cafes, restaurants, pubs, and specialty shops. For a more complete list of what's on offer, visit www.pec.on.ca.

The Bean Counter Coffee Co. & Gelaterie LIGHT FARE/ICE CREAM   One of the many good choices on Picton's main street, this open and airy cafe serves fair-trade coffee, homemade cakes, light lunch fare, and more than 20 flavors of ice cream made in-house. A perfect spot for refueling after a day on the dunes.

172 Main St., Unit 101, Picton. ✆ **613/476-1718.** www.beancountercafe.com. Sandwiches from C$5. AE, DC, MC, V. Mon–Fri 8am–9pm; Sat & Sun 9am–9pm.

Buddha Dog LIGHT FARE   Healthy hot dogs: The concept might be hard to swallow, but in fact, these tasty little dogs—more like sausages, really—are made using local, small-scale farm goods. Since starting out in the County, the owners have also opened shops in Toronto. Expect to eat at least two. There are a number of excellent sauces to pile on, too.

172 Main St., Picton. © **613/476-3814.** www.buddhafoodha.com. Hot dogs from C$2.50. AE, DC, MC V. Mon-Fri 11am-4pm; Sat & Sun 11am-5pm.

Harvest Restaurant ★ CANADIAN/ECLECTIC   Probably the County's top gourmet destination, this friendly, stylish restaurant is a favorite for locals, as well as foodie-focused travelers. Chef Michael Potters is a fine craftsman, and his passion for supporting local farmers means that you get a virtual tour of the County's best produce, meats, dairy, and wines in dishes such as Wild BC red spring salmon with sauce a la *Grecque,* or chicken and dumplings in a wild mushroom and chive flower broth.

106 Bridge St., Picton. © **613/476-6763.** www.harvestrestaurant.ca. Main courses C$13-C$30. AE, MC, V. Wed-Sun 5-10pm.

Miss Lily's Café CAFE   Situated in Books & Company, the charming Picton bookstore on the town's main strip, this is a local hang-out and a great place to relax over a cup of coffee, light breakfast, or lunch.

289 Main St., Picton. © **613/476-9289.** Main courses from C$5.50. AE, MC, V. Mon-Fri 7am-9pm; Sat 8am-9pm; Sun 9am-5pm.

Slickers ICE CREAM   The County is known for a healthy sense of pride in local foods, and even the ice-cream shops are in on the trend. This small spot with a pretty patio in Bloomfield serves up an eclectic collection of flavors, each one inspired by what's in season. Flavors include rhubarb ginger, local cantaloupe, apple pie, and even a maple walnut made with local syrup. They're all delicious. Open in summer only.

271 Main St., Bloomfield. No phone. www.slickersicecream.com. Single scoop from C$3. No credit cards. Daily 11am-9pm.

FAST FACTS

TORONTO

Area Codes Toronto's area codes are **416** and **647;** outside the city, the code is **905** or **289.** You must dial all 10 digits for all local phone numbers.

Automobile Organizations Motor clubs will supply maps, suggested routes, guidebooks, accident and bail-bond insurance, and emergency road service. The **Canadian Automobile Association (CAA)** is the major auto club in Canada, and its South Central Ontario branch is in Toronto. Within Canada, call ✆ **800/222-4357** or 416/222-5222. If you belong to a motor club in your home country, inquire about CAA reciprocity before you leave. You may be able to join CAA, even if you're not a member of a reciprocal club; to inquire, call CAA or visit **www.caa.ca.** If you are a member of the American Automobile Association (AAA), the CAA does provide emergency road service.

Business Hours Banks are generally open Monday through Thursday from 10am to 3pm, Friday 10am to 6pm. Most stores are open Monday through Wednesday from 10am to 6pm, and Saturday and Sunday from 10am to 5pm, with extended hours (until 8 or 9:30pm) on Thursday and often on Friday.

Drinking Laws The legal age for purchase and consumption of alcoholic beverages is 19 throughout Ontario; proof of age is required and often requested at bars, nightclubs, and restaurants, so it's always a good idea to bring ID when you go out.

Bars are usually open until 2am in Toronto, except during special events like the Toronto International Film Festival, when many venues are open later. A government monopoly runs liquor sales: **Liquor Control Board of Ontario (LCBO)** stores sell liquor, wine, and some beers. Most are open daily from 10am to 6pm (some have extended evening hours). The nicest shop is the **LCBO Summerhill** (10 Scrivener Sq.; ✆ **416/922-0403;** subway: Summerhill). Built in a former train station, this outpost hosts cooking classes, wine and spirit tastings, and party-planning seminars. Another good branch is at the **Manulife Centre** (55 Bloor St. W.; ✆ **416/925-5266**). See **www.lcbo.com** for information about products and special in-store events.

Do not carry open containers of alcohol in your car or any public area that isn't zoned for alcohol consumption. The police can fine you on the spot.

Driving Rules See "Getting There & Getting Around," p. 35.

Electricity Like the United States, Canada uses 110 to 120 volts AC (60 cycles), compared to 220 to 240 volts AC (50 cycles) in most of Europe, Australia, and New Zealand. Downward converters that change 220 to 240 volts to 110 to 120 volts are difficult to find in Canada, so bring one with you if you need it.

Embassies & Consulates   All embassies are in Ottawa, the national capital. They include the **Australian High Commission** (50 O'Connor St., Ste. 710, Ottawa, ON K1P 6L2; ✆ **613/236-0841**), the **British High Commission** (80 Elgin St., Ottawa, ON K1P 5K7; ✆ **613/237-1530**), the **Embassy of Ireland** (130 Albert St., Ottawa, ON K1P 5G4; ✆ **613/233-6281**), the **New Zealand High Commission** (727–99 Bank St., Ottawa, ON K1P 6G3; ✆ **613/238-5991**), the **South African High Commission** (15 Sussex Dr., Ottawa, ON K1M 1M8; ✆ **613/744-0330**), and the **Embassy of the United States of America** (490 Sussex Dr., Ottawa, ON K1N 1G8; ✆ **613/238-5335**).

Consulates in Toronto include the **Australian Consulate-General** (175 Bloor St. E., Ste. 314, at Church St.; ✆ **416/323-1155**), the **British Consulate-General** (777 Bay St., Ste. 2800, at College St.; ✆ **416/593-1290**), and the **U.S. Consulate** (360 University Ave.; ✆ **416/595-1700**).

Emergencies   Call ✆ **911** for fire, police, or ambulance.

Gasoline (Petrol)   Gasoline is sold by the liter, and taxes are already included in the printed price (unlike most products in Canada). Fill-up locations are known as gas stations or service stations.

Holidays   Toronto celebrates the following holidays: New Year's Day (Jan 1), Family Day (third Mon in Feb), Good Friday and Easter Monday (Mar or Apr), Victoria Day (Mon following the third weekend in May), Canada Day (July 1), Simcoe Day (first Mon in Aug), Labor Day (first Mon in Sept), Thanksgiving (second Mon in Oct), Remembrance Day (Nov 11), Christmas Day (Dec 25), and Boxing Day (Dec 26). For more information on holidays, see "Calendar of Events," in chapter 3.

Hospitals   In the downtown core, the **University Health Network** (UHN) manages three hospitals: **Toronto General,** at 200 Elizabeth St.; **Princess Margaret,** at 610 University Ave.; and **Toronto Western,** at 399 Bathurst St. The UHN has a central switchboard for all three (✆ **416/340-3111**). Other hospitals include **St. Michael's** (30 Bond St.; ✆ **416/360-4000**) and **Mount Sinai** (600 University Ave.; ✆ **416/596-4200**). Also downtown is the **Hospital for Sick Children** (555 University Ave.; ✆ **416/813-1500**). Uptown, there's **Sunnybrook Hospital** (2075 Bayview Ave., north of Eglinton Ave. E.; ✆ **416/480-6100**). In the eastern part of the city, go to **Toronto East General Hospital** (825 Coxwell Ave.; ✆ **416/461-8272**).

Hotlines   **Poison Information Centre** (✆ 800/267-1373), **Distress Centre** suicide-prevention line (✆ 416/408-4357), **Toronto Rape Crisis Centre** (✆ 416/597-8808), **Assaulted Women's Helpline** (✆ 416/863-0511), and **AIDS & Sexual Health InfoLine** (✆ 416/392-2437). For kids or teens in distress, there's **Kids Help Phone** (✆ 800/668-6868).

Insurance   Even though Canada is just a short drive or flight away for many Americans, U.S. health plans (including Medicare and Medicaid) do not provide coverage here, and the ones that do often require you to pay for services up front and reimburse you only after you return home. As a safety net, you may want to buy travel medical insurance. Travelers from the U.K. should carry their European Health Insurance Card (EHIC), which replaced the E111 form as proof of entitlement to free/reduced cost medical treatment abroad (✆ **0845/606-2030;** www.ehic.org.uk). Note, however, that the EHIC covers only "necessary medical treatment," and for repatriation costs, lost money, baggage, or cancellation, travel insurance from a reputable company should always be sought (www.travelinsuranceweb.com).

For information on traveler's insurance, trip cancellation insurance, and medical insurance while traveling, please visit **www.frommers.com/planning**.

Internet Access   Even budget hotels in Toronto now provide Internet access—and often Wi-Fi access. If you don't have a computer with you, there's **Insomnia** (563 Bloor St. W.; ✆ **416/588-3907**). Another option is **FedEx Kinko's.** There are several in the city, but one sure bet is the location at 505 University Ave., at Dundas St. W. (✆ **416/970-8447**).

There's also a not-for-profit group called **Wireless Toronto** that's dedicated to providing hotspots. You'll need to register online at **http://wirelesstoronto.ca**; after that, you'll be able to get 20 minutes of free Wi-Fi at places such as Harbourfront's York Quay (p. 126) and Yonge-Dundas Square (p. 210). A complete list of hotpots is available on the website.

Laundromats   **Bloor Laundromat** (598 Bloor St. W., at Bathurst St.; ✆ **416/588-6600**) and **Laundry Lounge** (527 Yonge St., at Wellesley St.; ✆ **416/975-4747**) are both conveniently located. **Careful Hand Laundry & Dry Cleaners Ltd.** has outlets at 206 Dupont St. (✆ **416/923-1200**) and 1844 Avenue Rd. (✆ **416/787-6006**); for pickup and delivery, call ✆ **416/787-9119.**

Legal Aid   If you are pulled over for a minor infraction (such as speeding), you'll be given a ticket that you pay at a later date. Pay fines by mail or directly into the hands of the clerk of the court. If accused of a more serious offense, say and do nothing before consulting a lawyer. Here, the burden is on the state to prove a person's guilt beyond a reasonable doubt, and everyone has the right to remain silent, whether he or she is suspected of a crime or actually arrested. Once arrested, a person can make one telephone call to a party of his or her choice. International visitors should call their embassy or consulate. If you need to get a lawyer while in Toronto, contact the **Law Society of Upper Canada** (✆ **800/668-7380** or 416/947-3300; www.lsuc.on.ca).

Lost & Found   If you leave something on a TTC bus, a streetcar, or the subway, call the **TTC Lost Articles Office** (✆ **416/393-4100**), at the Bay Street subway station. It's open Monday through Friday from 8am to 5pm.

You can also contact the **Toronto Police Service** about lost or found items at ✆ **416/808-2222.**

Mail   Postage for letter mail (up to 30g/1 oz.) to the United States costs C$1; overseas, it's C$1.70. Mailing letters within Canada costs C57¢. Note that there is no discounted rate for mailing postcards. For more information, go to **www.canadapost.ca**.

Postal services are available at some drugstores. Almost all drugstores sell stamps, and many have a separate counter where you can ship packages from 8:30am to 5pm. Look for a sign in the window indicating such services. There are also post-office windows in **Atrium on Bay** (✆ **416/506-0911**), in **Commerce Court** (✆ **416/956-7452**), and at the **TD Centre** (✆ **416/360-7105**).

Medical Conditions   If you have a medical condition that requires **syringe-administered medications,** carry a valid signed prescription from your physician; syringes in carry-on baggage will be inspected. Insulin in any form should have the proper pharmaceutical documentation. If you have a disease that requires treatment with **narcotics,** you should also carry documented proof with you—smuggling narcotics aboard a plane carries severe penalties.

For **HIV-positive visitors,** Canada does not require testing to enter the country on a tourist visa. However, a traveler can be denied entry to Canada if they are assessed as requiring health services during their stay. (Canada does not cover medical costs incurred by travelers.)

Newspapers & Magazines   The four daily newspapers are the *Globe and Mail,* the *National Post,* the *Toronto Star,* and the *Toronto Sun. Eye* and *Now* are free arts-and-entertainment weeklies. *Xtra!* is a free weekly targeted at the gay and lesbian community. In addition, many English-language ethnic newspapers serve Toronto's Portuguese, Hungarian, Italian, East Indian, Korean, Chinese, and Caribbean communities. *Toronto Life* is the major monthly city magazine. *Where Toronto* magazine is usually free at hotels and some Theater District restaurants.

Passports   See **www.frommers.com/planning** for information on how to obtain a passport. See "Embassies & Consulates," above, for whom to contact if you lose yours while traveling in Canada. For other information, please contact the following agencies:

For Residents of Australia   Contact the Australian Passport Information Service at ✆ **131-232** or visit the government website at www.passports.gov.au.

For Residents of Ireland   Contact the **Passport Office** (Setanta Centre, Molesworth Street, Dublin 2; ✆ **01/671-1633;** www.irlgov.ie/iveagh).

For Residents of New Zealand   Contact the Passports Office at ✆ **0800/225-050** in New Zealand or 04/474-8100, or log on to www.passports.govt.nz.

For Residents of the United Kingdom   Visit your nearest passport office, major post office, or travel agency or contact the **United Kingdom Passport Service** at ✆ **0870/521-0410** or search its website at **www.ukpa.gov.uk.**

For Residents of the United States   To find your regional passport office, either check the U.S. Department of State website www.state.gov or call the **National Passport Information Center** toll-free number (✆ **877/487-2778**) for automated information.

Police   In a life-threatening emergency, call ✆ **911.** For all other matters, contact the **Toronto Police Service** (40 College St.; ✆ **416/808-2222**).

Smoking   The Smoke-Free Ontario Act, which came into effect in 2006, is one of the most stringent in North America. It bans smoking in all workplaces and in all enclosed public spaces. It's all but impossible to smoke at Ontario restaurants because the law banned designated smoking areas; even patios that have any sort of covering have also had to go smoke-free.

Taxes   As of July 1, 2010, the Ontario government implemented a "harmonized" tax system, with a 13% sales tax on virtually everything for sale. (Previously, the federal GST was 5% and the Ontario sales tax was 8%, but the Ontario sales tax was not applied to purchases such as fast-food meals.) Taxes are added when you purchase an item, rather than being included in the original price as is common in much of Europe. The Canadian government suspended the GST Visitors' Rebate Program in 2007.

Within the city of Toronto, there is a new bylaw, introduced in 2009, that obliges retailers to charge a minimum of 5¢ per plastic bag. There are no exceptions to this rule. (The funds collected are not really a tax, since they go into the store's coffers and not the city's, but some people consider this a tax on shoppers.)

Telephones   Many convenience stores and packaging services sell **prepaid calling cards** in denominations up to C$50; for international visitors, these can be the least expensive way to call home. There are fewer public pay phones each year; those at airports now accept American Express, MasterCard, and Visa credit cards. **Local calls** made from pay phones in most locales cost C50¢ (no pennies). Most long-distance and international calls can be dialed directly from any phone. **For calls within Canada and to the United States,** dial 1 followed by the area code and the seven-digit number. **For other international calls,** dial 011 followed by the country code, city code, and the number you are calling.

Calls to area codes **800, 888, 877,** and **866** are toll-free. However, calls to area codes **700** and **900** (chat lines, bulletin boards, "dating" services, and so on) can be very expensive—usually a charge of C95¢ to C$3 or more per minute, and they sometimes have minimum charges that can run as high as C$15 or more.

For **reversed-charge or collect calls,** and for person-to-person calls, dial the number 0 then the area code and number; an operator will come on the line, and you should specify whether you are calling collect, person-to-person, or both. If your operator-assisted call is international, ask for the overseas operator.

For **local directory assistance** ("information"), dial ✆ **411;** for long-distance information, dial 1, then the appropriate area code, and 555-1212.

Time   Toronto is on Eastern Standard Time. When it's noon in Toronto, it's 9am in Los Angeles (PST), it's 7am in Honolulu (HST), 10am in Denver (MST), 11am in Chicago (CST), noon in New York City (also on EST), 5pm in London (GMT), and 2am the next day in Sydney (UTC).

Daylight Saving Time is in effect from 1am on the second Sunday in March to 1am on the first Sunday in November. Daylight Saving Time moves the clock 1 hour ahead of standard time.

Tipping   Tips are a very important part of certain workers' income, and gratuities are the standard way of showing appreciation for services provided. (Tipping is certainly not compulsory if the service is poor!) In hotels, tip **bellhops** at least C$1 per bag (C$2–C$3 if you have a lot of luggage) and tip the **chamber staff** C$1 to C$2 per day (more if you've left a disaster area for him or her to clean up). Tip the **doorman** or **concierge $2 or more** only if he or she has provided you with some specific service (for example, calling a cab for you or obtaining difficult-to-get theater tickets). Tip the **valet-parking attendant** C$1 or more every time you get your car.

In restaurants, bars, and nightclubs, tip **service staff** 15% to 20% of the check, tip **bartenders** 10% to 15%, tip **checkroom attendants** C$1 per garment, and tip **valet-parking attendants** C$1 per vehicle.

As for other service personnel, tip **cab drivers** 15% of the fare; tip **skycaps** at airports at least C$1 per bag (C$2–C$3 if you have a lot of luggage); and tip **hairdressers** and **barbers** 15% to 20%.

Toilets   You won't find public toilets or "restrooms" on the streets in Toronto, but they can be found in hotel lobbies, bars, restaurants, museums, department stores, railway and bus stations, and service stations. Large hotels and fast-food restaurants are often the best bet for clean facilities. Restaurants and bars in resorts or heavily visited areas may reserve their restrooms for patrons. There are also restrooms throughout the underground PATH system near the various food courts. There are restrooms at major subway stations, such as Yonge-Bloor which are best used in the daytime when the subways are busy.

Visas   For citizens of many countries, including the U.S., U.K., Ireland, Australia, and New Zealand, only a passport is required to visit Canada for up to 90 days; no visas or proof of vaccinations are necessary. For the most up-to-date list of visitor visa exemptions, visit **Citizenship and Immigration Canada** at **www.cic.gc.ca**.

Visitor Information   The best source for Toronto-specific information is **Tourism Toronto** (✆ **800/499-2514** from North America or 416/203-2600; www.seetorontonow.com). The website includes sections on accommodations, sights, shopping, and dining, plus up-to-the-minute events information. There's also a "Special Offers" section, which has package deals for hotels, and attractions or shows.

For information about traveling in the province of Ontario, contact **Tourism Ontario** (📞 **800/ONTARIO** [800/668-2746]; www.ontariotravel.net). While in Toronto, visit its information center in the **Atrium on Bay** (street level) at 20 Dundas St. W.—it's just across Dundas St. from the Sears store at the northern edge of the Eaton Centre. It's open daily from 8:30am to 4:30pm; hours are extended during the summer, often to 8pm.

Toronto.com (www.toronto.com), operated by the *Toronto Star,* offers extensive restaurant reviews, events listings, and feature articles. A couple of other great sources for local goings-on and news: the **Torontoist** blog (www.torontoist.com) and **blogTO** (www.blogto.com). If you love to shop, check out **SweetSpot** (www.sweetspot.ca) for its extensive Toronto coverage of local designers and boutiques. **Martini Boys** (www.martiniboys.com) also offers plenty of up-to-date reviews of hotels, nightclubs, restaurants, bars, and shows around town.

BlogTO produces some of my favorite local maps: You can pick them up for free at shops and restaurants around town. At press time, they have produced maps for West Queen West, Leslieville, Parkdale, and Little Italy. *Where Toronto* also prints good neighborhood maps in the magazine. Online, take a look at **Google Maps** (http://maps.google.com) for details on getting from Point A to Point B.

Water   Toronto's tap water is safe to drink, and it is tested continuously to guarantee public safety. For details, visit the City of Toronto's water information page at **www.toronto.ca/water**. However, while you'll see many locals swimming in Lake Ontario, this is not a good idea if you want to stay healthy; the lake contains high levels of E. coli, which causes nasty bacterial infections.

AIRLINE WEBSITES

Canadian Airlines

Air Canada
www.aircanada.com
Porter Airlines
www.flyporter.com
WestJet
www.westjet.com

Major Airlines

Aeroméxico
www.aeromexico.com
Air Canada
www.aircanada.com
Air France
www.airfrance.com
Air India
www.airindia.com
Air Jamaica
www.airjamaica.com
Air New Zealand
www.airnewzealand.com
Alitalia
www.alitalia.com

American Airlines
www.aa.com
British Airways
www.british-airways.com
Caribbean Airlines (formerly BWIA)
www.caribbean-airlines.com
China Airlines
www.china-airlines.com
Continental Airlines
www.continental.com
Cubana
www.cubana.cu
Delta Air Lines
www.delta.com
El Al Airlines
www.elal.co.il/elal/english/states/general/
Emirates Airlines
www.emirates.com
globespan
www.flyglobespan.ca
Hawaiian Airlines
www.hawaiianair.com

Iberia Airlines
www.iberia.com

Lan Airlines
www.lan.com

Lufthansa
www.lufthansa.com

Qantas Airways
www.qantas.com

TACA
www.taca.com

United Airlines
www.united.com

US Airways
www.usairways.com

Virgin Atlantic Airways
www.virgin-atlantic.com

FAST FACTS | Airline Websites

Index

Accommodations

Restaurants

Frommer's®

See the world by walking with Frommer's Best Hiking Trips!

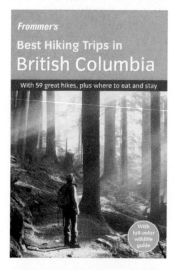

Frommer's
Best Hiking Trips in
British Columbia
With 59 great hikes, plus where to eat and stay
With full-color wildlife guide

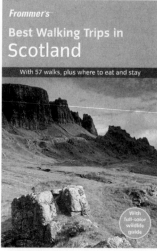

Frommer's
Best Walking Trips in
Scotland
With 57 walks, plus where to eat and stay
With full-color wildlife guide

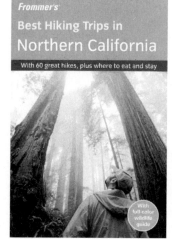

Frommer's
Best Hiking Trips in
Northern California
With 60 great hikes, plus where to eat and stay
With full-color wildlife guide

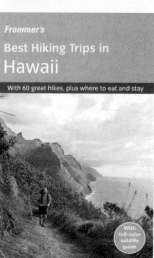

Frommer's
Best Hiking Trips in
Hawaii
With 60 great hikes, plus where to eat and stay
With full-color wildlife guide

Every book comes with innovative features and great resources in the Frommer's style:

- Two-color maps for every route
- Accommodation and restaurant reviews for businesses close to the trails
- A full-color introduction and wildlife identification guide
- GPS coordinates for every trailhead and waypoint

Discover Canada with Frommer's™!

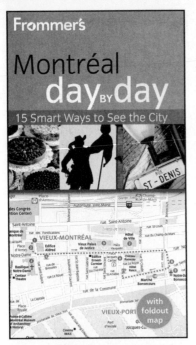

Frommer's

Montréal

day BY day

15 Smart Ways to See the City

with foldout map

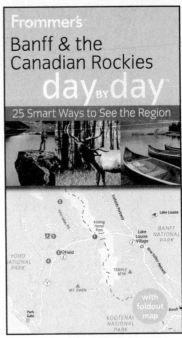

Frommer's

Banff & the Canadian Rockies

day BY day

25 Smart Ways to See the Region

with foldout map

Frommer's®

Vancouver & Whistler

day BY day

17 Smart Ways to See the Region

with foldout map

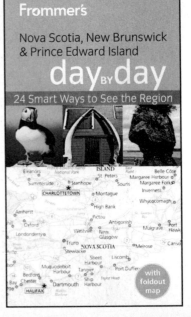

Frommer's

Nova Scotia, New Brunswick & Prince Edward Island

day BY day

24 Smart Ways to See the Region

with foldout map

Frommer's® 500 Places

These destination-packed global guides bring together practical travel information and armchair inspiration into one irresistible package.